PRAISE FOR *SO MAN*

CW00539792

THIS is an entertaining story of the life   ---, technology and education throughout the g........ part of the 20th Century. The thought that came to mind on first reading was that no man has the right to leave his mark on so many institutions and disciplines and influence so many people in a single lifetime, albeit one so long. From the delightfully disarming cover illustration (designed and executed by the author's wife) to the fitting epilogue, the book is a compelling read.

I regard the book as a significant contribution to the history of the 20th century from the 1920s to the end of the century. It is easy for anyone to read. I thoroughly recommend it.

–James R. Whitehead, Principal Science Advisor, Government of Canada

You have given your family and friends a great gift by writing this book. I have learned much from it. I have even had some nagging uncertainties resolved. Most of all, reading it was pure pleasure.

–Professor Peter Forsyth, University Of Western Ontario

A fine read...a testimony to a life of dedication, curiosity and many-faceted interests. I kept it by my bed until the last page.

–Robert N. White, Wake Forest University

So Many Hills gives an engrossing account of the rich personal and professional life of a prominent engineer, scientist, and administrator.

–Prof. Keith Smillie University of Alberta,
Review, IEEE Annals of the History of Computing

Your memoir was a delight to read!

–Professor Charlotte Fischer, Vanderbilt University

So Many Hills to Climb

Published in the United States by
Beckham Publications Group, Inc.
Second Printing, Revised October, 2006

ISBN: 0-931761-08-5
10 9 8 7 6 5 4 3 2

Arthur Porter

So Many Hills

TO CLIMB

*My Journey as a
Computer Pioneer*

THE Beckham
PUBLICATIONS GROUP, INC.
Silver Spring

Books by the Author

Introduction to Servomechanisms
Cybernetics Simplified
Towards a Community University

For my wife Patricia,
John and Kathryn,
my grandchildren,
my family and my friends

CONTENTS

PREFACE TO SECOND PRINTING

ESSENTIALLY, because the title of my memoir has been interpreted literally, rather than metaphorically as intended, I have concluded that a more appropriate sub-title should be "My Journey as a Computer Pioneer." This is the sole justification for a second printing.

It was during the early 1930's when, following in the pioneering footsteps of Vannevar Bush at MIT, that I became intrigued with the idea that many complex mathematical problems, especially related to science and engineering, could be solved by a machine—the differential analyzer. Consequently, in 1933-34 through the guidance and leadership of my mentor, teacher and friend, Professor Douglas Hartree at the University of Manchester, I actually built a model of the Bush machine largely from "Meccano" components (a child's toy construction set). And it was outstandingly successful in solving several problems, notably in determining approximately the structure of the chromium atom.

But, from my personal standpoint, the important consequence was my being recruited as a member of the Rockefeller Differential Analyzer (RDA) staff under the inspired leadership of Dr. Bush at MIT. The largest and most elegant computer of its kind ever built, the RDA contributed during World War II to the Manhattan Project (the Atom Bomb) and to radar and ballistics research. My personal involvement related to the conversion of digital to analog information and a few years later gave birth to the Porter-Stoneman converter system. The latter was ultimately adopted in air traffic control and space technology. Incidentally, in 1967 when the U.K. National Physical Laboratories sponsored a series of audio tapings, "The Computer Pioneers," to record our impressions of the evolution of computing since our early work in the thirties and forties, I was interviewed together with F.C. Williams, T Kilburn, A.D. Booth, Jay Forrester and Grace Hopper to name a few.

But the most rewarding reference to the model differential

analyzer, together with my M. Sc. thesis is the remarkable volume, *A Computer Perspective* published by Harvard University Press in 1973. To quote the Introduction by I. Bernard Cohen:

"*A Computer Perspective*" is an illustrated essay on the origins and first lines of development of the computer. The complex network of creative forces and social pressures that have produced the computer is personified here in the creators of instruments of computation..."

The exhibition upon which the volume was based, was assembled by the IBM Corporation. Subsequently, a portion of the Hartree-Porter model and related artifacts were put on permanent display in the National Science Museum, London.

In the summer of 1939, shortly after my return to Britain and two exciting years at MIT, World War II broke out in Europe. My first appointment during the war was at the Admiralty Research Laboratories, and it is fascinating to note that my first assignment was closely related to my work on the differential analyzer. The anti-aircraft predictors of the day were essentially special purpose analog computers. Accordingly, my earlier experiences were invaluable when subsequently, I was stationed on the ZS20 A.A. gun site during the Battle of Britain.

The revelation many years later, that the differential analyzer was a bridging technology has in fact had a profound effect on my career. It undoubtedly gave birth to my lifelong interest in interdisciplinary activities notably in biomedical engineering, educational reform—and with my colleague Marshall McLuhan, culture, the arts and technology. Metaphorically speaking, "there have been many hills to climb." Now in my 96th year, I am still fascinated by the differential analyzer and by no means least the realization that Dr. Vannevar Bush's dream of a visual approach to the teaching of the calculus, may now be achievable.

Arthur Porter
Bermuda Village, NC
September 2006

ACKNOWLEDGEMENTS

WORDS cannot convey my love and gratitude to my wife Patricia for her inspiration and for her dedication to the arduous and boring task of editing the manuscript, and her creativity in designing and fabricating the cover page. She has been, as always, a tower of strength and devotion.

I am deeply indebted to Lynn Hall without whose encouragement, patience and computer expertise these memoirs would never have been completed. She literally interpreted and transcribed 32 tapes and provided me with a perfectly executed manuscript. As well, her insights and advice helped appreciably in the structuring of the work.

It is a pleasure and privilege to acknowledge my indebtedness to my friends and fellow residents of Bermuda Village, Hank Lauerman, Professor Emeritus of Law, Wake Forest University and Ralph Church, Professor Emeritus of English, Juniata College. Hank parsed and analyzed the early chapters and was responsible for an important restructuring, and Ralph read the hard copy printout of the manuscript and identified a host of grammatical transgressions. My cousin Edith Mabbutt has been extremely helpful in providing me with a plethora of information relating to the English Lake District. Thank you, Edith. I am most grateful to the Hartree family, especially Richard, for providing the superb photograph of the model differential analyzer and the photograph of Douglas Hartree and Vannevar Bush. I am grateful as well to Professor Charlotte Fischer, biographer of Douglas Hartree, for her many helpful consultations.

Several former members of the Ferranti Electric Research Division, notably Les Wood, Gord Lang, Jim Williams, Herb Ratz and George Collins have encouraged me by showing that the halcyon days we spent together have not been forgotten. Thank you, guys! In this regard I am particularly grateful to Vincent Taylor, son of Kenyon.

I acknowledge with gratitude the help of Lorraine Pickavance of the Lake District Peninsulas Tourism Partnership for providing photographs of Ulverston and other material. Anne Lockes and Jane Evans of the Institution of Electrical Engineers have been most helpful in supplying photographs extracted from the Archives relating to the Centenary Celebrations. I acknowledge permission to publish these. As well, I acknowledge permission to include a photograph taken by the Dorchester Hotel Photography Department. I am grateful to Patricia's life-long friend

Daphne Keith for taking care of the London contacts. I wish to acknowledge most gratefully the help of Harold Averill, archivist of the University of Toronto in providing photographs of Omond Solandt and Marshall McLuhan.

During the past three years, the residents and staff of Bermuda Village, Advance, North Carolina, have provided a perfect haven for the writing of this memoir. My wife and I are most grateful. The role of medical science in a rather unique way is acknowledged as well. For several years, I have suffered from impaired vision and consequent physical balance problems. My son John concluded that a medication normally prescribed for dementia, might be helpful. Subsequent consultations with my physician Steven Wittmer supported the conclusion. Consequently, after two years' treatment, not only has my balance improved, but there has been an extraordinary enhancement of my memory. To Drs. Wittmer and Porter I owe a special debt.

Finally, I acknowledge the expeditious manner in which the Beckham Publications Group have handled every aspect of the publishing process. It has been a special pleasure to have had such cordial relations with Barry Beckham and his fastidious indexer, Joe Zang. Any mistakes in the text are solely my responsibility.

Arthur Porter
Bermuda Village
February 2004

"Those to whom the harmonious doors
Of science have unbarred celestial stores,
To whom a burning energy has given
That other eye which darts thru earth and heaven."
                                    William Wordsworth

"That which purifies us is by trial,
And trial is by what is contrary."
                                    John Milton

"Yet fish there be that neither hook nor line,
Nor snare, nor net, nor engine can make thine;
They must be groped for, and be tickled too,
Or they will not be catch'd whate'er you do."
                                    John Bunyan

PROLOGUE

IN embarking on such a major project as my memoirs is likely to be, I realize that in my 92nd year, I'm stretching my remaining memory neurons to the absolute limit. However, the spirit is willing and I'm encouraged by my wife, Patricia, and by a passage I unearthed recently in Hunter Davies biography of William Wordsworth. Referring to the poet he wrote:

> *He realized as an old man that the characters of youth and age were very similar — the inherent variety and originality of youth merged into dull uniformity in middle age, but then repeated afresh in old age."*

I've something, albeit regrettably little, in common with Wordsworth—we were both English Lake District men.

Chapter 1

GATEWAY TO THE LAKE DISTRICT

ROUGHLY 10,000 years ago, an Ice Age held most of Britain in its grip. But its impact is nowhere more evident than in the Lake District. The ice carved out the romantic fells and, dells and, during the massive thaw that followed, left behind the glorious landscape that was to enchant the Lakeland poets. I was born on the fringe of this wonderland at Lightburn Road, Ulverston on December 8, 1910. My birthplace, a market town of ancient lineage, being mentioned in the Domesday Book circa 1089 AD, is located in the Furness District of Cumbria, Northwest England.

The histories of the town and District have been well documented.[1] Of special interest is the fact that Druidism, a religious faith of Celtic origin — evidence of which exists in the form of a Druid Circle about two miles from Ulverston — flourished during the second century B.C. Christianity was widely practiced as early as the second century AD.

The District has been the site of several invasions. The Roman Legions, for example, who invaded Britain prior to 100 AD, established the most northerly outpost of their Empire in Cumbria. There is a great deal of evidence of their occupation. For example, Hadrian's Wall protected the northern counties of England from the marauding Scots, while the network of Roman roads exists even today. The Vikings invaded and subdued the whole of northern England and left their imprint, not least their language and dialect, and many memorials including place names. For instance, Ulverston was originally "Ulfer's Ton." It was the Vikings and Anglo Saxon stock that successfully defended the Furness District when the Norman invasion occurred during

---

[1] The Story of Ulverston, Henry F. Birkett, published by Titus Wilson

the 11th century. The 13th and 14th centuries were periods when border skirmishes were common. Scottish national heroes, William Wallace and Robert Bruce and their armies, terrorized the local population and repeatedly destroyed many Lakeland villages. Hostilities were resumed three centuries later when Mary, Queen of Scots, invaded Britain, but their sojourn was comparatively short. The final invasion during the early years of the 17th century was by Oliver Cromwell's parliamentary forces who defeated King Charles' army at the critical battle of Marston Moor, which was fought on the moors of the Pennines, adjacent to the Lake District. But Cumbrians remained loyal to the king.

With the establishment of the union between England and Scotland in 1707, peace was restored, although the Jacobite Rebellions, especially Bonnie Prince Charles activities in 1745, gave rise to more border clashes. Peace has reigned since then except on the rugby football field during the annual matches between England and Scotland when there is intense rivalry.

The Furness District owes a great debt to the monks of Furness Abbey. They were very successful sheep farmers. They cleared the primeval forest and established agriculture in the region. Unfortunately, King Henry VIII and Queen Elizabeth I were responsible for the dissolution of the monasteries during their respective reigns and the monks were disbanded.

Known to countless generation of Ulverstonians as "Lile Oostan," the town has a population of about 9,000. As a result of its comparative geographical separation from major urban centers, the townsfolk were reserved and proud of their lineage and speech. The local dialect, which I spoke fluently as a boy, is almost incomprehensible to "foreigners" dwelling in the rest of Britain. But the town's reputation for hospitality dates back many years, as witness the remarks of Father West, a visitor to the town in 1754:

> *"The people of the Furness District and Ulverston in particular, are civil and humane; to strangers hospitable. This universal civility and good manners is characteristic of Furness and distinguishes the District from those parts of the country (i.e. England) where an importunate curiosity degenerating to rudeness and barbarism is so flagrant and offensive amongst those of the lowest station."*

Perhaps the good Father's impressions were influenced by the number of pubs in Ulverston, which was well above average in those days. He noted as well that, "the air of Furness is salubrious, so the inhabitants live to a good old age." And I am grateful for this!

My pride in my birthplace is not only a result of the magnificent scenery and my heritage, but as well it is due to the fact that it was the birthplace of so many eminent people. To mention a few: — Sir John Barrow, born in a tiny cottage at Dragley Beck within the town's boundaries, rose to become secretary to the Admiralty during the times of Viscount Horatio Nelson. He was a noted explorer, especially of the Arctic Ocean and Alaska — several towns and geographical locations are named after him i.e. Point Barrow and Barrow Bay. The sesquicentennial of the Barrow Lighthouse Memorial, located at the summit of Hoad Hill, beneath which the town nestles, was celebrated at the end of 2000 A.D. Ulverston also was the birthplace of the internationally-known actress Harriet Melon, afterward Duchess of St. Albans; of Stanley Laurel of Laurel and Hardy fame born in 1890; and of Lord Birkett, Lord Justice of Appeal, perhaps Britain's most brilliant advocate, born above a draper's shop. He eventually became a prominent figure in the Nuremberg Military Tribunal following the conclusion of WWII, and he also represented Mrs. Wallis Simpson when she filed for divorce prior to marrying King Edward VIII. As well it was the birthplace of Basil Weston and Frederick Jefferson, both of whom attended my old school and both of whom obtained Victoria Crosses, the highest military honor in Britain during WWII. It is worth noting as well that George Fox, founder of the Quakers, established the first Friends' Meeting House in Swarthmoor close to Ulverston in 1688. He was a close friend of William Penn, founder of Pennsylvania, who also visited the town at the end of the 17th century.

Memories of my boyhood days in Ulverston remain fresh in my mind. There were no films, no radios, no televisions, no motor cars, no airplanes. But there were great compensations.

The exciting cricket and soccer matches — the back street games and races. The coach tours drawn by four splendid horses provided transportation. The Town Crier in uniform making public announcements after ringing a large bell — "Oh Yez, oh Yez!" And most vivid of all, the Ulverston Hospital Saturday Parades on Whit Saturday, culminating in the crowning of the Rose Queen at the Grammar School Sports Field. Accompanying the "royal carriage" and retinue were mounted police, marching brass bands, fire brigades and town dignitaries. In successive years, ages eight to 10, I was a page boy to a Lady in Waiting, a page boy to the Queen, and my pinnacle of fame was reached when I was the Queen's falcon bearer in the procession. My costumes were 17th century — velvet coat and breeches, lace trimmings, silk stockings, shoes with silver buckles and in my last appearance, a stuffed falcon clamped on my wrist. For several weeks prior to the big day we practiced in the Drill Hall. How many times I walked around and around the Hall to the strains of the Merry Widow Waltz played on the piano by Mr. Rogers the local grocer? They were many. Pointed toes, erect posture, uniform steps. Indeed, at that very early age I learned the trade of royal courtier, but it was by no means wasted time, because the hospital parade raised a tidy sum for the local cottage hospital, and to this day my favorite dance is the waltz, especially to the strains of that old familiar tune.

Other attractions were the Martinmas and Michaelmas fairs staged in the Gill. Round-a-bouts, swings, coconut shies, a boxing booth, fortune teller, magic lantern shows and ice cream vendors. My parents always contrived to save a few shillings for those wonderful occasions. The circus came to town almost yearly. After Sunday School, my family invariably took walks on Hoad Hill and even as far as Kirby Moors. At age 11, I was bequeathed my mother's bicycle. It opened up new and exciting vistas, especially Bardsea Beach on Morecambe Bay, which for several years was my favorite haunt. Family picnics, bathing in the warm waters of the Bay, cricket games on the sand and camping during the summer holidays readily come to mind. I recall as well lengthy bike rides to several of the lakes. Because of the many steep hills, these were strenuous and time consuming: an average of about eight miles an hour was good going.

Because Ulverston was the Furness Railway Junction for the branch line to Lakeside, at the southern end of Lake Windermere, it was in effect the "Gateway" to the Lakes.

The Lake District, one of England's most beautiful regions, remains one of the few places in the country where it can truly be said that man has come to terms with nature rather than taming it. Wordsworth and Coleridge and Keats got their inspiration there. Indeed, Wordsworth, one of my favorite poets, in his autobiographical poem, "The Prelude," recalls his many mystical experiences and his happiness as a child:

> *"Bliss it was in that dawn to be alive,*
> *But to be young was very heaven."*

The English landscape painter J.M.W. Turner, a frequent visitor, captures superbly the Lake District as I remember it. The sense of grandeur, not when the sun was shining, but when the swirling mist partially enveloped the country side and brought the fells and dells into stark relief. Awe inspiring!

Although the Lakeland poets and J.M.W. Turner probably take pride of place with the general public, it is worth noting that at least three distinguished writers dwelt there. Beatrix Potter, the beloved creator of Peter Rabbit; Hugh Walpole, author of the Herries Chronicles, which give unrivaled descriptions of the Lake District and which were read and reread by my father; and John Ruskin, the noted art critic and formerly Slade Professor of Poetry at Oxford. I am proud to mention John Dalton, born in Cockermouth, Cumbria (the birth place of Wordsworth and incidentally of my maternal grandmother) who, with no formal education, propounded the atomic theory of matter and thereby laid the foundations for all modern physics and chemistry.

On countless occasions I've been struck by the dramatic changes in scenery within a few miles as I've hiked Lakeland trails with rocky crags with water cascading from the heights; the picturesque white-washed stone farmhouses; the ancient granite churches; and the ever-present flocks of Hardwick sheep. The latter are especially noteworthy with their guardians the hardy border collies and their masters who perform incredible feats on the treacherous fell-slopes. Characteristic of the district as well are the century old dry stone walls and sheep shelters, miracles of muscle and craftsmanship, which enrich the slopes with bewildering patterns. These are monuments to the indefatigable Cumbrian men and women, descendants of the Vikings, who have survived blizzards and grievous winds to eke out frugal livings in this lonely and lovely part of England.

It is gratifying, largely due to the efforts of the likes of Beatrix Potter and especially of Lord Birkett, that large tracts of the Lake District are now protected by Acts of Parliament. Indeed, in recognition of his dedication to his native lake country, a "Fell" has been designated "Birkett Fell." My only personal recollection of him is on the occasion in October 1929 when as Sir Norman Birkett he presented the prizes at my old school. At the end of the proceedings as Head Prefect I rose and called "School! Three cheers for Sir Norman." Forty-two years subsequently, I recalled this event when I gave the prizes and addressed the school.

Chapter 2

THE FAMILY

THE Porters were for countless generations sheep farmers of hardy Lake District stock. Their main claim to fame appears to be in the traditional English sport of fox hunting. Let me hasten to add that this activity in the Lake District has for centuries been an economic necessity. While many animal lovers consider the sport as cruel and blood-thirsty, the Lakeland farmer's livelihood depends on the protection of his sheep herd, and the foxhounds have been the only means yet known to keep the fox in check.

The family was not only active as Huntsmen and Masters of the Foxhounds, but as well were highly respected breeders of the hounds. Quoting from "The Chronicle of the Horse," an American publication devoted to fox hunting:

> *"Great men like the wonderful Porter family, hereditary masters of the Eskdale and Ennerdale Hunt, have studied in depth the breeding of these incredible animals."*

My father was inordinately proud of the family tradition. Shortly after our marriage, Patricia and I stayed for a few days with my parents at Birkrigg and Dad, shortly after our arrival, proposed that on the following day we should visit what he obviously regarded as a "Porter Shrine." Threlkeld, Cumberland, in the northeast Lake District was to be our destination. Some 50 miles distance from Ulverston through rugged country, this would be quite an adventure. Furthermore, a month's gasoline ration would be used up in a single day. But it was well worthwhile because it gave Patricia her first opportunity of seeing the glorious scenery of my native heath.

Made from local granite, the memorial is located in the church yard of Threlkeld parish church. It is erected in memory of the Masters and Huntsmen of the three prominent Lake District Hunts. — The John Peel, the Blencathra and the Eskdale and Ennerdale. Carved in the granite faces are their names and fairly prominent among them is the name Porter. It was quite a shock to note that so many of my ancestors were killed at comparatively young ages hunting fox on the steep slopes of those unforgiving fells.

My family's propensity for fox hunting, even to the present, is manifest in the fact that we regard the traditional hunting song "John Peel" almost as a family anthem. But it is much more than that. It is one of the best known refrains throughout the British Commonwealth dedicated to the famous huntsman. It was a marching song of the troops during World War I and II. The first verse, which I've sung so lustily many times is:

> *D'ye ken John Peel with his coat so gray*
> *D'ye ken John Peel at break o' the day*
> *D'ye ken John Peel when he's far far away,*
> *With his hounds and his horn*
> *In the morning.*

My paternal grandparents, Robert Porter and Jane Irving, were born in 1854 and 1858 respectively. My grandfather deserted the family farm at an age of about 15, walked to Ulverston, about 40 miles distance, and started an apprenticeship as a house painter and decorator. My grandmother, at an early age, got a job as a housemaid in one of Cumberland's stately homes. But after a year or two in a highly disciplined environment, she decided, like my grandfather, to emigrate to Ulverston. They married in 1878.

Because my grandfather died in 1917 when I was six years old, I have only the vaguest recollections of him. But I have fond memories of my grandmother, the matriarch of the family who lived eventually at 26 Clarence Street, Ulverston. She raised a family of five children — John William (my father, always called Ron by family and friends), Robert Irving, Charlie and the twins Ethel and Frank. Uncle Frank, a corporal in the King's Own Infantry Regiment during World War I, was killed during the first day of the infamous battle of the Somme in June of 1916.

There is no doubt that grandmother Porter was a very determined and ambitious woman. During the early 1900's she purchased the relatively large Clarence Street house in order to take paying guests. A few years later she had accumulated enough capital to pay for a small house painting and decorating business in Keswick, Cumberland. Sadly the deal did not materialize, because, and Patricia insists that this rather shameful episode in our family history be recorded, my grandfather literally "blew it." He traveled to Keswick by train and horse-drawn char-a-banc with the money and returned to Ulverston about four weeks later without the business and without the money. Apparently, he had had a "rip-roaring" time in the pubs of Keswick. I leave to the imagination of the reader to reflect on the outcome — my grandmother was very displeased.

Because of the close proximity of Clarence Street to the Grammar School, my brother Ronald and I frequently had lunch with our grandmother. The whole family congregated there during the afternoons of every Christmas Day from the end of World War I to 1925. Subsequently, when we were settled at Cabinet Bank, it was impractical to continue the tradition because no public transportation was available and a three-mile walk, mostly on narrow country lanes, frequently inclement weather, in the dark was not particularly appealing. But the several activities of those rather somber years, the family gatherings at Christmas and New Year's Day remain happy memories. The delicious pastries, home-made of course, the trifle laced with sherry in which silver three-penny coins wrapped in waxed paper were hidden, and following tea, the party games and singing. Recall that in those days — pre-radio and television — the piano was the centerpiece of most drawing rooms. Virtually every member of my family, notably Uncle Irving who was organist at St. Jude's Church, played and sang around the piano. That was a universal family tradition which has regrettably disappeared and ever since there's been nothing to replace it.

In 1922, Aunt Ethel and her husband, with their two young sons, Frank and Fred, immigrated to the United States — they were processed through Ellis Island, where coincidently in 1906 my father had preceded them. My son John discovered this quite recently, albeit serendipitously on the Internet. My grandmother and this demonstrates her indomitable spirit, in 1928 and 1931 respectively, then in her 70's, visited her daughter and family in New Jersey. She traveled alone, crossing the Atlantic in a small Cunard Liner. She loved America. On her return I remember her saying, "Arthur, if ever you visit America, you must see Coney Island." Fortunately she lived to welcome her eldest grandson back to England in July, 1939 after my two wonderful years at MIT. But perhaps not surprisingly, she was disappointed that I had not made the pilgrimage to Coney Island.

Due to the outbreak of WWII and the difficulties of travel, I did not visit Clarence Street again and with the death of my grandmother in December, 1939, an eventful period in my life ended.

My maternal grandparents, Frederick William Harris and Lois Watts, were born in 1856 and 1857 respectively in Peterborough, Lincolnshire, and immigrated to the Lake District during the early 1870's. My grandfather, the eldest of 12 children, demonstrated his independent character by "running away" from home when he was 14.

His first job was as a plate-layer's helper with the Furness Railway Company. As it happened, my maternal great grandfather, Israel Watts, was also a plate-layer. The Furness Railway connected the Carnforth Junction, on the main London-Glasgow Railway with Whitehaven, Cumberland. It not only helped to integrate an isolated region of England, but more importantly, provided ready access to the Lake District. My grandfather was obviously ambitious and hard working. Within a period of 20 years he was promoted from the lowest level to the top level of the company. After several years at Millom, Cumberland, he was appointed as one of the three directors of the company with responsibility for the maintenance of the permanent way. About this time my mother was born in January, 1882. However, the promotion involved the family moving to Ulverston and residing in a comparatively large house close to the Railway Station. It was called Station House. Large wrought-iron gates and a high fence gave the house and its grounds a rather austere appearance. In many respects it fitted my grandfather admirably, because even after his retirement, while still living in Station House, he was always impeccably dressed. Indeed, I do not recall ever seeing him in casual attire. But this was not uncommon in those days — the days when George V reigned over the widespread British Empire.

A notable consequence of the English innate love of gardens was the attractive appearance of the small country Railway Stations. My grandfather was prominent in promoting the annual station garden competition in which all Furness Railway Stations competed for the "Best Garden." A handsome silver trophy was awarded to the winner. I recall on at least two occasions that Ulverston was the winner and the trophy was displayed for all passengers to admire at Ulverston Station. Because the garden of Station House was included in the display, Grandfather Harris was particularly proud of the achievement.

The "nasturtiums" bordering the walkway to the front door, ablaze with color, were his pride and joy — he fertilized them using an ornate brass spray pump, always brilliantly polished and still in my possession.

Grandma Harris in contrast to my paternal grandmother was very reserved and lived in the shadow of her husband. She was undoubtedly my favorite grandparent, not least because of her afternoon teas with fabulous fruit pastries and the fact that she rarely failed to supplement my meager weekly allowance with a "three-penny piece." The children, Aunt Laura, born in 1880, my mother (Mary Ann), born in 1882, and Uncle Fred, born in 1888, adored her. She was not only a wonderful cook, but a talented seamstress as well. A photograph hanging in my den, taken about 1900 shows Grandfather Harris in an elegant business suit with Victorian collar and tie, and Grandmother in a beautiful silk coat (self-sewn of course) and a fashionable hat with her ubiquitous parasol. She bequeathed her culinary and dressmaking talents to Aunt Laura and Mother respectively, while Uncle Fred, who became chief engineer of the famous J.J. Cash Company of Coventry, inherited his father's business acumen. After being stricken by a heavy cold in 1931, Grandfather Harris developed pneumonia and died within a few days. My grandmother, who always seemed impervious to illness, followed four days later. She had literally devoted her entire adult life to her husband and the task being completed, she relaxed and passed peacefully away.

My Mother and Father

What can I say about my parents whose love, devotion and self-sacrifice were pivotal in my upbringing and that of my brothers? Even financially they helped appreciably because unlike the USA and Canada, summer jobs for students were virtually nonexistent in Britain. My debt to them, which regrettably I did not fully appreciate until after my education was completed, is inestimable. The example they set inspired and encouraged all of us.

The summary that follows of my recollection of parents, whose major goal in life was to ensure their sons had a college education, does not do justice to them, but with their innate modesty, I think they would approve.

My father, John William, was born on June 2, 1880 in Ulverston. He was educated at the National School and completed his schooling at age 14, the mandatory school leaving age in 1894. Two years later, he began his apprenticeship as a tool and die maker at the Ulverston Iron Works. On completing his journeyman's qualification in 1900, he joined Vickers Ship Building Company at Barrow-in-Furness. During the following few years, my father met and courted Mother and they were engaged in 1905. For some obscure reason, albeit in light of my future, perceptive, he decided to immigrate to the United States and was processed through Ellis Island in 1906. After only a year he returned to England because Mother adamantly refused to leave Ulverston. They were married at Ulverston Holy Trinity Church during the summer of 1908. I was born in 1910 and my brother, Ronald, was just 19 months younger, so that we grew up together with a close relationship, while Robert was eight years my junior.

During the First World War my father rose steadily at Vickers becoming successively assistant foreman, foreman and assistant manager. At one stage he had over 1000 women working for him. In 1917 he was presented to King George V and Queen Mary when they visited the shipyard — a very distinct honor for a non-executive employee.

My father was in every sense of the word a practical problem-solver with obviously some management skills. At Vickers several of his ideas were patented, but because of company policy he did not benefit financially. It is noteworthy as well that he had an understanding of quite complex systems. During the 30's for example, when I was studying the theoretical behavior of chemical process controls, my father made several valuable suggestions. He understood the basic principles of feedback control without knowledge of calculus through sheer intuition bordering on genius. Fortunately, my son John has inherited some of his grandfather's abilities.

During the depression years when the naval ship building industry was brought to a virtual standstill, Dad lost his job. In retrospect, Britain's disarmament policy during the 1930's almost had disastrous consequences as history will confirm.

However, shortly before WWII started in 1939 my father was recalled by Vickers Armstrong and served throughout the war years in the design department. His daily commute from Cabinet Bank to Barrow-in-Furness involved a two mile walk and an hour's bus ride often in inclement weather conditions. But my father rarely missed a day's work during those long dreary war years. He eventually retired during the fall of 1945 at the age of 65.

But the potential of Cabinet Bank, our home at the time, my father's technical ability and Mother's innate management skills clearly saved the family from appreciable hardship, if not downright poverty. They converted a veritable wilderness into a highly productive vegetable garden and orchard, built a small greenhouse and grew tomatoes, vegetable-marrows and cucumbers, and established a small poultry farm. My father designed and built an incubator for rearing chickens and incorporated the necessary temperature controls. The latter was a magnificent example of ingenuity and improvisation. There was always home produced food in abundance, and coupled with the dairy produce, milk, butter and cheese, supplied virtually for free by our neighbors the Riggs of Cowran Farm, adjacent to us, we lived very well. During harvest time there was always a surplus of vegetables and fruits from our garden and a ready market existing in the local village — this supplemented my parents' income and provided for clothing and new books for us boys, as well as the occasional luxury. Candy, ice cream and an occasional Saturday afternoon at the movies were greatly treasured.

Of my father's many creations, two deserve special mention. The first, and most incredible was the electric lighting system he installed in Cabinet Bank. Oil lamps and candles were inconvenient, expensive and especially in a Victorian house of its size and vintage, a constant fire hazard. Replacing them would be a major challenge.

Fortunately, my parents, inveterate auction sale attendees, were always on the lookout for bargains — and they found one: a second-hand DC electric lighting system!

I well remember the day — a Thursday (market day in Ulverston) — when the Riggs, with my parents aboard, drove their horse and trap into town. My parents returned greatly excited. They had made the winning, albeit very low bid, on a generator set which consisted of a small gasoline engine, electric generator and a 60-volt battery of large lead accumulators. The equipment was delivered by van the following day. It weighed well over a ton.

Over a period of two months, in addition to his normal chores, my father assembled the system in the "wash house" adjacent to the house and wired the kitchen, morning room, dining room and drawing room using only primitive tools. As well he recharged the plates of 30 cells with lead oxide and repaired a fairly sophisticated control panel. The whole family gathered around for the official "switch-on" and our rejoicing when everything worked perfectly was Dad's reward. Needless to add, I've rarely seen him more thrilled.

Still, he wasn't satisfied, even after several months of successful operation, because he figured the fuel cost could be reduced significantly. How? By replacing gasoline as fuel with a mixture of kerosene and super heated steam, reasoned by father. If ever there was a superb example of "Heath Robinsonism" (corresponding to "Rube" Goldberg in the USA) it was my father's solution to the problem. Having primed the engine with an egg-cup full of gasoline, the super-heated steam was produced in a coil of copper tubing wound around the engine exhaust pipe and mixed with kerosene vapor in the carburetor. A constant flow of water (the flow rate was critical and gave rise to much experimentation) was gravity-fed from a tin canister to the coil. And it worked; an example of sheer intuitive genius!

As a fascinating corollary to the achievement, it is interesting to reflect that the fuel of the modern jet airliner consists essentially of one part kerosene and three parts water vapor. I am virtually certain that in 1926 there was no literature on such combustion processes and even if it existed, my father would have been completely unaware of it. In other words, I like to think he was about a half a century ahead of his time.

The second example of his imagination and enterprise was the "still." Although my father drank alcohol very sparingly, he loved a pint or two of beer in the local tavern and as a treat an occasional glass of whiskey. But during the depression years these were rare luxuries. To remedy the deficiency, he built a small distilling apparatus in the basement of Cabinet Bank. I do not remember details of the still except that it consisted of a primitive retort and a series of glass jars interconnected by glass tubing. The source of the heat was a "primus" stove and the alcohol vapor was condensed through a coil of glass tubing cooled by constantly running water. He experimented with a variety of grains and potatoes to produce the fermented mash. The resulting liquor was clearly a success as witness the hilarity of his friends after one of his parties. Regrettably, after a couple of years operation, the still exploded and fragments were imbedded in the basement ceiling. My mother, who strongly disapproved of the operation, was fortunately not at home at the time. But my father redeemed himself, especially at Christmas time because as an expert toy-maker he insured that the family was entertained over the holidays with a magic lantern, toboggans and a wonderful steam engine. These remain cherished memories.

Mother attended the Millom one-room village school until she was 14. From an early age, she had a natural talent for sewing — a skill which served our family in good stead in later years. When Grandfather Harris was promoted to his executive position and the family moved to

Ulverston, mother was employed as a seamstress by the leading couture of the town — May Duff.

The Victorian era was fading and the Edwardian dawning when mother was in her prime — carefree days when her main recreational interests were cycling and dancing. In those days ballroom dancing was extremely popular and far more elegant than today. Such dances as the Viennese Waltz, the Valeta, and Sir Roger de Coverley were traditional, and the fox trot, when introduced a century ago, was a sensation. There were several dance halls in Ulverston, one of which was where my parents met. In spite of having a shy disposition, mother shone on the dance floor, partnered in the competitions, not by my father, but by his brother, Uncle Charlie, another star performer. They won first prize on many occasions and were even invited to compete in more distant locations.

Lightburn Road, where my brothers and I were born, was my parents' first home. It was a perfect location because of the close proximity of the schools, shops and churches. As well, it was only a few minutes walk from the Railway Station, from which my father traveled daily to Barrow-in-Furness, leaving at 6 a.m. and returning at 6 p.m. weekdays and 1 p.m. on Saturdays on the "Workman's Train." The small house had no indoor toilet or bath and with their growing family, my parents, by the mid 1920's decided that a more spacious dwelling was essential. In 1925 they made a critical decision and at an auction sale, bought Cabinet Bank, Pennington. Although at a bargain price and with a large mortgage, I'm still at a loss to understand how they managed on a wage of five pounds a week. In light of what transpired subsequently, it proved to be the most inspired decision of their lives. My parents complemented each other perfectly at Cabinet Bank. My father the innovator and provider, my mother the manager and driver. Neither of them ever complained.

In light of modern household conveniences, it is difficult to give a realistic impression of the magnitude of mother's chores. With no domestic help, she scrubbed weekly on "hands and knees" the flagstone floors of three rooms, and the hallway, cooked meals on the kitchen stove, did the laundry by hand in the wash house, cleaned carpets by "beating" them on a clothes line and maintained the large house in pristine condition. As well, she sewed and darned endlessly during the long winter evenings. For five years when her sons were ravenously hungry teenagers always needing winter clothing, she lodged and fed three paying guests — the principal of Pennington Elementary School and his family. But as the years rolled by her dreams were fulfilled and her boys went to college. Cabinet Bank having served its purpose magnificently became neither necessary nor viable, and we persuaded our parents to move to a small bungalow on the fringe of the ancient Druid encampment at Birkrigg Common. It is incongruous to recall that a 50kgm bomb actually exploded on the Common a mere 400 yards from the bungalow.

The location was historic. The Common housed the secret burial grounds of the early Quakers, about two miles from Swarthmoor Hall, the original Friends Meeting House, and a large Druid Circle. The mushrooms which grew prolifically on the Common were the most delicious I have ever tasted.

Equally distant from Ulverston, but more accessible than Cabinet Bank, especially when my father acquired a second-hand Morris Minor car, my parents lived a relatively stress-free life until my father was stricken with a rare form of cancer, which had been caused by his inhalation of nickel dust while working at his bench some 60 years previously. In spite of the wonderful care provided by our good friend Dr. John Edge, he suffered severe pain for about 18 months, but never admitted it. His courage was extraordinary. Not surprisingly, mother did everything possible to help ease his suffering and endured many sleepless nights. Such devotion and self-denial and sheer guts were an inspiration to all of us. A few days before my father died on July 4, 1954, Patricia and I visited him at Barrow Infirmary. He was alert and comparatively free from pain. In his fine baritone voice he sang several verses from some of his favorite songs — "Danny Boy," "I'll Take You Home Again, Kathleen," and the vaudeville hit he loved so well, "The Belle of New York."

Essentially, because her neighbors were "the salt of the earth," Mother continued to live at Rondane for another 10 years. Fortunately for us, her greatest joy was to entertain her boys and their families. She always excelled as a pastry cook and had few if any equals. How we loved staying with her in her small but impeccably kept home — about two miles from where I was born.

But there came a time when her physician decided that she would be far better off living in a small private home for elderly ladies. Dr. John Edge knew the ideal place. It was run by one of the kindest people we have ever known — Kay Brown. The home was called Water Yeat Mill and was located a mile from Ruskin's home on Coniston Lake. It consisted of eight small one-room apartments in which the residents could be surrounded by their most treasured possessions. All the residents were in their 70's and 80's.

The Mill atmosphere was extremely congenial. It could not be otherwise — Kay Brown saw to that. The housekeeper, Mrs. Toose, came in daily and cooked mid-day meals in true Cumbrian fashion. It was served in a small dining room, and as the saying goes, the ladies were waited on hand and foot, most of them for the first time in their lives. That certainly applied to Mother. For breakfast and supper, the residents fended for themselves, but Mother after about 12 years in residence, received special treatment. Mrs. Hudson, a fellow resident, adopted her and very deservedly, she lived a life of comparative luxury. Patricia and I paid our last visit to the Mill a month before her death in September, 1978. She was in her 97th year. A few days after her burial next to my father in the Ulverston Cemetery, I received a letter from Paul Palmer, a neighbor, and it is fitting that I should quote a couple of sentences:

> *"We shall neither of us readily forget the charm which your mother spread and feel so very glad that you did in fact come and visit her when you did. Kay Brown said that it was so peaceful and easy. A really nice end for a really valuable and long life."*

As a memorial to my parents, it is also fitting that I should outline the achievements of my two brothers.

Ronald's career, after a brilliant record at grammar school culminating in the award of an Open Scholarship at Queens College, Cambridge in 1931, lived up to everyone's high expectations. In his bachelor's degree he obtained the highest honors achievable (A Wrangler) and earned the Master of Arts degree of Cambridge University. Subsequently, he achieved the rare honor of Membership of the Order of the British Empire. He was commissioned major (Royal Signals) in World War II and appointed scientific advisor to General Sir Frederick Pyle, C-in-C Anti-Aircraft Command. After the war he became headmaster of Audinshaw Grammar School and ultimately headmaster of Penrith Royal Grammar School. He authored nine books on mathematical subjects and achieved distinction in several sports, being vice captain of the Queens College Cricket XI and the college soccer team. He was elected a member of the Penrith Council and was treasurer of his local parish church. Ronald was an ardent fly fisherman and in this regard followed in the footsteps of my father. He shared with me a love of rock climbing and I recall an episode which occurred on Easter Saturday when we were home on vacation from our respective universities. We decided that conditions were perfect for some serious climbing, and the group of fells called Dow Crags which border Coniston Water about 20 miles distant was the ideal place.

The designated climbs on Dow Crags range from easy to severe. However, these classifications apply only when the climbing conditions are ideal. Ice and snow-coated rocks obviously increase the difficulty of all the climbs. Ice axes are essential, and I soon discovered that the so-called "Easy Gully" would provide all the excitement I could tolerate.

Although the snow-covered track leading to the Crags at first sight was featureless, at second sight it certainly wasn't. Naturally, they were bleak. That's a Lakeland feature, especially during the winter and early spring. Certainly uninviting except to devotees like Ronald and myself. As well, the scene would have been inviting to the incomparable British landscape painters J.M.W. Turner and John Constable, and the Lakeland poets, especially William Wordsworth, who have given us glorious visions of their mystery and majesty and timelessness through images and words..

As we approached the Crags, their most distinguishing features, the gullies, which carve huge slashes in the mountain side, showed up with increasing clarity. On that day they were essentially miniature glaciers. It was fortunate that the ubiquitous mist which so frequently enshrouds the fell slopes, was absent.

Nevertheless, in retrospect, it should have been obvious that the climb we envisioned would be more difficult than we had contemplated. Undaunted, we laid out the rope, about 30 feet in length, secured it to our sturdy leather belts and, with Ronald in the lead, set off. My brother, albeit younger, was the more experienced and accomplished climber. This was in part due to the fact that at six feet two inches, he was four inches taller than I, and this turned out to be a crucial factor during our climb.

The first stages of the ascent were easy — not too steep scrambles in loose rock with a scree-like quality. However, the scree-like slopes soon became quite hazardous and it was comforting to be roped to by brother.

Fortunately, there was only a light wind, and apart from the seagulls with their raucous chattering, we appeared to be alone on "Easy Gully," and probably on all of Dow Crags. I can still remember the sheer exhilaration of the climb; the quickened pulse rate and the tingling toes that provide the thrill. But there was something else. There is something intangible and unique to the psyche of all who love climbing rocks and mountains. It is identifiable in a single word — "excelsior" — and it casts some light on the response of George Mallory, the renowned Everest climber, who when asked, "Why climb Everest?" replied "Because it's there."

As Ronald and I climbed higher, the nature of the gully changed from scree to patchy snow and ice. Extra caution was required. But Ronald was equal to the task. Obviously, we were taking a risk — youth and recklessness are usually synonymous. But it never occurred to us that the higher we climbed the gully, with the increasing hazard of "black ice," the greater the risk. Fortunately, our ice axes were a Godsend — my brother carved rudimentary steps and I followed about 10 feet behind.

All was going well until we were faced with the only really difficult problem of the whole climb — a boulder which blocked the gully and hence the route to the top. In Lake District climbing parlance, such a boulder is referred to as a "chock-stone." And there was inevitably an overhang — eight feet high and coated with an inch of black ice.

To negotiate it we had to climb the "chimney" between the sides of the gully and boulder. This was in fact our only choice because descent of that steep, ice gully was not an option. Indeed, it would have been suicide to attempt it. Happily, the chock stone provided shelter from the continuous cascade of snow falling from the cornices at the top of the gully. The memory of crouching there beneath the boulder preparing for our assault on the chimney is a vivid one. But not as vivid as the 30 minutes or so that followed.

Ronald, after a couple of false starts, eventually squirmed (the only appropriate description) his way up and around the chock-stone and disappeared from sight about 12 feet above me. His advantage in height gave him the extra leverage he needed. The technique was to jam oneself between the walls of the chimney — knees on one side, back on the other — and to inch one's way up the chimney and I mean inch literally.

Then it was my turn. Not helpful was the fact that my hands were numb with cold, as the icy surface precluded wearing gloves. After I should imagine about 20 minutes of futile and frustrating struggle, I had climbed not one inch.

Fortunately, it was very still and Ronald and I had no trouble communicating. After a few minutes silence, he called down, "I think

I've got a belay,"[2] he added. "I've anchored my axe in a rock fissure." Being roped to it, I surmised he was sufficiently secure to withstand my weight if I should fall in negotiating the chimney. I took him at his word and was suffused with a tremendous burst of energy.

Although recollections of the next five minutes or so that passed as I inched my way up the chimney have dimmed over the intervening years, I definitely recall that there was continuous tension on the rope. My brother was not only willing me to press upward, he was giving me a physical assist.

Rarely in my life have I been more relieved than when my head emerged from the chimney. Indeed, it was more than a relief. It was a salvation, made all the more so when I found that my brother's belay was very superficial. He had taken a tremendous risk because had I slipped, he could not possibly have held on, especially with his icy footing. We would both have hurtled with increasing speed down that treacherous gully.

Still in a state of shock, I believe I said something like, "You crazy son-of-a-gun. You took a hell of a risk," or words to that effect. But in his usual modest way, he just grinned and we carried on.

Now all was plain sailing or more to the point, plain climbing, and we reached the summit of the gully well before sunset. The descent to Torver, via Walna Scar was incident-free and the bus left right on time.

On Easter Saturday in the year 2000, I telephoned from my home in Bermuda Village, North Carolina, to Ronald's in Hedgerows, Margate Cross, Cumbria, and we shared our recollections of that day. His memories of the event I've recorded here were as vivid as my own.

Robert, my younger brother, left an enviable legacy. Athlete, educator and visionary, he was a man of rare sensibility who unfortunately died at the age of 65 from cancer. During the war as a parachute instructor in the RAF he trained many Allied agents and dispatched them over enemy-occupied France. After several years as a teacher, he was appointed Inspector of Physical Education for Manchester City High Schools. But his crowning achievement after a tremendous struggle raising funds was the establishment of an educational/recreational facility for underprivileged children in the Lake

---

[2]A belay is a fundamental procedure in rock climbing when two or more climbers are roped together, especially on difficult pitches, i.e. stages of the climb. The lead anchors himself using the rope, to a solid rock base in order to support the weight of climbers below should they lose their footing. Modern climbers now have the advantage of pitons and special rope attachments, something we had to do without those many years ago.

District. It is located at Ghyll Head, Lake Windermere. Regrettably, he was never given the credit he deserved for this venture. In a letter published in the Manchester Press, the mother of a son who had benefited wrote:

> *"Sole recognition for the project was given to the City Fathers and no acknowledgment was made of the late Mr. Robert Porter. It was he who had the vision to realize the potential of such a venture. Bob Porter was one man ahead of his time."*

Accordingly, in their respective ways, my parents and brothers have left their mark on the Lake District and thereby maintained centuries old traditions.

Chapter 3

THE EARLY YEARS

MY first memory is of a sea voyage with my parents. It was on August 4, 1914, the day after the outbreak of World War I. We crossed the Irish Sea in a ferry steamer in very stormy weather and mother and I were violently seasick. Our summer holiday in the Isle of Man had been abruptly terminated after only a few days because my father, a very conscientious individual, decided that his job at the shipyard took precedence.

After that rather unpleasant beginning to life, I recall little until the unforgettable day I started school. Miss Probert's School for Boys and Girls aged four to six years was home-based. A small living room comprised the classroom. There were about 10 children armed with slates and we sat on the floor. Miss Probert, an elderly spinster, was a superb teacher with a fine reputation throughout the town. Her fees were about five shillings a week per student or about six percent of my father's income.

A strict disciplinarian, she taught us the elements of reading, writing and arithmetic, but most important of all, she demonstrated to her young pupils that learning was fun. After a lifetime, spent first as student and then as teacher, I heartily agree with her. And of course teaching and learning are synonymous. My attendance at this small "academy" was indeed the first manifestation of my parents' determination that my education and that of my brothers was top priority.

After two years under Miss Probert's tutelage, I was eligible to attend at age seven the local elementary school. It was the Lightburn Council School and it was free. Fortunately, the school was located only 200 yards from my home. On my first day I recall attending the morning school assembly and the very first hymn we sang on that Monday morning was "Onward Christian Soldiers." By any standard, the teaching staff was first class. The headmaster, Mr. Hibbard, tall, slender and austere, was about 50 years old. He was a strict but fair disciplinarian who did not hesitate to use the cane when it was deserved. Fortunately, I can only recall one occasion when I was delinquent by playing around in the school wash room and justifiably I was caned on the right hand with a yard-long cane — it hurt! I progressed from standard one to standard five without distinction, but I held my own. Each year I had a different teacher, but in my last year Mr. Athersmith was my favorite. He taught all the subjects, but excelled in elementary mathematics, which consisted essentially of the elements of arithmetic. But as well, at the early age of 10, I was introduced to algebra and this has held me in good stead ever since.

My first real examination came at the end of my fourth year when I sat the examination for the County Junior Scholarship. At the time virtually all secondary schools in our county were fee-paying, and although the fees were comparatively small, about eight pounds sterling a term, or 24 pounds a year, they were quite beyond my parents' limited resources. It was essential, therefore, that I win a Junior Scholarship. For entrance to the Ulverston Victoria Grammar School, only five scholarships were available and I was fortunate to win one. I was fifth on the list — providence was on my side. The scholarship not only paid my tuition fees, but also covered the cost of school books.

It might be of interest to note that in contrast to all modern schools, my elementary school had no facilities for swimming, gymnastics, etc. — no pool, no gymnasium. The only recreational facility was a small playground with a shelter at one end with no equipment of any description. Nevertheless, a large vacant area, subsequently the Ulverston Park, was available for soccer and cricket in season.

During 1915-1916 when I was a pupil at Miss Proberts and subsequently at the Lightburn School, the war was being waged with increasing ferocity and on an increasing scale and I recall, albeit vaguely, many stories of the action. Our single source of information was the daily newspaper which my father brought home after work. I learned that the German army had invaded and swept through Belgium and that many Belgians were refugees. The inhabitants of Ulverston received several families of these unfortunate people and I recall meeting a few of them in the market place. There was tremendous activity in Barrow-in-Furness, especially in the shipyard where my father was employed. Work proceeded on an 24-hour a day basis and special trains from Ulverston had to be put into service. Clearly everything possible had to go into the war effort and, even as young as I was, I appreciated that a dangerous situation existed for our country.

As the war progressed, an increasing number of soldiers and sailors were conscripted and transported to either the front lines in France or to naval barracks in southern England. We were told of the horror of trench warfare and of the awful hardships suffered by the men in trenches, especially when the weather was cold and wet. The whole population of Britain suffered increasingly because of the activities of the German U-boats. We relied heavily on food imports from the United States and Canada, and as the merchant ship losses escalated, our meager food rations suffered. Fortunately, the farming community around Ulverston thrived and we were rarely short of milk, but butter and eggs were strictly rationed and meat was a rare luxury. However, Mother, as always the ideal housekeeper, succeeded in feeding her family not well, but adequately. From time to time there was good news from the war zones, notably the British navy's successes in the Battles of Jutland and the Falkland Islands.

Tragedy struck the family when my Uncle Frank, aged 26, was killed during the first day of the Battle of the Somme in June, 1916. This was one of the most infamous battles of the war which, in retrospect, appears to have been very ill-advised. More than 30,000 men died on a single day when they became entangled in vast areas of barbed wire fences and subjected to deadly enemy machine gun crossfire. Most families in Britain suffered grievous losses as the war seemed endless.

The Germans made frequent air attacks on various parts of Britain, which were bombed from the fearsome Zeppelins. These were large airships whose appearance in the sky must have been a terrifying experience for people living in the large cities, especially London. Although we were spared such atrocities in the northwest of England, toward the end of the war in 1918, I recall seeing a British airship flying over our town. It was an incredible sight and a big thrill.

The United States entered the war at a very critical period and I recall that the news was received with considerable relief. Within a year the armistice was signed at 11 a.m. on November 11, 1918, and at the age of eight I entered into the joyous celebrations at the Coronation Hall with great fervor. The excited crowd milled around the square waving Union Jacks and blowing horns. The town band tried to compete, but with little success. Of course a national holiday was declared and my whole family rejoiced together. On the following Sunday we attended a

Service of Thanksgiving at Holy Trinity Church where I sang in the choir.

Ulverston Victoria Grammar School, a co-educational foundation where I was to spend eight very happy years, was founded about 1890. It is a most attractive building with a large playing field for cricket and rugby football and where the annual sports day is held. It is within a stones throw of Grandmother Porter's home in Clarence Street. The school is situated beneath that wonderful landmark Hoad Hill. I can still recall the School Song which I sang on many occasions:

> *"And at times will rise the image,*
> *Of the School beneath the hill*
> *Of the field where once we sported,*
> *And our hearts again will thrill.*
> *Per laborem ad honorem."*

The headmaster, Mr. G.A. Daniel, was a distinguished elderly man two years away from retirement. Unlike most headmasters of the times, he used the cane sparingly and was greatly respected by pupils, staff and the townsfolk. Always gowned, he presided at morning assembly when the whole school attended for prayers, a lesson from scriptures and announcements. The staff, all wearing gowns, sat on either side of the headmaster, men on one side and women on the other. My favorite teachers whom I recall with pride and pleasure were George Calderbank, physics, and Miss Bowe, history. But there was not a single teacher whom I did not admire. George Calderbank was a phenomenon to whom I owe a very great deal.

About 400 pupils were crowded into a comparatively small school hall — standing. We wore uniforms, boys in blazers and short or long trousers, girls in gym slips. Both boys and girls wore the school tie.

Virtually from our very first year, Form I, we were classed as science or arts. The science Forms were designated (b) and the arts (a). However, to a large extent the classification was arbitrary until Form V when specialization began. For example, as well as mathematics, physics and chemistry on the science side, I took English, French, Latin and geography on the arts side. Regrettably, I dropped Latin after my first year and took the alternative subject, geography. Each year we were assigned our Form room where all subjects except physics and chemistry were taught. Classes in the latter were held in very well-equipped laboratories.

It is worth noting that in the early 20's and for many years subsequently, school teaching was a very honored and respected profession, and the headmaster was regarded as equal to the senior physician in the town and the local Bishop. Furthermore, salaries were commensurate with the teacher's stature. The idea that there might come a day in the future when teachers would be "unionized" would have been abhorrent to not only the teachers but the population as a whole. It is not surprising that from an early age my ambition was to become a physics teacher.

Sports were well-organized with good competition between the various Houses — Red, White and Blue. I played both rugby and cricket for the Red House and one, for me memorable occasion, I actually saved my House from certain defeat on the cricket field when I opened the batting, kept my end up through out the inning and as a direct consequence, I was awarded my House colors. I wore my House tie with great pride. Nonetheless, compared with my brother Ronald, I was a mere "rabbit." My brother Robert excelled on the rugby field and at the annual sports when in successive years he won the Gold Medal and was acclaimed "victor ludorem." I played both rugby and cricket for my school without distinction, but enjoyed every minute of the matches, especially when we traveled by train to schools as far away as St. Bees at Whitehaven.

I faced my first scholastic hurdle in 1926 when I sat for the so-called Northern Universities Joint Board Matriculation School Certificate Examination. For some unaccountable reason, probably because of the many hours I spent practicing cricket at the nets, I did not take the examination seriously and was completely unprepared for it. We sat at individual desks in the school hall; a master and a mistress, duly gowned of course, invigilated. At the stroke of 9 o'clock, each morning the examination papers were distributed and two or three hours later were retrieved. The papers were set and graded by an independent body of academics in Manchester. The results were posted through the mail about two months later, and not surprisingly, I had failed. My father's only remark was "Arthur, I'm very disappointed." This really made me realize how I had let him down and I resolved to do better.

As a result of my failing to pass this examination, I was obliged to repeat my Form V year. It turned out to be a blessing in disguise for reasons which will emerge subsequently. Instead of spending the six weeks summer vacation of 1926 playing cricket and other pursuits, I spent many hours each day studying. When school resumed in September, I was confident that I would succeed. Indeed, it was essential because Ronald, hitherto a year behind, caught up and we were together in the same Form. Apart from the classes in French, always the "Achilles heel" of the Porters, I did well. Homework, which normally took two or three hours in the evenings, was pursued diligently and especially in my favorite subject — physics — I excelled. Furthermore, now living at Cabinet Bank, the whole environment was more conducive to study. Indeed there was little else to do. I was fortunate as well, to be coached by my French teacher, Miss Hobley, two or three evenings a week. It was absolutely essential to pass the French examination for entrance to university.

I took the examination in early July, 1927 and the results were announced in early August. I shall never forget the morning when the postman delivered the small book in which were listed the successful candidates. I eagerly scanned the book, found the Ulverston Grammar School list and there was my name and to my great joy, opposite it was the letter "d"* [3]physics, chemistry, history. Most unfortunately, Ronald's name was not listed. He'd failed in French and like myself, was required to repeat the year. A surprising fact was that my distinction in history was the only one in the whole school — not one of the arts side candidates had achieved distinction.

The summer of 1927, especially after hearing about my success in the Matriculation Examination, was very happy and carefree. A notable event was the total eclipse of the sun, which very rarely happens over England. The band of total eclipse was only about 50 miles wide and one of the best viewing places was Giggleswick on the Yorkshire moors. The school arranged for the Ribble Bus Company to take a group of pupils to the site. We left early in the morning to drive the 80 miles because totality was due at about 9 a.m. There was considerable excitement when we learned that the vehicle ahead of us — about a quarter of a mile or so — carried the Prince of Wales. Equipped with "smoked glass," we found an excellent location near the village. The early stages of the eclipse began after about 30 minutes wait. Unfortunately, but not uncharacteristically for this part of England, there were frequent cloudy periods and our viewing was interrupted. A minute or two before totality, the phenomenon of "Bailey's Beads" occurred and I observed it, but then the clouds moved in and I missed seeing the corona, which is the most spectacular phenomenon in a solar eclipse. This was a great disappointment. Two miles away where the Prince was watching, the crowds were very fortunate and saw the whole exciting display. It is

---

[3]"d" meant Distinction, the highest grade

interesting to note that during the eclipse, the degree of darkness of the sky was quite remarkable — birds stopped singing and all the characteristics of the night occurred. It was the only time in my life when I've seen a total solar eclipse or about 99 percent of it, and it was a morning I shall never forget.

When I returned to school in early September there was a new headmaster, Dr. Herbert W. Cousins. Austere and erudite and a fine rugby player in his youth (he was "capped" by the University of Durham), he had a profound impact on my career. Together with Mr. George Calderbank, the physics master who taught the VIth Form, they instilled in me an insatiable curiosity which has served me well throughout my lifetime.

The final two or three years in English high schools, and indeed in European high schools as a whole, unlike their American counterparts, are highly specialized. In Form VIb I attended classes in only three subjects — pure mathematics, applied mathematics and physics. On the arts side, Form VIa, the subjects were English, history and a language, either French or Latin. This very restricted curriculum was, and unfortunately still is, regrettable in so far as it is not education in the true sense of the word. The fault essentially is due to the universities and the fact that the undergraduate programs are only three years in duration, even the honor courses. Not surprisingly, I was introduced to the elements of calculus, coordinate geometry and trigonometry at an early age. The Higher School Certificate examination at the age of 18 or 19 is highly specialized — only three subjects. The examinations are the basis for university entrance, as well as for scholarships.

I must confess that apart from history, I was not a good student in the English language and literature courses and certainly not in the French language, which I had been obliged to take for matriculation. But I was in my element in the VIth Form because I had a wonderful teacher in George Calderbank and pretty good teachers in mathematics — Mr. Helm and Mr. Crosland. I was fortunate as well to be appointed a School Prefect. Although the total number of students in the upper VIth Form was more than 20, only six Prefects were appointed. My appointment was certainly not based on my sporting ability.

I sat for the Higher School Certificate Examination, which was also set by the universities, in July, 1929 at the age of 18. I passed the examination with good grades and obtained my Higher School Certificate. But unfortunately my grades were not high enough for me to win a university scholarship. Only 10 State Scholarships and 20 County

Scholarships were awarded for the whole county of Lancashire each year. It should be emphasized that these scholarships were awarded solely on the basis of academic achievement in the examination and did not take into account a family's financial resources. In retrospect, my failure to win a scholarship was a blessing because my whole career would have been very different if I'd gone up to university in September, 1929 rather than a year later. Why? Because it is doubtful that I would have met my mentor and friend, Professor Douglas R. Hartree, F.R.S.

Accordingly, I returned to school in September, 1929 to repeat the final year. My brother Ronald again caught up and we were in the same class. To my surprise, but great pleasure, the Headmaster appointed me Head Prefect, effectively Head Boy of the school, and I had diverse responsibilities, not least of which was reading the lesson at morning assembly. Repeating a second year at Grammar School was not the norm for a student who would aspire subsequently to professorships in several universities. But for me it had its compensations, most importantly was the fact that Ronald and I were in the same class and he was a keen competitor.

Together with Mr. Calderbank, I explored various avenues for university scholarships and made application to two of them. The first was to the University of Sheffield where I sat for the Edgar Allen Scholarship in February, 1930. The following month I sat for the Royal College of Science Scholarship at Imperial College University of London. Either of these scholarships would have provided adequate funds for me to attend one of the respective universities. The mathematical papers were very difficult and I failed to win a scholarship. It is interesting to reflect that 25 years after the failures, I was offered the Chair of Electrical Engineering at Sheffield, which I declined and the Chair of Light Electrical Engineering (I inaugurated the Chair) at Imperial College, which I accepted. In July of 1930 I sat the Higher School Certificate Examination for a second time and I was not only successful, but achieved distinction in physics and most importantly, was awarded a Lancashire County Major Scholarship. I had the satisfaction as well of being informed (in those days grades were only revealed to the school staff and not to the student) that I had achieved the highest grade in physics ever earned by any pupil at the Grammar School. For this I was given a special prize — a textbook of physics which proved extremely useful when I reached university.

A few months previously, I had decided that if I were to win a scholarship, I would attend the University of Manchester. This was an inspired choice, and I applied for a place in the Honors School of Physics. My County Scholarship was worth 60 pounds sterling a year, which was inadequate to cover fees, living expenses and books. But at the time I was determined to attempt to follow in the footsteps of my idol, George Calderbank, and become a teacher of physics in a Grammar School. Accordingly, I applied for a Department of Education grant which would cover all of my tuition fees, plus 35 pounds sterling a year for supplemental expenses. Both my applications were successful.

Chapter 4

THE UNIVERSITY OF MANCHESTER

AFTER a carefree summer camping at Bardsea Beach, I registered as a first year student at the University of Manchester on October 7, 1930. I was the first Porter of my family to attend university because Ronald's entry to the University of Cambridge as a scholar at Queens College had to be delayed a year because he had failed the language qualification — par for the course!

A few words about my alma mater may not be out of place. Owen's College, the University of Manchester's founding institution was chartered in 1851. Although I was unaware of it at the time of my application, the University's Physical Laboratories had a revered name in nuclear science and X-ray crystallography. Let me summarize its claim to fame. Lord Rutherford, the founder of nuclear science, was professor and head of the laboratories from 1909 to 1928. During this period he carried out experiments which laid the foundation for the subsequent development of nuclear energy and a host of related fields. He was succeeded by Sir Lawrence Bragg, who together with his father pioneered the determination of molecular structure utilizing X-ray spectra. This work eventually led to such profoundly important developments as the determination of the structure of the DNA molecule. Professor Sir Lawrence Bragg, who was to play such an important part in my future, ultimately became Cavendish Professor at Cambridge. Both Rutherford and Bragg were awarded Nobel Prizes. Notably, my professor received the award at the age of 27 — the youngest Nobel laureate in history. The list of alumni and staff members is a veritable "Who's Who" in physics. Let me mention a few of them: J.J. Thomson, who discovered the electron and subsequently became Cavendish Professor at Cambridge; Niels Bohr, who was first to formulate atomic structure; James Chadwick, who discovered the neutron; John Cockcroft, who, together with Walton, was the first to split the nucleus of an atom. All won Nobel Prices. It was in the footsteps of these giants that I followed in October of 1930.

I will not dwell on my academic performance as a freshman because it was influenced by my being involved in so many extracurricular activities. For instance, I acted on the stage of the Manchester Opera House in February, 1931, when the university's annual review "Shrove Pie" was staged. Rehearsals were very time consuming and my studies suffered. Furthermore, my first residence in 19 Limegrove, adjacent to the university, was not conducive to academic endeavor. As one of the only two freshmen in residence there, I was subjected to a whole variety of rather rowdy experiences. As a member of the University Union (of which I'm a Life Member), I recall in particular Saturday night socials (i.e. dances) when I used to meet my date inside the dance hall in order to avoid paying the one shilling admission. At the end of the dance she was invariably escorted to a street car. A few years later I attended the formal dances in the University's Halls of Residence which were "card" affairs and necessitated my acquiring a second-hand dinner jacket.

But there were some highlights. I shall never forget, for example, "Jimmy" Nuttall's first lecture on electromagnetism. He was the joint inventor of the Gieger-Nuttall Counter, one of the key instruments in the study of radioactivity. It was an awe-inspiring experience, not least because of the boisterous behavior of the majority of the students who were upper classmen.

Within a week or two of the end of the third term as a freshman, I suffered a somewhat debilitating sickness which precluded my taking the examinations at the end of the year. Fortunately, I was given an "agrotat" which meant I was excused attendance at the examination without penalty. This was very fortuitous in so far as I was reasonably certain my performance would have resulted in my being near the bottom of the class of about 36 first-year Honors Physics students. My second year was in marked contrast to my first for two reasons. First, through the enterprise of a good friend, Wilfred Thatcher, we obtained a new place of residence. It was with Mr. and Mrs. Hodgson in Crumpsall, about three miles from the University and an easy bike ride. Secondly, I was determined to study more intensely. In the examinations at the end of my second year, I placed third in the class and was awarded the H.G. J. Moseley Memorial Prize. (Moseley was the brilliant young English scientist who discovered the fundamental structure of the X-ray spectra of the elements.) Regrettably, he was killed in the Gallipoli Campaign of WWI at the age of 27 — it was a tragic loss for world physics because he had demonstrated such brilliance at such an early age.

During my second and third years at university, I was fortunate enough to establish a good friendship with Bert Toft. He became famous for his Rugby Union playing activities in later years. After being "capped" for the Lancashire County Team, he was rapidly elevated to international stature and was "capped" for the England XV no fewer than six successive years. Bert became famous as probably the finest "hooker" (center of the front row forwards) in the many international matches he played. He was captain of the English team for several seasons before retiring from the game. In those days the game was strictly amateur, although more recently I understand a degree of professionalism has been introduced.

In preparation for my third year as an undergraduate, I spent many hours studying during the summer vacation of 1932. During the months of June through September at Cabinet Bank I was comparatively secluded and my parents cooperated magnificently. I knew that the coming year would be the most critical of my life. A notable feature of the third year curriculum was the comparatively few lectures a student was expected to attend — only eight lectures a week, three of which were given by Professor Bragg on Physical Optics. But it was expected that he would spend at least 20 hours in the laboratories on experimental work. Consequently, the student was left very much to his own devices and independent study was encouraged.

The period November '32 to April '33 proved to be both exciting and exhausting. During the mid 1920's, physics had undergone a major transformation from classical to quantum physics. The contributions of Planck, Rutherford, Schrodinger and Heisenberg were breathtaking. These scientists, all Nobel Laureates, had an important influence on my life and career. Their work was reflected in the lectures I took in my final undergraduate year.

Because of my involvement, some four decades subsequently, with nuclear power, and the centrality of the neutron in all nuclear reactions, it is fascinating to observe that this fundamental particle had not even been discovered when I was attending lectures on atomic structure.

Indeed, prior to the discovery of the neutron by James Chadwick in 1933, it was assumed that the constituent particles in atomic nuclei were protons and electrons. In fact, of course, the constituents are protons and neutrons. But this was not realized until a year or two after my graduation.

I completed my first final year laboratory experiment satisfactorily and then came the crucial question which essentially decided my career. Dr. Brentano, the laboratory supervisor asked: "What are you interested in?" After my first suggestion had been rejected because it was apparently too sophisticated for a third year undergraduate, I reflected momentarily on the fact that very morning I had picked up at random a recent volume of the *Proceedings of the Cambridge Philosophical Society*. Opening it, again at random, there was a paper by E.C. Bullard on "The Solution of Second Order Differential Equations Using a Moving Coil Galvanometer." I had been intrigued. Hence my spontaneous reply to Brentano was — "calculating machines." He was obviously surprised because the probability of a physics student being interested in such a topic was virtually zero. But he was quick to respond, "That's very interesting because today I had lunch with Professor Douglas Hartree (then professor of applied mathematics) who has just returned from the United States where he visited the Department of Electrical Engineering at MIT. Hartree inquired about the possibility of any third year student being interested in helping to build a machine to solve differential equations. I suggest you go immediately to see Professor Hartree."

Douglas Hartree, then aged about 33 and very young for professorial rank, was sitting at his desk, on which, to my absolute astonishment, was a structure made entirely of Meccano parts. The main component was a small wheel at the end of a rod resting on a wooden disk, which could be rotated. I explained that I had come at the suggestion of Dr. Brentano," whereupon Hartree's eyes literally "lit up." He told me about his visit to MIT to see the Bush Differential Analyzer. "Would I be interested in assisting him in developing a model of the Bush machine?" I was intrigued, albeit completely ignorant of the implications and replied in the affirmative. He immediately telephoned Brentano and it was confirmed that my participation in the project was quite acceptable as a requirement for the B.Sc. degree. My initial assignment was to build a model "torque amplifier" and to determine its behavior using a variety of materials. I will not pursue details of the system. Suffice it to say, it was based on the well-known "capstan" principle.

Fortunately, the physics laboratories were equipped with excellent machine-shop capabilities and I had no difficulty in building the apparatus and carrying out the investigations. The main conclusion was that such a system would be adequate for incorporating in a model differential analyzer(d.a.). Douglas Hartree was delighted.

It was understood that if I succeeded in winning a graduate research scholarship based on the results of my final examinations, which were held in early June 1933, Hartree would proceed with the building of the model machine with me as his assistant. I worked diligently and when the final results were announced, I was awarded the B. Sc. degree with first class honors in physics and was ranked number one in my class. Consequently, I was awarded the top scholarships — the Samuel Bright Scholarship, and a graduate research scholarship — the combined income from which would be adequate for my fees, accommodation and supplementary expenses.

My first step on the academic ladder had been completed successfully, indeed beyond my wildest dreams. My many hours of study had paid off. The graduation ceremony in Convocation Hall, attended by my mother and father, was a happy occasion for all.

Before proceeding to the next step — graduate school — let me record an episode which throws some light on my radical attitudes as a young man. Although, during the early 1930's my university in unison with most British institutions of higher learning, was a comparative beehive of political activity, mostly left-leaning. I had neither the time nor the inclination for such activities. But this was an exception.

During the spring of 1933 the Student's Union of Oxford University had passed the Motion: "That this house will in no circumstances fight for King and Country" by a large majority. During those dark and menacing days when Hitler was creating international tensions as a result of his dictatorial powers — concentration camps and persecution of the Jewish population, armaments build-up on an unprecedented scale, scornful brushing aside of international arms limitation treaties — the times were not conducive to complacency, especially in Britain. But we students thought otherwise.

Following Oxford's lead, the student unions of many British universities staged the same debate and the "Oxford Motion" was approved with the same degree of enthusiasm. In retrospect, it was an inglorious episode in recent British history.

Within a few days of Oxford's initiative, my own university staged the debate and I attended. Regretfully, I voted for the motion. I say regretfully because rather more than six years later I did in fact "fight" for King and Country and so did the vast majority of my peers.

There was an interesting aftermath albeit some 30 years later when I participated in a Hart House debate at the University of Toronto. These debates adopted parliamentary procedures in every respect. The Order paper that night (the House was called to order at 8 p.m.) announced the motion: "That this house condemns scientists who conduct research knowing it is for war." For the "Ayes" was a second year law student and Professor Chandler Davis; and for the "Nays" it was a second year engineering student and Professor Arthur Porter.

Chandler Davis, an associate professor of mathematics, was the most vociferous political activist on the campus and in particular he was the leader of the anti-nuclear movement. My views were dramatically opposite and I became increasingly incensed with some of Davis' allegations. Eventually I challenged him to a public debate on any topic of his choosing. He accepted my challenge and selected the above mentioned subject. It was appropriate because the "cold war" was being waged incessantly.

During the 1960's most university campuses were involved with many protest movements and Toronto was no exception. Not surprisingly then the debate attracted widespread interest, so much so that the Hart House Debates Chamber was crowded with standing room only.

The Speaker of the House was John Bosley, a senior arts student (subsequently to become the Hon. John Bosley, Speaker, Canadian House of Commons from 1984-86) who presided very professionally.

Not having participated as a principal in any public forum in my life, I found the "rules of procedure "and the debate environment somewhat intimidating. Fortunately, I had followed several parliamentary debates on television and was aware of the need for a speaker to portray a "commanding presence" and to lace his rhetoric with a modicum of humor. In the event I believe I achieved the first objective by striding aggressively up and down the center aisle and emphasizing debating points by jabbing my right hand in the direction of the opposition. I seem to recall incidentally that the "Ayes" benches were more crowded than the "Nays," which was not a good omen.

By far my most telling debating point related to the Oxford "peace" debate referred to previously. I suggested that the fact that a majority of university students in Britain had endorsed the motion "that they would fight for neither King nor country" must have encouraged Hitler enormously. The extent to which such a declaration had done so is a moot point, but very surely he was not discouraged in his aggressions. Ergo! I proclaimed with excusable gusto the present question for debate would likewise gladden the hearts of the potential enemies of our country.

As I indicated earlier, my friend, Arthur McIlwain, a second year applied science student, and I were the underdogs, but in the event, we won the debate handily.

In September 1933 I was enrolled as a candidate for the degree of M.Sc. at the University of Manchester. A unique feature of graduate programs in the 1930's was the fact graduate degrees were awarded solely on the basis of a dissertation (i.e. thesis). No written examination or lecture course materials were required. Although I attended two classes in nuclear and atomic physics, the majority of my time was spent in the laboratory and workshop building the Meccano model. From my point of view this was a wonderful state of affairs. It was one of the most fascinating experiences of my life. I was building an apparatus, using mostly components from a large Meccano set to build a machine that would solve differential equations. In no sense of the word was it work. It was play! And I spent most weekday evenings, as well as days, in the laboratory.

Professor Hartree was an ideal advisor — easy-going, enthusiastic and unlike many university teachers of professorial rank (I recall that in each department there was one and only one professor, the other members of the staff being readers, senior lecturers or lecturers) he was both my teacher and my friend and remained so for the following 25 years until his death. At the time Hartree, already a Fellow of the Royal Society, a rare distinction for one so young, was an internationally recognized authority on atomic structure as a result of his pioneering work in determining the self-consistent field of several atoms. It was a great privilege to work under the guidance of such a wonderful man. There was another advantage as well; I was working in a field virtually unexplored at the time and it was certainly not in the mainstream of physics. Furthermore, it was essentially cross-disciplinary, the first of several such that I have been interested in. It crossed disciplinary boundaries, especially physics — engineering. In light of the fact that our model was the first of its kind in Europe, a brief review of computers in general is worthwhile.

Computers can be categorized as digital or analog in operation. The former are exemplified by the "modern computer" and complementary devices such as printers, videos and camcorders. Their operation is predicated on digital (binary) technology, and based on binary arithmetic.[4] Although we feed decimal numbers into a computer, these

[4]The binary numbers equivalent to decimal numbers 0,1,2,3,4,5,6, — are 0,1,10,11,100,101,110

are converted by the machine into their binary equivalents and all information processing is carried out in binary notation. Theoretically, the accuracy of the digital computer is limitless and its speed, presently in order of billions of operations per second, is limited only by the speed of light. Even a simple hand-held solar powered calculator costing about $10 can determine the square root of a seven-digit number virtually instantaneously.

On the other hand, the operation of analog computers such as the differential analyzer and the slide rule is based on measurement — in the case of the d.a., rotations of shafts; in the case of the slide rule, lengths. The accuracy of these computers is limited by the accuracy of measurement, which, even in the most sophisticated machines, rarely exceeds one-tenth of a percent. But during the 1930's there was no alternative. Many complex problems, especially in engineering, military technology and science were virtually unsolvable. So the analog machines, especially the differential analyzer, were invaluable. Even today I suspect the optimum way of solving certain very sophisticated problems is by means of hybrid computers using both analog and digital techniques. This is not surprising in view of the fact that the human brain, the most imaginative, comprehensive and sophisticated "computer" ever created (by God), is essentially analog/digital in its mode of operation. In common with a digital computer, the differential analyzer requires software, but of an entirely different kind. The interconnections between the integrators, the input tables and the output table can be regarded as the network. Perhaps better still as a mechanical communication system. The configuration of components required to solve a specific problem is unique. In the final stages of its determination, a symbolic representation of the machine shows the location of gears, shafts and initial settings of the integrators and tables. This is essentially the software. It is literally transferred to the machine. When operating, the differential analyzer can be regarded as a simulator in so far as it is a dynamic representation of the behavior of system variables and indeed as such can provide guidance relating to the determination of initial conditions. But that is a rather sophisticated concept indescribable in words and only realizable by an operator well-versed in the system's characteristics.

A one-integrator model built almost exclusively of Meccano components (shafts, gears, wheels and a couple of small electric motors) mounted on plywood boards was ready for testing in December, 1933. It worked well in solving a simple first-order differential equation and

Douglas Hartree gave me the go-ahead to build two more integrators and associated components — he funded everything out of his own pocket. The only components apart from the torque-amplifiers, not fabricated in Meccano were the support brackets for the integrator wheels. Fortunately, Uncle Charlie, my father's younger brother, came to the rescue. He arranged for a total of six brackets to be caste in bronze at Vickers-Armstrong Barrow-in-Furness where he was employed. The ultimate objective was to solve the Hartree Self-Consistent Field Equations for initially the atom of hydrogen and then the more complex atom of chromium using the model. My master's dissertation was based on the construction of the model and its use in atomic structure calculations. Only the vision of D.R.H. could anticipate that such an apparatus, which anything less scientific would be difficult to imagine, could actually solve a complex mathematical problem. Running it created a cacophony of noise which resonated throughout the basement of the laboratories. It was ready for operation in early April 1934.

There are moments in our lives, especially if we are poets or painters or scholars or engineers or scientists, when in a figurative sense we "strike pay dirt." I don't mean this in a pejorative sense, but rather in the sense of a revelation. Such a moment occurred when the model d.a. produced for the first time a series of graphs of, for me, unsurpassed beauty — wave function of an atom — first hydrogen and then a few weeks later, chromium.

In spite of marked sloppiness in the gear trains and vibration in the rotating shafts, a graph of remarkable smoothness and clarity was plotted automatically on the output table of the model.

I am still, some 70 years later, completely mystified as to how such quality was achieved. D.R.H. was delighted. Suffice it to say, that a selection of the actual graphs are included in my M.Sc. thesis and that the latter is on display in the Mathematical Calculation Machine Section of the National Science Museum in South Kensington, London. (Some time ago I had an opportunity to show my two grandsons the exhibit — for me it was a very proud moment.) Because of the wealth of historic material available, the exhibits are rotated, but to my certain knowledge, the Model Differential Analyzer was displayed until 1998. Incidentally, while not on display, my PhD. thesis is on permanent loan to the museum. It is stored in the archives. Somewhat surprisingly, because during the 1930's science was not particularly newsworthy, members of the press were interested in this rather bizarre device and several stories were published in local and national newspapers, and at least one publication in the U.S. — *Popular Technical Journal*. Although we didn't appreciate it at the time, the model was in fact the first analog computer for the solution of differential equations outside the U.S.A. For me, the period 1933-34 was one of the most exciting of my life.

The success of the model d.a. was not only manifest in the several complex problems which it handled successfully, but as well in the fact that several other universities built similar models. In particular I recall Professor Lennard-Jones and Maurice Wilkes (subsequently Sir Maurice) whom I visited at Cambridge, built a model and also Professor Harry Massie built one at Queen's University, Belfast. Because of its size, the model illuminated for me the basic principles of calculus and gave me insights into the solutions to differential equations which would otherwise have escaped me. This facility is not quite so apparent with the large machine. It was fascinating, for example, to see the solution of a differential equation unfolding before my very eyes. This provided insights not otherwise readily obtainable and demonstrated that in fact the model simulates the actual behavior of processes and systems. A digital computer solving similar problems does not possess such a characteristic.

Because the University of Manchester's physics laboratories had an international reputation, many eminent physicists visited to give lectures, and invariably, Professor Hartree and Professor Bragg brought them to see the model in operation. I'll never forget the afternoon Lord Rutherford himself appeared. I have rarely been in contact with such a towering intellect and such a commanding presence. But he was by no means intimidating. Indeed, he had a knack with young graduate students and I felt at ease, not least when he told me that our basement laboratory was where he had carried out the experiments which showed that the nucleus of the helium atom was in fact an alpha particle; just one of the earth-shattering discoveries that have had such a profound impact on civilization.

After explaining the operation of the model and the problem set up, I was surprised and delighted when the great man — not only great intellectually, but in stature as well — asked if he might operate the machine. And he did, controlling the input cursor cross-hairs with high precision and thereby feeding information into the integrators. A grin of pure delight showed how much he was enjoying the experience. Needless to add, so was I!

Of the many visitors to the laboratory, several of whom have been identified previously, five deserve special mention: Professor James

Chadwick; Professor G. P. Thomson, another Nobel laureate, son of the legendary Sir J.J. Thomson; Professor John Cockcroft; Professor Charles Darwin, grandson of Charles Darwin who formulated the theory of evolution. It is noteworthy that a few years later during WWII, Patricia and I worked under John Cockcroft at the Air Defense Research and Development Establishment and later under Charles Darwin at the National Physical Laboratories in Teddington.

The fifth notable visitor was Professor J.D. Bernal, professor of physics at Birkbeck College, University of London. Apart from his X-ray crystallography research, he had written extensively on the social and political implications of advances in science. His book The World, The Flesh and The Devil (1929), which incidently was followed by several equally controversial books, caused a minor sensation in scientific circles. Perhaps not surprisingly, he was awarded the Stalin Peace Prize in 1953. He devoted at least 10 minutes to operating the model and his concentration was so great that he leaned over the input table and gear systems to such an extent that by the end of the period, his blonde hair was streaked with lubricating oil!

So much for the more formal visits: There was a lighter side as well. Virtually every graduate student in the department and all members of the staff came to see the model, and it was a very salutary experience for a lowly graduate student. Perhaps the most memorable visit occurred during the fall of 1935 when the Physical Society Exhibition was held at Manchester and the physical laboratories were open to the public. The model was one of the attractions. During a Saturday evening, the last of the Exhibition, I was demonstrating the model to a few teenagers when quite dramatically there was a surge of men and a few women who filled the room to overflowing. They were all wearing colorful rosettes. It immediately occurred to me that they were soccer fans, visitors from a distant city whose team had been playing the redoubtable Manchester United in an English Cup Semi-Final match earlier in the day. It was an occasion worthy of the Guinness Book of Records in so far as of all the attractions available (i.e. pubs, movies, etc.) they had chosen to visit a physics exhibition. In those days, fortunately, the hooliganism that has characterized British soccer during the past decade was unknown.

Suffice it to say I was agreeably surprised when the group of about 20 people listened attentively to my five minute talk and were obviously fascinated to see an assembly of Meccano components actually solving a mathematical problem. But the climax came at the end when one of the fans in a broad north of England accent said, "Gents, this young fella has done us real proud — let's give him a big hand." whereupon they all clapped and as befitting an embarrassed young physicist, I blushed!

My master's thesis was duly completed and I was awarded the degree. D.R. H. decided that papers should be prepared for potential publication in the *Proceedings of the Manchester Literary and Philosophical Society.* The first written exclusively by my professor, although jointly authored, described the construction and operation of the machine, and the second, which I authored (my first real publication) presented the results I obtained using the machine in the determination of the atomic structure of the chromium atom. It is regrettable that during the bombing of Manchester during 1941, the headquarters of the Society were destroyed and all off-prints of the papers are unavailable. Fortunately, I possess single copies.

Another exciting possibility for applying the model arose as the result of an inquiry from the research division of the Imperial Chemical Industry (I.C.I.), Britain's greatest chemical company. Albert Callender, a senior scientist with the firm was interested in the possibility of using a differential analyzer to solve the equations relating to the automatic control of temperature during a chemical process. Characteristic of such a system is a finite time-lag within the control loop. This gives rise to difficulties in studying the dynamic performance of such systems by standard methods and it was here that D.R.H. came up with the idea that the model differential analyzer input table might be modified in order to handle such equations. Because finite time-lags arise as well in other situations such as the study of stability of electric power transmission lines, it was considered to be a very worthwhile modification. Indeed, it was subsequently incorporated into the design of the full-scale differential analyzer.

Through the support of Professors Bragg and Hartree, in 1934 I was awarded the Beyer Fellowship, the most prestigious award available to graduate students in physics. This ensured my financial independence for two academic years, 1934-36, and D.R.H. decided that my work to date justified my registering for the PhD degree. The topic was "The Differential Analyzer and Some Applications." The fact that the results obtained with the model were far beyond our expectations was sufficient to encourage my professor to seek funding for a large-scale machine. Although I had added a fourth integrator to the model in order to handle the chemical process control problem, it was still quite inadequate to handle many problems in science and engineering and not surprisingly, its accuracy was strictly limited. But it is important to note that the rough results obtained in the study of quite sophisticated problems provided a basis for more in depth investigation.

Unquestionably, a differential analyzer with an accuracy of about a percentage point had proved to be a valuable research tool. Furthermore, there was evidence even in our own department that several problems were being side-lined because of the lack of computational facilities. Indeed D.R.H. himself, using a Brunsviga desk calculator (and he was an incredibly fast worker) spent many hours determining the atomic structures of comparatively light elements. But for the heavier elements, such methods were prohibitive. It was fortuitous that about this time, the summer of 1934, Robert McDougall, a member of the governing body of the university, and a philanthropist, came to the rescue. He had seen the Meccano model machine operating, was duly impressed, and offered to finance the construction of an eight integrator differential analyzer on the lines of the Bush original machine, but larger and more accurate. Another good friend of the university and as it turned out subsequently, a very good friend of mine, Sir Arthur Fleming, Director of Research at the Metropolitan-Vickers Company, was approached and offered to build the machine. Mr. James Starling, a senior mechanical engineer at the company was designated to undertake the design. The generosity of Dr. Vannevar Bush of MIT, creator of the first differential analyzer, was manifest in the fact that he provided a full set of blueprints upon which the design of the Manchester machine might be based. This saved many months.

The machine was built in record time and installed in the large laboratory adjacent to the small room that housed the model. When fully assembled, I recall it was in early 1935, it was an impressive structure about 30 feet long and 15 feet wide. It was powered by an independent motor-generator set. After a few teething problems, it worked perfectly, and nobody was more thrilled than my professor. Today, half the machine is housed in the Manchester Museum of Science and Technology and the other half in the National Science Museum in South Kensington.

The commissioning of the large machine was essentially a landmark in the history of analog computers. It was the first machine of its kind outside the U.S. Hartree and I worked as a team and I have rarely seen my professor so enthusiastic, so much so that frequently we worked late in the laboratory — 11 p.m was not unusual and dinner was forgotten. In such circumstances it is not surprising that a close relationship between professor and student developed. I dined several times with Douglas and

Elaine Hartree at their home at 1 Didsbury Park in South Manchester. On another occasion, a Saturday morning during the spring of 1935, D.R.H. asked me if I would like to join him and his two boys on a visit to the main "Signal Box" at Manchester's Exchange Railway Station. All his life Hartree had been fascinated by railways and it was his idea of relaxation to spend an afternoon observing the operation of the switches and signals controlling railway traffic into and out of the station. Regretfully, I made some excuse and missed a rare opportunity to enhance my education. About a dozen years later I recall watching Hartree, then my close friend, helping my son John assemble a model railway set on the floor of our living room in Toronto, Canada.

In 1934, the requirements for the degree of PhD, in British universities, unlike those in the U.S. and Canada, did not include compulsory graduate lecture courses or indeed a comprehensive examination before work on the dissertation could be started. This was fortunate because I could devote my time exclusively to working with the McDougall Differential Analyzer. In retrospect I probably averaged more hours working in the laboratory per week than ever since. As well I attended a course of lectures in quantum theory given by Dr. Hans Bethe (who later became a Nobel laureate and professor of physics at Cornell) and Dr. Peierls, professor of physics at the University of Birmingham, (who subsequently became Sir. Rudolf). Both scientists had escaped from Nazi Germany.

As a PhD candidate I was given the privilege of using the staff room and this was particularly rewarding when on most days I joined my former teachers and visiting scientists for a "cup of tea." After 6 p.m. the laboratories were comparatively quiet, and so I spent most evenings working with the machine. I rarely left the laboratory before 11 p.m. My very first lecture to staff, visitors and graduate students was in the 1934-35 Junior Colloquium Lecture Series in which graduate students were expected, although it was optional, to give a talk on their research. My lecture was given in the large physics lecture theatre, which held about 200 people, where such greats as Lord Rutherford, Professor Chadwick, Professor Cockcroft and Professor Thomson had lectured. It was a nerve-racking experience and I was apprehensive, to put it mildly. But William Kaye, the senior laboratory steward, came to the rescue. In the preparation room behind the theatre, I recall him saying, "Mr. Porter, the great man himself (Lord Rutherford) was always nervous before giving a lecture and I can assure you it is a good sign." Incidentally, he prepared all my lantern slides, three-inch glass slides and operated the lantern.

William Kaye was a treasure and the successes of the physical laboratories were in no small measure due to his dedication and expertise. I will always be grateful to him. The university subsequently bestowed on him the degree of M. Sc. *honoris causa* in recognition of his distinguished service.

As I mentioned previously, the model d.a. while satisfactory for some problems, was unsuitable for more complex problems, although I managed to obtain rough solutions for the I.C.I. control problem. It was, therefore, a delightful experience to set up the large D.A. and to observe the machine generating on the output table solutions to the problem. Over a period of several months I determined the behavior of the control system using a wide range of values of the control parameters. Plotting the final results in the form of a contour map was a thrill — this constituted an important component of my PhD program.

There is little doubt that our work made an important contribution to chemical process controls, as witness the publication in 1936 of the paper "Time-Lag in a Control System" in the prestigious *Philosophical Transactions of the Royal Society of London* and of the paper "Time-Lag in a Control System II' the following year in the *Proceedings of the Royal Society of London*. The first paper was authored by Callender, Hartree and Porter and the second by Hartree, Porter, Callender and Stevenson. It is gratifying to note that in 1974 these papers were included as two of the 21 landmark papers selected for inclusion in the volume "Automatic Control — Classic Linear Theory," edited by George Thaler of the Naval Postgraduate School, Monterey, California. This volume traces the development of the theory and practice of automatic control during the period 1868 to 1950. Douglas Hartree's dreams were fulfilled, but in a much more spectacular manner than either of us imagined at the time.

Although I had no appreciation of it then, studies of control system behavior played a major role in my subsequent career. Indeed they paved the way for most of my World War II activities and as well introduced me to what I think of as a holistic and interdisciplinary approach to a wide variety of problems, both technological and societal.

At intervals of about a month, we tested the differential analyzer for accuracy. This was necessary, especially during the first few months of operation because gears and screws needed a running-in period. We followed the procedure initially devised by Dr. Bush and known as the "circle test." The machine is set up to solve a simple second-order differential equation, the solution of which can be displayed on the output table as a perfect circle. The machine's accuracy is determined by the extent to which the curve at the start and the finish join. Perfect accuracy arises when there is no error in joining, and we found that our machine was accurate to within one-tenth of a percentage point.

Late one evening, when I was carrying out such a test, (the operation was completely automatic with no manual input), I observed a slight malfunction in a gear train. I was standing close to the output table and leaned over the main assembly to make a closer inspection. In a single instant my necktie got caught between the main gears of the drive shaft. Divine providence intervened, first because the machine was operating at a slow speed, and secondly, the portable control panel which might have been at least 20 feet away, providentially was in fact lying atop the adjacent integrator cabinet within easy reach. My reflexes as a young man were excellent. Although I could not actually see the control panel, I crashed my right hand down and by sheer good luck, hit the master control button which stopped the machine instantaneously. My head had been pulled down to within six inches of the gears and it took at least five minutes to untangle my tie (I should have kept it as a souvenir). There was little doubt that within a matter of two or three seconds I would have suffered strangulation. Subsequently, I never wore a tie when operating the machine and neither did D.R.H. who was distressed when I told him about the incident.

The differential analyzer was, because it could solve both linear and non-linear differential equations, a tool for all disciplines. However, during the three years when I was in charge of operations so to speak, albeit with the powerful support of my professor, the machine was applied exclusively to problems in science and technology. I list a few below:

- The problem of "terminating" high power electrical transmission lines to protect them from lightning strikes is of profound importance, especially in geographical areas subject to many thunderstorms. In practice, "thyrite" elements are utilized as "lightning arresters." These elements are located at strategic positions along the line. When the latter is subjected to a lightning strike, a surge travels along the transmission line and a reflected electrical disturbance occurs. The problem was submitted to us by a A.K. Nuttall, an engineer at Metropolitan-Vickers Company, and D.R.H. with his usual perspicacity, determined the differential equations which described the phenomenon. The equations included a finite time-lag and were readily solvable by the machine. The results obtained on the differential analyzer compared very favorably with those obtained in practice and demonstrated how the machine might be utilized in the design of transmission line lightning protectors. The results obtained on the output table were quite dramatic as shown in a paper published subsequently, "The Application of the Differential Analyzer to Transients on a Distortion-less Transmission Line." (Hartree and Porter, Institution of Electrical Engineers, November, 1938). Machine solutions are shown for line conditions and arrester characteristics. A companion study which was carried out in collaboration with A.K. Nuttall of the Research Department of Metropolitan-Vickers, related to the response of an electric circuit incorporating a thyrite lightning arrester when an impulse is applied. The object of this investigation was to clarify some anomalies which had appeared in a practical test of the thyrite material. From our point of view it was another example of a problem in electric power system design which demonstrated the extraordinary flexibility of the differential analyzer. A paper was subsequently published in the *Proceedings of the Cambridge Philosophical Society*.[5]

- A problem of quite a different nature was referred to us by David Meyers, then at the Engineering Laboratory at the University of Oxford. He was interested in the behavior of vacuum tubes (triodes) of a special design. I recall that during the 1930's, many years before the advent of the transistor, vacuum tubes were widely used in all electronic equipment, especially radio communications and control systems. Our results corresponded closely to those obtained experimentally. Of special interest is the fact that rather more than 20 years subsequently, Meyers and I were Deans of Engineering in two Canadian universities, the University of British Columbia and University of Saskatchewan respectively. The studies of the space-charge and secondary current in a vacuum tube had given me an introduction to electronic technology and this proved valuable when I became involved in electronic digital data processing systems. Our results were of general interest to electronic engineers of the times and were considered appropriate for publication. A paper was published in January, 1937 under the joint authorship of Meyers, Hartree and Porter.

---

[5]Proceedings: Cambridge Philosophical Society. Vol. 22, Part 2, May 1936

- The 1930's were a period when public interest in gramophones and radio receivers was blossoming, and high fidelity of reproduction was the goal, as it is even today. It had been observed in certain loud speaker systems that under certain circumstances sub-harmonics might arise. The question was — under what conditions? One enterprising company suggested to Professor Hartree that the differential analyzer might prove useful in solving the dilemma. Because the theoretical behavior of the key element of a radio loud speaker could be represented by a non-linear differential equation, it was obvious that the differential analyzer could in fact solve the problem. In order to demonstrate the existence or non-existence of sub-harmonics, the machine was set up to generate "Lissajous Figures." Under normal conditions these are generated on the output tables as asymmetrical ellipses — single loops. However, if a sub-harmonic is present, the joining-up does not occur as anticipated, and a second loop is generated before joining occurs. For several weeks I wrestled with the problem. The key was obviously the nature of the non-linearity in the loud speaker element. A wide range of possibilities had to be explored and I had failed to determine the conditions which gave rise to sub-harmonic behavior. But my luck changed. Providentially, it was during the visit of Professor Charles Darwin to the laboratory. Professor Hartree introduced me and suggested that we should demonstrate the machine. Just prior to the visit I had set the input conditions more or less at random, and much to the surprise of our distinguished visitor and indeed of Hartree and myself, the machine proceeded to generate a double loop. What was unusual, however, was a minor "blip" on one of the loops. I had in fact noted during the machine operation that at one point Darwin was so intrigued with the generation of the figures that inadvertently he leaned on the output table. Hartree also noticed this and promptly described it as the "Darwin Bum Effect," whereupon Darwin roared with laughter.

- One of the most enterprising, and indeed in many respects, rewarding problems we tackled on the machine was a study of the temperature distribution in a dielectric material when placed in an alternating field. In light of modern electric power technology, the study anticipated developments which were completely undreamed of at the time. The problem was particularly interesting as well because it necessitated the solution of "partial differential equations," which Professor Hartree succeeded in converting into ordinary differential equations; it had been submitted by the Metropolitan-Vickers Company Research Division at the time under the direction of Dr. Willis Jackson. Previously he was professor of electrical engineering at Imperial College, University of London. I followed in his footsteps several years later.

In retrospect, albeit somewhat tangential, our investigations were a prelude to the "chaos theory," which has assumed such great importance in recent years. The Hartree formulation of the problem and how the temperature distribution, step-by-step, was generated on the output table of the differential analyzer was certainly one of the high points in the history of the machine. A very small change in the initial conditions at the boundary of the dielectric had spectacular effects, and indeed, in the ultimate condition gave rise theoretically to the complete breakdown of the dielectric material through a sudden increase in temperature. Many years later there was an analogous effect in meteorology — the so-called "butterfly effect" — when it was hypothesized that the fluttering of a butterfly wing in West Africa might cause a hurricane to hit the southern states of the U.S. This was a highly speculative example of the nature of chaos. Prior to this investigation, I had operated the machine on my own. Clearly opportunities for other graduate students to become familiar with and to operate the machine existed. D.R. H. recruited two prospective master's students, Cecil Copple and Harry Tyson. Of considerable personal interest is the fact that Harry Tyson was born in Ulverston, at 12 Lightburn Road, next door to me, and the project was in fact his thesis topic for the M. Sc.

Because my PhD thesis required a fair proportion of my time, Copple and Tyson were very welcome additions to the differential analyzer team. Moreover, the machine's solution of equations, such as those describing the temperature distributions in a dielectric, essentially non-linear, requires the satisfaction of a boundary condition at each end of the integration process. The machine solution can only be carried out by trial and error methods. This is a time-consuming process and many machine solutions were required, not least because of the extreme sensitivity when the condition of thermal breakdown is approached. Although we did not appreciate it at the time, the solution of a non-linear, partial differential equation by the differential analyzer was the first investigation of its kind. It is gratifying to recall that the solutions we obtained compared favorably with the result of experiments carried out in the Research Department of the Metropolitan-Vickers Company under conditions approximating the ideal conditions we adopted for the theoretical investigation. The paper, "The Evolution of Transient Temperature Distributions in a Dielectric in an Alternating Field" by Copple, Hartree, Porter and Tyson was published in the "Journal of the Institution of Electrical Engineers" in July, 1939, shortly after my return from the United States. Let me hasten to add that my personal involvement in preparing the publication was minimal.

My involvement with the machine virtually ceased in December, 1936, but I was fortunate to have the opportunity to use the machine in 1943 for a project relating to radar research.

My PhD thesis entitled "The Differential Analyzer and Some Applications" included a broad range of topics and many diagrams had to be drawn. The only suitable location for the actual writing and preparation of tables of results was a table at the end of the differential analyzer itself. For example, the actual set-up diagrams (the software) were large and unwieldy and required plenty of space. I was fortunate to find a final year undergraduate in honors mathematics who was intrigued with the machine and who volunteered her help. Marguerite Mitchell spent many hours assisting me, sometimes working until midnight in the laboratory. One night about 11 p.m. Professor Hartree suddenly appeared. He had forgotten whether or not the motor generator had been switched off and returned to make sure. I do not recall the extent to which he was embarrassed to discover a young lady helping his graduate student, especially at that late hour. I suspect that I was more than a little embarrassed myself. Incidentally, Marguerite Mitchell's help was acknowledged formally in the thesis. It was completed and submitted in July, 1936.

The thesis was examined by an external examiner, Professor John Cockcroft of the University of Cambridge (subsequently Sir John, and a Nobel Laureate) and an internal examiner, my advisor, Professor Douglas Hartree. The oral examination was in September, 1936 and took place in D.R.H.'s office. I stood at the chalk board and was very nervous. I was expected not only to defend my thesis, but also to be familiar with related materials. In light of the broad range of topics I'd researched, this presented a formidable challenge. However, I was fortunate to have two sympathetic examiners. Most of the questions related specifically to my thesis per se and only marginally to the underlying physics. Indeed, the topic was atypical of a PhD in physics. One question asked by Cockcroft dealt with the process control problem and I knew instantly I was in trouble. After perhaps five minutes of futile scribbling on the board, it was obvious to the examiners that I did not know the answer.

Fortunately, D.R.H. intervened and asked, "Do you know the answer, Cockcroft?" Whereupon, Cockcroft replied, "No!" My professor responded, "That makes three of us." This was another example of my professor "bending over backwards" on my behalf because he certainly knew the answer. The examination took about an hour and then I withdrew to the outer office. After about 15 minutes, D.R.H. emerged smiling and I knew I had my PhD. Lunch with the two eminent professors followed and it was an unforgettable experience.

The convocation ceremony held in Whitworth Hall of the university in early December, 1936, was attended by my parents. To say the least, it was a proud occasion for them, and it was very special, not least because when my name was called, Professor Hartree proceeded to take me by the hand and walk with me to formally present me to the Chancellor[6] who then "hooded" me in the traditional manner. From my perspective, this was a wonderful gesture by a man to whom I owed so very much.

Early in September, 1936, I was appointed, together with Bernard Lovell (subsequently Sir Bernard of Jodrell Bank Radio Astronomy fame) to an Assistant Lectureship in Physics. This, (although the bottom rung of the academic ladder), was a major achievement, especially in those days when lectureships were so very scarce for a budding academic. At the same time as Lovell, my brother Ronald (then a mathematics master at a grammar school in the city) and I were appointed Associate Tutors at Hulme Hall, a university men's residence. Our duties were nominal amounting to little more than attending a few seminars and our compensation amounted to free board and lodging. This was my first taste of "institutional food" after the delicious meals prepared by Mrs. Hodgson in my previous lodging. It was quite a come down. I said good-bye to the Hodgsons with real regret. They had provided me with a "home away from home" for my five critical years as undergraduate and graduate student. Their role in any of the academic successes I had achieved was by no means trivial.

Although at the time Bernard Lovell was working in a field quite different from my own, we nevertheless became good friends. I shall always be grateful to him for introducing me to classical music. My initiation came one evening when Bernard persuaded me to join him in attending a concert by the Halle Orchestra in the Free Trade Hall, Manchester. The program included a Beethoven Symphony and Brahms second Piano Concerto. The soloist was the internationally acclaimed German pianist Artur Schnabel. I was enthralled. From that day I became

---

[6]Of the 20 doctoral candidates presented, I was the only one to be so honored.

a music lover in every sense of the word. Some four years later, I was able to share my enthusiasm with Patricia, my future wife, on our first date in July, 1940 — a Promenade Concert at Queen's Hall, London (later destroyed by bombs) and conducted by Sir Henry Wood. From that evening, she has been a classical music lover, and music has been a catalyst that continues to strengthen the bonds between us. Unforgettable was our 55th wedding anniversary, July 26, 1996, which we celebrated most appropriately by attending the Promenade Concert at the Royal Albert Hall in London. Coincidently, it is not far from the church where we were married.

During October, 1936, an event occurred which had profound consequences for my future. Professor Bragg was appointed a member of the "Awards Committee" of the Commonwealth Fund Fellowships. Having an overview of the potential of the fellowship, he considered that I might be a suitable candidate. Not least because it was obvious that if awarded one, I would opt to spend two years at the Massachusetts Institute of Technology, working under Dr. Vannevar Bush. Having spent several highly productive months at MIT, Professor Hartree was equally enthusiastic about my spending two full years with Dr. Bush, whom he greatly admired. With such encouragement, I had no hesitation in applying and completing the application form in which I was required to name three references: they were Dr. H. W. Cousins, Professor Hartree and Dr. A. P. M. Fleming, director of research of the Metropolitan-Vickers Electrical Company. As a matter of fact, I had never met A.P. M. Fleming, a highly respected engineer and member of the University of Manchester governing council, but D.R.H. was of the opinion that his support might be quite critical. He convinced Fleming that my spending two years at MIT could prove very helpful to his company and perhaps even to the country in case a European war was declared. The point was that differential analyzer techniques were directly applicable to the control of anti-aircraft and naval guns, and for somebody to be at the cutting edge so to speak, could prove an asset. My application was submitted in January, 1937, and I received word two months later to the effect that I was one of 50 candidates selected for the interview at the London headquarters of the Commonwealth Fund Fellowships.

The interview, held in early April at 30 Portman Square, was an experience I shall never forget. I waited in a small anteroom on the second floor of this glorious mansion, to be called. Quite suddenly double doors at one end of the room opened and the whole Committee of

Awards under the chairmanship of Sir Walter Moberley (vice chancellor of the University of Manchester) and consisting of about seven members, appeared seated at a beautiful mahogany table. I learned subsequently that the committee included such eminent men as Lord Halifax (then the Foreign Secretary of Great Britain), Sir James Irvine, Principal of St. Andrews University, Mr. Benians, Master of all Souls College, Oxford, Sir Richard Southwell, Rector of Imperial College of Science and Technology, Professor A.V. Hill, University of London, and fortunately the familiar face of Professor Lawrence W. Bragg of my own university. I have a feeling that if it had not been for the presence of Bragg, I might have had a disastrous interview because I had not the slightest idea of how elaborate the proceedings would be. But it was a friendly group and although I began the interview very shakily, I felt comfortable when I was asked the question: "If you are awarded a fellowship, what would you like to do in the United States?" Of course I told the committee about the work of Dr. Bush at MIT, about Hartree's and my own work at Manchester and in particular that I would benefit greatly by spending two years in an American university. The committee must have been duly impressed because a few weeks later I heard that I had won the Fellowship. I recall that about 200 applications were considered and being one of the 24 successful candidates was quite a feather in my cap. It was a prestigious award as witness some of the fellows who had preceded me — Alistair Cooke, noted broadcaster and television personality; Lord Crowther, Lord Ashby, Master of Emmanuel College at Cambridge, and author Eric Linkletter to name a few.

A revised extract of this chapter has been published in the IEE Annals of the History of Computing, Volume 25, Number 2, April — June 2003.

Chapter 5

THE COMMONWEALTH FUND FELLOWSHIP — THE MASSACHUSETTS INSTITUTE OF TECHNOLOGY (MIT)

THE Commonwealth Fund is a charitable Foundation established through a Harkness family trust. It is devoted essentially to the support of research in medicine and related disciplines, and the Harkness Pavilions are well-known adjuncts to several major hospitals in the United States. In 1924, however, the directors of the fund expanded its mandate to include a so-called "Commonwealth Fund Fellowship Program." At the time there existed nothing in the United States corresponding to the Rhodes Scholarships offered to Americans. The basic concept of the fellowship was to offer young men and women of "character and ability" from the British Commonwealth an opportunity to study for two years in an American university. The fellowships would be open to graduates of British universities who had been nominated by the head of their university. Between 20 and 30 fellowships were to be awarded annually and the selection of the fellows rested exclusively in the hands of a British Committee of Award. The award was not based on the results of a competitive examination, but rather on recommendations and on the result of an interview. The choice of the American university was in large measure determined by the fellow himself. In fact in any one year, it has been found that fellows would be working in as many as 20 institutions of higher education. This differs markedly from the Rhodes Scholarship in which tenure is exclusively at the University of Oxford. Two classes of fellows were awarded, the junior class being new graduates at the baccalaureate level and the senior class being graduates at doctoral level.

All fellows must agree to two conditions: first it is required that they spend between two and three months traveling in the United States in order to see the country first hand, and second that after their two years residence in the United States, they must return to the British Commonwealth for at least two years.

The three months subsequent to the announcement of the awards and prior to my embarkation were not heavy in so far as my teaching load was minimal and my work on the differential analyzer was complete.

At Portman Square in London I met three of the newly appointed fellows with whom I was to share many exciting occasions. They were Arthur Armitage of Queens College, Cambridge, destined to study law at Yale, Oscar Puls from Reading University destined to study physics at MIT, and Wilfred Merchant of Oxford, also destined for MIT. By far the most exciting event in London was the Commonwealth Fund Fellowship annual dinner in honor of the new fellows and Awards Committee members. It was held at the Ritz Hotel. Somewhat disappointedly, His Royal Highness, the Prince of Wales, later King Edward VIII, who had been Honorary Chairman of the Committee of Award had abdicated a few months earlier and did not attend. As a matter of fact, he had attended all of the annual dinners since the fellowships had been established. The dinner was spectacular in every possible regard, white tie and tails no less, and sitting next to Lady Bragg was a thrill. Indeed, without a shadow of a doubt, I appreciated at that time that my life would be changed markedly. I was literally within the course of a few weeks transported from a north of England country boy into an environment which I had never dreamed even existed. The dinner included about six courses with wine and champagne. From that day until the day when I returned to Britain, almost two years later, I lived in a veritable wonderland.

I sailed from Liverpool in early September, 1937. Although taken for granted today, a transatlantic voyage during the 1930's (shades of the Titanic) was regarded as an adventure. Emotional farewells at the docks were the order of the day. For me, embarkation on the Cunard Liner, RMS Laconia, was a happy occasion. All members of my family, including Aunt Laura and friends Harry Tyson and Alan Blades and wife, saw me off after they had had a tour of the ship.

We were all struck by the sheer opulence of the ship, especially the dining room and various lounges. In particular I recall the elevator and the gentleman who operated it. We cast off at about 3 p.m. on that lovely Saturday afternoon and I remember waving good-bye to my family and friends lining the dockside. A few minutes later we were hauled out into the channel by two tugboats. The ship's whistle was blown and my great adventure had begun. The Liver Building, a landmark of Liverpool dockland, was gradually left astern. Years later I visualized that scene when I met the Beatles, the immortal rock group who began playing guitars there.

After unpacking, itself an exciting process and getting to know Oscar Puls, my cabin-mate, I recall climbing up to the top deck and watching the coast of my native county of Lancashire slowly recede. Much would happen before I saw my homeland again.

The first two or three days of the voyage were stormy and the ship, having no stabilizers, pitched and rolled rather alarmingly. But it was such a novel experience that I was too excited to feel any ill-effects. By the Monday evening, everybody, certainly in the first class lounge and dining room, was in very festive moods. We had cocktails, a sumptuous six-course dinner and dancing subsequently. Especially noteworthy were the Captain's Dinner held on Tuesday evening and the Carnival Dinner on Thursday. Both were white tie and tails affairs. I recall Arthur Armitage saying to me, "Can you imagine we are actually being paid to do this!"

One of the most fortunate consequences of the voyage was my meeting the Spelman family returning to the United States from their annual pilgrimage to Europe. The Spelmans were a banking family with ties to J.P. Morgan and the Harkness family, of the Harkness Family Trust.

We docked at Boston on Friday at about 10:30 a.m. and Armitage and I promptly went ashore and spent a fascinating hour or so in a dockside tavern. This was my first contact with America.

The excitement of seeing the New York skyline, Staten Island and the Statue of Liberty was manifest in all of us. The taxi ride from the New York docks to the Harvard and Yale Club on the Avenue of the Americas was unbelievable in so far as in my life I had never seen any building taller than about 15 stories.

After visiting Harkness House (the former New York residence of the Harkness family), which was a tradition for new fellows, Armitage and I decided to explore the city. After dinner we found ourselves on Fifth Avenue among a crowd of people waiting to see the activities of the Shriners, a national philanthropic organization. As a major part of the annual celebration, a massive parade, stretching at least three miles, took place along the Avenue and included marching bands, big floats representing everything under the sun, and other facets of parades to which I subsequently learned Americans are addicted. But unfortunately, we found ourselves on the wrong side of the Avenue, and in order to return to the Harvard and Yale Club where we were staying, it was necessary to run across the wide Avenue between the marching bands. On the other side of the Avenue we were halted by a tall Irish American cop. When we explained our dilemma, he muttered, "G.D. limeys — do the best you can!" I'll never forget that incident or the grandeur of the Shriners Parade which was certainly in a different league from the Ulverston Hospital Saturday Parade in which I'd participated about 17 years previously.

My overall impression of New York City was essentially one of incredulity — the skyscrapers, the density of traffic, the noise, the hustle and bustle, the shops on Fifth Avenue and Broadway. Armitage and I also took an elevator to the top of the Empire State Building, then the tallest in the world, and I believe remains so at present as the result of the tragedy of September 11, 2001. As well, we attended the theatre at the Rockefeller Center and saw the famous Rockettes Chorus Line — sheer fantasy. Since those "heady days," I've returned to New York City quite a few times and even driven the full length of Manhattan, but the adrenaline never flowed as profusely as it did on that first visit. It is sad to reflect that my friend and fellow participant in so many adventures, beginning with Boston docking and finishing with the epic 1938 summer travel and train journey from Denver to Chicago, Arthur Armitage died on February 1, 1985. As a matter of fact, our last "big bash" together during our fellowship years was in Times Square, when we were present in the huge crowd which had gathered to celebrate the arrival of 1939.

Chronologically, I've leapt too far ahead. So let me return to September, 1937 when I took the train from Grand Central Station in New York City to Boston and had my first glimpse of my future home. My first impression of MIT was of a rather austere conglomeration of buildings which contrasted markedly with the university campus with which I had hitherto been familiar. But one thing was quite different. An air of excitement pervaded the campus and I was struck immediately by the enthusiasm of virtually everybody I met. In fact, it was this revelation that endeared me in the very first place to the United States.

Being lodged on the ground floor of Runkle House, which together with other houses in a quadrangle housed graduate students, gave me ready access to the Walker Memorial Dining Hall and to the Electrical Engineering Department. As well, there was a "diner" about quarter of a mile distant which provided my friends and me with good food and good fellowship in a typically American environment.

But it was my first meeting with Dr. Vannevar Bush which gave me the biggest thrill. I met him in the Dean of Engineering's Office. At that time he was both vice-president and dean. I was immediately struck by his friendly manner and his enthusiasm. A post-doc fellow could not possibly have had a warmer welcome to MIT and unquestionably it was the beginning of a life-long "love affair' with the institute. Because of the central role he has played in my career, I have outlined just a few of the subsequent achievements of Vannevar Bush.

After leaving MIT at the end of December, 1938, he took up the position of President of the Carnegie Institute of Washington, and subsequently during WWII became Director of the Office of Scientific Research and Development. This was coupled with the post of scientific advisor to President Roosevelt and later to President Truman. It is especially gratifying to note that while at MIT, Vannevar Bush was my advisor, but I little knew at the time that he would also become advisor to two American presidents. As a member of the top-level advisory committee on the atomic bomb (serving with President Conant of Harvard and Dr. Arthur Holly Compton of the University of Chicago), he played a critical role in the decisions relating to the strategic use of nuclear weapons and, by no means least, the dropping of the bombs on Hiroshima and three days later on Nagasaki.

But as advisor to the President, Dr. Bush not only played an important role in the conduct of WWII in the United States, but as well in Britain. When I met him for the last time during the fall of 1954, while I was assigned to Project Lamp Light, he told me with great delight about some of his meetings with Winston Churchill. He said, "Although I did not always agree with him, I liked the old so-and-so and we got on very well." For his services to Britain, Vannevar Bush was "knighted" by King George VI and received the title of "Honorary Knight of the British Empire." This was a rare distinction for an American and very certainly Dr. Bush deserved it.

In spite of this very distinguished career, or perhaps because of it, I will always recall Dr. Bush in his role as Director of the Rockefeller Differential Analyzer Group. He inspired all of the young men working under him and I recall especially the "illuminated address" we presented to him on his leaving MIT. Indeed it so very sincerely sums up my feelings that I cannot do better than to quote it here:

> *To V. Bush, Greetings: "To Doc" would perhaps be a better salutation for this note of farewell and Godspeed, for among ourselves we have always called you Doc as the title most appropriately expressing the affection and respect we have felt in working with you.*
>
> *We would not have you leave without saying that it has been fun to build a Differential Analyzer with you. We think you will agree that it has been fun, but we are not going to ask you to agree with some other feelings of ours, for of those we are better judges than you. We know, for example, the many ways in which we have felt your influence: in your generous praise for our successes, in your sympathetic analyses of our failures, in the enlivening breezes you have brought to our developmental doldrums.*
>
> *We shall miss these constant incentives, but the finest contribution you have made to our progress will remain. We mean your intuitive and inspiring faith in young men. To our minds this faith overshadows all else, is more lasting and important than your tangible scientific achievements, however, important we know them to be. It has given us a sense of accomplishment, a self-confidence, a realization of challenging opportunities at a period in our careers when the effect is profound. This faith remains with us and all the other young men who have worked with you at MIT.*
>
> *For this and for the other fine qualities that have inspired and delighted us we are grateful, and we want you to know it.*
>
> *This is the explanation then, if explanation is needed, of why we, the undersigned, thus say Hail and Farewell, and bid you visit us as often as your new work will allow.*
>
> > *With faith and affection*
> > *we remain,*
> > *Doc,*
> > *Your Differential Analyzer Staff*

The members of the team with which I was most closely associated were Sam Caldwell, Larry Frost, Jake Jaeger and Dick Taylor. Sam and Mrs. Caldwell became especially good friends and entertained me on several occasions at their beautiful home not far from MIT. I recall in particular a party which they gave in my honor at Graduate House in October, 1938. I was fortunate as well to count among my friends at MIT the great professor Norbert Wiener, founder of Cybernetics, who played a central role in the development of the computer; Professor Harold Edgerton, inventor of the high speed "stroboscopic camera;" Dean Harold Hazen, dean of the graduate school, and who together with Mrs. Hazen became close friends in subsequent years; Gene Stratton, professor of physics who later became president of MIT, and Gordon Brown with whom Patricia and I have had a close relationship since I left MIT. Gordon became one of the most illustrious deans of engineering at the institute. The interesting fact is that these friendships, which were begun in a rather superficial way during my fellowship years, have blossomed markedly since then. In no small measure, the close United States collaboration with Britain in science and technology during WWII was the result of the pioneering work of those MIT professors.

I was particularly gratified by the warm welcome I received from the differential analyzer team. I was fortunate as well to share an office with Claude Shannon who was the research assistant responsible for operating the original differential analyzer. Claude was a genius. After graduating with a master's degree, he joined the Bell Telephone Laboratories and became world famous as the pioneer of information theory which has provided the scientific basis for all modern communications and by no means least, the Internet.

Because it was the key reason for my being at MIT it would be remiss if I did not introduce, albeit briefly, the Rockefeller Differential Analyzer. Under Dr. Bush's direction, work started in 1936 rather more than a year before I joined the team. At the time it was no exaggeration to state that this machine, which was ultimately used in WWII for critical mathematical studies, was by far the most ambitious computer development of the time. The completed machine would incorporate more than 2000 vacuum tubes, more than 100 electric motors, a small telephone exchange and weighed approximately 30 tons. Furthermore, it was uniquely both analog and digital in operation. All information, including that required to establish interconnections between the basic integrator units, was digital in the form of punched cards. But the critical mathematical operations such as integration were carried out mechanically utilizing highly precise mechanical mechanisms because of the much greater accuracy achievable. When completed, the machine incorporated 16 integrator units and half a dozen input units. The output consisted of tables of numerical data.

My work was almost solely in connection with supplying the machine with analytical and empirical input information. In the original differential analyzer, and also the Manchester machine, this information was fed into the machine as graphs with the consequent inaccuracy arising from the thickness of the pencil curve, possible distortion of the paper and inaccurate tracking by manual operators. Bearing in mind the highly accurate basic elements of the new machine, this would constitute a serious deficiency. Accordingly, replacement of all operators and analog input tables was essential.

The fundamental idea of the "function unit," as it was called, was conceived before I arrived at MIT, but details of its operation had not been worked out. This was my job. I worked on a comprehensive analysis and proposed a preliminary design of the unit. This was subsequently modified and incorporated into the machine.

I was never particularly happy with my design because it was based very much on "trial and error" procedures. It was not until a dozen years later when I was working at the Military College of Science in Shrivenham, England, that a much more elegant solution to the problem emerged. Major Frank Stoneman, a student at the College, anxious to obtain a doctorate degree at the University of London, approached me and I decided that it would be worthwhile to resuscitate my original work and to update some of the original ideas. Stoneman came up with a brilliant solution which I will introduce later because it has much broader ramifications than its application in the design of a differential analyzer.

Although my work on the function unit was time-consuming, albeit exciting, especially to be a member of such a highly creative team, I did not neglect my social obligations. Recall that a major aim of the fellowship was to encourage fellows to familiarize themselves with American culture. This I believe I succeeded in doing in a variety of ways.

For this present purpose it is probably more interesting to introduce some of my extracurricular activities, not least because they give a broader perspective of my fellowship years than would a detailed review of my academic activities. During the first year, 1937-38 and roughly in chronological order some of the more noteworthy events are outlined here.

About three weeks after taking up residence, Oscar Puls and I were invited to a Rotary Club meeting in Marble Head, Mass. This gave us our first view of the beautiful Atlantic coast a few miles from Boston. Never having attended a Rotary Club meeting before, I was struck by the impressive ceremony, but somewhat to our surprise, we were obviously regarded as the guests of honor. This was confirmed later when the chairman announced that "our speakers for today will be Oscar Puls and Arther Porter, both of MIT." I don't recall who was more surprised, but suffice it to say I, being two years senior, was the first to speak. My subject? The only topic I could think of on the spur of the moment was "The British Universities." Each of us gave a talk lasting about 10 minutes and we stressed in particular the Commonwealth Fund Fellowships and their importance.

Then came the questions. What was our opinion of "Wally Simpson?" Recall that about seven or eight months previously King Edward VIII had abdicated the British throne and curiosity on this side of the Atlantic was even greater than in Britain. Regrettably during the 15 minutes or so of questions, not a single question was asked about the British universities and all the questions related to the Royal Family and the erstwhile Prince of Wales. Oscar Puls and I, I believe, handled the questions quite discreetly and pointed out in particular the only reason that Baltimore-born Mrs. Simpson had not become Queen of England was due to the fact that she was a twice divorced woman and it was this fact and this fact only that precluded her from becoming Queen. This was the first of very many occasions to follow when I observed how much Americans at large are interested in the Royal Family of Britain. There was a further manifestation of this when King George VI and Queen Elizabeth visited Boston in May, 1939 en route to Washington on a state visit.

During the Royal couple's visit to the United States, one of the escorting cruisers, HMS Southampton, docked at Boston Harbor, and Oscar Puls and I were thrilled to be invited to meet the Warrant Officers in their wardroom, and subsequently to take them to lunch. Never having been aboard a naval vessel in my life, this was quite an occasion, not least being "piped aboard" by a welcoming party. Some time later we entertained the officers at lunch at Hartwell Farms in the Boston suburbs.

My comparatively recent (1936-37) introduction to classical music thanks to Bernard Lovell, turned out to be a boon during my fellowship years. MIT students could obtain tickets for the Boston Symphony and Boston Pops orchestras at a third the normal cost. Consequently, I had the privilege of attending several concerts conducted by the great conductor Serge Koussevitzky and a few Pops concerts conducted by the very popular Arthur Fiedler. It also was fascinating to hear some details of Koussevitzky's family life and his addiction to the double-bass violin when, on the occasion of a Harvard — MIT picnic on Columbus Day, October, 1937, I had the pleasure of walking for at least an hour with the conductor's niece, then a student at Radcliffe (Harvard) College.

It became clear after a month's residence that a car was essential and indeed most new fellows purchased used vehicles during the fall of 1937. The only realistic way of touring the United States, especially during the summer months, was by car. I quickly discovered that while in Britain a car was regarded as a luxury, in the United States it was regarded as a necessity. Having previously arranged with Arthur Armitage that we would travel together in the summer of 1938, and the Commonwealth Fund having approved our plans, we decided as a trial run on a winter vacation together in the snowy wonderlands of New England. Fortunately at that time traffic on the highways was light and the snow clearance operations were excellent. New England during the winter, notably the small towns and villages with their white clapboard residences and beautiful churches, was everything "Grandma Moses" has portrayed in her beautiful pictures.

We stayed at the Pinckham Notch Lodge in New Hampshire for the Christmas holiday week, purchased skis and accessory equipment and managed to learn the rudiments of skiing, without taking lessons, which in retrospect was probably a mistake. Be that as it may, together with several other beginners we skied down the lower slopes of the Carriage Road reasonably successfully. Because of the Meteorological Station at the top of Mt. Washington, the Carriage Road is kept open during the winter — fortunately only official travel is permitted. But our efforts on the appreciably more difficult George Sherbourne and Wild Cat trails were unrewarding from a skiing point of view, but fun otherwise. At the end of the day we were ravenously hungry and did justice to the sumptuously delicious New England dishes served at the lodge. This was our first introduction to true Americana in so far as the guests included students, male and female, from several northeastern colleges and we sat around a roaring log fire and talked and debated the problems of the world. We were in our element. After a week at the lodge we drove over to a friend's chalet in Vermont where we'd been invited for the New Year's holiday. The chalet estate incorporated a ski hill and miniature ski jump. Great fun, but extremely hazardous. It was a holiday to remember.

Although I did not participate actively in any sport, I nevertheless became involved in some special events that deserve mention. They included cricket and baseball. The cricket episode in particular had fascinating long-term implications — afternoon tea tête-à-tête, with an internationally acclaimed stage and screen actress, Helen Hayes! Not a usual occurrence in the life of a graduate student, albeit a post-doc student. But it happened.

Returning to my room after breakfasting at my favorite diner one Saturday morning in June, 1938, I found a rather surprising message. Would I telephone as soon as possible Mr. X, President of the Harvard Dramatic Society at a given telephone number? I did so and spoke with an undergraduate whose name I have long forgotten. Apparently he had been informed by my friend Norman Jones (CFF — Commonwealth Fund Fellow and University of Manchester graduate) that I was a cricketer. I pointed out that although I played for my school, I was not de facto a cricketer. Did I know the rules? I probably replied, "Most of them."

He indicated that the Harvard Dramatic Society had been challenged to play a cricket match by the male members of the cast of "Victoria and Her Hussars" currently performing at a Boston theatre. All the necessary paraphernalia for the game, bats, balls and wickets, had been acquired and a field was available. Would I umpire the game? Needless to say I agreed, little knowing what I was letting myself in for! It turned out to be one of the most hilarious occasions of my fellowship years.

Even the simple process of "taking guard" (to ensure that the batsman and bat are positioned correctly relative to the wickets) proved difficult for the Harvard team. And although their "Victoria" opponents were comparatively literate concerning the rudiments of the game, they too needed coaching by the umpire. As the sole official, I spent most of my time "traipsing up and down" the pitch between the wickets, at one end helping a batsman with his guard, at the other end instructing the bowler on his delivery.

After a shaky start, characterized by baseball style swings by the Harvard batsmen, and theatrical antics on the part of their opponents, the likes of which I'd never seen on any cricket ground, the "match" settled down to a game reminiscent of games we played at Lightburn Park, Ulverston when I was about eight years old.

The event, played as it was on one of Harvard's traditional playing fields, attracted a lot of attention. No fewer than 200 "fans" attended. They were very vociferous and very partisan. Nor did the umpire escape unscathed, albeit without rancor. It was great entertainment and nobody enjoyed it more than Victoria, in the person of Helen Hayes, the star of the show.

From my point of view, the best was yet to come. Mr. X and I were invited to take tea with Miss Hayes at her hotel, The Commander Hotel in Cambridge, and that was memorable.

There was a fascinating sequel about 30 years subsequently. Helen Hayes was playing the lead role in a play at the Royal Alex Theatre in Toronto. Patricia and I were in attendance. On the spur of the moment I wrote a brief note to the actress — "Did she recall attending a cricket match at Harvard and subsequently taking tea at the Commander Hotel with a young Englishman?" An attendant took the note to Miss Hayes dressing room and the response was immediate. "Yes. Would your wife and you care to meet me in my dressing room after the show?" We did and it was a delightful experience.

Within a couple of weeks of the "cricket tea," Jake Jaeger, a prominent member of our differential analyzer team, asked if I would like to attend a baseball game with his fiancee and himself. The Boston Red Sox were to play the New York Yankees on the following Saturday to which Jake had complimentary tickets. I accepted with alacrity. What I did not realize until the game was that Dot Cronin, Jake's fiancé was the only daughter of Joe Cronin, legendary manager of the Red Sox. Consequently, I attended my first of many baseball games in a box reserved for the manager's family and friends at Fenway Park, one of the truly traditional ball parks in the United States. I was fortunate to be introduced to Dot's father and he said he hoped the game would appeal to a guy who was much more familiar with a cricket bat than a baseball bat.

It was not only the game that fascinated me, but equally the fans. About 40,000 of them and for the first time in my life I experienced the popcorn, peanuts, pretzels and beer vendors. Indeed there is nothing more American than a professional baseball game, especially the Red Sox playing the Yankees at Fenway Park. As an erstwhile cricketer I quickly appreciated the high skill of the players — the pitchers, batters and by no means least, the miraculous performance of the fielders. As an interesting sequel to this my first game, it's noteworthy that about 50 years subsequently the Toronto Blue Jays who were non-existent in the 1930's won back-to-back World Series Championships. Patricia and I were well-established Torontonians at the time and enthusiastic supporters.

The Summer Travel Program (June-September, 1938)

One of the biggest adventures of my life started effectively on June 18, 1938 when I left Cambridge and was driven by Sam Caldwell to Washington, D.C. to attend the Annual Convention of the American Institute of Electrical Engineers. This gave me an opportunity to visit, albeit transiently, several New England towns and see the verdant countryside in full bloom. It was an auspicious start.

The Convention, the first of many I have since attended and participated in, was both a social and a professional event. I met representatives of several universities and industrial organizations, by no means least, the Bell Telephone Laboratories. My early exposure to analog and digital computers provided the key to what was to become one of the most fertile areas of technological development in history. My brief talk on the utilization of the differential analyzer in solving partial differential equations was received warmly. Needless to add, the basic approach was due entirely to Douglas Hartree and I merely indicated how his ideas had been applied in practice. The talk was given to a final session of the Convention and immediately afterward, I hurriedly packed, met Arthur Armitage for dinner and subsequently left the Mayflower Hotel at about 10 p.m.

We headed due west for the mountains of West Virginia in Armitage's 1936 Ford sedan — fully loaded. Shortly after leaving the city we settled down to listen on the car radio to one of the historic World Heavy Weight Boxing Championships. Joe Louis of the United States was matched against Max Schmeling of Germany. Coming as it did at a time of great international tension when the Nazi movement under Hitler was very much on the offensive and an increasing threat to world peace, the fight had international political implications. Hitler had no doubt that Schmeling would triumph over his African American opponent. But he was in for a rude shock. And so were we, because after a single round, Joe Louis had proved victorious. A triumph for the democracies followed the triumphs of Jessie Owens, the black American athlete in the 1936 Berlin Olympics, when Hitler became so incensed that he refused to attend the final ceremonies.

After traversing the mountains where we camped by the roadside in sleeping bags and on camp cots, we were treated to the most gorgeous spectacle of the Shenandoah Valley. On to Knoxville, Tennessee and Chattanooga. I remember very well the latter city because after having been entertained by friends for dinner, we discovered we had no accommodations for the night and the only prospect was to set up our camp beds in a public parking lot and to settle down for a few hours sleep. Fortunately in those days the authorities did not intervene and we proceeded to drive to Decatur in southern Illinois. The city is noted for the log courthouse in which Abraham Lincoln first practiced as a lawyer and where he was subsequently, in 1860, endorsed for the Presidential nomination by the Republican Party.

Driving due south we found ourselves paralleling the mighty Mississippi and even spotted several of the large side-paddle steamers reminiscent of the musical "Show Boat." Cotton plantations galore and stately southern mansions were the order of the day. This was indeed the true south, and certainly during the 30's was not even remotely akin to the United States of New England. Our destination was Oxford, Mississippi, a small university town almost on the fringe of the Mississippi swamps. During his first year at Yale in the graduate faculty of law, Armitage had been befriended by Professor John Fox, who was on a sabbatical leave from the University of Mississippi. We were fortunate insofar as Professor and Mrs. Fox entertained us for almost a full week in their beautiful home on the outskirts of the university campus. We were introduced to quite a different life-style to that which we had become accustomed and we certainly enjoyed the southern cooking. However, the outstanding event of the visit was the "cat-fish fry' which was held in the extensive backyard of the Fox residence. This of course is a southern tradition. We were obviously privileged guests because the Mayor and Mayoress of Oxford attended the event in which copious quantities of barbecued chicken and a liberal supply of "Mint Juleeps" were much in evidence. Toward the end of the evening, when the mayor heard that we would be leaving Oxford the following morning, he was quite perturbed and even went to the extent of offering to get us jobs under the auspices of the city council.

During the 1930's, Mississippi and several other southern states were "dry" — alcohol beverages in all forms were banned. But this did not seem to inhibit the local inhabitants from enjoying their parties. The party in honor of Armitage and me was no exception. During the afternoon none other than the Mayor himself picked us up and drove us into the country, and to my utter astonishment, located in the woods a solitary cabin dedicated to the making of "moonshine." This liquor is in fact bourbon whiskey and very potent. It was the main ingredient of the "Mint Juleeps" which were made by pouring the liquor over a tumbler full of cracked ice and inserting a sprig of mint.

Heading south to our next destination, New Orleans, introduced us to the many vicissitudes of traveling during the summer in a non-air-conditioned car. Fortunately there were no mechanical problems. During this leg of the trip we discovered camping sites adjacent to the river in which at night the noise of insects and other swamp like creatures created a jungle-like environment in which the strident call of the bullfrog was a dominate feature. In such circumstances, my inherent dislike of reptiles was to a large extent suppressed. But it was a relief to reach civilization again; and New Orleans proved to be a city of many and diverse attractions.

I cannot emphasize too strongly how much we benefited from southern hospitality in every possible form. In the city of New Orleans, for example, we were entertained lavishly by an attorney, John Deutsch and his family. Armitage had met their son at Yale and although only a casual acquaintance, he suggested that we should contact him on our arrival in New Orleans. It was a very hot and humid day and the motel in which we found accommodation was not air-conditioned. The prospect of a three-day stay was not particularly encouraging. On the second day, out of the blue, Armitage recalled his fellow student at Yale and contacted him by telephone. The upshot was that the family invited the two of us to stay with them for a few days, sent one of their servants to help us pack, settle the bill at the motel and guide us to the Deutsch family home. It turned out that he was the most prominent attorney in New Orleans and his home was in every sense of the word a southern mansion. We had a wonderful time, not only in exploring the city and its night life, but as well taking a day's excursion to the Mississippi Delta for "soft shell" crab fishing. In order to ensure that we benefitted to the full from our stay, Mr. Deutsch senior took several days vacation. On the final evening of our stay, the Deutsch family arranged a farewell dinner for us which included at least 30 guests at the Hotel Roosevelt. It was July 4, 1938. Toasts to King George VI and President Roosevelt were proposed, and much to our embarrassment, to Armitage and myself. The hotel orchestra played several British patriotic songs, including the national anthem and "Rule Britannia." I frequently recalled that occasion two years subsequently when we were enduring some of the darkest days of WWII during the London Blitz of 1940-41 and I felt instinctively that it would not be too long before the United States joined the Allies in our battle against Hitler.

Leaving New Orleans on July 5 with many memories of a wonderful city and a wonderful people, we proceeded to drive to Houston, Texas without incident, and then to Dallas. Fortunately the traffic was light and we made excellent time. Indeed, compared with the English roads, it was a joy to drive on superb pavement at speeds ranging up to 80 miles per hour. But en route to San Antonio with me at the wheel, our exuberance was suddenly shattered by the sound of a police siren and suddenly a Texas State Trooper on a motor bicycle came into view in the side mirror and indicated we should pull onto the side of the road. Pulling out his notebook, he asked for my driver's license and other facts. But when I informed him we were visiting students from Britain and that there were effectively no speed limits in Britain, he became very friendly and inquired about our stay in the United States and our plans. Obviously we were unique and apart from giving us a comparatively mild caution, he then proceeded to show us another manifestation of southern hospitality. He offered to communicate with his home base in San Antonio and to ask the "boys" to show us the night life of the city. To my mind this was an incredible offer and when we reached San Antonio I was keen to pursue it. But Armitage, ever the lawyer, was very reluctant to spend the evening visiting some of San Antonio's night spots with a couple of Texas "cops" as our guides. I've always regretted missing such an opportunity because it would have been quite memorable.

A brief visit of several hours to Juarez across the international border from El Paso provided me with my first introduction to an entirely different culture. Colorful, uninhibited and extremely friendly, the Mexican people we met regarded us almost as superior beings from outer space. As a memento of my all too brief visit to this delightful country, I acquired some native pottery and a glorious hand-woven runner, still in the possession of my family.

Although it is not my intention to present a travel catalog of the national parks of the western United States, my experiences in visiting some half dozen of them were so extraordinary and have such far-reaching consequences, not least the Dartmouth connection, that a reasonable record of that eventful summer of 1938 seems appropriate. We encountered one wonderland after another, and the focal points were always the national parks. Indeed, our travel plan was strongly predicated on visiting as many of them as time permitted.

Proceeding in a northerly direction into New Mexico, we crossed the "Continental Divide" and were officially in the true west — where all streams and rivers eventually flowed into the Pacific Ocean. Our next objective was the Carlsbad Caverns, a national park. This incredible underground structure had only been explored about 14 years previously. It consisted of several interconnected chambers of which the largest is 285 feet high and 625 feet wide. It was so fascinating that we spent several hours exploring the interconnected caverns and taking many photographs. Each of the chambers is a veritable art gallery with the most colorful and beautifully shaped structures imaginable. The stalactites hang from the roof and the stalagmites rise from the floor and when they meet, columns, some at least two feet in diameter, are formed. An interesting feature was the enormous number of bats clinging to the roof. I understand there are almost a million of them and it must be quite a sight to see them emerge at nightfall to hunt for small rodents and insects.

When motel accommodations weren't available in the widely scattered towns and villages (which was rare), we slept in our sleeping bags on camp cots. The night sky, especially at an elevation of a few thousand feet, was a revelation. The dry atmosphere, zero pollution conditions and the eerie silence contributed to breathtaking views of the universe — planets, stars, the Milky Way and even several galaxies, notably the Andromeda which I'd never seen previously in such clarity.

Northern New Mexico and Arizona are sparsely populated, a notable feature being the huge tracts of country which were dedicated to Navajo Indian Reservations. I was extremely impressed with the Navajos. Reserved, but quite friendly, they initially treated us with suspicion as we were so obviously foreigners. But this quickly dissipated when we took their photographs for which privilege we paid a dollar or two and admired their native costumes, especially the jewelry. As a matter of fact, the Navajo are talented craftsmen in the arts of the silversmith, basket making and blanket and rug weavers. Their wares displayed on trestle tables, included silver and turquoise bracelets, necklaces and belts, decorative baskets and traditional rugs. I purchased several items of jewelry and notably a hand-woven wall hanging which embodied native icons. Some half century later, the latter was presented to the Caledon Township Public Library in Ontario and is on display there. Patricia treasures two of the beautiful silver bracelets acquired so many years ago in that faraway Navajo village.

The Caverns were the first of several national parks we visited during the following weeks. Within a few days we were enthralled by those wonderlands of unsurpassed beauty. Even their names — Painted Desert, Petrified Forest; Grand Canyon, Bryce Canyon and Zion Canyon are indicative of something special. We were not disappointed, and indeed the mountainous terrain of northern Arizona was typical, where peaks rise above 10,000 feet and must be an artist's delight. Although perhaps doing injustice to others, I've singled out one of the parks visited for special treatment.

Not surprisingly the Grand Canyon has been described as one of the seven natural wonders of the world. Excavated out of limestone and other ancient rocks over a period of one million years, essentially by the Colorado River, the Canyon is more than 200 miles long and between five and 20 miles across. In places it is more than a mile deep. Outcrops of rock and lava characterize the canyon and their colors — shades of greens, browns, yellow and reds — are constantly changing from sunrise to sunset. My first glimpse of this remarkable kaleidoscope of color was from the south rim. It remains during my long life the most remarkable spectacle I have ever seen.

We stayed for three days in the park lodge and on one day descended about 2,000 feet below the rim by a well-trodden track — we preferred walking to the alternative which was being precariously balanced on the back of a mule. As a matter of fact, we met a park ranger ascending the canyon wall in a state of exhaustion. His canteen of water was dry and his food supply was zero. We were able to escort him back to the rim of the canyon and his gratitude knew no bounds.

Fortunately during the summer of 1990 on a bus tour of the western national parks, I was able to prove to Patricia that my stories of the Grand Canyon, Zion and other parks were not pure fantasy. She was as thrilled, perhaps even more so because of her artistic attributes, than I was.

Zion Canyon, in the state of Utah, is about a days drive north of the Grand Canyon. Characterized by vivid colors and spectacular precipices, the park's most prominent feature is the major canyon which is deep, narrow and vertical-walled. The almost perpendicular cliffs are 2000 feet high. The canyon holds a special place in the hearts of the Porter family. But before giving the reason, a brief introduction may be appropriate. I can picture the log-built lodge with its massive stone fireplace and comfortable chairs even today. It proved an ideal spot from every point of view — nature walks, swimming pools and several interesting climbs. For example, we discovered that several of the 1000-year-old cave dwellings were accessible and they proved to be a fascinating attraction. During the afternoon of our last day at the lodge, walking in the narrowest portion of the canyon only about 50 years wide, we met three Dartmouth College students — Bob Schwartz, Adrian Weiss and Gerry

Ullman. From the moment of meeting, a life-long friendship was established. Indeed within the last few minutes, taking a break from my dictation, I've telephoned Bob Schwartz at Pine Ridge, North Carolina, and Adrian Weiss in Miami, Florida. Sadly, both Armitage and Ullman died about 15 years ago..

The group, five of us, soon discovered that our travel plans were very similar and we decided to team up and to travel together for at least six to eight weeks. It was a lucky break for all of us. The meeting and subsequent friendship must have been "ordained from above" insofar as on two separate occasions in the future, we were to lose contact, in the second case for about 50 years, and to regain it in the most incredible fashion.

As a fitting beginning, we all attended a concert given that night by the student staff members at the lodge and having found partners among the guests, we spent an enjoyable hour or so after the concert dancing.

Las Vegas, at the time a town of no more than 4,000 inhabitants with a single casino, was the first objective of our group. One of the few hotels available agreed to the five of us sharing one of their guest suites and consequently we had very inexpensive accommodations. This applied on many other occasions during our travels together, another advantage of traveling as a group. The temperature in Las Vegas that day reached an incredible 118 degrees F in the shade and most of our day's stay in the town was spent in the cool water of Lake Mead. With no air-conditioning in the cars, we considered a drive across the 150-200 mile wide Mohave Desert with virtually no conveniences or gas stations, to be a potentially hazardous undertaking. The alternative, which we chose, was to leave Las Vegas about 11 p.m. when the temperature had dropped to about 100 degrees F and to drive through the night. We planned to rendezvous at the first motel we encountered on the outskirts of San Bernardino in California.

It is interesting to reflect on the remarkable changes which have taken place in the area during the past 70 years. Today Las Vegas, carved out of the desert terrain, glitters with gambling casinos and high-rise luxury hotels. It is a tourist Mecca.

Unfortunately our Dartmouth friends did not reach the motel until the following afternoon because two flat tires during the desert crossing had delayed them considerably. In the meanwhile, Armitage and I assumed that they'd changed their plans and accordingly we drove into Los Angeles. Furthermore, because our own plans were quite indeterminate, we had no idea where we would be spending the following few days. After staying overnight in Long Beach, we decided to spend two or three days in the much more attractive community of Santa Monica. Having located an inexpensive apartment-hotel, we, through the good offices of the British Consul General's office in Los Angeles, obtained guest membership in the prestigious Deauville Beach Club, whose membership included well-known film stars and two other clubs in the vicinity as well. We enjoyed their facilities, especially the opportunity to swim in the warm waters of the Pacific Ocean. Consequently, we extended our stay to four days. But on the third day, in the afternoon, to our utter amazement, we discovered that the Dartmouth men had checked into the hotel — the first of two extraordinary coincidences I referred to previously.

It was a joyful reunion which changed markedly our program of activities. For example, the Dartmouth men had several friends in southern California and we benefitted greatly from some of these connections. Elissa Landi, the stage and screen actress was one of them and we were invited to her beautiful home and to play tennis on her court. As well, she arranged for us to visit a Hollywood film studio. It gave me a real appreciation of the complexity of film making, especially the production of some of the sets. Some of these were familiar and I identified them with films I had seen in the past.

The drive along the Pacific Highway through the gorgeous redwood forests with glimpses from time to time of the ocean was one of the most spectacular of my life. After 200 miles or so, we left the coast road and drove in an easterly direction through increasingly huge redwoods until we reached perhaps the oldest plantation of trees on earth. It is the Sequoia National Park. We spent a day driving through groves of the celebrated Sequoia and we actually drove through the trunk (with a diameter of almost 40 feet) of one of them. Considered to be the largest living organism in the world, the Sequoia tree can reach a height of more than 250 feet and is estimated to be in some cases more than 3,500 years old. When Christ was born, hundreds of these trees were flourishing and most had not reached middle age. Fortunately the trees are virtually indestructible except by fire, the ravages of which can be seen in various parts of the park. In "The National Parks Portfolio," which I acquired in 1937, several photographs portray the magnificence of the trees under the heading, "Wilderness of Giants." I came across the statement: "To walk and wonder through these woods, even for a few hours, is to feel an emotion which can be duplicated nowhere else." I agree.

Almost contiguous with the Sequoia Park is my favorite — the

Yosemite National Park, which covers no fewer than 1,100 square miles. Its most prominent feature is the Yosemite Valley carved out by a massive glacier millions of years ago. John Muir, the noted naturalist and founder of the Sierra Club, one of the most influential of all environmental-interest societies, described it simply as "The Land of Enchantment." I cannot think of a more appropriate description. Despite the beauty and grandeur of several of the parks we visited, Yosemite holds pride of place, probably because, as a group, my four comrades and I found so much there to see and do. We spent a week in the valley sleeping under the stars with a spectacular view of the world's highest waterfall (according to the park ranger), the Yosemite Falls has a drop of 1,400 feet, and about five times that of Niagara Falls. Equally impressive are the breathtaking granite precipices of Half Dome and el Capitan. As well we were in a good strategic position to view the man-created "fire falls" — at 9 p.m. each evening a stream of fiery embers descends from a height of several thousand feet, an awe-inspiring sight. As a mountain lover all my life, I had never been quite so thrilled, but there was more to come.

After exploring and photographing from many angles the wonderful falls (Bridalveil, Nevada, Vernal and the lower Yosemite falls, all having drops of more than 300 feet), we decided to climb Half Dome. It rises precipitously 4,000 feet from the valley floor.

It was a breath-taking experience in more ways than one, and although my companions at a height of about 3,000 feet called it a day, I persisted and eventually reached the summit. In front of me in "The National Parks Portfolio" is a large photograph of the Half Dome and I marvel that once I gazed with awe down that precipitous face to the valley below. Needless to add, I climbed from the remote side of the Dome where the gradients are appreciably less than the front face, and indeed for the last few hundred feet, a roped "stairway" greatly facilitated the climb. At the summit in a bronze container was a book, dedicated to climbers. There were only about 300 signatures inscribed, the names of those who had climbed the Dome in 1938. I appended my name with considerable pride, especially when I noted that there were very few Englishmen among the climbers.

Leaving our site at Camp Currie, we drove to a remote area of the park — the Tuolumne Meadows. High up in the Sierra Nevada range, they gave ready access to Mt. Dana, which was our objective. The mountain has an elevation of more than 13,000 feet and my companions and I all reached the summit, albeit somewhat breathless. Notably we encountered huge snowdrifts in spite of the fact that it was mid-summer in California.

The drive north from San Francisco followed another "redwood" highway and it was a delightful experience. The road would wind for miles between the huge trees and then without warning, the glitter of sun on the ocean would occur. In the short space of a hundred yards, a scene strangely reminiscent of Cornwall and the coast of southwest England would unfold. We were making a beeline for two national parks — Crater Lake and Mount Rainier. The former is said to be the deepest and bluest fresh water lake in the world. It consists essentially of the remnants of a collapsed volcano. I cannot do better then quote from the article in The National Parks Portfolio devoted to Crater Lake:

> *"It is a gem of wonderful color in a setting of pearly lavas relieved by patches of pine green and snow — a gem which changes hue with every atmospheric change and every shift of light. It is a lake of mystery."*

Our stay in the park was unfortunately transitory because we were anxious to reach Mt. Rainier Park before sundown. We did, and in time to see the rays of the evening sun glittering on some of the largest glaciers I've ever seen. This is the land of expired volcanoes and Mt. Rainier is the most prominent.

After dinner at Paradise Lodge, we five intrepid adventurers took a stroll to stretch our legs after our long drive. The full moon was rising over the summit of Mt. Rainer. It was a wonderful scene, indeed, one of the unforgettable occasions of our visit to the western wonderlands of the United States. The next morning was cloudy and not conducive to serious climbing. But we did, in fact, climb the lower reaches of Pinnacle Peak and obtained a bird's-eye view of one of the spectacular glaciers which gave rise to Mt. Rainier being referred to as "the frozen octopus." There are a total of 28 glaciers and the one we saw in-depth was the Nasqually — a river of ice flowing down the mountain side. The extensive wild flower parks, several thousand acres in extent, provided a perfect framework to a scene which unfortunately our black and white photographs captured inadequately. Although our two-day visit to the Mt. Rainier Park permitted only a superficial appreciation of this glacier wonderland, we at least experienced scenes which were unique, unimaginable and certainly inspiring.

Our next destination was Victoria, British Columbia via the Puget

Sound ferry. The Princess Marguerite steamer sails daily, round trip, from Seattle to Victoria.

It was interesting how we, especially Armitage and I, reacted to a complete change of scenery and lifestyle. It was almost a year since we'd left Britain and we were struck immediately by how very British the city of Victoria is. Indeed, more British than Britain itself! This was manifest in a variety of ways, especially in the tempo of everyday life which was markedly different from that to which we had become accustomed — much more relaxed. The gardens, notably the Bouchard Gardens, in many respects surpassed their peers in Britain. The roses in particular were superb. We spent an unforgettable afternoon culminating in tea at the Empress Hotel. It was served in traditional style with all the trimmings, notably the real Fortnum and Mason's brand of tea. It was a refreshing, albeit nostalgic interlude which in at least one regard brought us "down to earth." The headlines of the Canadian newspapers were to put it mildly, very disturbing. We became aware for the first time in many months of political and military developments in Europe from Britain's point of view. Clearly our native land was responding to the seriousness of the threat posed by Nazi Germany. This of course, was manifest about three months later when Neville Chamberlain, the Prime Minister, visited Hitler in Munich. This rather dampened our spirits, but not for long because our travel plans still anticipated some exciting prospects.

We planned to stay several days in Canada with Banff, Alberta as our base. Even in 1938 the town, essentially because of its strategic location on the Canadian Pacific Railway, was an all-year round resort and convention center. It provided ready access to the Canadian Rocky Mountains. The vista was dominated by the Banff Springs Hotel, surely one of the most picturesque hotels in the world. Although we preferred camping out in the large well-equipped campgrounds to the more civilized life of hotel living, we nevertheless used some of the hotel facilities and notably the hot spring baths. We enjoyed as well a day trip to Lake Louise and the view of the glacier which flows into the northern shores of the lake. I've rarely seen a more vivid scene than the sunshine shimmering on the emerald green waters of the lake. It provided a fitting finale to my first footing in Canada, little realizing at the time that I would subsequently spend the majority of my working life as a citizen of this great country; albeit in the province of Ontario, some 2,000 miles to the east.

Driving due south through the city of Calgary, we eventually reached

Yellowstone Park. Regretfully, it was here after a few days camping that we parted company with our Dartmouth companions after six weeks of good fellowship and a multiplicity of adventures. As I will record subsequently, my retirement years have been greatly enriched by an amazing coincidental reunion in 1986 with the Dartmouth men and their wives. They traveled back to their homes in Westchester County, New York, while Armitage and I continued to enjoy the wonders of Yellowstone Park — the oldest, (established in 1872) and the largest (8400 square miles) of all the national parks.

A belt road interconnects locations of special interest and we had no difficulty during our five-day stay in viewing some of the best-known attractions. But I must stress that a comprehensive exploration of the park would take several of the summer months and for the hardy explorer braving the winter climate, a year or two. It is fortunate that in spite of the extensive forest fires that often devour thousands of acres of forest, the park remains pristine, in no small measure due to the elite core of park rangers, with whom I had several fascinating conversations. From them I learned that the park is one of the largest game preserves in the world. Hunting has been prohibited since 1872. While the herds of bison, deer and antelope were commonplace, I recall seeing in the distance a few elk and moose and on one rare occasion I obtained a glimpse of a few big horn mountain sheep. But it was the sight of black bear (there were grizzlies in the park as well but not in our immediate vicinity) that proved rather intimidating. However, these animals showed little fear of humans and I have close-up photographs of a black bear with two cubs ambling across a paved road, and another photograph of a large bear standing upright with two feet planted on the top of our car! I recall having to take extraordinary precautions to protect our food stuff and frequently we strung large canvas bags containing food over branches of trees out of reach of the bears.

When Patricia and I returned to Yellowstone Park in 1989, the situation was completely different. Apart from a single small herd of bison, the wildlife had completely disappeared, no doubt as a result of the massive increase in the tourist populations and a corresponding escalation in the number of automobiles. Armitage and I were indeed fortunate to have seen the park in a state not much different from the wooded wilderness that existed almost a century earlier.

Lasting impressions of Yellowstone include the glowing canyons carved by the Yellowstone River, the Great Falls of the river, and twice the height of Niagara, the innumerable boiling hot springs, the Petrified

Forest and by no means least, the geysers of which there are more in the park than in the rest of the world combined. It would be impossible to forget "Old Faithful" which was as regular as clockwork, erupting to a height of 170 feet for about four minutes, at intervals of 60 minutes on average. It attracts thousands of visitors during the summer months. Only the giant geysers spouting 250 feet for an hour each eruption is more spectacular. But because its frequency is less often — four to sixteen days — we unfortunately missed seeing it.

Our next destination, 100 miles south of the boundary of Yellowstone, was the Grand Teton National Park. We approached it from the east side — Jackson's Hole — once a notorious rendezvous of outlaws. The small town had matured into a tourist resort. The Grand Teton mountains, ranging between 7,000 and 14,000 feet in altitude, spring abruptly from the valley floor, granite bastions and precipices of unsurpassed grandeur, albeit in some respects reminiscent of my native Lake District, they dominate the Wyoming skyline. We obtained extraordinary photographs when we rowed a boat across Jackson's Lake and caught the sunset over the mountain tops. Some 50 years later (1989) during the bus tour of the National Parks mentioned earlier, Patricia and I took the ski lift (gondola) from Jackson's Hole to the summit of the Grand Teton mountains. We were rewarded with a magnificent view and as well saw first hand the severity of some of the ski runs of subsequent Olympic fame.

Although during most of our entire tour we had a minimum exposure to press and media (Victoria was an exception), we were fortunate at Jackson's Hole to learn that John Cobb, the racing car driver from the United Kingdom was due to make an attempt on the land speed record within a few days at the Salt Lake Flats in Utah, which was about 500 miles south. Not surprisingly, we felt the opportunity was too good to miss. While Salt Lake City was not included in our original itinerary, it turned out to be a historic and fascinating interlude. The venue for the world's land speed record attempt was, and I believe still is, a huge salt flat with an area of several hundred square miles, adjacent to the Great Salt Lake of Utah. The surface is granular and hence ideal for motor vehicle traction. It is also perfectly flat. Armitage and I were warmly welcomed by John Cobb and members of his team, especially the notable car designer, Reed Railton at their headquarters which had been established a few miles distance from where the attempt would take place. Being an event of international importance, a small village of trailers occupied for the most part by members of the press, had been assembled and we camped out in the vicinity. The vehicle designed especially for the occasion was called the "Railton Special" and incorporated two large aero engines of WWI vintage. The machine was a thing of beauty as it glistened in the sunlight and I obtained a few photographs, several of which are presently in the possession of my son, John, whose knowledge of vintage cars and all matters relating thereto, is truly encyclopedic.

Running in a south/north direction across the Salt Flats is a 10-mile long, one-foot wide strip of black tar. The middle one mile stretch, as well as the one kilometer stretch is monitored electrically. This is the "measured mile."

The day before the attempt, Armitage and I were driven the full length of the strip in a Hudson sedan automobile driven by none other than John Cobb himself. The object was to check for irregularities in the surface and to inspect the strip itself for inconsistencies. It was an incredible experience to be driven by, at the time, the world's fastest individual on land.

During the record runs, the vehicle is accelerated over a distance of six miles, reaches maximum speed and the time for the measured mile is recorded. At 400 mph, for example, the approximate record of the day, the time is 9.0 seconds and timing was accurate to 100th of a second. This corresponded to about five feet in distance, and then decelerated over a distance of six miles.

Unfortunately, although we did not actually see the record broken that day as the attempt was about five mph short, it was an unforgettable sight to see. I took a photo of John Cobb and the car immediately after. About a month later, Cobb succeeded in his attempt to set a new record.[7]

Shortly before leaving Salt Lake City headed for Denver, we received a telegram. Once every two weeks we telegraphed Commonwealth Fund headquarters in New York requesting our mail be forwarded to specific locations and we received a confirming telegram with the ominous and somewhat prophetic words, "Don't try to emulate Cobb's feat on the mountain roads."

In spite of the fact that we drove circumspectly on the treacherous roads over the mountains (I was at the wheel at the time) I encountered very loose gravel shoulders and within a fraction of a second, the car

---

[7]John Cobb held the official world speed record in Railton designed cars first in September 15, 1938 at the speed of 350.2 mph. Later, on August 23, 1939 he reached the speed of 368.9 mph and lastly on September 16, 1947 at a speed of 394.19 mph. Several years later in an attempt to break the water speed record on Loch Ness, Scotland, John Cobb was tragically killed.

skidded and proceeded down a slope finally coming to rest "upside down" some 40 feet off the road. We made a hasty exit and rapidly removed our possessions. The car was abandoned. Fortunately, within minutes on that sparsely traveled highway, we were rescued by the driver of a Kraft Cheese Wagon. With true western hospitality, he helped with our bags, drove us to the Colorado town of Kremmling, acted as witness of the accident at the police station and located a motel. The insurance claim involved a couple of days and we were then fortunate to obtain transportation to Denver. Incidentally, the insurance claim was settled reasonably satisfactorily although I felt guilty in so far as I was driving Armitage's car at the time and it was he who had to suffer the consequences.

We traveled on an overnight express train from Denver to Pennsylvania Station, New York and from there I proceeded by train to Boston. Armitage went on to Hartford, Conn. We parted on the very best of terms having spent three months of high adventure together and having seen more of the United States than the majority of our fellow students.

As a postscript it is worthy of mention that our train trip from Denver to Chicago was, in keeping with the whole tenure of our trip, exciting to say the least. Shortly after departing from Denver, we adjourned to the club car for dinner and refreshment. There were only two other diners and they agreed when we suggested that perhaps we should join them. Some 14 hours later, after having dined and wined very adequately with our companions, we were still very wide awake. The reason was quite incredible. One of our dinner companions was the renowned film star Spencer Tracy and he lived up to his reputation. Garrulous, but very charming, he entertained us during the entire railway journey. I wish I could recall some of the conversation, but not surprisingly, in light of the alcoholic beverages we consumed, these remain pleasant, albeit very vague memories. But it was a journey to remember and a fitting conclusion to one of the most fascinating three months of my life.

Back at MIT early in September 1938 my first job was to change residences. Runkle House had been converted to a senior undergraduate residence and I moved to the newly established Graduate House located at the northwest corner of the intersection of Memorial Drive and Massachusetts Avenue, Cambridge. Previously it had been a block of apartments. Because it was advantageous to share a two-room apartment, Fred Merrill became my roommate. A University of Liverpool graduate and Commonwealth Fund Fellow (1936-38) he had obtained a research assistantship and stayed on at MIT for an additional year. One of the major advantages of the new Graduate House was the excellent dining room and common room facilities. Furthermore, the Master, Avery Ashdown, became a good friend and wise counselor. His pioneering work in establishing the new facility was subsequently recognized when Graduate House was designated Avery Ashdown House. Fifty years after taking up residence as one of the first group of about 100 students, Patricia and I returned in May, 1988 to celebrate the 50th anniversary of the opening of Avery Ashdown House. During that reunion I met several other former graduate students who shared with me the experience of becoming founder members, so to speak, of MIT's first Graduate House. Especially joyful was our sharing the anniversary celebrations with Frank Lewis and his wife, Beatrice. Frank, a former electrical engineering graduate student, had been a close friend. In the next chapter I shall recall Frank's surprising "last minute" arrival at Patricia and my wedding in July, 1941, and how he entertained me at the Mayflower Hotel, Washington, D.C. in February, 1945 at the beginning of my war-time mission to the United States.

Let me try to put into perspective my impressions on my rejoining the RDA group after my summer travels. I received a warm welcome — everybody was anxious to hear about my impressions of the United States because I had seen more of the country than most of my colleagues. My many photographs had then been developed and I was able to show some of the highlights of the trip. Unfortunately, most of these photos during the past several decades have disappeared, although a few of the most memorable are still in my possession.

In spite of the fact that the fall of 1938 was one of the most stressful periods in modern European history — the increasing stranglehold by Nazi Germany on most of the continent of Europe culminating in Munich. Life in Cambridge, Mass. was relatively unaffected and this applied to the United States as a whole. Even visitors to the Institute from Britain during this period with their stories of preparations for war did not appreciably affect the overall optimism at MIT, which not surprisingly was due in large measure to the economic recovery of the United States after the devastating depression of previous years.

It was a period when science and technology were burgeoning and increasingly affecting the everyday lives of the public, notably in the fields of communication, air travel and the mass production of automobiles. This gave rise to increasing cooperation between research-oriented universities and industry. Consequently, the Engineering

Department at MIT under the dynamic leadership of Dr. Bush with his broad vision for the future and his many contacts in industry and government, benefited enormously. It is worth noting in particular, that the fruits of this collaboration were manifest especially during World War II at MIT with the establishment of the Radiation Laboratory, the Servo Mechanisms Laboratory and special laboratories in magnetic materials, gyroscope stabilization investigations, etc. These undoubtedly played a central role in the prosecution of the war.

A specific example of Dr. Bush's influence and contacts was the initiation of the gift by the Bell Telephone Laboratories to the RDA project. They donated the entire crossbar telephone switching system required for the 16-integrator machine. Recall that the RDA was essentially analog/digital in operation. Because of its centrality, let me expand on the introduction to the basic concepts of the RDA I presented earlier in this chapter. They played a not insignificant role in my future career.

The mathematical processes such as multiplication, integration, addition and function plotting were carried out by high precision analog/digital components and the interconnection between components was in effect a miniature telephone exchange with digital inputs (punched cards). In retrospect I marvel at the sheer elegance of the basic concept and engineering of the RDA. The precision wheel and disk integrators, the novel servo mechanisms, which were the electrical equivalent of the mechanical torque amplifiers of the original digital machine and the infrastructure of the machine, were engineering achievements at the very cutting edge of pre- World War II technology. In retrospect my personal involvement with the development of the function unit especially in light of future developments, constituted a comparatively minor contribution to the project as a whole.

Replacement of the time-consuming and laborious process involved in setting up the mechanical interconnections of the original differential analyzer by punching a deck of cards was the most novel feature of the RDA. The cards in effect acted as digital switches which activated the crossbar switches which in turn directed the flow of electrical signals to control a host of small electrical motors, at least 100.

But I certainly did not appreciate at the time or indeed until more than a decade subsequently (1950) the sheer complexity of the network of electrical switches. It constituted a monumental achievement. It anticipated in many respects the design of the basic logic circuits of a modern digital computer. During the summer of 1938 when I was enjoying "the grand tour," this was the major problem being addressed by Dick Taylor, who incidentally was the guy who introduced me to "draw" and "stud" poker and to the Friday evening games in which several of the RDA team participated.

However, a break-through was not achieved until early September shortly after my return and I was present, albeit as an onlooker. It was a Friday afternoon and Dick Taylor had dropped into Claude Shannon and my office to finalize arrangements for the weekly poker games (each participant had a chore — several cans of beer, Coca Cola, some crackers and cheese were basic requirements). I recall him saying, "Claude, I've been struggling with the crossbar switching problems stated previously. We need an analytical procedure to determine how the switches and the related punched card patterns should be programmed." More simplistically, the problem is to determine the configuration of switches required to control the flow of information between elements of the RDA and to use punched cards to provide the input data. In those days this was by no means a trivial problem in spite of the fact that considerable progress had been made in the design of large-scale telephone exchanges.

Being familiar with the basic concepts of the RDA, although not an active member of the team, Claude Shannon had no difficulty in formulating the problem and after a few minutes thought he said, "I'll take a look at it over the weekend."

Early the following week, Shannon outlined a novel approach to the problem. Together with Dick Taylor I was present, although I must confess I had only the vaguest idea of what was being proposed. In effect, the method was predicated on mechanizing the symbolic logic associated with binary arithmetic. Boolean algebra had been rediscovered by Claude Shannon! This was an incredible achievement for a young graduate student in electrical engineering. It sticks in my memory as an occasion when history, especially in the light of the developments within the last 60 years, was being made. As a matter of fact, Shannon subsequently used these ideas in the thesis he presented for his master of engineering degree. In my experiences during my academic career I can state quite unequivocally that Shannon's master's thesis is the most original I have ever encountered. In Chapter Eight I introduce another occasion when Shannon played a significant role in assisting me personally. By that time he had achieved international stature because of his seminal contributions to information and communications theory. I am thrilled to note that his work has been recognized at the Bell

Telephone Laboratories where "Claude Shannon Day" is celebrated annually on Claude's birthday.

During the month of October, 1938, New England was devastated by a hurricane which caused several hundred fatalities. Although I was about 80 miles from the epicenter of the storm, the damage in the Boston area was severe. Downed power lines caused by falling trees were particularly hazardous. I recall this occasion especially well because it coincided with a very special social event. Because of our nascent friendship with members of the Spelman family, Oscar Puls, Arthur Armitage and I had been invited to the "coming-out" party of Dorothy Spelman and Gene Tierney to be held at the Spelman's Fairfield, Conn. home four days after the hurricane struck. It took Oscar and myself about eight hours to drive from Cambridge to Fairfield (Armitage, of course, being at Hartford, missed that horrendous drive) negotiating those partially blocked highways was an adventure in itself as most of them had been open only for 24 hours. Providence, R.I., was an unforgettable sight; comparatively large sailing vessels and a small freighter had been blown ashore and were stranded virtually in the center of the city. Several years later during the London air raids, driving through the bomb-damaged streets, reminded me of the drive through Providence on that October day.

We stayed at the Spelman guest house located on the several acre estates. The party, typical of American upper class society, was unique in my experience; white tie and tails for the men, spectacular gowns for Dorothy and Gene and the ladies; sumptuous buffet, champagne cocktails. Following dinner there was dancing, singing and entertainment. In retrospect the party assumes ever more glamour because Gene Tierney, a very attractive young lady of 17 at the time, blossomed a decade later into one of Hollywood's most acclaimed film stars. Another guest who was achieving international fame and who had revolutionized the card game of Bridge was another neighbor of the Spelmans, Ely Culbertson. He was the inventor of the Culbertson System of bidding in Contract Bridge. During the morning after the party, I had the pleasure of partnering Mrs. Culbertson, a redoubtable Bridge player in her own right, in a single rubber. But of course, although not mentioned previously, at the time due essentially to the tutoring of my erstwhile friend Wilfred Thatcher at Manchester, I was a fairly good player.

While I was enjoying such events in the United States, it is salutary to recall that the political climate in Europe, exemplified by the "Munich

Agreement" was worsening.

During the whole period of my fellowship it is especially gratifying to report that Douglas Hartree not only updated me with respect to publications we had jointly authored, but as well commented on public affairs in Britain. I have for example in front of me an eight page letter he wrote on 22, October 1938 — exquisitely hand-written as always. His writing style was very artistic; tiny and precise. Let me quote from a single paragraph:

> *"Your letter came just as the international crisis last month seemed to becoming really acute, and when we were busy both at home and in the university trying to do what we could to meet the situation we were expecting; I don't know what the prospects seemed to you, but on the Tuesday and Wednesday before Chamberlain went to the meeting at Munich, it seemed to me that there was about one chance in 10 that we wouldn't be at war within a week; and it wasn't at all a comfortable thought!"*

DRH obviously had no illusions about Britain's future prospects, and more than once he emphasized the importance of Chamberlain's "scrap of paper" as being the country's savior because it gave a sorely needed period to build up the country's defenses. Far from regarding Chamberlain as an "appeaser," Douglas Hartree, and I agreed with him completely, considered him to be a savior.

The final months of my fellowship saw the completion of the design of the function unit and ancillary equipment, and there was much social activity. Notable were the several "senior proms" at local women's colleges, as well as the MIT senior prom, and several concerts at Symphony Hall.

Still vivid in my memory are the celebrations ushering in the year 1939 in Times Square, New York. Armitage and I attended what were to be the last peace-time New Years Eve parties we would attend for six long war-time years. We were obliged to park the car about a mile from Times Square and returning to the car in high spirits we had great difficulty in locating it. All New York Streets, especially at 2 a.m. on New Year's Day, appeared to be the same. Sadly it was Armitage's and my last celebration together.

Another notable occurrence was my emergency surgery in the Massachusetts General Hospital for acute hernia (the first of the three I have experienced). I was out of action for more than two weeks, but was greatly encouraged by the visitations of MIT friends and not least by a kind letter I received from Dr. Bush, then president of Carnegie Institute of Washington wishing me well.

Let me close this important chapter of my life by quoting in full a letter which Dr. Bush sent to Professor Hartree on the termination of my fellowship. In many respects it provides a perfect summing up of my two years in the academic wonderland of MIT. It is interesting to note that because of his eminent position as Presidential Advisor, to Franklin Roosevelt, the letter is included in the Vannevar Bush letters and papers presently housed in the "Collections of the Manuscript Division of the Library of Congress."

> *Dear Professor Hartree:*
>
> *The time has nearly arrived for Mr. Arthur Porter to return to England after a period of study at the Massachusetts Institute of Technology of approximately two years. His work was largely under my general direction, for he worked throughout his interval of study on analyzing machines which were very much my concern before I recently left my post as Vice President at MIT. We at that institution very much appreciate the fact that you made it possible for Porter, who had previously served as your assistant, to continue in the study of analyzing equipment under new auspices. He proved to be a very valuable member of the group, carrying on the development of such equipment. Although he was present in the status of a graduate student, he nevertheless became a member of the group and carried on one particular aspect of the work on his own responsibility, making the analyses and some of the engineering designs, and supervising one part of the work. I feel sure that the experience which he thus gained will be very valuable to him indeed, and the design of mechanical apparatus of high precision. He showed himself competent at both aspects of the work.*
>
> *I can assure you that he was thoroughly incorporated as an operating member of the organization, and was a very popular individual among his associates and the workers. He has a cheerful*

disposition, combined with the ability to devote his self with much concentration to the work in hand, which makes him a desirable member of any organization. I feel that he will go far on development work, and that he will be especially valuable to some commercial organization dealing with the development of new mechanisms or new instruments.

I look forward to a satisfactory career for him in his chosen work in England, and we will be very happy if his experience in this country has substantially contributed to that end.

Very truly yours,
V. Bush
May 1, 1939

Chapter 6

THE WAR YEARS

TOGETHER with Oscar Puls and Wilfred Merchant, I sailed from New York on June 20, 1939 aboard the "S.S. American Exporter." By no means as luxurious as the "Laconia," it was adequate — a one class ocean liner with reasonable accommodations. Although I was looking forward to a reunion with my family and the excitement of a new yet-to-be-ascertained job, I was nevertheless sad to leave a country which had provided me with so many wonderful friends and so much inspiration and adventure.

My parents and brothers met me at the Liverpool docks and we drove to Ulverston through the very familiar Lancashire countryside. Little had changed in spite of the international tensions which would lead to the outbreak of war in less than three months. After a wonderful holiday with the family exploring Cornwall and Devon, my first visit to this picturesque and historic region of England, the remainder of the summer was spent at Rondane and I resumed my love affair with the Lake District and the idyllic days in marked contrast to those that followed. It was not all relaxation, the job prospect, albeit promising, remained unresolved.

On one hand Professor Blackett, who had succeeded Professor Bragg as Langworthy Professor at Manchester, and Professor Hartree felt my experiences at MIT would be valuable in facilitating the Manchester d.a. program, especially in light of prospective developments which would arise if war broke out in Europe. Accordingly, after my meeting with the Vice Chancellor of the University of Manchester, Sir John Stopford, I was offered an assistant lectureship in physics. I was sorely tempted to accept, especially in view of the fact that I was familiar with Manchester and especially with the prospect of working again with Douglas Hartree.

But on the other hand, Professor Bragg, then director of the National Physical Laboratory and later to become Cavendish Professor of Physics at Cambridge, was particularly anxious for me to join one of the service laboratories. Indeed, he contacted Sir Charles Wright, Director of Scientific Research at the Admiralty. Sir Charles was a very distinguished individual with whom I was to have cordial relations until his retirement. Canadian by birth, he had been educated at Upper Canada College, Toronto, and the universities of Toronto and Cambridge. In 1912 he had been senior scientist on the Captain Scott Antartic Expedition, and in fact led the small party which eventually discovered the tent with the remains of Scott and his companions. After serving in various capacities in WWI, he joined the Department of Scientific Research at the Admiralty and after serving as Superintendent of the Admiralty Research Laboratories (A.R.L.) he was appointed Director of Research in 1934. The upshot was that I was interviewed by Sir Charles and offered a post at A.R.L. as a scientific officer. But in light of the Manchester offer, I was reluctant to accept and I wrote to Sir Charles expressing my preference for academic work. On receiving my letter, Wright immediately contacted Bragg and the latter wrote to me, and I am quoting his letter verbatim because it admirably sums up the position.

> *Dear Porter,*
>
> *I have just had a letter from Wright. I realize that you must have a difficult decision to make in choosing between the Admiralty post and an academic career and I must not try to sway you too much. I think it is fair to say this, however. If you take the Service work and find after the present crisis is over that you would like to get back into academic life, I feel confident that with your record, you would not be stranded. Also, there is a desperate need for men with research training in the Services just now and we are actually seconding men from university posts or scholarships for two years for temporary service with the Admiralty. A fortiori, it seems to me there is a case for a man who is temporarily free and would go without breaking any ties and who is needed by them, to do this particular job for his country at the present time. I cannot help hoping you will take on the Admiralty job because I feel academic needs must take second place for the time being.*
>
> *Yours sincerely,*
> *W.L. Bragg*

A young man with future academic aspirations could not possibly ignore such a letter, especially one from a Nobel Laureate and I very speedily changed my mind. Accordingly, I wrote a letter regretfully to Manchester and one to Sir Charles Wright accepting the ARL offer — the starting date was September 4, 1939.[8]

I left my parents' home by car (a newly acquired, albeit second-hand, 1935 Morris) on September 1 — a Friday. Early that morning the German Army invaded Poland. Their propaganda suggested that Polish border guards had crossed the Polish-German border and killed several German soldiers. In fact it was proved subsequently, that the dead men were occupants of a German concentration camp and were transported to the border and murdered by Nazi S.S. troops.

After spending the night with my aunt and uncle in Coventry, I left early on the Saturday morning. The weather was perfect and the drive to Teddington, Middlesex uneventful. However, a somewhat disturbing feature of the drive was the fact that a very heavy volume of traffic was streaming north out of London while the southbound traffic was virtually negligible. Clear evidence that London might be bombed within a few days.

I arrived at Teddington during the afternoon of September 2 and was welcomed by Mrs. Pemberthy, owner of the house at the corner of Station Road and Main Street where I was staying. Because it was less than a quarter of a mile from both the Admiralty Laboratory and the adjacent National Physical Laboratory (NPL) on the outskirts of Bushy Park, it was an ideal location. There were several ARL and NPL scientists in residence.

Sunday morning was eventful. At 11 a.m. Mrs. Pemberthy and most of the residents assembled in the lounge around a radio set to hear Prime Minister Chamberlain's historic announcement to the effect that Germany had failed to comply with Britain's ultimatum and continued with the invasion of Poland, a state of war was declared. This in itself was not unexpected, but what was not quite expected was the air raid siren that sounded within minutes of the speech. The next 30 minutes remain vivid in my memory.

Mrs. Pemberthy was an Air Raid Warden attached to a post about three miles away. In an air raid alert situation none of us knew what to expect, but it was obvious that Mrs. Pemberthy would be unwise to

---

[8] In retrospect while I didn't appreciate it at the time, the youngest Nobel Prize winner and a prospective Nobel Prize winner, Patrick Blackett, were competing for my services. I felt very flattered.

bicycle, which was her usual method of travel to the post. A massive air raid on London and environs was certainly not inconceivable. As the "junior" resident, I felt it was incumbent on me to volunteer to drive her. So while the other residents descended into the basement into a makeshift air raid shelter, I drove Mrs. P to her post. It was a bit scary in so far as the streets were completely deserted — no people, no vehicles and an eerie sense of disaster. Not surprising in light of the fact that we'd been at war with Germany for about 30 minutes. Having dropped Mrs. Pemberthy at her post, on my return I was stopped by a policeman. During the early days of the war, the police were especially vigilant — spies around every corner and "5th columnists traitors" as well! And justifiably, after explaining my mission, he told me to drive back to a public air raid shelter as quickly as possible, but shortly thereafter, the "All Clear" sounded and I returned without incident to my lodging. It was a relief. Incidentally, the warning had been sounded because an unidentified aircraft had been spotted headed for London! But in retrospect, such security precautions, especially during the early phases of the war, were by no means intrusive — contrast precautions being enforced during the War on Terror 2002. I recall vividly hearing on the BBC 9 o'clock news on September 3 that during the afternoon of that first day of war, a Cunard Liner – had been sunk in the Irish Sea with many casualties. I learned later that a friend and future colleague, (University of Toronto and Saskatchewan Power Corporation) David Cass-Beggs, his wife and young family were rescued, albeit having been separated for several days.

On Monday morning, September 4, I reported to work at ARL. A security guard stood at the gate. He was a retired Royal Navy Petty Officer. P.O. Jones, RN was quite a character with an incredible sense of humor. He had served in WWI and I will always identify him with ARL as a real "sea-dog" — he was chief of security. To his credit he was one of probably a very small minority of the population at the time who had any appreciation of the role of scientific research in naval warfare. His respect for his "young scientific gentlemen" was very genuine.

My start at the laboratories was not particularly propitious, essentially because questions were raised about my having lived abroad for nearly two years previously. I may have been an enemy spy! I was segregated in the non-classified section of the ARL Library for almost three weeks. This was extremely frustrating and in my opinion, not really necessary because, after all, I was a bona fide British citizen who had been studying at an American university. Subsequently, I became cleared to the level of "secret" and duly signed the "Official Secrets Act." Furthermore, in common with many academics having degrees in science and/or engineering, I was designated as being in a reserved occupation. Persons so designated were not permitted to join the Armed Services as I discovered a few months later.

I shared an office at the laboratory with three other scientific officers, one of whom, Reg Parker, became a good friend.

Having spent two years working with the Bush/Caldwell R.D.A. team which was unquestionably the most advanced group working on analog technology at the time, I expected to be assigned a project in the field of naval gun fire control, thereby utilizing my experiences. Note that the contemporary gun control systems were all essentially analog computers. This applied to the Army anti-Aircraft gunnery systems as well — the Sperry and Vickers predictors. But I was surprised and very disappointed when Norman Warren, my immediate supervisor, gave me a comparatively simple problem relating to the accuracy of performance of the tracking component of a Bofors (a light 40 mm AA gun designed and manufactured in Sweden) and Mark III predictor, and more specifically to the accuracy of tracking which, predicated on an aided "tracking" unit, measured the rate of change of the bearing of a target.

Already set up in the laboratory was a simulated target system. A "cross-hair" target was projected and traversed a long board mounted at the end of the laboratory. The "target" was tracked using a telescopic sight. The angular rate was recorded automatically and I was required to determine the accuracy of measurement using a range of values of the tracking "time-constant" — the so called "lambda/mu ratio" — a ratio which is deeply ingrained in my consciousness!

I spent many hours tracking the target and analyzing the results. A more boring exercise it is difficult to imagine and two or three months later a young technician was assigned to me to speed up the investigation. Although I did not appreciate it at the time, the experiment was in fact an exercise in "human factors" engineering, which in modern phraseology is described as ergonomics — it has become an essential feature in engineering design. It occurs to me, and this is a hindsight observation, that if my knowledge of statistics at that time had been greater I might have carried out a truly classical investigation of the "man/machine" interface. But in fact, the tracking experiment did not bear much resemblance to the conditions encountered in actual practice, i.e. severe vibration due to firing the gun, apprehension of the operator when under attack by hostile aircraft and extreme weather conditions. I stressed this in my report.

By February, 1940 I was truly frustrated and decided to try to improve the rate measuring systems of the predictor by introducing a non-linear factor. At least theoretically, this did in fact improve the accuracy of angular rate measurements, but whether or not it would work in practice is problematical. But from my point of view, the theoretical work relieved the monotony of the tracking experiments and I wrote a short report on my proposal and sent it to my supervisor.

The very next day I was "requested" to see Col. Kerrison, the superintendent of ARL and reputedly the inventor of the Mark III Predictor (the Kerrison Predictor). To say that I was given a "dressing down" is to put it mildly. Kerrison struck out page after page of my report without giving any reasons as to its validity. At the end of his ten minutes harangue, he made a comment to the effect that his opinion of my mentor, Douglas Hartree, was about the same as his opinion of my report. I was horrified.

Fortunately, there was a ray of light in early December after the dismal and somber months of September, October and November. The Battle of the River Plate off Montevideo, Uruguay when three British light cruisers harried and ultimately defeated the much more heavily armored and gunned German pocket battleship the Graf Spee, which was attacking Allied shipping in the South Atlantic. This event was heralded with great joy in Britain. The pocket battleship had sought refuge in the harbor of Montevideo, was refused sanctuary and her commander, Captain Langsdorff, scuttled his ship and then committed suicide.

From Britain's point of view this victory had a salutary effect because our confidence in the Royal Navy soared. We considered that our island fortress was impregnable. A victory parade of the crews of the victorious British cruisers who had fought in the battle was celebrated in London when a review by H.M. King George VI took place. There was great rejoicing.

The early months of 1940 were for me uneventful. We had become accustomed to such inconveniences as food and clothes rationing, and the "black-out," and I was resigned to carrying on the tracking experiments. Then an exciting event occurred.

One afternoon in March I was ordered by my immediate superior to travel up to Admiralty headquarters at Admiralty House, Whitehall and report to Sir Charles Wright. Recall that seven months previously I had met the director in connection with my initial appointment. My first reaction was to the effect that the "fat's in the fire!" — I had not been a particularly shining light at ARL. But it wasn't.

I was relieved when he greeted me effusively, and after a few pleasantries, he told me that the topic we were about to discuss was extremely sensitive — top secret. I could not help but wonder — why me? I soon found out!

I was told that a new type of German mine had been washed ashore in the Thames estuary two days previously. It was activated magnetically and was in fact a magnetic mine. Miraculously, without incident, two young naval lieutenants had removed the fuse mechanism — an act of extreme bravery and discovered it was essentially a magnetic needle mounted in such a way that the changing magnetic field caused by a moving ship would activate it. The R & D group at Admiralty had examined the fuse, determined its behavior and expressed it as a differential equation, but the group had failed to solve the equation. The director recalled that I had worked with D.R.H on the Manchester differential analyzer and after showing me the equation and how it was derived, he asked — "Could it be solved by the differential analyzer?" Even a cursory examination revealed it could. I was directed to telephone Douglas Hartree to request him to clear the machine for an urgent problem.

I was fascinated to see how the very sensitive material was packaged and sealed with the Admiralty seals. It was placed in a plain large brown envelope and I was provided with a somewhat nondescript document case to carry it. It was considered too risky for me to travel north to Manchester unaccompanied. Accordingly Eric Leese of the Mathematics Division of ARL, a friend, was asked to accompany me. I was in effect to be an official government "courier."

Eric Leese and I traveled by the night train from Euston Station and even though we arrived reasonably early, we discovered the train to be loaded to capacity. Indeed, I recall that virtually all through the night we stood in the corridor of a third class coach — it was quite an achievement even to reach the toilet. We arrived at London Road Station, Manchester about 5:30 a.m. and proceeded by street-car up Oxford Street to the university.

Not surprisingly, although the hour was little after six a.m. DRH was in his office on the top floor of the physical laboratories (the d.a. was in the basement). I say "not surprisingly" because Douglas Hartree was one of the most meticulous persons I have ever met. I recall one occasion when he was about 15 minutes late for a meeting at the Ministry of Supply, which he was due to chair and to present some calculations on servo mechanism behavior. He apologized for not having completed the work. He had had to stand in the corridor of the train all night and passengers jogged his elbow when he had tried to use his slide-rule.

After greeting us, he examined, albeit cursorily, the contents of the sealed envelope. I shall never forget him saying, "Why don't you fellows go across the street and have breakfast at the all-night café and we'll tackle the problem afterwards."

About 40 minutes later we returned to Hartree's office to be greeted with his conclusion that the machine was not in fact required. Douglas went on to say that he had thought of two methods of approach to solving the equation, neither of which involved the machine. I seem to recall that one of the methods was predicated on "spherical harmonics." Furthermore, he said, "if you can delay your return until the late afternoon, I think I can produce an approximate solution." He did! Much to the amazement of the mathematicians at Admiralty headquarters, I handed it in the following morning.

What followed was a crash program to "de-gauss" (i.e. de-magnetize all British and Allied naval vessels and some freighters). One key figure was Edward Bullard, whom I mentioned previously in connection with my first meeting with DRH. Without his incredible efforts and that of his colleagues, Britain might have been in real trouble. Magnetic mines, plus U-boats, could have seriously interfered with food and munitions supplies from Canada and the U.S.A. The extent to which the Hartree solutions to the equations were utilized in the "de-gauss-ing" operations is not to hand, but I suspect it was a vital step.

But the magnetic mine affair was not the only notable event in my life during those months of the so-called phony war. At the end of March I changed my lodging from Teddington to Hampton (not far from Hampton Court). The move had profound consequences, most important of which being meeting my future bride. This is how it happened.

Early in 1940, both Reg Parker and I had become disenchanted with the Pemberthy guest house and Reg began a systematic hunt for new lodgings. In a war environment with universal rationing, especially gasoline rationing, this was no easy task but after about a month, he discovered Mrs. Anderson's guest house at "Newlands" in Hampton, about three miles from ARL. He moved there in February. As his office-mate, I was of course kept fully informed of the merits of the Anderson menage, and from every point of view it was clearly an ideal place to live. Accordingly I followed Parker about a month later.

Prior to the outbreak of war the guest house had been the home of several Hampton Grammar School male teachers, all of whom had been called up for national service. As a result, Mrs. Anderson had about five vacancies.

There were in fact, two adjacent houses which she owned and operated. She was assisted by her three daughters (Jo, Bette and Rae) and provided the guests with breakfast and dinner and a very comfortable living room. Of interest is the fact that one of the pre-war guests was the famous British fighter pilot, Group Captain Douglas Bader, who was an "ace" in spite of having lost both legs.

During the course of my residence at Newlands, it became quite a "marriage bureau." In fact, I met Patricia there on a Saturday afternoon in June, 1940 after I'd spent the afternoon playing cricket for ARL against NPL. She was a very close friend of Bette and had been in the same class at Twickenham County School for Girls. Patricia frequently spent Saturday nights at Newlands and we literally met on the door-step. And coincidently, she met my brother Ronald at the same time.

Three marriages subsequently occurred as a direct consequence of Reg Parker's discovery of Newlands. In addition to Patricia and mine, Reg himself married Bette Anderson, and Ted Lee, a former friend at the University of Manchester, married Joan "Johnnie" Pearson, a school friend of Patricia's. I mention the Lees especially because they became our closest friends in England. Because Ted, who also topped his class two years after I did, and my paths did not cross again until the fall of 1939 when he joined ARL and eventually became a guest at Newlands, I had completely lost touch with him. While I was at MIT, Ted was completing his PhD at Cambridge. However, since those days in 1940-41, the Lees and Porters have maintained close ties to this day, sixty years later in spite of most of the time being separated by 3,000 miles. Sadly, Ted died in December 2001, but we remain in contact with Johnnie.

In the meantime "all was not quiet on the European front." April heralded the de facto beginning of hostilities when Germany invaded Denmark and Norway. As well, the U-boat campaign against Allied shipping intensified and losses in our vital shipping lanes escalated. For a few weeks it appeared, albeit transiently, that the Nazi juggernaut would be halted by the stubborn résistance of the Norwegian forces in spite of the counter-activities of the traitor Quisling. And the Royal Navy lived up to its reputation in the gallant attempt to recapture the Norwegian port of Narvik. Although unsuccessful, we were cheered to hear of the exploits of the small force which resulted in the release of about 100

British POWs from the German prison ship the Althouse. But soon after Norway was completely occupied the great German offensive in Western Europe began.

I'll never forget the night of May 9, 1940 when Holland and Belgium were invaded. These were traumatic times for Britain. Soon thereafter, Winston Churchill replaced Neville Chamberlain as Prime Minister of Britain. In spite of the fact that as a result of Munich, Chamberlain had gained an invaluable 12 months for Britain to re-arm and thereby saved us from inevitable defeat, he did not have the confidence of the British people which Churchill did. "Tears, toil and sweat" were all that Winston offered, but his speeches energized Britain and indeed the free world in a most remarkable fashion. Even when, within a few weeks of crossing, on May 14, the Luxembourg-French border, the German armored divisions reached the Channel ports the spirits of the British people did not falter and the last ditch stand and subsequent evacuation of 350,000 men (a miraculous operation involving thousands of small ships) from Dunkirk on June 4, 1940, only strengthened our resolve that we would eventually win the war.

I recall having my sandwich lunch with friends on the lawn of the National Physical Laboratories and hearing the guns at Dunkirk. Shortly after the French surrender on June 22, the Churchill speech to the nation: "I expect the Battle of Britain is about to begin. Upon this battle depends the survival of Christian civilization...."

These were stirring times. Just four days previously, June 18, the Prime Minister had stated unequivocally, "Let us brace ourselves to our duty and so bear ourselves so that if the British Commonwealth and Empire last for a thousand years, men will say: 'this was their finest hour.'" The instincts of the British people to the effect that Churchill was their heaven-sent leader were justified.

Life at the ARL proceeded with scarcely any changes, i.e. working from 9 a.m. to 5 p.m. five days a week — shades of Sir Frances Drake "let's finish our game of bowls and then we will deal with the Spaniards."

Because of the possibility of a German invasion, the government established the Local Defense Volunteers (LDV) which was subsequently renamed the Home Guard, early in May, 1940. All my colleagues at ARL volunteered and we mustered under the command of Lt. Weston, who incidentally shared my office. As a private in the LDV, I was required to attend drill sessions using a broomstick in lieu of a rifle, stand guard on the roof of ARL, two hours on, four hours off, two nights a week — and spend at least one Saturday afternoon on the firing range. My initiation as a rifleman was not particularly auspicious. We used the standard Lee Enfield rifle and each of us fired five rounds. Never having fired a rifle before, or indeed any hand gun, the experience was unforgettable; not only did I miss the target completely, but my right shoulder was badly bruised. My tenure as a Local Defense Volunteer was not to be prolonged and my release from ARL came much sooner than I ever dreamed.

It was a Friday morning in early July when members of the government's Senior Scientific Advisory Committee visited ARL — members included Professor Patrick Blackett and Sir Henry Tizard, who became a good friend and advisor a few years subsequently. Fortunately, that morning I was — and it was comparatively rare during that period- in my laboratory instead of my office. Otherwise, Blackett would not have seen me. As it happened, he spotted me, walked over and said, "Hello, Porter. How's it going?" My response was "Not too well. For God's sake, get me out of here." Blackett said "I'll do what I can."

He was as good as his word because a few days later an order came through from the Admiralty that I was to report as soon as possible to Frederick Brundrett, deputy director of Research and Development. The meeting lasted about 20 minutes. I was informed that Blackett, acting on behalf of the Commander-In-Chief of Anti-Aircraft Command had requested my transfer to a small operational research group. It was headed by Blackett himself and was affectionately referred to as "Blackett's Circus."

The purpose of the group was to facilitate the introduction of "radio location" (later called radar) equipment into the London anti-aircraft defenses. Because air raids, especially on London were expected momentarily, the replacement of optical tracking and range-finding instruments during daytime air raids, and of sound locators and search lights during night time raids was urgent. The notorious cloudy conditions, coupled with impenetrable London fogs which I had experienced on many occasions, were not conducive to visual methods of defense.

Brundrett stressed the secrecy of the operation. I was forbidden even to mention it to my colleagues at ARL. He told me that while the Admiralty was very reluctant to let me go (I smiled inwardly) the Blackett project had very high priority, not surprising in view of the fact that minor air raids on coastal towns were already occurring.

I reported to Blackett the following morning at the offices of the

Army Operations Research Group, the official designation of the group, in the War Office, Whitehall. Within a few months the office was moved successively, first to Brettenham House (where we shared space with Lord Suffock and his amazing crew of unexploded bomb experts), then to the Adelphi and finally to Petersham near Richmond-on-Thames. The latter location had a James Bond flavor. We were housed in the hall of a de-consecrated church. The location was so secret that the local inhabitants were completely mystified. No guards were mounted. We were identified by a map reference known only to senior personnel and the code "Thy Kingdom Come" was adopted. (These were the words engraved over the entrance.) Incidentally, Patricia and I revisited Petersham during the summer of 1992 and the hall was still standing, albeit rather derelict.

When I joined Blackett's Circus it consisted of Blackett, L.E. Bayliss, a physiologist at University College, University of London, David Hill and Andrew Huxley, both physiologists from Cambridge, and me. Later we were joined by an astronomer and another physicist. Our main job was to calibrate the recently developed elevation finding (EF) attachment to the GL MkI radar equipment which determined target range and bearing. I'll not go into details except to say that we used barrage balloons to hoist signal generators and subsequently we tracked Lysander "spotter" aircraft. On one occasion I recall my Lysander having to flee from a German fighter who appeared suddenly from the south. He escaped. Each member of our group was attached to a gun-site in the Greater London area. My site was located in Richmond Park near the Sheen Gate. This was within two miles of where Patricia and I established our first home in Sheen Court. It was designated ZS20 and was essentially a four AA guns (3.7 inch caliber battery) with radar units, a Sperry Predictor and a Command Post. The sound locator and search lights had been discarded. I spent many hours at ZS20. The advantage of having no military rank and being a civilian — I could treat the Battery Commander as an equal and I messed with the officers.

As well as calibrating the radar equipment, we did experimental work with wire netting mats which surrounded the radar set. Because the EF attachment relied on a reflected signal, it was important to minimize noise and to provide an effective reflecting surface. Recall that centimetric radar (10 cm wave lengths and less) was not available during the summer of 1940 and much longer wave lengths were in use e.g. 20 meters with corresponding lower resolving power and hence accuracy.

Another critical problem was the performance of the predictors (essentially analog computers). These were designed to operate with "smooth" data obtained from the manually controlled tracking telescopes and hence were only operable during the daylight hours. As noted previously, in the pre-radar era during nighttime raids, the sound locator-search light combination proved virtually impractical because it was impossible to feed smooth and continuous target information into the predictor. However, because of the losses they began to suffer, even during the desultory daylight raids over southern England in May — August, 1940, the enemy decided to concentrate their main bombing effort during nighttime. Accordingly our main goal was to optimize the performance of the AA guns and this necessitated replacement of predictors by novel plotting technologies. We developed several and they proved greatly superior to the procedures in place. But it was essential that I should be available at ZS20 whenever a raid was anticipated. Accordingly, the battery commander arranged to have me telephoned at Newlands, Hampton in the event of pending action, especially night action. I would receive messages often during the night such as "50 bandits crossed coast." Whereupon, I would drive over to Richmond Park; and be at the anti-aircraft battery in about 20 minutes.

We were hard pressed for qualified staff during those early days of air attacks and the High Command decided to develop a radar training School at Petersham under the directorship of J.A. Ratcliff, a Reader at Cambridge who was an authority on telecommunications. Regular army officers, even those in the Signals Corps, were not knowledgeable in the new and sophisticated field of radar. I recall a meeting of staff officers, supplemented by our Operations Research Team, called by Sir Frederick Pile, C in C Anti-Aircraft Command in which this question was addressed. With my brother Ronald in mind — at the time he was a 2nd Lt. in the infantry attending a catering course in Northern Ireland, prior to serving in South East Asia, I suggested that there must be a large number of former teachers of science and mathematics who would be admirable recruits for the radar school. The General responded. "Good suggestion, Porter. If you have anybody in mind please inform G1 after the meeting."

Suffice it to add, I suggested Ronald, who had an M.A. from Cambridge in mathematics, and an old friend from Ulverston, my next door neighbor Harry Tyson with an MSc degree from Manchester, also a 2nd Lt in the infantry, that they would be excellent candidates. Much to the chagrin of his C.O. at the camp in Northern Ireland with whom Ronald was not particularly friendly, he received urgent instructions from the War Office in London to report to Petersham Radar School. He arrived within 48 hours. Because of his flare for science and technology, Ronald rapidly became an expert in radar and was singled out for rapid promotion. Successively, he became a staff officer at A.A. command, was the officer in charge of anti-aircraft defenses against the V-1 flying bombs which involved the re-siting of many of the London batteries and eventually, with the rank of Major, he became General Frederick Pile's scientific advisor.

Shortly after this secondment to Petersham, Ronald and I designed and successfully tested a modification of a Sperry Predictor aimed at smoothing the raw radar data. It was referred to as the "Porter Smoothers." However, it was never adopted in the field because of potential production problems.

There were several night raids on the Hampton area including Bushy Park during May and June 1940 and the excitement was intensified when news of Hitler's plan to invade Britain, code named "Sea- Lion" was reported. A few thousand invasion barges docked at the Ports of Calais and Boulogne were evidence that this was a serious threat.

Two incidents of special interest are worth recording. During a raid on the southwestern suburbs of London, which included Hampton, a comparatively small bomb (50 kilograms) landed literally between the two Anderson houses and created a small crater. It was a narrow escape; 40 feet would have made quite a difference. In the event, the only casualty was my small Morris car which was almost completely covered with soil and debris and as well suffered a cracked windshield. Another near miss occurred when I was driving from Newlands to ZS20 and responding to a "bandits call" one night in late July about midnight. There was a huge flash in the rear view mirror and it was accompanied by a loud explosion. I saw a building literally being demolished by a bomb. I had passed the building, which I learned subsequently was the Royal Oak pub on the Staines bye-pass, probably three or four seconds earlier. It was roughly 100 to 120 yards behind me. Coincidently, I had passed a car traveling in the opposite direction from where the pub was located and some five years later when Patricia and I were living at Warwick Close, Hampton we learned that our next door neighbor Jock Cantrell was "the guy driving the other car." That night we were two very lucky guys!

These were the early days of the Battle of Britain. In order for "Sea-Lion" to be successful, Hitler had to first subdue the RAF fighter squadrons. This proved to be a much tougher proposition than he had anticipated. Nevertheless, he was confident of victory in this, probably the most important battle in the history of air warfare and boasted that "he would ring Britain's neck like a chicken." To which Churchill responded, *"Some chicken — some neck."* I shall never forget this aphorism nor will I forget the scornful manner in which he said it.

While the threat of invasion continued, it is interesting to reflect on Britain's response. Let me quote from Jon Lake's excellent volume *The Battle of Britain* in which he sums up the situation brilliantly.

> *"They dug trenches and dugouts right through the center of their beloved flower beds and carefully tended lawns. They donated their aluminum pots for aircraft production and took down the iron railings protecting their front gardens. When the curtain actually rose on the sinister drama, they were at least morally prepared."*

In anticipation of heavy air raids on London coming in the fall of 1940 (the Blitz) and at a time when the Battle of Britain was at its height, Professor Blackett recommended a major change in London anti-aircraft defenses. This was wise because the bombing of provincial cities was intensifying and the need for radar was urgent. Actually, radar sets were being transferred from London to these cities. Something had to be done about it.

Recall that forty anti-aircraft gun batteries were defending London, each having four 3.7-inch guns. The idea, endorsed by Anti-aircraft Command was to select 20 of these batteries and to convert them into eight gun batteries, thereby freeing 20 radar sets. This was not as straightforward a problem as it may have sounded. In effect, I was given the job of determining the locations of the supplemented batteries based on such factors as the radar characteristics; maximizing the concentration of anti-aircraft fire to protect critical targets such as Buckingham Palace, power stations, Whitehall offices, Parliament buildings, etc. taking into account the brigade and regimental structures.

Incidentally, an important decision on re-siting the batteries was taken. In order to improve radar performance, especially at extreme ranges, we recommended that every night an hour before sundown that the barrage balloons should be lowered and raised again an hour before sunrise. Most London residents were unaware of this operation which, of course, was kept secret. Radar and barrage balloons were incompatible during air raids because the echoes from the latter obscured the cathode ray tube display.

To help me I was assigned a young South African physicist Frank Nabarro, and to look after the brigade problems, a junior Army officer, Captain Raybould. The three of us worked very well together. Blackett had stressed that he must have our recommendations in a form readily communicable to AA Command by 11 a.m. on the following Thursday. It was then Monday afternoon so taking into account traveling to and from Hampton; we had about 60 hours to complete the assignment. I had decided to work at Newlands for two main reasons, first because the likelihood of air raids was less in the suburbs than in the city and secondly there would be no interruptions. A further advantage was that, if necessary, beds would be available for "cat-naps."

The project was approached essentially by trial and error techniques, and because of the large number of variables was very time consuming. More by good luck than by logical thought, and in spite of three minor air raids in the vicinity, we finished the job about six o'clock on Thursday morning. We had had very little sleep but the adrenalin was flowing rapidly facilitated by many mugs of tea.

We produced three copies (one each) of the master plan of Greater London showing the new gun battery locations, the density (in color) of the gun barrage for enemy aircraft flying at an altitude of 17,000 feet, and the locations of strategic targets. The final product looked quite impressive.

I left Newlands in my trusty old Morris car about 7 o'clock for the War Office; a trip which under normal circumstances would take no longer than three-quarters of an hour. But I had not counted on the after-effects of the previous night's air raid on Central London. Countless roads were blocked by fire trucks, fire hoses threading across the streets, debris from bombed buildings, notably glass fragments, and many police-controlled diversions. It turned the drive into a nightmare. I was lucky to reach the War Office about 11:35 a.m. But I recall that Blackett was not particularly pleased because he had arranged to see Sir Frederick and several senior staff officers to present the plan at 11:30 a.m. In any event I briefed him (Blackett was a very fast learner) and he hurried away with two copies of the master plan. I retained one copy. It was of course a top secret document.

On his return to the office, he apologized for "balling" me out and told me that the plan had been accepted in its entirety. There was a sequel to this operation that I did not reveal until many years after WWII had ended for obvious reasons!

Early the following Monday I had to inspect some radar equipment at a gun battery situated literally in the grounds of Wormwood Scrubs Prison — a notorious institution situated in the near suburbs of London. I then had lunch at a small café in nearby Shepherd's Bush, drove back to the War Office in plenty of time for a meeting I was due to attend at 2 o'clock. I had been asked to brief a government scientific advisory panel, chaired by none other than my PhD examiner, Sir John Cockcroft. It was to brief them on the proposed re-organization of the London A.A. defenses. There were about 20 people at the meeting and I noted my contribution to the agenda was item eight. Seated several places from the chairman, I shall never forget the shock I suffered when reaching for my briefcase, it wasn't there! Where was it? Few moments in my life have been more traumatic. I concluded I must have left it at the café. I was very conscious of the fact that the master plan was a top secret document and even the remotest chance of it falling into unfriendly hands, especially in view of the fact that the re-siting of the guns was already in hand, was unthinkable. Even the fact that it had been mislaid was sufficient to put me in a very embarrassing, even serious, situation. Within seconds of the original shock, I left my seat and approached Sir John Cockcroft and whispered, "May I be excused for a short while. I'm not feeling too well." It was an understatement. However, the chairman, glancing at the agenda said, "I hope you can be back in about an hour."

Suffice it to say that I ran to the parking lot, started the car (always a relief those days) and drove at high speed west from Whitehall to Shepherd's Bush, about 10 miles in 15 minutes. Fortunately the debris of raids which had occurred three and four nights previously had been cleared and speeding tickets were virtually unknown.

I entered the café with a pulse rate which must have been twice normal. To my tremendous relief I spotted the briefcase in exactly the same position where I had left it under the table at lunch. Nobody was in the café but the owner. He said, "I thought someone would return sooner or later to retrieve it." And so ended a very nerve-racking incident. Incidentally on returning to the meeting I presented the plan and left it in the safe keeping of Anti-aircraft Command! The only excuse I have in retrospect is that after several sleepless nights I must have been suffering from more than my usual forgetfulness.

A climax to the whole episode was that I recall with pleasure how very thrilled I was a few days later when I observed an Army convoy of AA guns and mountings and other paraphernalia moving along Richmond Road heading for ZS20; and later to see the equipment being installed at high speed in readiness for the next air raid. It is noteworthy that the radar and gun control positions were manned by men and women — the latter being members of the Auxiliary Territorial Service (ATS). My sister-in-law, Mary, Ronald's wife, was an officer in this service. At such a time one could not but be proud of one's fellow countrymen and women. I breathed a sigh of relief on seeing those convoys, my mission had been completed.

During the summer months when the Battle of Britain, and the RAF and Luftwaffe fought in the skies over Southeast England we witnessed some spectacular sights. The sky was often festooned with intricate vapor trail patterns and occasionally we saw a fighter develop a plume of smoke, a parachute would emerge as the plane dived to the ground. These "dog-fights" were frequently preludes to the arrival of the bombers a few hours after sunset. However, few of us realized at the time that the Battle of Britain was "a very close-run thing." The RAF Reserves, certainly by the middle of September, were low, virtually zero. On the other hand, there was evidence of heavy enemy losses and the fact that "Sea-Lion" was obviously being abandoned gave credence to our optimism.

However, in so far as the bombing of London was concerned, the worst was yet to come, but Churchill's confidence was compelling. It was about this time, September, 1940, that he expressed the debt we owed to the RAF pilots. "Never in the history of human conflict have so many owed so much to so few."

I am proud to recall that Patricia's only brother, John, was one of the few. A Hurricane fighter pilot, he fought in the air battles over France, in May 1940. Quoting from Jon Lake:

> *"Of the 261 Hurricanes dispatched to fly from French aerodromes, only 66 returned and some of these were so badly damaged they were unceremoniously scrapped."*

Escaping from France at the time of Dunkirk, John subsequently served in a Hurricane squadron during the Battle of Britain where only three out of every 10 pilots survived.

I was "best man" at John's wedding to Elsa in London on August 31. As a matter of fact, I was brought in at the very last moment because John's closest friend and a friend of the family, another fighter pilot, were in the air fighting the enemy on that day. The reception at Overstrand Mansions was memorable, and particularly, Patricia and I after a few months of stress, were relaxed and happy, although little did we know that evening that the bombing would begin in earnest with a mass attack on the London docks and the east end. As I dictate this, Patricia has been speaking to Elsa on the telephone- July 18, 1999-49 years after those hectic days. Sadly, John passed away on December 18, 1998.

Before I recount the events identifiable with the Blitz on London, this is an appropriate time to introduce the Dixon family.

Mabel Dixon, my future mother-in-law and Patricia, until our marriage in July, 1941, lived in an apartment in Overstrand Mansions on Prince of Wales Drive which parallels Battersea Park. Lt. Col Dixon was commanding officer of the A.A. Batteries defending the strategic ports of Portsmouth, while Carol, Patricia's sister, because of her war-time duties as first an Air Raid Warden and later as an Auxiliary Constable in the Metropolitan Police, both extremely hazardous occupations, had her own apartment in Chelsea.

The ninth and top floor of Overstrand Mansion on Prince of Wales Drive, which was adjacent to the River Thames, was about as dangerous a place to live as anywhere in London during the Blitz. It was far more dangerous a location than my own dwelling in Hampton, even when I was serving at ZS20. At times, indeed most of the time during the night, it was extremely noisy and the noise was amplified after the installation in Battersea Park of the Z-Rocket Batteries. They were probably less than half a mile from the Mansions, and I can assert *a fortiori*, that the Battery created the most terrifying sound I heard throughout the war, even more so than the V-1 flying bombs.

Mabel Dixon served as a Red Cross nurse in WWI where she met, nursed and married Vernon Dixon. In spite of the fact that most of the residents of the Mansions had moved away, Patricia and her mother stayed, but moved from the top floor to an apartment on the ground floor with a bomb shelter in the basement. I recall this was rarely used in spite of the intensity of the bombing, which during the winter of 1941 was a nightly occurrence. As an example of my mother-in-law's indomitable spirits during those days of the Blitz, and it exemplifies the spirit of Londoners as a whole, she took a dim view of the fact that local authorities replaced her windows after raids because they were usually blown out again within a few days. Quite a lady was Mabel Dixon — the great grandmother of Jennifer, Ian and Gregory and John and Elsa's grandchildren Kate and Joe. Great grandfather Vernon Dixon, a hero of WWI, having been awarded the Military Cross for Bravery in action in

France, was at camp in the Territorial Army in September 1939 at the outbreak of WWII. He was later awarded the Order of the British Empire for services as a Regimental Commander in A.A. Command, so he played a very conspicuous part in both wars. It is especially noteworthy that after my father-in-law left Portsmouth, he commanded three batteries in southeastern London, one of which was at Wandsworth Common. After an air raid alert had sounded, invariably the first guns in action were Col. Dixon's'.

In the meanwhile, Patricia demonstrated her courage virtually every day during the scary days of the Blitz when she traveled from Overstrand Mansion to the Westminster Bank Head Office, adjacent to the Bank of England in the very heart of the city. She worked in the Income Tax Department, replacing one of the young men who had been called up. Alone she walked about half a mile, took a London bus and then the City Underground to Bank Station. This would be somewhat of a forbidding undertaking even during peace time on a sunny spring day. But during the Blitz when so many streets were damaged by bombs, blocked by fire trucks and fire hoses as well as unexploded bombs, virtually no taxis and scores of air raid alerts, the situation was to put it mildly diametrically different. Only those who experienced those times can appreciate the hazards Patricia faced. For example, returning home one rainy night in January during the blackout (and it was a real black blackout.) she arrived at the apartment with her face streaming with blood. She had walked straight into an iron railing near the Mansions. Her mother opened the door to her injured daughter and promptly took her to the nearest hospital emergency room where they sutured her wound.

The month of October turned out to be one of the most anxious times of my life. At the beginning of the month Patricia was suddenly stricken with typhoid fever with a temperature of 105 degrees F, and she was taken to South Middlesex Hospital on the outskirts of London. For many weeks she was confined to her hospital bed and could not be moved during air raids to a shelter. However, she made a remarkable recovery, so much so that in early December she was fit to travel north to Nantwich, Cheshire to stay a few weeks with her aunt Grace and uncle Kenneth Evans away from the bombs and hazards of life in London.

During this period when London suffered its heaviest air attacks, on the nights of October 14 and 16 respectively, 951 and 912 civilian deaths were recorded, as well as terrific damage to property. These were 1000 bomber raids, the first we experienced. Churchill summed it up as follows:

"London is like some huge prehistoric animal. Capable of enduring terrific injury, tangled and bleeding from many wounds, yet preserving its life."

During the winter of 1940 and 41, Patricia and I lived through quite a few incidents during the Blitz on London, but few were more dramatic than the evening of September 7, 1940 when we had a grandstand view of the first major night bombing attack on the city. We were crossing the River Thames by the Albert Bridge when the air raid warning sounded and within minutes the whole eastern sky erupted in a bright red glow. Every A.A. gun in the London area was in action, and coupled with the explosion of the bombs, the noise was terrific. Unfortunately, I missed the activity at ZS20 having had a weekend leave. We lingered at the highest point of the bridge and stared in awe as the conflagration gradually extended covering the whole of the east end and dock area. It seemed as if all of London was in flames. After perhaps fifteen minutes, we were ordered off the bridge and to go to an air raid shelter as quickly as possible. But we preferred proceeding directly to Overstrand Mansions and fortunately there were no bombs in the immediate area.

I was able to obtain a few days furlough over the Christmas season. Although there were no festivities planned — the bombing, black-out and petrol rationing combined precluded much frivolity — I planned to make the most of it. Not having seen Patricia for about three months I decided to drive to Nantwich and stay at a local hotel. Patricia's sister Carol and Ted Lee accompanied me, and despite not very pleasant driving conditions, the 180 miles were completed in about five hours — good going at that time.

We found Patricia to be in good health and spirits and my brief vacation was one of the happiest in my life. One incident worth noting, although it didn't show me up in a particularly good light, was while walking from the hotel to the Evans' home on Christmas Eve, I decided to test the ice on a small pond. It wasn't a good idea because a couple of yards from the edge the ice cracked and I went through it, to about 18 inches- enough to soak my slacks up to my knees. On arrival at the Evans' residence, I was greeted by Ken Evans, who never minced his words, with "You B–y fool, can't you recognize thin ice!" This was not the impression I meant to make on my future aunt and uncle-in-law. A few months later Patricia told me that Ted Lee had confided to her at the time that she was about to receive a proposal from me.

And she did. We became engaged sitting in my car early in January, 1941. We had had dinner and subsequently danced at the Castle Hotel, Richmond. Ted Lee was the first to be told when I awakened him after midnight on that memorable evening. His response, "I've known for months." Many years later during a visit to Britain in 1996, Patricia and I revisited "the Castle." Regretfully, it had been demolished, but we recognized many of our old haunts, and as I mentioned previously, by no means least, Petersham.

The great incendiary bomb attack on London occurred early in February. I was staying at Overstrand Mansions that Saturday night with Patricia and her mother. Shortly after the air raid warning had sounded the incendiary bombs rained down literally in tens of thousands. The whole London area was carpeted in bright magnesium flares. Many of the incendiary bombs were laced with explosive material and miniature explosions were occurring all over the place. Many fires were started. The smoke hanging low in the sky added mystery to an unforgettable sight.

To obtain a better prospective on how we were faring locally, I went outside and was shocked to see the top floor (the 9th) bathed in bright light. A bomb had penetrated the roof and set fire to the flooring. I raced up the stairs to find the top apartment unoccupied and failed to open the door. But fortunately within minutes, several volunteer firemen arrived, broke down the heavy glass door with a fire axe and quickly found the bomb. It was embedded in the floor boards having already burned a beautiful carpet. The flames were spreading rapidly, but we managed to cope with the situation. Indeed, I was fascinated to see how quickly the firemen, using pails of sand subdued the fire within about 10 minutes and the very hot bomb was transferred to a fireproof container. At the time I do not recall any of us thinking of an explosive device being assembled in the bomb. One in ten bombs was explosive. We were lucky.

Later the same evening I spotted another bomb which had fallen in the small front garden of the apartment building. In retrospect, somewhat foolishly, I lifted a bucket of sand, not a light weight, to the top of the railing and balanced it precariously. In climbing over the railing unfortunately I fell very close to the bomb and in twisting my body to avoid it, I suffered a severe hernia. The bomb was extinguished but I spent a frustrating 10 days subsequently in the Nightingale Nursing Home, Twickenham recovering from the surgery.

The fact that the Blitz (79 consecutive night raids with more than 200 bombers) persisted throughout my convalescence did not improve my temperament. Many of London's historic buildings and locations were severely bombed. They included the Houses of Parliament. Buckingham Palace, Victoria Station and Leicester Square. But by April, 1941 there was a marked decrease in air raids over Britain largely because, although this was not in evidence at the time, the Luftwaffe was being transferred to the Soviet border in preparation for the invasion of the Soviet Union on June 22. This came as a complete surprise because of the Soviet-German non-aggression pact of two years previously. The respite could not have come at a better time because Patricia and I were getting things organized for our forthcoming wedding. Most importantly, we located our future home, albeit a home for only a few months, at Apartment 177 Sheen Court, Richmond on the top floor of the building. Because of the incidence of many air raids in the vicinity, most top floor apartments were vacant and the price was right — rock bottom! Further it was ideally situated — only a couple of miles from ZS20 and about six miles from the Petersham headquarters. What we did not foresee even in our wildest dreams was that Sheen Court was to be the first of our 35 more or less permanent homes in the future. They have been located in Britain, Canada and the United States. We've jumped from hither to thither, i.e. London England to Saskatoon Canada, with incredible abandon. Many influential people have been responsible for our moves and at each of our destinations we have made many friends. We're still making friends in Bermuda Village in North Carolina, which will be our final destination, number 35!

What a fascinating journey we've had from Sheen Court to Bermuda Village; sixty-one years and counting. Some of the highlights and there have been very many, are recorded in these memoirs. Certainly number one was our wedding day, July 26, 1941.

While my brother Ronald was billeted in the near vicinity, my youngest brother, Robert had to travel down from Manchester where he was serving as an instructor in the parachute regiment of the RAF. Regrettably, Mary, Ronald's wife, a first officer in the Auxiliary Territorial Service (ATS) was on duty and unable to join the family. Alas, Patricia's brother John was stationed with a R.A.F. squadron in Dumfries and couldn't get leave to be with us either.

We three brothers in traditional English style had a stag party (the bridegroom to be on his last night of "freedom" is treated in the vernacular, to a "pub crawl" with all the trimmings such as bangers and chips). Robert, the best man to be, led the festivities in no uncertain manner. It remains a mystery as to how I managed to drive the car back from the local hostelries to the apartment in the blackout without an accident. There was one unfortunate incident, however. In those days, a car's traffic indicators were essentially small lighted arms which projected from the side of the car. Unfortunately, these required a reasonably large electrical current to operate, and if operated inadvertently for more than about 15 minutes, the car battery became completely discharged. Perhaps, not surprisingly, because we were "feeling no pain" and consequently not very observant, a traffic indicator was left switched on for about 10 hours. I mention this incident because of the resulting consequences. The dead car battery caused several problems during the morning of our wedding day and indeed persisted throughout the day. Suffice it to say that in Britain in July 1941, it was almost impossible to find a service station open on a Saturday. Furthermore, "jumper cables" which would have at least got the engine running, were rare commodities. We were in a quandary! My parents were due to arrive at Euston Station at about 11 a.m. and I'd promised to meet them.

During the war the journey from Ulverston to London took at least six hours and the trains were crowded. Mother and Dad had only visited London a couple of times in their lives and my failure to meet the train would have been a real shock for them. Fortunately, as a last resort, I telephoned the Petersham-Quartermaster's Office and the Quartermaster, Capt. Fletcher, came to the rescue. He dispatched an Army utility vehicle immediately and with the help of a tow rope my car was started albeit reluctantly. We met the train with only a few minutes to spare. How we managed to keep my car operating for the rest of the day remains a mystery. But I do recall that the only way to restart the engine was with the "starting handle" and many a wrist has been broken by resorting to this method. At least we avoided any such mishap. However, to ensure that "the honeymoon car" was mobile during the reception, Robert literally kept his foot on the accelerator for about half an hour or so it seemed.

My family and I arrived at the church on time. It was gratifying to see so many relations and friends gathered at the church, especially in view of the fact that the weather was temperamental and thunderstorms were threatening. The occasion was unique as well in that only one half of the roof of the Battersea Parish Church was intact. A bomb had removed the other half which had been replaced by huge sheets of tarpaulin.

I can still picture Patricia entering the church on the arm of Lt. Col.

Dixon. Because flash photography was virtually non-existent at the time because of the needs of the Armed Services, no photographs of that scene were taken. My bride and her father had a rather perilous walk down the aisle. A tremendous thunder clap coincided with their arrival and they had to avoid large raindrops descending from the roof. But of course, Patricia and her father, were veterans in so far as they'd survived so many disasters and they were certainly not daunted by a mere thunderstorm. The ceremony went off perfectly although when the vicar asked me "will you take this woman, Phyllis, to be your wedded wife," Patricia was a little bit taken aback because all her life she has been called Patricia or Pat and Phyllis, although her first name, was unexpected!

In retrospect, recalling that food and clothes rationing in Britain were more stringent than in any other country in the world, our wedding was a "tour de force," organized solely by my mother-in-law, sister-in-law Carol and of course my bride. Attending the reception at Overstrand Mansions were many friends I had not see for years. The biggest surprise, however, was the arrival of Frank Lewis, a fellow graduate student in electrical engineering and resident of Graduate House at MIT. I had not the slightest idea that Frank was in England. As it happened, he had arrived two days previously to join the scientific staff of the US Embassy. As a wedding present he brought us a nest of three beautiful trays, two of which are still in daily use. Talking about wedding presents, I must mention three, and I do injustice to many; the leather and wooden stool made by hand in Kendal, Cumbria and given to those of us who had had the privilege of being Professor Hartree's students; the Waterford glasses given by Air Chief Marshall Sir Christopher and Lady Courtenay, and a spectacular green vase which still adorns our sideboard, given by Mr. and Mrs. Weston, my roommate at A.R.L. We are still using them. When we drove away from the reception with the cheers of relatives and friends ringing in our ears, and a cloud of confetti, I recall especially that cacophony of sounds created by a variety of tin cans and the like being towed by the car. My brothers were determined that the ceremony should end in style. Our honeymoon was spent in our apartment in Sheen Court. Regrettably, it only lasted three days which were spent buying second-hand furniture and other necessities.

During the fall of 1941 and the spring of 1942, I was still involved in the development of modifications to the Sperry Predictor. One of the Operations Research Group with whom I had close relations was Andrew Huxley — the brilliant Cambridge physiologist who in 1968 shared the

Nobel Prize for Medicine and Physiology. After our work at Petersham was concluded, Andrew and I have had numerous contacts and he was a guest in our home on several occasions.

One event which occurred during our time at Sheen Court is indelibly embedded in Patricia and my memories. It was the B.B.C. Radio news broadcast at 9 p.m. on December 8, 1941 (my 31st birthday). The dramatic announcement that the U.S. Naval Base at Pearl Harbor had been attacked by Japanese bombers was electrifying. World War II had taken on an entirely new complexion. Britain and her Commonwealth — notably India, Canada, South Africa, Australia and New Zealand — would no longer have to shoulder alone the heavy responsibility of resisting the Nazi and Fascist threatened world domination. Being only 22 miles distant from the enemy, and it should never be forgotten that Dover and its environs were well within range of the German coastal artillery batteries and suffered shelling for many months, meant that we felt particularly vulnerable, especially after the fall of France in June 1940.

Nor should it be forgotten that Britain was carrying an almost unbearable economic burden as well as the threat of starvation because the German U-boat campaign was proliferating. American assistance in providing armaments and food had been indispensable, albeit very costly until President Roosevelt pushed the Lend-Lease legislation through Congress. Incidentally, the 50 WWI, U.S. destroyers in exchange for several important naval bases proved to be a very good bargain for the U.S. But without doubt, the U.S. entry into the war in December 1941 was a great morale-booster to we beleaguered Brits.

There were soon to be major changes at Petersham and in particular the program of the Operations Research Group which had been expanded to include armed fighting vehicles, field artillery, signals, etc. The Blackett group was melded into this organization. Blackett himself headed a small group at the Admiralty working on anti-U-boat operations. Andrew Huxley joined him, together with an old friend, E. J. Williams, whose lectures I had attended during my final year at Manchester.

Of special interest was the appointment of Dr. Omond Solandt, a physiologist from the University of Toronto as head of Army Operations Research. Subsequently Omond had a profound influence on my career, especially in so far as the move to Canada in 1949 was concerned and even after. Coincidently, about the same time I left the group and joined the Air Defense Research and Development Establishment (ADRDE) based at Christchurch near Bournemouth on the English Channel. [9]

Sir John Cockcroft was responsible for this move. After being appointed head of the Establishment, whose main concern was the development of advanced radar equipment, he was anxious to introduce automatic controlled radar to replace the current manual control. With the advent of centimetric (10 cm) radar based on the Magnetron,*[10] the tracking data were so much more accurate than had been achieved hitherto with longer wave length radars that automatic tracking became essential. No doubt Cockcroft recalled, as my PhD. external examiner, that a major part of my thesis dealt with the automatic control of a chemical process. From then on I became a servo- mechanism specialist.

The move from Sheen Court to Christchurch was an epic. How we managed to pack all our worldly goods into a small Morris Minor car remains a mystery. Our second-hand furniture was put in storage. Gambling that the weather would be fair for the drive and this was the very first of what must have been literally hundreds of occasions during our married life when Patricia demonstrated her mastery of the art, and it is an art, of packing. The vehicle was a sight to behold! It was a cross between a gypsy caravan and an itinerant salesman's vehicle. We were destined to show it off in a most remarkable albeit somewhat embarrassing fashion. When we started the 80 mile drive to Christchurch on a sunny spring morning, and even during the war spring time in rural Britain was and is a veritable fairy land, we had no idea this was to be the day when H.M. George VI was to review the Grenadier Guards Armored Brigade then stationed at Aldershot Common. Tanks and a variety of armored fighting vehicles were positioned on either side of the main road from London to Portsmouth for a distance of between one and two miles. The Guards (officers, NCOs and private soldiers) in battle dress, but nevertheless resplendent as befitted Britain's most elite brigades, were drawn up on parade beside their vehicles. It was an impressive spectacle. If we'd been a few minutes later, the barriers would have been closed and we'd have been held up at least an hour or two. But fate was on our side because we were in fact the last vehicle allowed through the barrier before the arrival of His Majesty. We

---

[9]ADRDE was the major Ministry of Supply establishment for radar telecommunications, data processing, automatic control systems and electronics research and development. In 1945, it was renamed the Radar Research and Development Establishment and Dr. O.M. Sutton was appointed Superintendent.

[10]Many authorities consider the Magnetron and the Atomic Bomb to be the two most important scientific achievements of the Allies during WWII.

proceeded at about 20 mph in solitary state through the parade of armor, much to the amusement of the Guardsmen, although they did their best to hide it. Our loaded vehicle proceeding through those lines of battle tanks must have appeared a bit incongruous and, not surprisingly, we were very embarrassed.

We were billeted in Christchurch in a lovely white bungalow near the coast. Mrs. DeJersey, a physician's widow, was our most gracious hostess and we enjoyed very much the three months we stayed with her. However, I had no sooner got settled down at A.D.R.D.E., and familiarized myself with the state of the art, i.e. centi-metric radar equipment, when the order came through from the Prime Minster's office no less, to the effect that the Establishment must be evacuated. A few weeks previously, British and Canadian commandos, had raided a German radar installation on the coast of Normandy, and Churchill contemplated retaliatory raids by the enemy on A.D.R.D.E. at Christchurch and on the Telecommunications Research Establishment (TRE) at the adjacent town of Swanage. Both establishments were vital to Britain's war effort.

Our destination was to be Malvern, Worcestershire in the very heart of England, far remote from industrial centers and consequently unlikely to be attacked. Indeed, I'm reasonably sure not a single bomb was dropped on Malvern and its environs during the war. But before leaving Christchurch I witnessed a remarkable demonstration at TRE by "Freddie" Williams, one of Britain's most brilliant electronic engineers and another friend from the University of Manchester. We had been appointed assistant lecturers there at the same time. He had been seconded to TRE at the beginning of the war and was in charge of automatic tracking radar research. About a month after we arrived at Christchurch, Fred telephoned to say that he had something very interesting to demonstrate — could I come over to TRE? Probably, and indeed almost certainly, for the first time in history he demonstrated how a radar beam could be locked onto a target automatically. The target was the well-known "Needles Rocks" located off the south coast of England — the range from TRE Swanage was about 12 miles. I shall have more to tell about Fred Williams subsequently in these memoirs. Suffice it to say that he and his wife, Gladys, became our very close friends.

The move itself was uneventful; after all we had had a dress rehearsal three months previously.

At Malvern, TRE was located in the extensive buildings and grounds of Malvern College, a boys' public school, and ADRDE was located at

Malvern Link in a conglomeration of prefabricated buildings and huts. The two establishments were about two miles apart.

Our billet in Malvern contrasted markedly from that in Christchurch. Our hosts were the Rev. and Mrs. Simon, a retired Anglican clergyman and his wife who were closely related to Sir John Simon, a member of Winston Churchill's Cabinet. Emergency defense regulations at the time were in force and the Simons, rather reluctantly, were required to open their doors to men and women in the Armed Services and civilians in war-related employment just like thousands of other residents throughout Britain.

I recall the suspicion we aroused among the Malvern establishment (mostly retired civil servants and professional people) when they were confronted with about 2,000 civilian scientists and their families literally invading the neighborhood. In the modern vernacular, we were regarded as "draft dodgers," and this was an affront to the worthy citizens of Malvern and the local press was not particularly friendly. It is worthy of note that this opinion was radically revised four years later when news was released that Sir John Cockcroft had participated in the design of the atomic bomb. Indeed, it was even suggested that the idea for the atomic bomb occurred when Sir John was strolling on the Malvern hills. The local newspaper headlines hailed the young scientists in their midst as heroes and the citizenry of Malvern followed suit. Unfortunately, Patricia and I had moved to London and so missed the revelry and adulation.

Not only did we feel unwelcome at the Simons', but we were under-fed as well. Admittedly, the food ration was not particularly generous, but during the six weeks of our residency, Mrs. Simon, who held our Ration Books, rarely provided a meat dish and we subsisted largely on green salads. Patricia has just reminded me that we frequently hid fruit and other "goodies" under our bed. Our room was so small that every square inch was utilized.

Shortly after our arrival in Malvern, more precisely, Malvern Link, Patricia was appointed Personal Assistant (PA) to Dr. John Dunworth, head of the GL Mark III Division at ADRDE. Prior to joining the Establishment, John Dunworth had been a lecturer at Cambridge and was a close friend of the Cockcroft family. This inevitably meant his group received many perks. One of Patricia's jobs was to provide tea for her boss and Cockcroft frequently dropped in at tea-time to enjoy "Mrs. Porter's tea." Of course, her job involved much more than tea-making. Indeed, she organized the filing system, prepared drawings and illustrations for secret reports and was usually at Dunworth's right-hand when Divisional meetings were held. As well, she had the responsibility of making arrangements for visiting dignitaries and there were many of these — mostly top Army brass who included a fair number of American military and scientific personnel. All-in-all, it was an exciting and very responsible job.

My own job was by no means well defined. My section was assigned to work on the manual and automatic control of radar systems. For example, Brenda Milner, a newly graduated psychologist from Cambridge, studied the manual control of G.L. Mk II, a Canadian designed radar system. Her experiments were probably the first of their kind and predated by several years the emergence of "ergonomics" — the study of the performance of man-machine systems. I am proud to record that Brenda held her first job in my section at ADRDE. Subsequently, she was appointed Dorothy Killam Professor of Neuroscience at the Montreal Neurological Institute, McGill University. In the intervening years, she has become one of the world's most distinguished clinical neuro-psychologists and has the distinction of being elected to the Royal Societies of Canada and of London.

A Polish army officer Lt. Col. Shymanski was attached to my section and shared an office with Brenda and her husband, Peter. An amusing anecdote relating to this is worth relating. One afternoon they came to my office and complained that although the Colonel was a delightful colleague, he invariably ate garlic sandwiches for lunch and they found the aroma very unpleasant. To resolve the problem, I arranged for a small office to be constructed in the corner of our laboratory and the Colonel loved it. Incidently, much to my embarrassment because he was about 20 years older than me, he insisted on addressing me as "Sir."

Shortly after our move to Malvern, I teamed up with Dr. Arthur Solomon, who was special assistant to the Superintendent. Art Solomon was a very delightful and brilliant Harvard man who eventually held a named chair in physiology at the university. Among his many attributes at the time, as an American citizen seconded to the British war effort, he had access to an apparently unlimited supply of nylon stockings. In those days, nylon stockings were an extremely precious commodity. The ladies loved Art Solomon!

One of the most challenging projects, certainly from a theoretical point of view I was involved in at ADRDE, was in fact a brain child of Solomon's. He envisioned a fully automated radar controlled Bofors 40 mm AA gun for defense against low flying aircraft. The complete radar and predictor units were to be assembled on the gun carriage. It appeared to be a worthwhile concept because it enhanced both the mobility and the accuracy of the gun. But as I will show, there was a fundamental flaw.

The project was designated with the code name AFT1 and my objective was to determine whether this system was inherently stable. Its dynamics could be represented by a fourth order linear differential equation. It was necessary to investigate a broad range of configurations and this involved obtaining the solutions to about 100 equations. The basic requirement was to determine the real and complex roots of the associated quartic algebraic equations (and a few quintic equations).

While at least two methods for solving the equations were well known, they both turned out to be laborious and time-consuming. Newton's method, in particular, proved to be the less satisfactory of the two. I spent at least two weeks struggling with the problem and in sheer desperation; I decided to use the Manchester DA which was free at the time.

I traveled to Manchester by train, which was quite an exercise in itself because it was "cross-country," and stayed with an old friend from my Lime Grove, Manchester days. Alan Blades and his wife welcomed me warmly. Now comes a most unusual happening.

I awakened in the middle of the night and on a notepad beside my bed, outlined a new method for solving quartic equations. In the morning I had only the vaguest recollection of awakening and even less so of outlining an approach to the problem. There is no doubt, however, that in fact I had outlined a solution to a problem that had been plaguing me for many hours. Consequently, much to the surprise of the Blades' family, I announced at breakfast that there was no need for me to use the differential analyzer and I hastened back to Malvern.

Within a few days I had obtained all the required solutions and proceeded to write a final report on the AFT1 proposal. Unfortunately, the concept proved to be insufficiently stable for operational purposes and it was pursued no farther. I learned subsequently that my former boss, Col. Kerrison, was strongly opposed to the idea in the first place and after he had read my report, he was delighted. I was no longer a heretic!

The report was subsequently published as an ADRDE report and included in a compendium of reports of special interest after the war ended. Also included in the volume were two reports written by a colleague, Cornelius Mack, both of which were based on my method.[11]

---

[11]A selected Government Research Report, Vol. 5 "Servo-Mechanisms," published by H.M. Stationery Office, London, 1952

During the war these reports were classified as "Confidential" and were not available for open publication. A few years subsequently in collaboration with Mack, a paper describing the method, was published in "The Philosophical Magazine," a prestigious journal published in London.

On the domestic front, after a six-weeks stay at the Simons', Patricia pulled off a "tour de force." Mrs. Simon, who was as anxious as we were for us to find more congenial accommodation, played a major role. She took Patricia to a local real estate agent and that very morning a house came on the market. With so many TRE and ADRDE "immigrants" in Malvern, one had to move very quickly and Patricia did! As a matter of fact, the house was next door to the Malvern Police Station and the rental was reasonable. The location was ideal, only two miles from ADRDE, an easy bike ride albeit, hilly. However, the house was much too big for the two of us and Patricia came up with the idea of sharing with another couple. She found an ideal couple, John and Eleanor Scott. John, a Cambridge mathematician, was attached to ADRDE. Patricia and I arranged a bed-sitter on the ground floor and shared the kitchen. We paid about a third of the rent. There was a small garden at the back of the house and as our food rations were so meager, not least the egg ration, Patricia and I decided that a few chickens would be a good idea. Furthermore, a small shed was available and we easily constructed a chicken run with wire-netting. The upshot was that we acquired four Rhode Island Red chickens. Our favorite hen, because her egg-laying capability was superb, was Belinda. Henceforth we supplied both ourselves and the Scotts with an adequate supply of eggs at minimum cost and effort.

The 12-months we lived at 37 Church Street, Malvern, were uneventful. In spite of our limited space, we managed to entertain many colleagues and several even spent a day or two in the Spartan accommodation we provided in the basement. Two of these were future Nobel Laureates — Andrew Huxley and Neville Mott. Hotel accommodation was almost impossible to find. So many rural hotels were full of evacuees who spent the war years there in residence after abandoning their homes in the city.

Our next move, necessary because the Scott family was increasing, was to Flat 1 Wellington House. Our stay there was brief, however, because we moved back to London in November, 1943.

In retrospect, one satisfactory outcome of the AFT1 investigation was the fact that it stimulated my interest in automatic control, especially in servo mechanisms. It is no exaggeration to state that the field has been both conceptually and practically central throughout my career.

Having seen at first hand Fred Williams's research for the RAF in automating centi-metric radar tracking for fighter aircraft (the AI System) it was obvious that such technology would be of considerable interest to many research and development people in all three services. The advent of radar had emphasized the importance of replacing manual control by servo mechanisms. Indeed, in the specific case of fighter aircraft, the pilot is 100 percent occupied flying the aircraft and the radar is required to "lock-on" and track a target automatically. Manual control would be impossible.

Under normal circumstances, it would be regarded as a gross breech of confidentiality to reveal technological secrets outside one's own branch of the service, and it was quite unheard of to discuss such matters with industrial personnel. Clearly there was a considerable degree of duplication of both theory and practice which should not be tolerated under war-time conditions. As a first step in remedying the situation, Art Solomon and I conceived the idea of establishing an inter-department, albeit comparably informal, mechanism whereby servo problems could be discussed in an "open forum."

The Servo Panel was born and we proceeded to schedule several meetings on a monthly basis. Although I do not recollect any discussion of our plan with our superiors, we proceeded as befits the enthusiasm of comparative youth, on the assumption that the Ministry of Supply would sponsor and administer the meetings. The whole concept was an instant success and accepted enthusiastically by both the Services and the appropriate industrial research and development establishments. However, I am convinced that it was one factor, and one factor alone which contributed to the acceptance and success of the Servo Panel. I argued that to carry a high level of authority and prestige, it was essential that the chairman of the panel should have national stature in both academic and government circles. Not surprisingly Professor Douglas Hartree was the unanimous choice. Fortunately, Douglas accepted the job in spite of the fact that he had so many other commitments and I found myself enjoying a new job, secretary of the Servo Panel and I've rarely enjoyed a job more, not least because the Hartree — Porter team was in action again. We were fortunate as well when Professor Kenneth Hayes, a future colleague at the Military College of Science, agreed to be vice-chairman. Kenneth was a tower of strength and continued to be years later when I joined the College.

It is noteworthy that the Servo Panel actually operated for a year (from March 1942 to April, 1943) without full-time staff. Both Solomon and I were involved with the AFT1 project as well as a variety of manual tracking studies. But because the early meetings of the Servo Panel were so successful, it became increasingly clear that the potential of the panel was being restricted because of the need for a full-time secretary. Furthermore, it was increasingly obvious that London rather than Malvern would be a more appropriate location for my office. A special branch of the Ministry of Supply — SR1A, under the general direction of Dr. F. Vick, was established to deal with the Servo Panel and related questions and I was appointed head. Peak membership of the Servo Panel, which included representatives from industry, notably Arnold Tustin of Metropolitan Vickers and A.L. Whiteley of B.T.H.[12] from the United States Services, as well as "official" members from government departments was about 75. Meetings were held in the large lecture theatre of the Institution of Electrical Engineers. Some of the more noteworthy topics were the "Metadyne" by Arnold Tustin, the "Amplidyne" by John Whiteley, and the "Velodyne" by Fred Williams. At the time their papers made notable contributions to servo theory and practice. The fact that the information was shared by all the Services was a distinct advantage.

A consequence of the new arrangement was that Patricia and I had to move to London. We did on December 16, 1943 and our move was to 87 Overstrand Mansions. We had come full circle since our wedding day. Patricia's mother very generously gave us temporary residence for about six months. Providentially, Patricia was on the spot when a couple of weeks after our arrival, my mother-in-law became seriously ill. Indeed for much of our stay in the apartment, she was in hospital located 20 miles away. Patricia undertook the journey twice weekly by bus and the London underground, and in the circumstances, these journeys proved to be very time-consuming.

Another complication was the renewed bombing of London by the Luftwaffe during the spring of 1944. At that time we had dispensed with the car and we were both dependent on public transportation, which fortunately, even during the worst air raid situations in London, remained remarkably efficient. The drivers and conductresses of the buses were some of the unsung heroes of London because they carried on in spite of air raids and, as a consequence, suffered many casualties. Being close to one of the most important targets in Britain, the Battersea Power Station,

[12]British Thomson Houston Company

as well as the River Thames, Patricia and I endured some rather terrifying moments. I recall for example the night Patricia was in bed with the flu and a high temperature when the Battersea Park Z Batteries opened up. We held hands throughout the raid. It was a hair-raising experience. But it was perhaps equaled and even surpassed in terror the night that a stick of heavy (1000 Kg) bombs was dropped less than a quarter of a mile from our apartment doing heavy damage to a whole street of houses with many casualties. We were "sheltering" behind a plaster-board partition about 15 feet from the window of the living room. It was the only time in my life when my "knees were literally knocking," a sure indication of real fright. Patricia was probably as scared as I was but she didn't show it. Although the peak of the bombing lasted for less than 15 minutes, it seemed like an eternity, and when we explored the damage on the other side of that partition — the living room — we realized how very lucky we had been; Divine intervention in a very real sense. The furniture and floor were covered by fragments of glass from the window. The grandfather clock had fallen flat on its face and incredibly the only damage was that a small piece of glass had been dislodged from the glass door which covered the clock. To this day, the evidence that this 200-year-old clock had survived the London Blitz still exists. It is in John's home — we declined to have the glass replaced! Perhaps the scariest sight was to see long splinters of glass embedded in the partition less than a foot from our heads. It was fortunate that Mrs. Dixon was not at home.

A notable event of my early days back in London was the establishment of the Ministry of Supply Technical Committee on Servo-Mechanisms. This was essentially formal recognition by the powers that be that the Servo Panel had served a useful purpose. The committee was chaired by Professor Kenneth Hayes and there were 14 members, notable among who were Douglas Hartree, Fred Williams, Arnold Tustin and Graham Sutton. I was secretary to the committee which met each month until the end of the war in Europe the following year. Because of its membership, which included representatives from all Services and industry, the committee was responsible for initiating several research programs in universities and it provided a much needed mechanism for minimizing duplication of efforts in the field of automatic and manual controls.

My new office was located at 23 Baker Street, adjacent to the Baker Street Underground Station and incidentally very close to the legendary home of Sherlock Holmes, which was 21A Baker Street. Although only about six miles from Overstrand Mansions, it was nevertheless not an easy journey, especially during air raids — half mile walk, a bus to Waterloo Station and then the Bakerloo Line on the Underground. With the renewal of air raids on London, occupants of buildings in the city were required to spend two nights each week in "fire watching." After the disastrous incendiary bomb raid of early 1941 when so many buildings were destroyed by fire, this was a wise precaution. During an air raid warning, armed with a "tin hat" and service gas mask (still regarded as essential) I walked around the roof of my new quarters. The only incident worth noting during my fire watching activities occurred on June 13, 1944 at 4:30 a.m. Incidentally this was exactly one week after the D-Day landings. About 10 to 15 miles due south, I observed what I assumed to be a plane crashing. I heard a huge explosion and assumed that a bomber had been shot down, although I had not observed any anti-aircraft gunfire. A few days later I learned that what I had seen was one of the first of several thousand flying bombs" to hit London.

Coincidently, later on the same day, Patricia and I changed our address once again. By this time my mother-in-law had recovered her health and it was fortunate that a house she owned in Hampton had just become vacant and was available for rental. It was 12 Warwick Close, adjacent to Bushey Park, (headquarters of General Eisenhower, Supreme Allied Commander-in-Chief — a highly secret location). It was a mile from Hampton Court Palace and the river. Although not particularly convenient for travel to Baker Street, it had several advantages; not least that it was a small detached house with a garden.

Within a few hours Patricia had organized the move and we were settled in and spent an uneventful night in our new home. I was back in the office early the morning of June 14 — it took slightly more than an hour — bus to Richmond, train to Waterloo and Underground to Baker Street. Later that day, I received a telephone call from Fred Williams asking if it would be convenient for Gladys and him to spend a few days with us starting on Thursday, June 15. The Williams had become close friends and we always enjoyed their company — bridge and playing "the game" — a form of charades.

The night of June 15 proved eventful. Although there was no official announcement to the effect that the flying bombs were actually reaching targets in London, in fact the first night of the Williams' visit proved that they were. In retrospect, the reason for the official silence (which lasted 36 hours during which period the air raid warning persisted) was to confuse the enemy who had no idea as to whether or not the new weapon was proving effective. Some 20 of the bombs exploded that night within a mile or two of Hampton, but it was not so much the noise of the explosions (we'd heard hundreds of these during the Blitz) it was the terrifying rhythmic beat of the jet engines (about 100 per minute) which rattled windows because they were flying at an altitude of only 3000 to 5000 feet. These were terror weapons. The terror resulted from the fact that when the engine stopped, we knew that the missile was descending to the ground. Twenty to 30 seconds elapsed before the bomb exploded.

The following morning, June 16, after a sleepless night the Williams decided to make a hasty retreat back to their home in Malvern. Traveling up to my office in Baker Street that morning was an eerie experience. The "All Clear" had not sounded even after 24 hours, nor did it for another 12 hours until after the BBC 9 o'clock news when it was announced that "a few flying bombs had fallen on the outskirts of London, but had done no damage."

Subsequently because of the random distribution of the attacks, the government decided to limit air raid warnings to specific areas rather than covering the whole of Metropolitan London. However, the warnings were supplemented when necessary by Imminent Danger Signals (piercing whistles) indicating that flying bombs were in the close vicinity. Amazingly, because we were veterans of the Blitz, most people ignored the air raid warnings and only reacted when the Imminent Danger Signal sounded.

Patricia and I decided to spend the night of Friday, June 16, in makeshift beds on the ground floor. But although only a couple of Imminent Danger Signals sounded and fewer than a dozen flying bombs were heard, (with subsequent explosions) we slept very little.

The only alternative was to sleep in a public air raid shelter fitted with bunks. No privacy! Fortunately, our designated shelter, which accommodated about 100 people, men, women and children, was located at the end of our road, a mere 100 yards distance from the house.

Carrying pillows and blankets, we descended about 50 steps below ground and this was a nightly ritual — usually between 9 and 10 o'clock. Being new to the neighborhood, it took a few nights for us to become acquainted with some of our neighbors. It was quite incredible that even the normally reserved Englishman or woman loses his or her reserve in an air raid shelter.

The prefabricated bunks were assembled in three levels and stretched along each side of the shelter — similar to a railroad sleeping car, but by no means as comfortable. We soon became accustomed to the gentle snoring of the occupants of adjacent bunks and on the whole we slept well. The sound of flying bombs was considerably muted. We were regular occupants of the shelter for three months until September 1944 when the Allied Armies occupied the flying bomb launching pads in northeast France (the Pas-de-Boulogne).

During the three months of flying bomb raids I recall just two near-miss incidents. Patricia was at home alone one evening when an Imminent Danger Warning sounded, and within minutes the roar of a flying bomb engine was heard. The whole house trembled. She immediately crouched underneath the staircase, the engine shut down and a tremendous explosion which shook the whole neighborhood occurred. The bomb completely demolished two or three houses about 150 yards away. One of the houses belonged to the local doctor, but it was unoccupied at the time, and as far as I know, there were no casualties. But all houses within 200 yards of the blast suffered superficial damage, mostly roof tiles displaced and broken windows.

My own near miss occurred at Waterloo Station on my way to work. Within a few minutes of the Richmond train's arrival, the Imminent Danger Warning sounded, followed by the familiar roar of a flying bomb. I immediately located the nearest station post and flattened myself against it. About five other people, including a RN Commander, literally hurled themselves at the post and we formed a veritable rugby scrimmage. Seconds later there was an eerie silence as the bomb descended. It hit and demolished a large section of the station roof, but I escaped unharmed. Quite a few people were not so fortunate and several ambulances were soon in evidence. It is obvious that without the Imminent Danger Warning system there would have been many more casualties.

An unexpected advantage of our new home was being within a couple of miles of both the NPL and the ARL where there were many job opportunities for Patricia. Her executive secretarial talents were again exercised when she became personal assistant to Dr. Smith-Rose, head of the Radio Division at NPL. The laboratories were within walking distance of Bushey Park. Although by no means well known at the time, it transpired subsequently that Smith-Rose was together with Dr. Robert Watson-Watt, co-inventor of radar. She subsequently enjoyed two happy and fruitful years at NPL where almost on a daily basis she "rubbed shoulders" with many eminent scientists, and by no means least the director, Sir Charles Darwin, to whom reference has been made previously.

Patricia is the first to admit that her limited exposure to physics and mathematics prior to the outbreak of war and meeting myself, underwent a dramatic change. Indeed, her education in the sciences has been hands-on and under the tutelage effectively of the likes of Cockcroft, Dunworth, Darwin and Hartree, a unique experience.

In the meantime, the monthly meetings of the interdepartmental committee and the panel served the purpose of providing information exchange admirably. Because of the rapid proliferation of research material it was clear during our early deliberations that there was a pressing need to standardize nomenclature and definitions. Consequently, a small sub-committee under the chairmanship of Kenneth Hayes was set up to prepare material for discussion by the committee as a whole. This proved an extremely laborious and indeed at times acrimonious task. But although it was subject to some criticism, especially in industrial circles, I believe the final report served a very useful purpose not least as the result of the sterling work of Chairman Kenneth Hayes. Not surprisingly, as well, Douglas Hartree played a key role as he did in the deliberations of several other specialist groups.

As the summer progressed there was a noticeable diminution of V-1 missiles reaching London. This was due in part to the increased effectiveness of the RAF bomber attacks on the launching sites, and as well, to the large number of missiles destroyed by AA gunfire and fighter aircraft. Incidentally, contributing markedly to the AA gun successes was the newly installed U.S. fire control equipment designed by the MIT Radiation and Servo Mechanisms Laboratories. Indeed, the fact that the missiles flew in a straight line and at a constant height and speed resulted in almost a 100 percent success rate.

As scientific advisor to the Anti-aircraft Command, my brother Ronald played a key role in the redeployment of the London guns to locations between London and the English Channel in order to intercept the missiles before they reached the metropolitan area. At this stage of the flying bomb offensive it was obvious that the defenses were in command and Patricia and I vacated the air raid shelter and returned to our own bed.

At the beginning of September, Patricia and I took the train from Euston Station to Ulverston for a brief holiday with my parents. This was our third visit to Birkrigg since we'd married and we made the most of it.

I recall especially how much my parents "spoiled" us. Mother preserved a fair proportion of the family's food ration and coupled with the several delicacies of the neighborhood, notably the sumptuous

Birkrigg mushrooms, Kirby Moor "blea berries," Plumption Viaduct black berries as well as the rabbit and hare available in the Ulverston market, she prepared many feasts "fit for a king." On these occasions I recalled the many hours as a boy I'd enjoyed both picking the fruit and eating the delicious tarts baked by my mother. We took advantage as well of the close proximity of Bardsea Beach — a two-mile bike ride — where I'd spent so much time camping and bathing during school and university vacations. We enjoyed several picnics and simple ball games on the sand. Sadly, those glorious sands of Morecambe Bay have by now been polluted beyond recognition. How lucky we were to enjoy them in such a comparatively pristine condition.

In the courtyard of Euston Station on our return from our vacation, we were greeted by a distant explosion and we saw smoke rising over west London, about 10 miles away. It was caused by one of the first V-2 rockets to hit the metropolitan area. The launching sites were about 200 miles away, located in Holland and still at least 300 miles from the advancing Allied Armies. The missile was virtually identical to the modern "SCUD rocket" and carried a 1000 pound warhead. During the fall of 1944 some 2000 V-2's were launched and did considerable damage to life and property. Unlike the V-1, their approach was soundless and no Imminent Danger Signal was possible. It is worth noting that during the Gulf War of a decade ago, no more than five SCUD's were launched by Iraq against Israel.

In retrospect, this second of Hitler's "secret weapons" was another terrorist device which caused far more psychological damage than material damage. Only one V-2 hit within a mile of Warwick Close — falling in open ground it created a large crater in the park, but did little damage. Of interest is the fact that the launching site of the V-2's was first detected by the late Wing Commander Douglas Kendall RAF, who headed up an air reconnaissance unit. In later years Douglas and I served together on several advisory committees in Canada, and the Kendalls were our friends and neighbors in the Caledon Hills, Ontario.

In January, 1945, I was fortunate to be nominated as the interdepartmental committee representative to visit the U.S.A. Douglas Hartree was too heavily committed at the time to spare the two months necessary. Since the early days of the Servo Panel, members of the staff of the technical section of the US Embassy had been enthusiastic participants. It was through them that the visit was arranged. Its main purpose was to exchange information on topics of mutual interest, and several organizations were identified as the key places to visit. It was not surprising that the RD work in hand at MIT was included in the itinerary. This was especially important for me personally because I knew several of the key people involved. To put it mildly, I was thrilled with the prospect of the visit and I was not disappointed.

My unique war-time adventure began on February 9, 1945 at Waterloo Station. At 8 p.m. I met John Womersley, head of the Mathematics Division of NPL, whose mission to the U.S., independent of mine, was related to computer development. We boarded a special Pullman car headed for "a secret destination." The secrecy was justified because a month previously a Pan-American Clipper in which the British actor Leslie Howard was a passenger had been shot down over the Bay of Biscay, and the port of departure of the flying boats had been changed since this disaster. We learned subsequently that the port of departure was actually Poole Harbor, Dorsetshire.

Accustomed as we'd been to strict food rationing, the dinner served was a gourmet's delight, as befitted the most luxurious train service in Britain. I still recall the roast pheasant. We spent the night at an unidentified seaside hotel and we were instructed to be ready for departure at 5 a.m. the following morning. Breakfast was served to a total of about 40 passengers and crew of the Clipper.

The secrecy aspect certainly contributed to the adventurous aspect of our mission. Even the dock where we boarded the tender was in total darkness.

My first impression of the Pan-American Super Clipper as we approached remains vivid in my memory. It was in fact 106 feet long and had a wing space of 152 feet. There was sleeping accommodation for 40 passengers and crew, a main lounge and a large suite for VIPs. In peace time this was the "honeymoon suite."

My seat which could be converted at night into a bunk-bed was essentially a miniature cabin. I was located at the rear of the Clipper and had perfect views of the various harbors on route to the United States. Recently I read *Night Over Water*, a novel by Ken Follett which gives a magnificent description of the Clipper and an almost disastrous night flight from Shannon, Ireland, to the United States. A plan of the aircraft shows the actual location of the various cabins and the main lounge and I had no difficulty in identifying my location — it has served as a remarkable stimulant to my recollections of that flight. Suffice it to say that the Pan-American Airways Super-Clipper is described in the novel as "the most romantic plane ever made," and I flew in it!

Although by no means as massive nor as powerful as a modern jet liner, the Clipper was nevertheless the largest commercial passenger aircraft in history to take off and land on water. It was an exhilarating experience to accelerate for a mile or two over the waters of Poole Harbor and to rise gracefully into the air. The cruising speed was 100 knots (equivalent to 115 mph) and we flew at an altitude of 10,000 feet. Breakfast was served in the Main Lounge shortly after take-off.

The first leg of a total of six legs of the flight, terminated in Lisbon, capital of Portugal. We touched down in the harbor after a six-hour flight and taxied to within two miles of the shoreline. The city and the mountainous background presented an awe-inspiring sight from the harbor on that sunny afternoon. After the Clipper was anchored to a pilot boat, we were taken ashore by tender. Before disembarking however, we were briefed on the importance of our acting as typical tourists because Lisbon was notorious during the war as a center for international espionage. A veritable hot spot of spies! As a matter of fact, several of the passengers were Naval and Army officers headed for the Bermuda headquarters of Allied Secret Service Missions; they wore civilian attire.

We were welcomed warmly by officials and given a brief history of the city. (Patricia and I visited Lisbon during a cruise in 1993. It was interesting to see how very many changes had taken place.) During a brief tour of the city highlights, we were particularly interested to see the German Embassy with its entourage of S.S. sentries, the elite corps of the German Army, in their resplendent uniform. The brief stay in Lisbon concluded with a gourmet dinner hosted by the city and each of us was presented with a bottle of vintage port wine. After more than five years living under total "black-out" conditions in Britain, it was quite a shock on emerging from the restaurant to be confronted with the glare of city lights — the first we'd seen since September 1939.

For security reasons the Clipper's flight schedule was predicated on a series of night flights and day stop-overs. From the passenger's point of view this was most desirable because it gave us an opportunity to explore albeit transiently, each of the five ports of call en route to Baltimore, Maryland.

The night flight to Bathurst was uneventful. However, I was agreeably surprised by the comfortable bunk beds, which together with the quiet engines were conducive to a good night's sleep. At 8 a.m. the following morning we docked at Bathurst, West Africa, again in glorious sunshine. It was in marked contrast with Lisbon — primitive thatched huts were in abundance. An interesting societal observation was that the women, many bare-breasted, seemed to do all the work. They carried large loads of either faggots of wood or pots of varying shapes and sizes on top of their heads — striding majestically with erect postures. While many of the men seemed to be occupied climbing huge coconut palm trees bare foot and extracting what I was told was a potent beverage from the fruits. It was a fascinating experience.

The fact that the Bathurst beach is adjacent to the town also appealed. Neither John Womersley nor I had bathed in the warm waters of the South Atlantic before and in spite of having no bathing suits, we spent a relaxing hour in the ocean. What a contrast to war-weary Britain. As well during our brief sojourn ashore we took advantage of the well-stocked marketplace — tropical fruits galore. We were fortunate in taking off that evening to have a calm sea. This, the third leg of the flight, took us across the South Atlantic from Bathurst to Belem, Brazil. We docked at 7 a.m. The city, largest in the massive delta of the river Amazon, has a wonderful harbor — perfect docking for the Clipper. For the first time in my life, I crossed the equator — Belem has a latitude of 2 degrees south.

We were ferried over to the Pan-American building ashore, but because of the extreme heat and humidity even during the comparatively early morning hours, I regret to say I only had a superficial view of the city. When we re-embarked about noon, the sun was virtually overhead.

Our next port of call was Port of Spain, capital of the Trinidad and Tobago islands. We had flown within sight of the South American coast for several hours when the captain announced we would be flying directly over Devil's Island, the notorious penal settlement off the coast of French Guiana. Because the inmates had so little contact with the outside world, we flew over the island at the reduced altitude of 5,000 feet. I still recall quite vividly seeing several hundred inmates in the precincts of the prison waving to us. For them the Clipper was a welcome, albeit transitory relief from their very boring existence. To us it was a sad sight.

During the afternoon of February 8, about half a dozen passengers, including Womersley and myself, who had had their first war-time flight over the Atlantic, were inducted into the "short snorter club." We were inducted by Commander Keith Walter, RN a "short snorter" who had several crossings to his credit. The certificate of membership to the club is a one-dollar bill on which the signatures of other members are written. These included the signature of the captain of the Clipper. Life membership in the club costs $1 — paid to the short snorter who performed the induction. On my return flight across the Atlantic, details of which will be given later, my short snorter bill was supplemented by a Mexican dollar bill and signed by the captain and crew of the Liberator Aircraft. I have introduced the short snorter club in a little detail because it has some historical significance, not least of which Winston Churchill was introduced as a member and this fact is recorded in his memoirs of World War II. Today my certificate of life membership in the club has been framed and hopefully may become a conversation piece for some of my descendants.

It was dusk when we touched down at Port of Spain and because the stop-over was essentially for refueling, we remained onboard. The flight from Trinidad to Bermuda was very bumpy as was the touch-down in Hamilton Harbor. At least half of the passengers, I suspect, were members of the staff of Sir William Stephenson, chief of British intelligence.

We touched down in Chesapeake Bay, Md. during the late afternoon of February 9 — the Bay was dotted with small ice floes, graphic signs of the severity of the 1944-45 winters in the eastern U.S.A.

Both Womersley and I took a local train from Baltimore to Washington, D.C. and registered at the Mayflower Hotel. The following morning I spent a few hours at the British Embassy and was briefed by staff of the Scientific Mission. The staff made all the necessary arrangements including travel for my visits to MIT, the Bell Telephone Laboratories and the laboratories of the GE Company Schenectady NY. It was estimated that my visit would take about two months. That evening I was warmly greeted by Frank Lewis who had completed his tour of duty in London and was stationed in Washington, D.C. It will be recalled that Frank, a friend from MIT days, attended Patricia and my wedding and we had many mutual interests in London. He had promised to treat me to the largest steak dinner available in the capital should I visit during war-time — and he did. We had an unforgettable dinner at the Mayflower Hotel. It was in marked contrast to the dark days of 1942 when we had last had dinner together in London.

Because the programs at MIT, notably the Radiation Laboratory and the Servo Mechanism Laboratory were of paramount interest, I spent the first five weeks of my visit at Cambridge, Mass. I was fortunate to locate a communal residence on Garden Street where a group of graduate students and faculty members from Harvard and MIT lived — a total of 10 residents. Coincidently, Holly Irvine, daughter of Sir James Irvine, vice-chairman of the Commonwealth Fund Committee of Award, whom I had met in London in 1937, was a resident. Another resident was Cyril

Henderson, a graduate student at Harvard — another remarkable coincidence in the "annals of the Porter family" because as I will indicate subsequently, he became a close friend of Patricia and mine in Canada.

In light of a prospective early end to the war in Europe, prior to leaving London I was requested by the Interdepartmental Technical Committee to concentrate my mission, especially on the application of control systems in industry. Although Britain had made dramatic strides in military technology during the war the country was nevertheless well behind the USA in the transfer of this technology to the industrial sector.

The Radiation and Servo Mechanisms laboratories at MIT offered an excellent starting point. I could not possibly have had a more sympathetic mentor than Gordon Brown, (an Australian by birth). Not only did he provide a survey of significant developments in the field of automatic control in US industry, but as well gave me introductions to key people at the Bell Labs and the General Electric laboratories. I also was fortunate to have profitable sessions with Jay Forrester, the computer pioneer who has remained a friend for the past 50 years, Professor Draper whose pioneering work on the design of gyroscopes revolutionized the technology and Professor Harold Edgerton of stereoscopic photography fame. These MIT "greats" gave unreservedly of their time and I benefited significantly. It was also a pleasure and privilege to renew friendship with MIT faculty members who had been so helpful during my previous sojourn at the Institute. In particular, from the graduate school I single out Harold Hazen and his wife, Kathleen, and Professor Sam Caldwell and Eva. These were the people who endeared me to MIT and I shall always be grateful to them.

As a visitor from Britain, a rare commodity at the time, especially one who had lived through the London bombings, I was invited to several dinner parties. At one party in Lowell House, Harvard, I was introduced by Arthur Solomon (recently returned from Britain to take up a faculty appointment) to Tom Lehrer, Associate Professor of Mathematics and composer and lyricist of many hilarious satiric songs i.e. "Be Prepared" and "Fight, Fight, Fight for Harvard." He entertained us at the piano.

My two day visit to the GE Company at Schenectady, N.Y., gave me new insights into the potential of military servo-mechanism developments in a range of peace-time industrial applications. I recall especially the development of massive electrical controls for the steel industry, notably steel rolling mills, and similar systems for the paper industry. Equally impressive were the designs of the instrumentation and controls of steam turbines and electric power plants. With the rapid expansion of the commercial aircraft business expected in the post-war period, there were as well numerous developments in navigation and instrumentation. Indeed I was introduced to such a plethora of state-of-the-art technology that I spent many weeks on my return to Britain digesting and communicating my findings.

The last of my prearranged visits was to the Bell Telephone Laboratories at Murray Hill, N.J., a few miles from New York City. I was especially anxious to meet three people:

- Henry Nyquist, whose landmark paper "Regeneration Theory" in which the ubiquitous Nyguist Criterion of Stability is developed, was and is the universally recognized pioneer of the so-called frequency response approach to feedback amplifier and servo system design.

- H. W. Bode, whose work complimented Nyquist's and related specifically to the optimum design of broad-band feedback amplifiers. He had developed the well-known and widely used "Bode diagrams." This design tool has been found indispensable not only in the development of feedback amplifiers but as well to automatic control systems.

- George Stibitz had designed the Bell Telephone Relay Calculator which used teletype punched tape as input. His pioneering work in developing the forerunners to electronic computers was based exclusively on telephone switching equipment. Of his many contributions to automatic computing the development of binary and "floating decimal point arithmetic" stand out.

In fact I met all three during the course of a two-day visit. My overall impression was that I had seen one of the greatest industrial laboratories in history notably in the field of communications and control. This visit concluded my mission and I took the night train from New York Central to Montreal. It was April 12, 1945. Arriving in Montreal the following morning I was shocked to see headlines in the newspapers announcing that President Roosevelt had died during the previous afternoon.

It was a sad ending to a mission which has through the years had a profound influence on my understanding of automatic control theory and concepts related thereto. During the early afternoon of April 13, I boarded a converted Liberator bomber aircraft for my return flight to Britain — Gander, Newfoundland; Goose Bay Labrador; Keflavik,

Iceland; terminating in Prestwick, Scotland. Not in the same league as the Clipper for comfort and quality of food, indeed the aircraft was neither pressurized nor air conditioned and we wore oxygen masks most of the time.

There were brief refueling stop-overs and because winter lingered on in the northern latitudes, these were not an imposition. The airports and surroundings were snow-covered, wild and bleak. It was a relief to see the green countryside of Northern Ireland and southern Scotland in the spring sunshine. We touched down at Prestwick at about 1 p.m. on April 14. Total time of flight was 17 hours. A non-stop express train journey from Glasgow to Euston London completed an unforgettable adventure and after an almost 10 week absence, I was thrilled to see Patricia waiting on the arrivals' platform to welcome me home.

Less than three weeks after my return, Hitler committed suicide on April 30, the German armed forces disintegrated and hostilities ceased on land, on sea and in the air. Victory in Europe Day (V-E Day) May 8 was celebrated. For Patricia and me the day started about 5 a.m. — we took an early train from Richmond to Waterloo and walked along the Thames Embankment to a convenient location 300 yards from Charing Cross. We claimed an excellent viewing position and literally squatted on the pavement to await the arrival of the V-E Day procession which was due to start at 9 a.m. from Trafalgar Square — proceed down Whitehall to the Embankment, hence to the City of London and return to Central London via Piccadilly and Hyde Park — a total of at least five miles.

It was by far the most impressive procession we had ever seen. In attendance were King George VI and Queen Elizabeth, Princesses Elizabeth and Margaret and other members of the Royal Family; Winston Churchill and members of the War Cabinet; Generals Eisenhower, Alexander, Montgomery, Bradley and other Allied Army commanders; Admirals of the Fleet and Air Marshals in limousines followed by the Guards regiments in full dress regalia including bearskin helmets; Royal Naval officers and men towing gun carriages; the RAF contingents; and representative regiments from all the Allied Armed Forces. We were particularly impressed by the young women members of the Armed Services marching with pride and precision. And there were many other women in the procession, members of the Metropolitan Police Force, the Nursing Services, the Auxiliary Fire Services, Air Raid Wardens and even the Women's Land Army.

Marching bands from the Services and civilian organizations were interspersed in the procession and played patriotic and popular tunes.

Thousands of Union Jacks were waving and one could not but notice the tears streaming down the cheeks of many of those present that day, including ours. After at least two hours of cheering and hollering as the parade passed us by, we ate our sandwich lunches and drank tea from a thermos together with thousands of our fellow countrymen.

I am still mystified as to how we reached Piccadilly Circus by the Underground after the crowds on the Embankment had dispersed. But we did. The revelry there was a sight to behold and to remember. Fortunately the Statue of Eros had been sandbagged since the beginning of the war and was safe. Rarely had I seen tens of thousands of Britishers so relaxed and exuberant. The noise was deafening. Both Patricia and I were veterans in so far as the London transport system was concerned and in spite of the chaos all around us we managed miraculously to board at least three buses that took us within half a mile of Buckingham Palace. Even at a distance of 100 yards, in the midst of a cheering throng, we were rewarded with the sight of the King and Queen, the Princesses and Winston Churchill waving from the balcony of the Palace. It was a fitting climax to the victory celebrations.

In more leisurely fashion we traveled home to Hampton, not quite in time for tea. During the evening we walked over to Avenue Road where we'd first met, and spent the evening comparatively quietly with Johnnie and Ted Lee, our oldest friends.

I should mention that within the last hour on Saturday, July 10, 2002, I have just spoken on the telephone to Johnnie and recalled the events I have just recorded. She was thrilled — she lives in the beautiful village of Weybridge on the banks of the River Thames about 50miles from London.

We were almost too "bleary"-eyed to watch the firework displays which ended a perfect day.

Back to work after the revelry, I was confronted with the problem of classifying and sorting the many reports and documents I had accumulated during my visit to the United States. Special meetings of the Interdepartmental Committee and the Servo Mechanism Panel were arranged and I made verbal presentations. At the time it was not my intention to identify the many and varied industrial applications of automatic control (these were subsequently identified in my final report)[13] but rather to present an overview of my impressions. To

---

[13]Ministry of Supply Interdepartmental Technical Committee on Servo-Mechanism Publication No. 2; Memorandum on "The Application of Control Systems in Industry," October 1945

illustrate my main conclusions, I quote below from the report:

> *Not withstanding the great interest shown by certain branches of industry in control applications it had become increasingly clear that America is far ahead of this country in this respect. It is little doubt that the applications of servo technique in the design of industrial processes is rapidly gaining ground in America and during a recent visit this writer was strongly impressed by the already wide range of applications. Three factors appear to contribute to the lead which America has gained in this field:*
> *(I) The American industrialist appears to be more "control-minded" than his counterpart in this country.*
> *(II) The number of research personnel engaged on control problems is far greater than the number so engaged in Britain.*
> *(III) The design and application of control systems is included as a subject for post graduate study at several American universities and technical colleges.*

In retrospect I feel that as a comparatively junior member of the British scientific establishment I was being rather outspoken, but as events transpired during the post-war years, my conclusions were salutary. Many years after the end of the war the director of a large British electronics company remarked that "If Britain had only taken Arthur Porter's advice in 1945, it would have helped."

Because my final report has probably for many years been consigned to the dusty archives of the Ministry of Supply, I take this opportunity to mention the following recommendations:

1. The formation of an Industrial Control System Panel is strongly recommended. The nucleus of the panel would consist of (a) key industrial and research personnel, (b) research personnel associated with the Industrial Research Associations, (c) personnel associated with the Central Advisory Service on Control Systems.

2. The formation of a research group to handle industrial control problems of fundamental importance and wide application.

3. The formation of an Advisory Service on the design and application of industrial control systems.

Throughout my career I've been a staunch advocate of interdisciplinary study and research. Suffice it to say that the seeds of this philosophy were sown during the formative days of the Servo Panel and the Interdepartmental Committees and by no means least during my visit to the United States in early 1945.

The situation in the Far East remained critical. Although in some sectors, Britain continued to play an important role, i.e. the Burma campaign and the Royal Naval Pacific fleet, the United States carried the brunt of the military operations against Japan. In Britain we were encouraged time and time again to hear of the heroic battles in which so many Pacific Islands were recaptured, notably Iwo Jima. It seemed increasingly clear however, that the Japanese would continue this struggle to the bitter end and particularly in defense of the Japanese homeland.

But dramatic events were to occur within a few weeks. On July 16, 1945 the first nuclear weapons test, code named Trinity, was carried out successfully in the New Mexico desert. It is difficult to describe my reaction. Certainly it was one of incredible amazement even though I had had some premonition that "something was in the works." Three weeks later on August 6, 1945, the Japanese city of Hiroshima was destroyed by the nuclear bomb, code named "Little Boy." Three days later Nagasaki suffered the same fate. In the circumstances, in spite of the horror of these attacks, I feel that the United States had no alternative — drop the bombs or suffer many months longer of mortal combat with Japan in which perhaps more than a million lives might be lost. Not surprisingly, Japan capitulated and WWII in effect ended on August 14, 1945 (the formal signing of capitulation on U.S. Missouri occurred on September 2, 1945). It is worthy of note that nuclear power, not nuclear weapons, would play a significant role in my future career.

A fitting climax to my war time activities was my visit to Germany in March 1946.

Shortly after the end of hostilities in Europe, there were prolonged discussions among the Allies regarding the occupation of Germany. Eventually the country was divided into four geographical zones — American, Soviet Union, British and a comparatively small French zone, while Berlin was treated separately, but in a similar fashion. The British zone covered the north east of the country. To facilitate the return of Germany to normality as quickly as possible, it was essential ipso facto that professional people, especially scientists, engineers and physicians should be encouraged to remain in the country. But there was increasing evidence that the Soviet authorities were using unethical and indeed illegal methods to kidnap and then smuggle key German scientists into the Soviet zone. One technique was to transport them across the zone borders, hidden in hay carts. On the other hand, some German specialists such as the inventor of the German V2 rocket, Werner von Braun applied for visas to reside in Allied countries.

To counter the threat of forceful removal of German nationals across the Soviet boundaries, the authorities recruited a group of scientists from Britain to investigate the situation and in particular to identify key German personnel who were targets. I was approached by Professor Blackett who was organizing the operation to ascertain whether I would be interested. I agreed to serve for a period of three weeks. Although not mandatory, for security reasons, I opted to wear an officer's uniform during the visit.

My headquarters was in the university city of Göttingen. The German authorities were extremely helpful. They were as anxious as we were to ensure that German citizens were protected. One of the most memorable occasions during my stay was my lunch at the University of Göttingen Faculty Club with Dr. Werner Heisenberg, director of the Max Planck Institute for Physics and winner of the Nobel Prize in 1932. He was one of the most renowned scientists of the 20th century being one of the founders of quantum theory and discoverer of the Heisenberg Uncertainty Principle. I told him about my work at Manchester and how his work had had such a profound influence. It was a very worthwhile meeting. Heisenberg was anxious to do everything possible to expedite our mission.

My visit to Germany was not only interesting from a practical and political point of view, but also because during my train journey, it gave me an opportunity to see at first-hand some of the devastation suffered by German cities. It was a sad experience — Hanover had been virtually destroyed and all that remained was mounds of debris and a terrible stench.

On the domestic front, Patricia had an extraordinarily busy time during the remaining months of 1945 and beginning of 1946. We were inundated with house guests. Two full pages of our guest book no less! Indeed, quite understandably members of our family from northern England delayed visiting us until the cessation of bombing. Patricia and I are in our element when entertaining, even during the immediate post-war period when food and gasoline rationing were at least as stringent as previously. She continued her full-time job at NPL without domestic help or laundry or cleaning services, Patricia succeeded in entertaining not only family but several "official" guests. During this period, Douglas Hartree, Freddie Williams and Kenneth Hayes were frequent visitors. They were key members of my various committees and had become close friends.

I single out Douglas Hartree for special mention. Not only had I been his first PhD. student and had developed a special relationship during those years, but especially during the war our friendship had blossomed. He was an ideal guest in every respect, even on many occasions helping in the kitchen. We were fortunate as well one weekend in November 1945, when Elaine joined us and inquired rather tentatively and shyly, "Would we be able to put Douglas up for a few weeks while he was on a special assignment at NPL?" Needless to add, Patricia and I were delighted.

Consequently, Douglas stayed with us for about two months. It was during this period that we discussed my immediate future. My Ministry of Supply job (I was in fact on loan from the Admiralty) was essentially temporary, although there was no urgency since my various committees were still extant.

Was it to be university, industry or government service?

I had already been approached by Vickers-Armstrong, the international armaments corporation, and my father's life-time employers, but I felt the prospects much too restrictive, especially in a peace-time environment. I recalled as well that Professor Bragg had suggested in July, 1939 that a post would be available at my old university, Manchester. But, and Douglas Hartree concurred, would there be enough challenge in operating the differential analyzer and would there be additional prospects? The answer was in the negative. The dilemma, if such it was, would be resolved rather sooner than I expected.

One morning early in January 1946 on leaving the train at Waterloo Station on my way to work, I noticed that a copy of the "Times" had been left by a fellow passenger. I retrieved it more or less out of habit. I mention this incident because it had quite significant consequences. Perusing the newspaper on my way home that day I noted in the Front Page Notices (in those days, uniquely, the Times devoted the whole front page to advertisements) an ad inserted by the War Office. It read "Applications are requested for the fully tenured post of Professor of Instrument Technology and Head of the Faculty of Instrument Technology in the Military College of Science, Shrivensham, Berkshire.

Applicants should have appropriate qualifications. The salary level is equivalent to that of a Deputy Chief Scientific Officer in the Civil Service and a residence will be provided on the campus." I understood from a previous conversation with Professor Hayes that the College was undertaking a major re-organization. During the war the College had been located on three campuses — Woolwich, Kent; Aldershot, Hampshire; and Bury, Lancashire; with a consequent lack of communication and indeed identity.

I reasoned that perhaps the War Office in light of this re-organization was seeking "new blood," and I had the temerity to think that perhaps I was qualified for the post — in spite of the fact that its standing in the scientific civil service was four grades higher than my existing appointment. On the assumption that I had nothing to lose, I duly applied for the professorship.

At the next meeting of the Interdepartmental Committee, I informed Kenneth Hayes of my decision and he felt it was a good idea in spite of the fact that he himself was obviously a candidate for the post. Indeed, both Hayes and Lee (Chairman of the Radar and Telecommunications Department) were equivalent in seniority with virtually identical qualifications, but the choice of one or the other would have created problems both practical and psychological.

Within a week or two of sending in my Military College of Science application to the War Office and promptly forgetting about it because it was such a long shot, I was requested to meet Sir Charles Darwin, director of NPL. (Douglas Hartree obviously had something to do with this.)

The meeting was most cordial, not least because he doubtless recalled the "Darwin Bum Phenomenon" which I described in a previous chapter. Sir Charles Darwin outlined his plan to establish a small computer and control section in the Metrology Division. Would I be interested in heading it? The post would carry the rank of Principal Scientific Officer. Without hesitating I responded affirmatively and started work at the NPL on April 1, 1946. I remember the delightful walk to work across Bushey Park, often with deer herds within a few hundred yards. It was spring time and the daffodils and blossoms were in full bloom.

Coincidently the day after starting work at NPL I received a letter from the War Office requesting that I appear for an interview on April 8 to be conducted by the Civil Service Commissioners in connection with my application for the Military College of Science professorship. The

Civil Service Commission was the body responsible for senior appointments to the government. The interviewing committee was chaired by no less a personage than C.P. Snow (later Lord Snow), chairman of the Commission, and a celebrated author and Cambridge don who had worked with Lord Rutherford. Fortunately, I seemed to thrive on interviews of this kind, as witness my performance in the Commonwealth Fund Fellowship interview. I concentrated on the importance of computers in the future of the College, and my experiences at MIT. However, although I was given a good, indeed cordial reception with C.P. Snow leading the questioning, I was not optimistic because of my junior status at the time.

My new job certainly provided plenty of opportunities. The NPL was the premier government scientific research establishment in the country and I was to be responsible for assembling a team of engineering physicists interested in computers. My first recruit was Dick Tizard, son of Sir Henry and a recent graduate of engineering from Oxford University. I also was fortunate to have the advice of a senior member of the Metrology Division who introduced me to members of the Division and to administrative procedures. Within a few weeks it was clear that I was confronted with a dilemma. During the last few years of the war, large scale electronic digital computers were being developed at the University of Pennsylvania (the ENIAC) and at Princeton (the EDVCA), both developments being funded by the U.S. Army, and Douglas Hartree had been informed of these developments. To what extent should the new section concentrate on digital computers? On one hand I was very familiar with analog machines, both mechanical and electrical, but on the other I was blissfully ignorant of digital computer developments. Indeed my initial reactions had been that the latter would contain thousands of electronic vacuum tubes and be correspondingly unreliable. Although justifiable at the time, in retrospect all I can add is that "how wrong I was!" Indeed I must confess that it was not until early 1950 that I became convinced of the fantastic potential of the electronic digital computer.

Most unexpectedly my dilemma was short lived. Early in June as I was leaving 12 Warwick Close to walk to work, the postman handed me a small buff OHMS (On His Majesty's Service) letter and I knew immediately it related to the Military College. I was so certain that I had been unsuccessful that I tore open the envelope and continued walking. But I was in for a surprise — on a small sheet of paper the letter read:

> *Civil Service Commission competition No.* ++++
> *Successful candidate: A. Porter*

It took a few moments for the contents to sink in before I realized that I had in fact got the job and I returned home immediately to inform Patricia. I was late for work that day. I was especially relieved, when later Darwin on being informed congratulated me and wished me well. I was gratified to learn subsequently that the great computer pioneer, Allan Turing[1] had been appointed in my place.

[1]See Chapter 7 — The Military College of Science

Chapter 7

THE MILITARY COLLEGE OF SCIENCE (M.C. OF S)

PATRICIA and I first visited the Military College of Science to meet the Commandant, Major General Shapland and Mrs. Shapland early in July 1946. We took the Southern Railway from Paddington Station to Swindon, Wiltshire, where an Army car took us through delightful country to Shrivenham — about 12 miles. This was our first visit to Berkshire and Wiltshire and we discovered a wealth of Georgian and Tudor houses on the way — a completely different landscape from my Lake District and Patricia's London homelands. The village is typical of the South Downs with an ancient church dominating the small houses and shops of the main street. Our first impression of the College campus was that of a large country estate with thousands of oak, ash and beech trees, a large house, Beckett House, typical of the stately homes of the Victorian era, and a small ornamental lake. At first sight the College buildings, mostly red brick, seemed rather incongruous in such surroundings. As a matter of fact, the MC of S had housed "the American University" which provided courses in European history and military affairs for US Army offices who having completed their tour of active duty spent a few months on the campus prior to their return to the United States.

While I was briefed on the basics of the instructional side of the College, Mrs. Shapland, a most forceful albeit elegant lady, showed Patricia around the residences, (officers' quarters) and introduced her to some of the social aspects of life in a military establishment.

The organization of the college is predicated on four faculties of science and technology of which Instrument Technology is one. Each faculty is headed by a full professor. The coordination of scientific and military studies is carried out by three military Directors of Study, each of colonel's rank. A Board of Studies, the senior academic policy making body in the college, consisted of the four full professors and the three colonels.

The major academic programs were, and probably still are, the Technical Staff Officers (TSO) course — a two year graduate program for graduates of the college and of universities, and a Young Officers course — for the training of junior officers in basic science and ultimately leading to the degree of Bachelor of Science in the University of London.

The TSO courses lead to the PTSC (passed technical staff course) certificate — the highest technical qualification in the Army and a necessary pre-requisite for senior appointments — colonel and above in the Corps of the Royal Engineers, the Royal Electrical and Mechanical Engineers (REME) and the Royal Signals (RSig). The first TSO course with 30 students in Instrument Technology was due to begin on October 1, 1946. I had a lot of work to do before that date.

Just prior to our departure for Shrivenham, I received an invitation to present a paper to the Institution of Mechanical Engineers to be delivered during the spring of 1947. The Institution is housed in a magnificent Victorian building on Bird Cage Walk, in the close vicinity of Buckingham Palace and the Houses of Parliament. As a matter of fact, I had never entered the building until the evening of my lecture. It was quite an honor for a non-member to be invited and, in accepting, I chose the topic "The Fundamental Principles of Automatic Control Systems." In spite of many matters to be attended to at the time, I gave the lecture high priority. It gave me an excellent opportunity to review my earlier work under the inspired leadership of Douglas Hartree on feedback control systems, my work on radar systems during WWII, and perhaps most importantly, to structure the material as a basis for subsequent lecture courses at the Military College and in the more distant future at Imperial College.

In particular I emphasized the importance of standardizing basic definitions and introduced the ideas of the Nomenclature Committee of the Servo Panel. As well, I introduced an idea, "disturbance feedback" which although innate in many industrial control processes, had not been analyzed theoretically. The paper was presented at a special meeting of the Institution in February of 1947. There was a huge audience because the subject was very topical at the time.

What I was not prepared for, however, was the lengthy, detailed and at times almost acrimonious discussion that followed my presentation. It lasted almost an hour.

Two discussants, in particular, were highly critical of certain aspects of my paper, and my response at the conclusion, in light of the complexity of the issues involved was, I am certain, not very convincing. I needed more time. Subsequently, just prior to publication when all the contributions were available, I prepared my response having identified the fallaciousness of the arguments raised by the critics. The full discussion and my response were published at the end of the paper in the Proceedings of the Institution in July of 1947.

A few months after the publication I was delighted to be informed that my paper had been awarded an Institution Prize 1947. It consists of a rather elegant parchment signed by the President of the Institution, Lord Dudley Gordon, and now hangs in my den. In 1977, just 30 years after its publication, the paper was included in the so-called "Benchmark Papers" on "The Control of Energy." I am particularly proud that of the 26 papers which comprised the volume, there were contributions from such notables as Maxwell, de Forrest, Wiener and Bardeen. The citation relating to my paper concludes with "Naturally there has been a very extensive development of the whole subject of control during the past quarter of a century, but Porter's paper still remains fundamental."

During our visit in July of 1946 we learned that 1 Park Avenue on the campus had been reserved as our future residence. With five bedrooms, dining room, reception room, two bathrooms, kitchen, laundry room and a large front and very large back garden, it was much too big for our needs. Even so, we were eligible on the basis of rank for an even larger "quarter." Indeed, two of my future colleagues insisted on the larger houses. We had a glorious view of the White Horse Hills across a beautiful verdant valley. The White Horse itself is an ancient (at least 1000 years) artifact, at least 200 feet long, and carved in chalk. It is visible for many miles.

On our return journey to Hampton we reflected on the incredible transformation in our life-style which would begin in a couple of months. We were thrilled at the prospects. I was 35 years old and Patricia was 25. We were, together with one other couple, the youngest members of the Board of Studies. I must confess that I felt quite embarrassed when saluted by uniformed members of the College staff of rank up to and including Lt. Colonel, several of whom were a decade or two older than I was.

There is little doubt that one of Patricia's attributes is the planning and executing of family moves, having moved to new locations, proceeding to adapt to new environments, new customs and in some cases virtually new cultures. This has been an absolute necessity during our married life. Our many moves, trans-national; trans-Atlantic; and trans-continental have only been possible because of this wonderful talent. I emphasize it because my personal contributions in these regards, to put it mildly, have been minimal.

The move from Hampton to Shrivenham provided a good trial run for what was to follow three short years later. To be separated from family, especially Patricia's and friends such as the Lees with whom we had endured so many exciting and at times life-threatening occasions during the war, was a real wrench. Needless to add, and there have been many during the past half-century, several farewell parties were organized to wish us "God-speed."

On the domestic front I should mention the enthusiastic assistance of two German prisoners of war. During the couple of years prior to their return to Germany they had painted the house, performed miracles in the garden and helped make our move almost a pleasurable experience. Gunther and Wilhelm were real assets.

Our first winter in Shrivenham was one of the coldest on record, temperatures dipping below freezing every night. English houses are not designed for these kinds of conditions; most of the plumbing is on the outer wall of the building. You can imagine the problems which everyone experienced with freezing water pipes. Then, later, when the weather warmed up and the pipes thawed, pipes were bursting and homes flooding. Everyone living at the Military College of Science experienced this problem, with water bringing down ceilings and spoiling carpets and furniture.

Fortunately, we were one of the few that did not experience such problems in our home, the reason being that every night during the freezing weather, Patricia and I drained all of the 20 water faucets in the house. This was a long, cold job, and necessitated my being outside where the main water valve was located. Each tap had to be drained singly and this we accomplished between us with a lot of running to and fro turning on and off taps as they emptied. But it was well worth the effort as we were spared the damage experienced by our friends and neighbors. The first few months at the College were eventful. While Patricia was busy furnishing our new home, planning the resuscitation of a much neglected garden, exploring the shops and facilities, I was familiarizing myself with the three departments which comprised my Faculty — Electrical Engineering under Kenneth Hayes; Radar and Telecommunications under Alan Lee; and Mechanical and Optical Instruments under Willie Coutts, who had 40 years of distinguished service to the College and was due to retire at the end of the year.

Until four months previously the whole faculty incorporating at least a dozen sophisticated laboratories had been located almost 200 miles away and through the dedication and expertise of these my future colleagues, literally tons of electrical, electronic and optical equipment and stores had been relocated and were now operational in Shrivenham.

A horticultural episode of epic proportions is worthy of special mention: it is unique certainly in our experience. Early in the spring of 1947 after one of the most severe winters of the century, Gunther and Wilhelm, to whom reference has been made previously, came up with a scheme to completely resuscitate our back garden. This would be their "swan song" as they were due for repatriation to Germany within a week or two.

Would I sign a requisition form giving them permission to drive an Army truck to a specific location and to obtain a load of granular fertilizer? Without inquiring too deeply into the proposal, I agreed. At that time the P.O.W.s were given all kinds of privileges — a few of them even returned to Germany with English brides!

Apparently our two German friends had located a sewage lagoon, which had not been used for about a century, in a field adjoining an abandoned farmhouse some 10 miles away. The residual material had decomposed and dried out during the decades until it approximated a dry granular black loom — it was completely odorless.

The following day a loaded truck was driven to our residence and the loam was taken by wheel barrel to the garden and spread more or less evenly to a depth of about two inches all over it. At the time, we were in the early stages of cultivation of the garden and except for a few fruit bushes and trees, it was fallow land. Neither Patricia, (pregnant with John), nor I, fully occupied with academic and administrative affairs, had much time for the garden. Even if we had our efforts would have been abortive, for within a few weeks the garden blossomed with tomato plants.[14] The subsequent crop was incredible — we supplied all our

---

[14]The "loam" contained a multitude of tomato seeds which had been dormant for at least 100 years. They provided evidence that tomatoes had been a prominent component in the diet of the farmers who lived in the early 19th century.

neighbors with tomatoes for several weeks. But the response of the fruit bushes to such nourishment was even more spectacular. In particular, the black currants were the size of grapes and we were persuaded to exhibit them at the annual Royal Swindon Agricultural Show during the fall of 1947. They won first price.

The Professorship of Instrument Technology was a newly established chair and I volunteered to give an inaugural lecture. It was the first of the three new chairs I have in fact inaugurated. I gave the lecture during the evening of May 1, 1947 in the main lecture hall of the College, and in attendance were the Commandant, Directors of Study, Faculty members and Army officers enrolled as students of the college. Patricia, almost six months pregnant with John, also attended. My title was "Closed Loop Systems — An Important Fundamental Concept." I illustrated the lecture with lantern slides. My main purpose was to stress the commonality of scientific and engineering principles in military and civilian enterprises. Incidentally I have always found military audiences to be extremely receptive and this was no exception — indeed I enjoyed myself and so did they.

After the lecture, the Commandant hosted a small cocktail party in Beckett Hall, officers' mess, which was the focal point for all social activities. Occasionally, especially during visits of V.I.P's to the College, mess dinners were formal with a military band playing background music. Invariably we were piped into dinner. What a thrill that was!

I was thankful that my white tie and tails, which had been so essential during my Commonwealth Fellowship years, still fit. But Patricia was not quite so fortunate because war time clothes rationing virtually eliminated the availability of formal evening gowns. However, as a talented seamstress and a wizard with a sewing machine (accomplishments which have served us well during the past 60 years) she improvised and fabricated several spectacular creations.

My academic career up to the M.C. of S. had been completely research-oriented both at Manchester and MIT. Not surprisingly I found myself at Shrivenham a full professor with some, albeit minimal, teaching commitments. For the first time in my life, I was required to give lectures to a class. However, four lectures a week to the TSO course on the Theory and Practice of Automatic Control Systems and Introduction to Analog Computers was by no means a heavy teaching load. Even so it took me a few weeks to become acclimatized to wearing an academic gown and being saluted by students and uniformed staff, and also to standing in front of a chalk board facing a class of some 60

Army officers with the rank of major and above. Fortunately, the class President, Jake Eaman, a full Colonel in the Canadian Army with a distinguished war-time service record, was a very sympathetic individual and we got along famously.

Apart from administrative chores during my first year, I devoted a great deal of time establishing two laboratories in the Mechanical and Optical Instruments Department — the Mathematical Machines Laboratory to demonstrate how various instruments could be used to solve mathematical problems and the Human Factors Laboratory for the investigations of human performance in the operation of military instruments. In light of my long love affair with the differential analyzer, I decided that one of the principal machines should be a model differential analyzer. Accordingly, with major assists from students and technical staff, I supervised the building of a four integrator machine. It was a greatly refined and somewhat larger version of the original Manchester d.a. Indeed I believe it was the largest of at least half a dozen to my certain knowledge of Meccano machines of its kind ever built. It turned out to be very popular with the students, essentially because it provided insights into the physical significance of differential equations as well as providing a useful tool in obtaining approximate solutions to problems that arise in military science, notably ballistics.

Of the "inner circle" of teachers, colleagues and friends who have greatly influenced my career, only one was associated with the College. Graham Sutton (later Sir Graham) had succeeded Sir John Cockroft in 1945 as senior superintendent of ADRDE, one of the most senior scientific appointments in government service, and it was a very pleasant surprise when it was announced in early 1947 that he had been appointed Bashforth Professor of Mathematical Physics (the only named chair in the College) and head of the Faculty. Graham Sutton, a distinguished micrometeorologist who was ultimately appointed Director-General of the Meteorological Office, became the "de facto" leader in the academic community. About the same time as the Sutton appointment, Professor C. H. Landers, professor emeritus of Civil Engineering at Imperial College, London, was appointed Dean of the College. Landers was essentially the senior statesman in the College and provided a close tie to the University of London. In view of the fact that there were a few "prima-donnas" in our midst (I was probably one of them!) the Dean showed considerable wisdom in handling some of the tricky relationships between senior military and senior academics. He was essentially the main conduit between the Commandant and the Faculty.

While over the years the College and its predecessors, especially Woolwich, had been responsible for some research and development, notably in ordinance and ballistics, this was not a high priority. In other words, our "ultimate masters" at the War Office were, not surprisingly, much more concerned with the education of our officer students than with research activities at the College. In this regard our philosophy differed appreciably from that of the universities and within a month or two of my taking up my appointment, I was on the lookout for research potential. But the majority of the students were "career officers" with the ultimate goal of receiving senior rank and research was not an option. However there were a few officers on short-term commissions whose career prospects were oriented toward business and industry. One of these was Major Frank Stoneman of the Royal Electrical and Mechanical Engineers (coincidently my brother Ronald retired from the Army at the end of the war with the same rank and regiment.) Major Stoneman expressed considerable interest in undertaking a research project, perhaps leading to a graduate degree of the University of London. Furthermore I had the germ of an idea for the project. Since leaving MIT, my thoughts had turned frequently to the "function unit." Before leaving I had obtained a provisional design, but always considered that there was a more general solution to the problem. Because of its novelty, it was an ideal topic for a dissertation, perhaps even at Ph.D level, especially since radar technology had developed so rapidly during the war. For example the original function unit converted tabulated information (digital) into graphical data (analog) and the graphs were fed automatically into the differential analyzer network, which corresponded to the mechanical bus-bar network of the original differential analyzer. However, there was a complementary problem which arose in connection with the Pulse Position Indicator (PPI) radar displays developed for airport air traffic control systems and hence in the process of digital-analog data conversion. (In simple terms the requirement is to plot graphs through the radar echo points on the display.) As well, there was the complementary, albeit straightforward problem of analog-digital conversion.

If a general solution to the problem could be developed it would have wide-spread application. This was Frank Stoneman's thesis topic!

When I sought official approval for the program, in effect a double graduate degree which I proposed for Stoneman, the Dean was somewhat incredulous. The TSO Course itself was a full-time two-year program with final examinations in six subjects (military and civilian), and a PhD normally required at least two and usually three years of study and research. Never before in the history of the College had such a feat been accomplished. Nor, as far as I know, has been accomplished since.

In retrospect I feel Frank Stoneman's graduating near the top of his TSO Class and obtaining the Ph.D degree of the University of London concurrently to be one of the most meritorious achievements by a student I have experienced throughout my career. I will not go into specific details concerning the research except to say that a paper was accepted and published in the *Proceedings of the Institute of Electrical Engineers* entitled "A New Approach to the Design of Pulse-Monitored Servo Systems" in October 1950. It provoked a lengthy discussion when it was presented. Of special interest as well is the fact that the book, *Digital Processes for Sampled Data Systems* by Alfred J. Monroe, a member of the Technical Staff, Space Technology Laboratories, Los Angeles, California, and published by John Wiley and Sons in 1962 included virtually two full chapters on the Porter-Stoneman Data-Extrapolation Methods.

August 5, 1947 was a memorable date. Our son, John Arthur Harris was born at 8:45 p.m. at the Radcliffe Infirmary, Oxford. The city of Oxford, seat of one of the oldest and best known universities in the world, is about 30 minutes drive from Shrivenham. Our 1938 Vauxhall car, which I'd purchased in October, 1946, (cars were very scarce at the time) in spite of a 12-inch crack in the engine block did the trip in record time, about 40 minutes arriving at 6:30 p.m. We did not have too much time to spare. My return drive was anti-climactic, the universal joint (i.e. Hardy Spicer) completely disintegrated. If it had happened on the outward journey, we would most certainly have had a serious problem, not least due to the fact that the road was not heavily traveled at the time. I was fortunate to be rescued by an Army vehicle and taken home, while the College workshops looked after the Vauxhall. The anxiously awaited telephone call came at 9 p.m. announcing the birth of our son. "Mother and son doing very well!" I visited Patricia and John early on August 6.

Patricia and John, accompanied by a wonderful nurse, Sister Wade, returned to Shrivenham on August 15. I drove them in the newly repaired Vauxhall. Sister Wade stayed with us at 1 Park Avenue until September 5 by which time the nursing mother and her baby and a very proud father were thriving. The baptism of John took place in the ancient Shrivenham Parish Church on the 1st of November. It was quite an occasion. John's Godfathers were my brother Ronald, Patricia's brother John, and our good friend Ted Lee. Patricia's sister Carol was Godmother. The organ was played by Colonel H.M. Patterson.

In the meanwhile during the summer of 1947 I was busy developing the new laboratories and in parallel a course of lectures for the second year TSO Course. It was intended not only as a "primer" on servomechanisms for army officers, but I also had a much broader audience in mind because at the time, although many scientific and engineering articles had been published, no textbook on the subject existed. The fundamental concept of feedback underpins so many disciplines for example, electronics, engineering, biology, medicine, psychology and economics to name the most obvious. The servomechanism can be regarded as a paradigm for all of them. In contrast to most control systems, it can be readily visualized as an automatic position control system which is actuated by the difference between actual and desired behavior (i.e. it is "error-actuated"), which is power-amplifying, and excellent for educational purposes. My ultimate objective, therefore, was to prepare a course of lectures and to expand them in to a textbook. The latter was in fact first published as a Methuen Monograph with the title "An Introduction to Servomechanisms," in December 1950. It must have achieved a degree of popularity because a second edition was published in November, 1952, reprinted twice and was finally published in revised form in 1961.

Because of its being the first of its kind in the British Commonwealth and in the western world, the College soon attracted a plethora of V.I.P.s. On these occasions, the Commandant and Dean acted as host and the faculty showed the guests some of the laboratories and, with the help of a small group of students and staff, managed to convey the aims and ideals of the College. The visits usually concluded with a lunch or dinner in the Officers' Mess. The most memorable visits were those of Prime Minister Clement Attlee; Minister of Defense Emmanuel Shinwell; Admiral Lord Mountbatten; Field Marshal Harding, the Chief of the Imperial General Staff (CIGS). Some of these encounters have had interesting sequels subsequently, notably Lord Mountbatten's visit. As well I paid an interesting visit to Lord Cherwell at the Clarendon Laboratory, Oxford University during September, 1946. Formerly Professor Frederick Lindermann, he had been Winston Churchill's close friend and confidante during WWII. I was especially interested to learn that he had had several meetings with Vannevar Bush.

In setting up the manual tracking (ergonomics) laboratory I sought the advice of several members of the original Manual Tracking Panel, in particular Dr.Hicks, a member of the Medical Research Council in the

University of Cambridge. A visit to the university in April 1947 proved more informative, and in some respects historical, than I had anticipated. Hicks and I were discussing some aspects of position control when quite suddenly the door of his office was opened and in walked none other than Professor Norbert Wiener, Professor of Mathematics at MIT who I had not seen since 1939. Surprisingly he recognized me and then, ignoring the nicety of being introduced, took off his jacket, hung it on a chair, walked to the chalk board and said "what do you think of this?" Whereupon for at least 30 minutes he promenaded up and down in front of the board and proceeded to outline a new approach to the general theory of control. The board was filled with a proliferation of mathematical formulas. Both Hicks and I were rather mystified until Wiener summed up his "off-the-cuff" lecture in a few cogent conclusions and then announced that he had fashioned the word "cybernetics" to describe "control and communication in the animal and the machine."[15] I like to think on that day Norbert Wiener raised the curtain for Hicks and me on a new philosophy and technology which within the course of a few decades would have a profound impact on civilization -e.g. "the internet" and "cyberspace."

A few weeks subsequently, Patricia, John and I drove about 250 miles north from Shrivenham to Birkrigg. The main purpose of the trip was to introduce John to his grandparents. He was their first grandson — it was an exciting occasion.

Just prior to the trip I sought the advice of Bob Pattenden, the acknowledged authority on motor vehicles in the College, regarding the 12-inch crack in the engine block. Leakage of engine oil into the radiator had become increasingly serious. I had tried several commercially available treatments, e.g. "Wonder Weld," without success and I was rather apprehensive about a long drive, especially with Patricia and John on board.

Bob proceeded to hoist the engine block out of the Vauxhall and as a last resort; so to speak, he packed a compound of white lead into the crack. After hardening it should prevent further leakages, he reasoned.

The drive was uneventful until we pulled into a service station to fill up with gasoline. With a worried expression on his face, the attendant came over and said "there's a milk-like fluid leaking from the bottom of your engine — I've never seen the likes of it before!" Neither had I! But I surmised correctly that the white lead seal had been compromised and

---

[15]Cybernetics by Norbert Wiener, published by John Wiley in 1948. It was the definitive text. Today the term has been applied widely e.g. cyber-space.

could not stand the heat of the engine. We managed to complete the journey albeit at a reduced speed.

My parents who lived a very quiet life on the outskirts of Birkrigg Common were delighted to see us and made a great fuss of Patricia and their first grandson. Because rationing was still in full force, my father had installed a greenhouse in the backyard — succulent vegetables, a rabbit pie and mother's glorious pastries greeted us. We were ready for them after our lengthy and adventuresome journey. Patricia was in her element because she always had a great deal of affection for my parents and she enjoyed every minute of our one-week stay.

Needless to say my father was very intrigued with the Vauxhall. He couldn't understand how his son had bought such a "lemon." I told him that there was little choice in those days because of the scarcity of cars for sale. With his usual intuitive approach to such problems as the cracked engine block, he announced- "Oatmeal is the answer. One tablespoon in the radiator should fix it," and it did! When a small amount of oatmeal porridge is dropped on a very hot stove plate it takes literally a hammer and chisels to remove. In the case of the cracked cylinder block, when the fragments of oatmeal permeate into the crack they are trapped and in aggregate, when the engine is hot, create a perfect weld. Much relieved, we drove back to Shrivenham and shortly after our arrival, I telephoned Bob Pattenden to update him on the state of the Vauxhall. Thereafter, for 18 months until the car was sold, it ran perfectly and the crack was permanently sealed.

At the College there was increasing interest in digital computers. The development of machines incorporating novel concepts, notably the Williams' Memory based on storing digital information on the display surface of cathode ray tubes was, proceeding at the University of Manchester and at Cambridge. Maurice Wilkes using mercury delay line memory systems had virtually completed the EDSAC in May 1949. As well, Alan Turing, who had anticipated the modern digital computer in 1936 when the "Universal Turing Machine" was first conceived, having joined the NPL shortly after I left, had started work on the Automatic Computing Engine (ACE) computer. It is well established, of course, that Turing's seminal paper set out the whole philosophy of the modern computer. Accordingly, when it was announced that Turing would give a course of 10 lectures on computer development, I responded immediately. The location was the Dollis Hill Laboratories of the British Post Office. This location was chosen because during WWII Dollis Hill had collaborated with Bletchley Park on code-breaking.

It is by no means well known that Turing's work on breaking the ENIGMA Code was greatly facilitated by "Colossus" the world's first large-scale electronic digital computer designed by Tommy Flowers of Dollis Hill. There were only five participants.

In spite of his brilliance, or perhaps because of it, Turing was not a good lecturer — he assumed that his "pupils" were as bright as he was! Furthermore, the design of a delay-line memory system-based computer was logically complex and not easy to explain. But the great virtue of the lectures was that I had the opportunity to get to know Turing. It is not surprising that several books have been written about the life of this incredible genius. For example, with the exception of John Nash, of "The Beautiful Mind" fame, Turing is the only other mathematician I've heard of about whom a Broadway play and a film have been produced.

But as well as his intellectual achievements, Turing was an outstanding athlete who ran the mile in little more than four minutes and was one of Roger Bannister's (first man to run a four-minute mile) running mates. A delightful feature of Turing's personality was the way in which he ignored conventions. Let me summarize two incidents. When the NPL Account's Department refused to accept his claims for taxi fares from Teddington to Dollis Hill and return (public transport by train, underground, bus and foot took about two hours and Turing was unwilling to sacrifice so much time) he donned his running attire and ran the 10 miles in about an hour. Arriving at the seminar room, he calmly donned slacks and a sweatshirt and proceeded with the seminar. A second example of his non-conventionality related to the design of delay-line memories. They were notoriously difficult to operate and maintain and mercury was a very unpleasant, indeed toxic, material to handle. An alternative suggested by Turing was "gin," essentially a mixture of alcohol and water, which appeared to have some of the desired properties. Whether or not it was ever tried, I don't know.

A few years later I was profoundly shocked to hear of Turing's untimely death at the age of 42. He was an intellectual giant.

Of the many memories of family at Shrivenham that I treasure, one deserves special mention. Ever since the age of a few months John, encouraged by his mother, has been fascinated by four-wheeled vehicles. Even before he walked, the sound of traffic on the country road, adjacent to our home, stimulated his interest and Patricia on countless occasions picked him up and carried him to the window to see what was going on. He quickly identified the characteristic sound of farm tractors and one in particular. It belonged to a local farmer called Knapp. I still recall the shriek of pure delight when aged about 18 months, John toddled toward the window of our living room and announced "Old Knapp's tractor." Together with his model cars and trains, this daily ritual triggered John's life-long hobby, the motor car, especially the antique motor car. His present collection of four antique Bentley cars which he conditions and drives in rallies as far distant as South Africa and New Zealand attest to this passion.

It was essentially through my friendship with Fred Williams and my Servo Panel activities, that I met Eric Grundy and became associated, albeit in an honorary capacity, with the electronics and electrical engineering company — Ferranti Limited. Eric was a director of the company. Patricia and I became close friends of Eva and Eric Grundy and enjoyed many dinners both formal and informal at some of London's most renowned restaurants, notably the Savoy Grill, the Ivy and the Dorchester.

Occasionally, Eric with his chauffeured car would pick me up at the College and we would drive to the Moston Plant near Manchester. These visits were extremely beneficial in so far as I was kept up to date in several branches of electronics, notably radar, digital computers and telecommunications. (In those days, Ferranti was a major government defense contractor.) Not infrequently I was supplied on "permanent loan" with a variety of technological marvels for my new laboratories in the College.

The most memorable of my visits to Moston was that of March, 1949. During the drive from the College, Grundy informed me that the company was in the process of establishing a research department as a component of their Canadian subsidiary — Ferranti Electric Limited in Toronto. Apparently, a few months previously a nucleus group of four Ferranti engineers, headed by Kenyon Taylor, whom I had known when we were fellow students at Manchester, and with whom I had had several contacts during the war, had obtained a Canadian government contract to explore the potential of digital data communications. Several young Canadian graduates in engineering physics had been recruited. There was considerable interest in expanding the group because the Defense Research Board (DRB) in Ottawa was anxious to build up a viable electronics industry in Canada. Of considerable interest moreover to me personally was the fact that Dr. Omond Solandt had been appointed chairman of the DRB. Our paths had crossed on many occasions and he was to become a close friend and advisor.

Grundy advised me that the future of the Canadian Research

Division was to be one of the topics the chairman, Sir Vincent Ferranti, wished to discuss with me. Furthermore, since it was improbable that Taylor would remain in Canada for more than a few months, a pertinent question was — who would I recommend to permanently head the new department? Did I have any ideas?

After my wonderful experiences in the United States during 1937-39, I was always conscious of a desire at some future time to live and work in America. Perhaps this was an opportunity to "get my foot in the door." Here was a challenge — a new wonderland to explore.

Impetuosity has always been one of my weaknesses and I must confess where my career has been concerned, selfishness. Literally on the spur of the moment after no more than a few minutes thought I made the fateful utterance, "Eric, I'll go!" Whereupon, Grundy said with alacrity — "Are you serious?" And we took it from there.

I will not go into details of the discussions I had during dinner with Sir Vincent except to say that he was pleased to hear that there was a good chance of my joining the company. He indicated that if I did, the salary would be generous, and it was. How to break the news to Patricia was my real concern. If she had balked at the prospect of leaving family, friends and country, and setting up home with our two-year-old son in far-off Canada, I am sure that I would not have formally accepted the job offer. But after expressing surprise, and a little shock, she agreed with virtually no reservations to what was to prove one of the two most dramatic moves of our lives.

Because I had already sampled and enjoyed life in North America, I was fully aware of the magnitude of the risks and potential benefits of the move. But for Patricia, still in her 20s, with a two-year-old baby, it must have been a daunting prospect. However, and the pattern has been repeated again and again during the past half century and more, she rose to the occasion with courage and devotion knowing full well that she would bear the brunt of the travails and uncertainties which confronted us. But in retrospect, we both feel that we made the right decision.

Let me try to assess the risks and benefits associated with the decision we were making. On one hand we would exchange a high security — both salary and pension wise — and high prestige job for one with an uncertain future in a foreign country. Close family ties and friendships would inevitably suffer; there would be the trauma of leaving Britain and establishing a home 3000 miles away. On the other hand I would have an opportunity to gain industrial experience in an organization which I admired and had the benefit of cordial relations with the chief executive and top management. The challenge of the burgeoning field of electronic technology, especially digital data communications and storage appealed. By no means inconsequential was the financial incentive. An unforeseeable wonderland beckoned. The decision to take the plunge was justified.

Fortunately, largely through the good offices of Graham Sutton, whose support and advice throughout my tenure at the Military College of Science was invaluable, I was spared the possibility of a less than friendly departure from the College. Indeed, the Commandant, Board of Studies and members of the Faculty of Instrument Technology, were most gracious in their acceptance of my resignation and in wishing myself and family well for our future in Toronto.

Chapter 8

AN INDUSTRIAL INTERLUDE

THE wonderland of Canada, and it is a wonderland in every sense of the word, beckoned, and largely due to Patricia's expertise in packing and managing, we were all set to leave Shrivenham at the end of August, 1949. We had had three wonderful years at the College, made many friends, and I had launched a few enterprises. Perhaps my brief tenure was a little too brief, but I had the satisfaction of knowing I would be succeeded by an excellent man. Professor Holt Smith, a close friend and former colleague of Fred Williams, had been a senior scientist at the Telecommunication Research Establishment (TRE), Malvern. As well, his appointment ensured the continuation of the liaison with the University of Manchester of which he was a graduate and with the Ferranti Company.

We were "seen" off in grand style by Eric and Eva Grundy, who hosted a farewell dinner for us at the Midland Hotel, Manchester. Patricia recalls that sitting at an adjacent table was Ivor Novello, the impresario who was launching a new show — she had been an admirer of his from her teens. The following morning the Grundys drove us to the Liverpool docks — homeland of the Beatles — for embarkation on the Canada Pacific Railroad Liner, the Empress of France. John, aged two, was fascinated by the whole procedure.

Within a day or two of sailing for Montreal on September 2, 1949, we discovered two former Commonwealth Fund Fellows and their families were also aboard. Richard Flood, a CFF at University of Chicago, 1936-38, Phyllis, his wife, and daughter, Betsy, became good friends. Maurice Lister CFF at Harvard 1938-40, traveling with his wife, Lois and family would be a colleague during my tenure at the University of Toronto. This was a remarkable coincidence especially since all three of us were headed toward Toronto. During the voyage, Betsy Flood, a few years older than John, became a constant companion of our son, and thereby helped in the transition phase we were enduring.

We were not so fortunate in Montreal on the Friday of our arrival. By the time we had completed immigration procedures we were too late to obtain the morning train for Toronto, and this meant spending about six hours in the city. By English standards it was hot, in the 80s and not knowing anybody or anything about the city, we had a tiring first day in Canada.

We boarded the Toronto train at 3 p.m. for the six hour journey and had two club car chairs, which was not an ideal way to travel for two adults and an active two-year-old! Not surprisingly, all the excitement of a day that had begun at 6 a.m. completely disorganized John's normal sleep patterns and he persisted in staying awake until we were within a few miles of Toronto.

While Patricia struggled with our baggage and eventually obtained a Red Cap, I carried John the not inconsiderable distance from the Union Station platform through the tunnel to the lobby of the Royal York Hotel.

We were met by Dr. John M. Thomson, president of Ferranti Electric and his wife, and given a very warm welcome. Unfortunately, however, our arrival had coincided with the opening of the Canadian National Exhibition, and the hotel was over-booked. After at least an hour, stuck in that crowded lobby, we were finally conducted to a small conference room — about 30 feet by 20 feet — that reeked of tobacco smoke with no beds! It was virtually midnight before two folding beds and a cot were assembled in a room in which there were no mirrors, no drawers, only a long conference table and chairs. Completely exhausted we slept and in the morning we were transferred to a room on the ninth floor of the hotel facing Lake Ontario.

The nightmarish quality of our first two days in Canada was not ended. During the Saturday night there was a continuing cacophony of police and fire department sirens and whistles which disturbed our rest for several hours. We were too exhausted even to draw the drapes to find out what was going on. It's fortunate that we remained ignorant until the morning. It was the night of the SS Noronic fire. The vessel, a Great Lakes passenger steamer, was fully loaded with more than 300 passengers when it caught on fire. It was docked about 200 yards from the hotel on Lake Ontario and in spite of being so close to shore, there were more than 100 fatalities.

The following morning I went down to the lobby early to obtain a newspaper. The lobby had been converted into a temporary hospital facility with at least 20 beds and several doctors and nurses in attendance. It was a shocking unforgettable sight. I contrived to have our breakfast delivered to our room so that Patricia and John would be spared from yet another unpleasant experience. Patricia must have thought — "what on earth have I let myself in for!"

Before reporting for work I tried to locate a suitable residence. This proved extremely difficult. After two weeks stay in the hotel, which was by no means a pleasant experience for Patricia and John, we were desperate.

Because my new job took up so much of my time and because Patricia could not possibly participate in hunting for accommodation, we were reduced to taking anything that was available. As a result, we ended up sharing a small apartment on St.Clair Avenue, a very busy city thoroughfare with a not very friendly landlady; another dreadful experience which lasted three weeks. Then we were rescued by the head of Ferranti's X-Ray Department, who obtained accommodation for us in Nanton Court, Rosedale, one of Toronto's most desirable residential areas and one with which we would become very familiar a few years down the road. We shared a small apartment with a delightful widow who worked at the Canadian Red Cross. Nanton Court, albeit not ideal because it was so isolated and not much fun for Patricia and John especially after the joy of living in Shrivenham, was nevertheless much superior to living on St. Clair Avenue.

In the meanwhile, through the good offices of a Toronto lawyer whom I met in an elevator in the Royal York Hotel, we were fortunate to reserve an apartment which would be ready for occupancy early in February, 1950. It was Bayview Court, Sheppard Avenue in northern Toronto.

A few words about the Ferranti organization may not be out of place. Founded by Dr. Sebastian Ferranti, an immigrant to Britain from Italy, during the 1870s, the company specialized in the design and production of electric power transformers and kilowatt-hour meters. It is worth noting that during the 1880's Ferranti designed and developed the world's first alternating current electric power station at Deptford near London. Incidentally, about the same time Edison built an electric power station in New York City which generated direct current electricity. The advantages of alternating current soon emerged.

The company grew rapidly due to electrification in Britain and abroad and they established headquarters in Lancashire. Appreciable expansion of the company occurred during both World Wars I and II and it became a prime government contractor for electrical research. Most importantly the idea of building a complementary research department in Canada was appealing.

My first few weeks at Mount Dennis were essentially a familiarization. I was certainly impressed with the work of Kenyon Taylor in laying the foundations of the research department. It was already well established with a total staff of a dozen engineers and technicians. Furthermore, it was gratifying that John Thomson, an electrical power engineer was content to give us a free hand.

Prior to my arrival a small government contract had been obtained. It was for the development of a digital data transmission channel between Toronto and Ottawa and ancillary terminal equipment. Because my personal experience was in mechanical analog computers (i.e. the d.a.), this new field was indeed a quantum jump. I must confess, largely because of my skepticism regarding the lack of reliability of large scale electronic systems, that it took at least a month before I was finally convinced that digital communications and data processing, rather than analog, were the more promising for the future. I spent quite a few hours studying the basics of such concepts as pulse — code — modulation and electronic digital switching. In this regard I was fortunate to have shared an office a decade previously with Claude Shannon whose seminal work on information theory had contributed so much to modern communications technology. Accordingly, although I did not expect to be involved in the detailed design of specific systems, at least I understood the basic principles.

As head of the department my responsibilities involved such activities as contract acquisition and negotiation, budgeting, recruitment of professional staff, and by no means least, sales. Research and development of the kind we contemplated were novel activities in Canada at the time and needed selling! New skills had to be acquired and applied; a salutary experience; for me a change in philosophy from that to which I had become accustomed as an academic.

I cannot praise too highly the small team Kenyon Taylor had assembled. Kenyon himself was a phenomenon, one of the most creative people I've ever encountered. He had a Faraday-like approach to problems — practical rather than theoretical. It's not surprising that after spending a year in university, he was "bored stiff" and quit before graduating.

Married at an early age to Maggie, who after the birth of their second son contracted polio and for the rest of her life was confined to a wheelchair, Kenyon designed and built a mechanical and electrical conveyance system whereby she could carry out normal household chores. She was probably the most remarkable woman I have ever known. Kenyon Taylor was in his element in the laboratory with a soldering iron, a few circuit boards and a cathode ray tube. Novel circuits and technologies were contrived within days, not months as might be expected. This unique ability inspired the four original graduates in engineering and radio physics from local universities — Tom Cranston, Les Wood, Gordon Lang and David Nuttall, who had been hired. Most importantly they were all "veterans" of the Canadian Armed Services having served during WWII and having attended Canadian universities subsequently under a G.I Bill similar to the United States. Together with John Harben, a former Ferranti employee who had immigrated with Kenyon Taylor, they were the nucleus of what was to become within four years a powerful R&D group numbering about 120 people (physicists, engineers, technicians and office staff).

The original plan, approved by Sir Vincent and the Board, was for Taylor to be "on loan" from the parent company for a year and then to return to the U.K. However, during my first few months we "hit it off" so well that with the approval of the parent company, he agreed to stay as deputy head and chief engineer. I breathed a sigh of relief because for me it was unthinkable to carry on without him. I should add, in parentheses, that he was not only a brilliant inventor, but as well a very talented musician. He played the piano extremely well, both classical and popular music, and could play with varying degrees of competence, the violin, clarinet and flute. To my certain knowledge because I was a member of the cast of "The Shrove Rag Review," 1934 at the Manchester Opera House, Kenyon composed all the music including the theme song which was published "She's my Sugar." As well, he designed and built a honky-tonk piano.

His athletic prowess on the golf course, tennis court and even cricket field, was the envy of all his friends. Not surprisingly the Taylor boys, Martin and Vincent, are equally talented.

The Taylor family embraced Patricia and John and me as virtually members of their family and it is a truism to say that without their help and encouragement, especially during the first few months of our sojourn in Toronto, our lives would have been far less pleasant.

I soon learned that, although Omond Solandt, chairman of the Defense Research Board, had been responsible originally for interesting

Ferranti Electric in the possibility of undertaking R&D in electronics technology, it was in fact a young officer in the Royal Canadian Navy, Lt. Jim Belyea, who provided the necessary impetus and most importantly financial support. It was he, for example, who drew up the original contract referred to previously.

About a month after my arrival, Jim Belyea, who was based in Ottawa spent a couple of days discussing his ideas for the next phase of the contract. He outlined what he considered to be the future needs of the RCN in information communications and processing. I learned, for example, that the RCN's major role in defense would effectively be in convoy protection. This was logical in light of the fact that the RCN had contributed greatly to the protection of the Atlantic convoys during WWII. But with major developments in centi-metric radar and sonar submarine detecting equipment in hand, Belyea envisioned radical changes in both inter-and intra — ship communications and information processing.

I was tremendously impressed with Jim Belyea. His ideas predicated on digital rather than analog systems (and if I had any lingering doubts on the superiority of the former before Belyea, they were quickly dispelled after our first meeting) would revolutionize Naval warfare. As it transpired a few years down the road, Belyea's basic idea of sharing precise real time radar and sonar data between all ships in a convoy, compensating for ship movement and distinguishing between friendly and enemy ships was years ahead of its time. Indeed, it was a quantum jump into the future and although I am by no means up to date at the time of writing (September, 2002) I am virtually certain that all modern naval task forces basically incorporate the Belyea concepts. I am proud to feel that I had the privilege of knowing Jim and benefiting from his genius. Most importantly, Kenyon Taylor and Jim complemented each other perfectly.

A primary requirement in implementing Jim Belyea's ideas was to demonstrate the efficacy of digital data transmission over comparatively long distances. An experimental radio link was set up with the transmitter at Mount Dennis and the receiver in the electrical laboratories of the RCN Ottawa. I don't recall technical details, not even the carrier frequency, of this first digital data transmission except that it was based on "pulsed code modulation (PCM)[16] of a carrier signal with various

---

[16]The technology has virtually exploded during the past half-century. The internet, digital television, satellite communications, etc., are all predicated on digital data transmission.

levels of noise superimposed. John Harben and I traveled to Ottawa in early December, 1949 to see the demonstration. Because Patricia and our son John had been confined to a small apartment for so long, they joined us. To keep Patricia company, Joy Harben came as well. I recall vividly our reaction, eyes glued to a cathode ray tube, when at the stroke of 3 p.m. the pulses slowly traversed the base line. Even when the "signal to noise ratio" was diminished markedly, the signal came through loud and clear. The first digital data link of its kind in Canada and one of the first in the world. It was essentially the success of this demonstration that encouraged DRB and Jim Belyea and "we were home to the races." The proposed system was designated DATAR (Digital Automated Tracking and Remoting). With the successful testing of the digital data transmission and shortly thereafter the storage of digital data on a rotating magnetic drum (thereby providing 64 parallel channels of digital information) and the associated "write-in" and "read-out" units, the key components were available.

Shortly after our visit to Ottawa we received the very welcome news that the Bayview Apartment would be ready for occupancy early in February, 1950. Our first few months in Canada, in spite of the help of several friends, had not been propitious especially for Patricia and John. On occasions we even had misgivings about our move to Toronto. But after moving to our new apartment, furnishing it and meeting several new friends, the situation changed dramatically. Our new neighbors were Carl, a transport manager for the Shell Oil Company, and Gladys Patch and their three-year-old daughter, Casey, who were from our point of view a "gift from heaven." In a real sense their friendship especially John and Casey, was the key factor in our final integration into Canadian culture and society.

Everything took a turn for the better and the Canada winter, with an above average snow fall, proved to be a God send. Snowmen and toboggans were new experiences for the youngsters, shops were within easy reach and so was John's future school. Being on a golf course (as we are now 50 years later) we were ideally located. Even driving our new car, a British Austin, on the snow-covered and sometimes icy roads proved an exhilarating experience.

Nor did we lose contact with several British friends and colleagues. Indeed, the first visitor from Britain to stay with us at Bayview Court was my former colleague at the Military College of Science, Col. H.M Patterson on an official visit to Canada. It was gratifying as well to welcome John Shapland, son of the Commandant to our home, not least because it demonstrated that, in spite of my early departure from the College, good relations still existed.

Another very welcome visitor from the College was Graham Sutton with whom I had continued to maintain close contact. But the most welcome guests of all were Elaine and Douglas Hartree who stayed with us for several days. It was great to hear that they had settled down so successfully in Cambridge and that Douglas was enjoying his new Chair at the university.

Gradually my department burgeoned and the enthusiasm of the young Canadian engineers was remarkable. Rarely did they leave work at normal finishing time and frequently spent several hours on the job at weekends. One of my most important responsibilities was to interview and hire new staff. The original members of the team, under Kenyon Taylor's leadership, had already proved themselves well beyond my hopes and expectations, and we needed more of this high quality.

Although I do injustice to many, I have singled out for special mention, just one of the men I hired. Fred Longstaffe was one of the two most brilliant young geniuses I have identified during my career. (The other was Jack Cowan, to whom reference will be made subsequently.) Fred, who is unfortunately deceased, was absolutely superb in the design of both the hardware and software of digital technology. It is no exaggeration to say he anticipated by a few years the software developed by Bill Gates which gave birth to the giant conglomerate Microsoft Corporation. Together with Tom Cranston, he invented the so-called "track-ball," which in principle is identical to the modern computer "mouse." I shall have more to say about these developments later.

Suffice it to say that the group was at the cutting edge of electronic technology. New ideas and concepts were emerging almost weekly. The project was the largest, most complex system of its kind ever built in Canada. I reflect on the amazing fact that a team of fewer than 50 young engineers and scientists would complete within three years in modern terminology a miniature internet incorporating 30,000 vacuum tubes.

It was soon realized that a project of such magnitude was going to be expensive. But with the outbreak of the Korean War (1950-53), funds for national defense throughout the western world become more readily available. Consequently, I spent a goodly proportion of my time on essentially contract negotiations.

It was obvious by the beginning of 1951 that the space available at Mount Dennis was neither adequate nor appropriate for the program we had in mind. I capitalized on the contacts I had made during my numerous liaison visits to Ottawa, especially to DRB and the National Research Council (NRC) to seek advice regarding a new location for the department. In light of the fact that the prospective field trials of DATAR would be started within a year or at most two, it was essential to find laboratories on the shores of Lake Ontario where target vessels could be deployed.

Through my blossoming friendship with Omond Solandt I had been introduced to Dr. C.J. McKenzie, the president of NRC. This was an extremely important contact because. C.J. as he was affectionately called was soon to be recognized as the "grand old man" of Canadian science. The meeting was providential. Indeed it not only resulted in my department obtaining an ideal future location, but from my personal point of view it had a profound influence on my future career.

The location was the NRC Field Station on Scarboro Bluffs overlooking Lake Ontaria, about 30 miles from Mount Dennis. It was perfect from every point of view; ready access, radar sighting, and security.

It reflects very positively on the high morale of the team that by this time I regarded them as a group of friends as well as colleagues, so that in spite of transportation difficulties, (most of them lived in the vicinity of Mount Dennis) they welcomed the move enthusiastically. Laboratories and workshops were in full operation within a few days and DATAR proceeded "full steam ahead."

So much of their ability to get things done in record time stemmed from the incredible propensity of those young Canadian engineers (mechanical, electrical and electronic) to improvise. This attribute sprang in part from the fact that many of them had grown up on farms in rural Ontario where improvisation was essential. Without it, in my opinion DATAR would never have achieved what I regard as a virtual miracle.

Apart from the design of literally hundreds of electronic circuits and such imaginative creations as the "track-ball" and the magnetic digital storage drum to which I referred previously, the success of DATAR depended on two complementary developments.

From the start of the project it had been recognized that the reliability of the system would depend essentially on the performance of the electronic vacuum tubes. With literally tens of thousands of the latter in operation simultaneously it was obvious, on a probability basis, which several failures would occur each hour of the active life of the system. This was a critical issue because system breakdown during active operation at sea would be disastrous. The answer, by no means perfect, but which I regarded as optimum at the time, was in the architecture of the system.

Each panel of electronic switches (vacuum tube diodes) was regarded as a "page" in the overall system. Each page consisted of "paragraphs" and "lines" of equipment which could be monitored independently. In the event of a failure on a specific page, an indicator signal (both visual and auditory) on a control board would identify the page involved and correspondingly the monitor would identify the specific paragraph and line in which the failure had occurred. Furthermore, and I won't attempt to give details, through the magic of error-detecting codes the fault could be literally detected and corrected within seconds — an incredible achievement primarily the brainchild of John Harben and Kenyon Taylor.

The second problem also related to reliability, it concerned the comparatively high levels of interference or noise characteristic of shipboard radio links, because of the ubiquitous operation of electrical equipment. Another member of the original group, Gordon Lang, a graduate of the University of Western Ontario, handled the problem brilliantly. With my MIT and WWII experience, I at least understood the nature of the problem, and when Lang presented his findings I was intrigued but not entirely convinced by his proposed solution. In technical terms what he suggested was a radio-link predicated on "Octal-Based Pulse Position Modulation!" At the time this was a very novel concept. It was also a crucial requirement — the radio link must operate reliably under very undesirable conditions (i.e. low signal to noise ratios). Although I had great confidence in Lang's ability I felt that an independent assessment was justifiable. It is fascinating to recall that Lang, with perhaps minimal input from me, had based his conclusion on, at the time, the highly original and sophisticated "communications theory" of Claude Shannon, my office- mate at MIT. If Claude approved, I was confident that we would be OK. I telephoned Shannon, who I had not been in touch with for 13 years, then on the staff of the Bell Telephone Laboratories and set up a meeting in New York City. It was highly successful, not only from my personal point of view since we had been good friends, but also because he confirmed that Lang had produced an optimal solution to the problem. Shannon went on further to state that as far as he was aware, Lang was the first person to apply his theories to a specific problem.

With the design of most electronic circuits and mechanical components well in hand, I persuaded a reluctant Tom Cranston, one of

the original MKT. team to take on the demanding job of chief engineer
of the DATAR project. It was an inspired choice because Tom succeeded
brilliantly in pulling the loose ends together and completing the project.
In the meantime MKT was reaching beyond DATAR and dreaming up
plans for the future.

During the fall of 1952 a conference was held in Toronto to update
academic and industry leaders on recent developments in computers. Of
special interest to me was the University of Toronto FERUT computer,
the first commercially available machine to be installed in any university
outside Britain. The machine had been manufactured by Ferranti U.K.
and incorporated Fred Williams' electrostatic memory system. The
meeting gave me opportunity to meet some of the university people with
whom a decade in the future, I would have close associations. It was
particularly rewarding to meet Professors Willie Watson, head of the
Computer Department, Pat Hume, and Kelly Gotlieb. Our paths would
cross frequently in the future.

At the same meeting the Ferranti Company exhibited a small game-
playing machine which literally played a game of "tic-tac-toe" against a
human opponent. It never lost! One evening, I was prevailed upon to
give a short talk and demonstration of the machine. Attending the talk
was Dr. Gordon Shrum, then chairman of the Physics Department at
University of British Columbia (UBC). After the talk we had a
fascinating conversation. He was obviously intrigued by the potential of
the digital computer in the university. He wondered whether of not I
would be interested in an academic career at UBC. Incidentally what I
did not appreciate at the time was that Shrum was one of the most
respected physicists in western Canada. It transpired subsequently that he
had concluded after our talk that I would be a good candidate for the post
of Dean of the Faculty of Applied Science and Engineering at UBC.
With his usual enthusiastic approach to such matters he arranged for me
to meet members of the engineering faculty, give a lecture, meet
members of the Board of Governors and stay at the President's house on
the campus.

Everything went perfectly during the visit and my lecture was well
received. Gordon Shum had obviously given me quite a build-up because
my reception by the faculty could not have been more cordial. Dinner
with the Board of Governors also went off well. Indeed it seemed to be
taken for granted that I would be the new Dean of Engineering. There is
no doubt that if invited, with Patricia's approval, I'm certain that I would
have accepted. But there was a snag.

At breakfast on the final day of my visit, the President, Dr. MacKenzie expressed his pleasure on the success of my visit, but before making me a formal offer, he felt it advisable to speak with the chairman of each department of the faculty to obtain their approval. I'll never forget the look of chagrin on his face when he appeared for lunch. He was extremely apologetic because the Chairman of Geology had not only declined to support my nomination, but asserted that he personally was interested in the Dean's job. In the circumstances, the President felt obliged, and I agreed with him, to submit the name of this gentleman to the Board and he, the President, felt that they would approve. In retrospect it is interesting to recall that the Chairman of Geology was appointed Dean, but only served for about three years before taking a consulting job in the mining industry in South Africa. It is interesting to recall as well that his successor as Dean was David Myers, the Australian graduate student with whom I had collaborated at Manchester several years previously and co-authored a paper. On my return to Toronto, I'm quite sure that although in the event of my being offered the Deanship Patricia would have agreed to go to Vancouver, she was at the time relieved that another major move was not in the offing. But a minor move was. Because with John's education in mind, Patricia and I concluded that it would be desirable for us to reside in the reasonably close vicinity of a good school.

Accordingly in April, 1953 we purchased a delightful ranch bungalow in one of the most pleasant suburbs of Toronto with a large lot and only about three hundred yards from Harrison Road School. It was also convenient for commuting to Mt. Dennis and our recently established laboratories at Scarboro Bluffs, because a major east-west highway (Highway 401) had recently been opened and thereby reduced my travel time to less than 30 minutes to each location.

Preparation for the major DATAR prototype demonstrations scheduled for the summer of 1953 proceeded apace and by early 1952 the department had a staff of almost 100. It was a privilege and pleasure to head up such a wonderful team. We were in fact a happy family: Maggie Taylor and Patricia took care of the many social events, ranging from golf games to backyard parties, while Kenyon and I looked after the welfare and well-being of our young colleagues in the laboratories, offices and the workshop. As an example of the camaraderie that existed, I recall receiving an urgent telephone call from the Toronto General Hospital one night at 11 o'clock. A janitor who had only been employed a few months had suffered a serious accident and required a large number of blood transfusions. Could I obtain as many donors as possible immediately? The first dozen staff members I telephoned all volunteered and we assembled at the hospital within an hour of the original telephone call. The janitor's life was saved — in those days blood banks were nonexistent.

I cannot praise too highly the efforts of my colleagues during those hectic months of 1952 and early 1953 in assembling the DATAR systems. Two were installed below the main decks of Royal Canadian Navy Mine Sweepers and the third at the Scarboro Field Station. It was a "tour-de-force" and necessitated many hours of evening and weekend labor. On several occasions I visited the mine sweepers during the night-time hours to find "my boys" sweating in temperatures over 100 degrees F under very restricted conditions. But the job was accomplished on schedule. More than 30,000 diodes and miscellaneous electrical and mechanical equipment, not least the large magnetic storage drums, were in operation. In effect three independent electronic digital computers were linked together, two aboard the mine sweepers and the other ashore, by digital data radio links. Never before had a system of this kind and complexity operated anywhere in the world. What an achievement. It anticipated the internet system, albeit on a miniature scale, by many years.

Demonstrations of the system took place during September and October of 1953. Attending were members of the Navy and several senior officers from the other Services and Defense Research Board. As well, at least 50 representatives from the United States Navy and some industrial contractors attended the demonstrations. What they witnessed in each ship and on shore were complete pictures on cathode ray oscilloscope of sonar and radar targets, some real, others simulated, and with the capability of individual target information being displayed separately under the control of a track-ball system. The information displayed was automatically corrected for our own ship's motion. It was pure magic.

On the home front, Patricia was fully occupied with furnishing our new home, planting shrubs in our huge backyard and converting a track of barren soil into a garden. But her most important activities related to John's education. After spending a year at a public school, he proceeded to grade one in the Harrison Road School. His teacher, Mrs. Rust, was an excellent teacher, although I suspect at the time her pupils regarded her with a little apprehension. John's first school friend was Tedder Staunton who lived on a road adjacent to ours. Today Tedder is Headmaster of St.

Andrews College, one of Ontario's best known private schools. Concurrently with school, John also took piano lessons. Incidentally much more successfully than his father, and I recall how very proud Patricia and I were when we attended an evening concert featuring the young pianist, and John opened the program with a piece composed for children by Joseph Haydn — "Little Fingers." Because of my frequent visits to Ottawa in search of new business, so to speak, Patricia bore the burden of raising our son in an environment which was very different to the campus of the Military College. She succeeded brilliantly.

It was during one of my visits to Ottawa that I had a flash of inspiration. In contemplating potential applications of the comparatively primitive electronic digital computers of the day, and in spite of such achievement as the ENIAC computer at the University of Pennsylvania and the computers built by Fred Williams and Maurice Wilkes at Manchester and Cambridge Universities respectively, the technology in the light of the fantastic modern developments was indeed primitive. However, it showed great promise, and it was obvious that within a few years the machines would be widely used in finance, business and industry.

Sitting at breakfast in Murray's Restaurant, the coffee shop of the Chateau Laurier Hotel, I envisioned an application of computers to trading on international stock markets which could have very deleterious consequences. This, in spite of the fact that my knowledge of all matters relating to stock exchanges at the time was abysmal. Recall that the year 1953 had seen a marked increase in tension due to the "Cold War." Assume, I conjectured, that the Soviet Union might consider the possibility of manipulating the New York Stock Exchange by building up strong positions in defense-related industries. Was this a feasible option? Could it be achieved with a high level of secrecy? I believed it could.

Still at breakfast I wrote a few tentative ideas literally on the back of an envelope. I argued as follows:

- Assume a group of Soviet agents located in several strategic financial centers, i.e. New York, London, Paris, Zurich, etc., each having access to a primitive computer incorporating a magnetic storage drum, diode registers, keyboard, and a low speed printer. The computer would be pre-programmed to carry out procedures related to stock transactions and matters related thereto. (In modern parlance, I was in fact, anticipating "programmed trading".)

- Identify key target defense-oriented companies.

- Establish telephonic links between the agents and maintain the strictest secrecy.

- A senior agent with support staff might be located, for example, in New York City and would have central control and a more sophisticated computer.

Why a "network" of agents? First, for security reasons, and secondly with proliferating capital resources available less suspicion would be aroused if each agent's share in the "pie" would be correspondingly less. Furthermore, by capitalizing on small differences in share prices between the various agents, and fluctuating currency, the ultimate objectives of an enemy might be achieved more quickly.

It was at this stage in my "day-dreaming" that my friend Willie Watson, to whom I referred previously, entered the restaurant. I joined him at his table. As Director of the University of Toronto Computer Center, he was fully up to date with computer developments. I quickly outlined my concerns and even suggested that if such a scheme was impractical, rumors of its spreading through Wall Street might be equally devastating. What did he think? He reacted very positively, and ignoring his breakfast, we proceeded to consider the next steps. Our mutual friendship with Omond Solandt suggested that he would be the most appropriate government official to contact.

Later that morning, we met with Solandt in his office. He was intrigued, even to the extent of immediately telephoning Col. Wally Goforth, at the time head of Canadian Army Intelligence. Goforth arrived in Solandt's office within minutes and the four of us discussed the implications of such a hypothetical situation arising. At the conclusion of our meeting, Goforth decided that the matter should be handled by the Canadian "secret service," and classified as "secret" or "top secret." It was code named PAW (Porter and Watson). Goforth proceeded to contact appropriate authorities in the United States and Watson and I "bowed out" of the operation. About a year later I heard from Solandt that the U.S. authorities had taken certain steps to secure the markets from such potential undercover activities. Of the four attendees at the Ottawa meeting, all but me are deceased.

Before I left Britain it had been suggested that at the end of a year in Toronto I should report personally to Sir Vincent and members of the board, progress and prospects in Canada. As well it would give me an opportunity to visit Fred Williams at the University of Manchester to be updated on his work on computers. During my absence of about two or three weeks, Patricia and John were the guests of Grace and John Thomson at their summer cottage on an island in the Muskoka Lake Country. This was a unique experience for them and beneficial as well in so far as John suffered fewer and less severe asthma attacks. Because of the hot summers in Toronto we quickly ascertained that the summer cottage was a way of life for many professional people. We did not take much persuading in obtaining a cottage of our own. There were many options, but to minimize traveling time we decided to investigate Western Georgian Bay, Lake Huron, about 120 miles distance from our home. Eventually we purchased a comparatively large wood-framed cottage with 120-foot lake frontage and a big natural stone fireplace. Although not blessed with modern conveniences, indeed rather primitive with a "privy" at the back, a water pump in the lake, an ancient wood stove, an ice box for food storage, somewhat dowdy furniture, but it was roomy and indeed we could sleep about a dozen people albeit several on the large veranda, and proved, not ideal but adequate.

Patricia and John spent four summers there while I commuted. Idyllic summers during which John in particular obtained relief from his asthma attacks, which always plagued him in Toronto. He reveled in the glorious Georgian Bay sands building, not castles, as is usual for his age (four to seven years), but motor car "cockpits" with a real steering wheel and short rods to simulate gear shifts and brakes. His fascination with the motor car took firm root at an early age.

Apart from keeping the family fed and clothed and the cottage a viable entity, no small achievement, Patricia had her work cut out entertaining many over-night guests, notably the Taylors, Fishers and the Seddons. But having enjoyed so many holidays in the past at sea-side resorts in Britain and having been taught to swim by her father, Patricia was in her element in the fresh clear water of the lake and she quickly taught John to swim.

It's remarkable how comparatively obscure episodes stick in my memory. One of these related to John's favorite swimming companion — "Bulgie," a large plastic whale. There was an off- shore breeze one afternoon and Bulgie was suddenly blown "out to sea." John, aged five, was extremely distressed to see his favorite toy gradually floating away, but Patricia on the veranda at the time, and realizing that she was a far stronger swimmer than I plunged into the cool lake and swam after Bulgie. It was a dramatic rescue, at least 200 feet offshore and the incident had been watched by many of our neighbors on the beach. As Patricia waded ashore clutching Bulgie, everyone applauded, especially John who was over-joyed.

We will always remember those summers spent on Georgian Bay and it was a sad time when we had to give up our Canadian cottage.

Having demonstrated that in principle DATAR was a viable system, what was the next step? The sheer size, power requirements and reliability of vacuum tubes clearly precluded large scale adoption of DATAR in its existing form. However, with the comparatively recent invention of the transistor and advances in solid-state physics, we considered that a transistorized version of DATAR was a possibility. This in itself was a risky conjecture because of our limited experience in solid-state circuit design, and by no means least, the high cost of transistors. A single transistor cost nearly $100, in contrast to today when in the form of silicon chips, one can buy millions of microscopic transistors for a few dollars. Notwithstanding an anticipated marked decrease in the cost of transistors within a decade or two, the Navy was unwilling, probably justifiably, to fund a solid-state version of DATAR. We had assembled a first class research facility and its potential demise was unthinkable, especially after the highly successful demonstrations on Lake Ontario. Alternative avenues must be explored.

There were two promising prospects — the computerization of mail-sorting, through a contact I had made as early as March, 1951 with Maurice Levy, and airline reservations, through a contact I had made more recently with Lyman Richardson. I shall deal with these subsequently. But first let me outline my experiences as a member of "Project Lamp Light" because they were essentially anti-climactic to DATAR. I was invited to become a member of the six-man Canadian delegation seconded to the project largely through the influence of Omond Solandt. My previous association with MIT was probably a major factor in my being invited because MIT was sponsoring the project.

As it transpired, Project Lamp Light was to become a highly confidential investigation related to the "continental defense of North America." Consequently, membership was restricted to citizens of the United States and Canada. Even representatives from the U.K. were originally excluded, and at the time I was a British citizen. This situation was resolved within a couple of weeks when I was duly sworn in by a Canadian judge as a citizen of Canada. I had no idea incidently, that the project would develop into a full time job located in Washington, D.C., the U.S. Naval Base at Norfolk, VA., and MIT. And that it would last six months from September, 1954 to March, 1955.

One major reason for the setting up of a broadly based study of the continental defense of North America was the fact that in July, 1953, the Soviet Union tested their first thermonuclear bomb with a yield equivalent of 400,000 tons of TNT, which corresponds to a bomb 40 times as destructive as that which destroyed Hiroshama, but less than the yield achieved at the same time by the United States. However, the USSR was only about two years behind the United States.

The primary purpose of Project Lamp Light was to examine the strategic and tactical factors relating to the continental defense of North America with special reference to recent advances in science and technology. Because the "Cold War" was intensifying, the project had been given the highest priority. It was directed by a remarkable MIT professor of physics — Dr. Zacharias (affectionately called Zach) who had been responsible for several inter-service and inter-departmental task forces in the past. He had the incredible knack of melding together a team of quite different individuals into a cohesive study group. In order to facilitate communications between naval officers, university scientists and industrial personnel, Zach recruited Vice Admiral E.C. Cochrane who subsequently became vice president of MIT.

To exemplify the diversity of the personnel let me introduce some of the personalities who became my colleagues — Jerry Wiesner, Jay Forrester and Ivan Getting of MIT; Charles Lindbergh; Dean Wooldridge (co-founder of Thomson Ramo Wooldridge-TRW) and senior scientists from IBM, the Bell Telephone Laboratories and Sperry.

The preliminary familiarization meetings, conducted by Zach were held in Washington, D.C., and Norfolk, aboard the aircraft carrier U.S. Enterprise and the Radiation Laboratory at MIT. After two weeks of plenary sessions the project was split up into specialized sections which studied topics such as the DEW Line[17]; fighter aircraft; naval operations; global navigation; communications and information processing. I was assigned to the latter section under the leadership of Jerry Wiesner. He was a dynamic leader and it is not surprising that a decade later he would be appointed scientific advisor to President John F. Kennedy and subsequently to the presidency of MIT.

All meetings of the information section and the plenary sessions took place at MIT, usually in the Radiation Laboratory. It may not be out of place to mention how the Radiation Laboratory came into being because,

---

[17]Distant Early Warning radar system

and I only discovered this recently while reading <u>The Making of the Atomic Bomb</u> by Richard Rhodes, my former boss and PhD. external examiner John Cockroft, played a central role. The following quotation not only reveals Cockroft's contributions, but as well enlightens us concerning the close military ties that existed between Britain and the U.S. as early as 1940:

> "But American science, spurred on by British appeals, was finally gearing up for war. Churchill had sent over Henry Tizard[18] in the late summer of 1940 with a delegation of experts and a black-enameled metal steamer truck the original black box, full of military secrets. The prize specimen among them was the "cavity magnetron", developed in Mark Oliphant's laboratory at Birmingham. (Incidently the operation of the modern microwave oven depends exclusively on the magnetron.) John Cockroft, a future Nobel laureate with a vital mission, traveled along to explain the high-powered microwave generator. The Americans had never seen anything like it before. Cockroft got together one weekend in October with Ernest Lawrence and multimillionaire physicists-financier Alfred Loomis,[19] the last of the gentleman scientists at Loomis's private laboratory in the elegant suburban New York colony of Tuxedo Park. That meeting laid the groundwork for a major new NDRC Laboratory at MIT. To keep its work secret it was named the Radiation Laboratory, as if serious scientists might be pursuing applications so dubious as those bruited by visionaries from nuclear physics."

I recall that our discussions, which were essentially seminars, related to the nature of the threat likely to arise in case hostilities broke out and the surveillance techniques complemented by information processing which would be required to contain it. Although much attention was

---

[18]* Note the important role played by Sir Henry Tizard, who was a member of my Commonwealth Fund Fellowship Committee of Award, and subsequently a friend and advisor.

[19]It is worth drawing attention to the fact that Loomis is the central figure in the recent book <u>Tuxedo Park</u>.

devoted to radar requirements and the complementary question of radar "jamming," my personal contributions related to the relative merits of communications and information systems being developed at the University of Illinois, IBM, Remington Rand and DATAR. While it was generally agreed, essentially as a result of the demonstrations, that DATAR had considerable merit, the majority opinion was that mass production of the system would present insuperable difficulties. Be that as it may, I recall with pride that at one stage during the discussions on the relative merits of the respective teams that Jerry Wiesner stated "Arthur, your team performed miracles in Canada. I doubt whether we could match them in the United States!" But in spite of such compliments we did not obtain a contract from the U.S. Navy for a transistorized version of DATAR

I have vivid recollections of a weekend in October 1954 when the full fury of Hurricane Hazel struck Toronto. During the early phase of Project Lamp Light I had contrived to return home for weekends. But on this occasion meetings of our section were scheduled for the Saturday. Coincidently, a major hurricane, Hurricane Hazel, was headed in our direction from the Atlantic Ocean. By the Friday, Boston appeared to be close to the projected location of "land-fall." In anticipation of a serious disruption of services, I telephoned Patricia early that morning to tell her that I was in a very secure building and not to worry if telephonic communications were cutoff. As the day progressed wind squalls of at least 60 miles per hour developed, but by the late afternoon it was obvious that the hurricane had changed directions and headed westerly well south of Boston. We breathed a sigh of relief!

However, Patricia and John were not so fortunate and I was shocked to read in the Boston Globe the following morning that Hurricane Hazel had in fact caused power outages, severe wind damage and worst of all disastrous flooding in the city of Toronto and vicinity. One whole street, Ettrick Crescent on the banks of the Humber River, had been undermined by the flood waters and many homes were literally precipitated into the river. There were more than 100 fatalities.

There was very heavy rain during the early afternoon of that Friday when Patricia, with John, driving our Austin car, picked up Tedder Staunton and his mother, and drove a further two miles to pick up the boy's school teacher. Afternoon tea was planned at our Old Colony Road home.

About five o'clock, with heavy rains and high winds persisting, Patricia dropped the Stauntons at their home just north of ours. Then, driving in appalling conditions, (there was about 18 inches of flood water beneath the Highway 401 underpass on Bayview Avenue) took the teacher home. By then it was dark and Hazel was reaching hurricane proportions. Driving back to Old Colony Road, Patricia ran into two feet of water at the under-pass. Not surprisingly, the Austin stalled and had to be abandoned. Fortunately, a motorist driving a much larger car than ours negotiated the flood and literally rescued Patricia and John and drove them to the end of our road. Arriving home after a quarter mile walk on the unlighted road, soaked to the skin, they discovered that electrical power and water supplies had been cut off. I was not aware of the ordeal they had suffered until late on the Saturday night when telephonic communication was restored. More than 11 inches of rain had fallen on Toronto in about the same number of hours. It was a major tragedy for the city which will always live in our memories.

In many respects Project Lamp Light was an educational experience which not only gave me some insight into corporate America, but as well into the structure of the defense-related government departments. These insights were gained not so much from the many seminars and plenary sessions which were held, but most importantly during the coffee and lunch breaks. Several of the participants (regrettably all male) were, or were to become, internationally known personalities. Of the academics who have influenced my thinking so much I must identify Jerry Wiesner and Jay Forrester (inventor of core storage and builder of "Whirland," one of the world's first major digital computers).

After five months of intensive research and debate, Project Lamp Light finally reached a consensus of opinion relating to the future defense of the North American continent. Major recommendations were formulated for presentation at a final plenary session, the main purpose of which was to brief the Chiefs of Staff or their representatives, senior members of the Department of Defense and leaders in the defense industries.

This memorable session, chaired by Professor Zacharias was held in the Schubert Theatre in downtown Boston. There were at least 200 attendees. Because of the highly classified material under discussion, the security arrangements were quite remarkable. Everybody, including officers in the services, were in civilian clothes with no identification whatsoever. But I understood that each attendee was scrutinized by unidentified FBI agents, and the theatre was checked thoroughly for "bugs."

During the morning of the second and final day of the briefings, I was alerted to an "urgent" telephone call from England. It remains a mystery as to how Professor Patrick Blackett, who had already had so much to do with my career, tracked me down to that secret location. But having rescued me from ARL in 1940 he decided to "rescue" me from what he regarded as a "dead-end" industry. Without mincing any words, Blackett said "Porter, would you be interested in a newly created chair in Light Electrical Engineering at Imperial College?" Furthermore, he mentioned that it was very probable that I would be receiving an invitation from the University of Sheffield to take the chairmanship of the Department of Electrical Engineering, and that he was anxious that I should be aware of the Imperial College situation. Needless to say, I had rarely been more favorably surprised in my life than by Blackett's telephone call. I responded positively, pending further information. I returned to my seat in the theatre with a feeling of euphoria and a glow in my heart. It was the last day of the Lamp Light final briefings and I returned to Toronto on the following morning.

On my arrival at Old Colony Road, Patricia and John sensed that I was bursting with some very special news. I did not waste any time in conveying it. To say that they were surprised, albeit excited with the possibility of a move back to our homeland and to London in particular, is to put it mildly. But undaunted by the prospect of severing our ties with so many Canadian friends, and this applied particularly to John and his friendship with Tedder Staunton, we were prepared for the new challenge which loomed ahead. Perhaps not surprisingly because even in those days we seemed to thrive on challenges. A few days later I received a letter from Imperial College giving details of the proposed chair in light electrical engineering and such details as salary, tenure, pension arrangements and the like. As forecast by Blackett, a letter from Sheffield University concerning the chairmanship of the Electrical Engineering Department arrived asking whether or not I was interested in the post. I felt very flattered, not least because a quarter of a century earlier I had failed to win an Edgar Allen Scholarship at this university, nor coincidently I had also failed to win an Imperial College Open Scholarship. In the event I accepted the Imperial College chair conditionally because I felt it incumbent on me to treat the Sheffield offer seriously by visiting the university on my return to Britain.

A letter from Vice-Admiral E.L. Cochrane, vice president of MIT awaited my arrival back at Ferranti in early March 1955. It was in reply to a letter I had written previously expressing my appreciation for having been invited to participate in Project Lamp Light. In retrospect it is clear that the project had been climactic in so far as it introduced me to new insights and many prospective contacts. The letter admirably sums up the epic proportions and glamor of the project and emphasizes the importance of inter-service and industrial cooperation — a theme central to my personal philosophy. It is worth quoting in full:

> *Dear Arthur:*
>
> *Both Dr. Zacharias and I appreciate your very nice letter of 23 February, in connection with your association with Project Lamp Light. You were a great comfort to both Zacharias and myself, and a refreshing addition to the group. We hope very much that you will look back on the months you spent here in Cambridge with as much satisfaction as we got from having you. There are always those who carp at efforts such as Lamp Light, and I had an almost amusing one from a man who worried over such use of scientists. In my reply, I could not refrain from pointing out that, so far as I was concerned, the very fact that having a group of such wide associations of both military, government and commercial backgrounds and from three nations produced values in association no less important than the technical results which were achieved.*
>
> *I personally cherish the friendships which grew out of the Project, and hope you will not fail to let us know if you are coming to this part of the country so that we may have the pleasure of seeing you. With kindest personal regards and best wishes, I am*
>
> Very sincerely,
E.L. Cochrane,
Vice Admiral, USN (Ret.)
Vice President

While Lamp Light had confirmed my belief that the DATAR system was unrivaled at the time, it also confirmed that the future development of the system in transistorized form by a Canadian organization was highly problematical. The United States computer industry was a much too powerful competitor. But it is comforting to reflect on the fact that many of the basic concepts and much of the technology developed in my department were adopted and paved the way for future developments.

One of the most dramatic episodes of my life occurred during the late spring of 1955. Project Lamp Light had concluded and it seemed fairly certain that we would be headed for Imperial College in the fall. But there were a few loose ends to be cleared up. First, I felt it incumbent on me to report the general findings of Lamp Light which related to information processing, to my peers in Ferranti U.K. Secondly, I had promised to visit Sheffield University to hear more about the chair of Electrical Engineering. The latter, in reality, was a courtesy because I had already decided to accept the Imperial College chair.

Much preferring day-time trans Atlantic crossings to night-time, I flew Trans-Canada Airlines (TCA) to New York and Pan Am from New York to London. My itinerary in England was completed in three days. It was on the return flight from London to Toronto that things didn't go according to plan.

Not unusually in those days when trans-Atlantic flights were still a novelty, there was a several hours delay in departure, and by the time I boarded the Pan Am Strato-Cruiser at London airport it was late afternoon. At about 8 p.m., when we were 800 miles west of Ireland, the Captain made the rather disturbing announcement to the effect that he had been obliged to "feather" No. 2 port-side propeller, that he would be jettisoning 16,000 pounds of fuel within a few minutes, that we would be returning to London, that there would be no smoking and that "for those fortunate enough to be in the lower deck bar," as I was, all drinks would be "on the house." Normally, I'm a very light consumer of alcohol, but on that occasion I probably exceeded my average consumption. Arriving at the London airport at midnight without incident, we passengers were both relaxed and relieved. In a conversation with the captain the following morning before the return flight, he told me that the engine failure of the previous evening and subsequent jettisoning of fuel was the first in his experience and he hoped it would be the last. After spending the night at Kensington Palace Hotel, and having sent a message to Patricia saying I would be delayed at least 24 hours, I boarded the Strato-Cruiser once again and after a refueling stop at Keflavik, Iceland, arrived in New York about 7 p.m. — too late to obtain the last flight of the day to Toronto.

Unfortunately in those days a visa was required for even an over-night stop-over, and this applied to Canadians. I didn't have one. Ergo! I was immediately placed in custody and my passport surrendered. A Pinkerton Security Agent drove me in a splendid limousine to a hotel in Queens in which the 6th and 7th floors were dedicated to "illegal aliens."

Armed guards were located at each end of the corridor. My room was quite comfortable and dinner was provided, but I was incommunicado — no telephone. After breakfast, a courteous Pinkerton agent drove me back to the airport and I was literally escorted and pre-boarded by two TCA stewardesses, still without my passport.

The final incident in this incredible episode occurred at Malton Airport (Toronto). I was again escorted from the plane to an immigration area. After a few minutes wait, I ascertained that the door was locked. It took many bangs on the door to attract the attention of an immigration officer. To my inquiry — "What's going on?"

He replied "you're in quarantine!" For sentimental reasons I'd always kept my original "landing card" for entry into Canada in my passport. It was almost identical in size and color to the "quarantine card" of the day. Eventually I was released and Patricia met me almost an hour after the plane's arrival. Neither of us will ever forget that day.

During my four months absence on Lamp Light, the department made impressive advances in the design of transistor circuits in anticipation of a burgeoning market in the future — in light of the incredible advances of solid state technology, especially digital computers, during the past half-century, this was a very perceptive development. The first application of the technology was in the development of a prototype automatic mail sorting system for the Canadian Post Office based on the ideas formulated by Maurice Levy and introduced previously.

Although preliminary work on the project, based on vacuum circuitry, had started in 1953, it was soon appreciated that such an approach was impractical due to the sheer bulk of the equipment and the difficulty of achieving adequate reliability. But with the advent of the transistor, Maurice Levy's dream became a reality and before I left Ferranti Electric later in 1955, the prototype was well in hand. It was a highly significant step in the annals of the history of digital computer technology, and the fact that it revolutionized mail sorting and many related societal technologies of which a check-sorting system installed in 1958 in the New York offices of the Federal Reserve Bank was the prime example, a brief description is not inappropriate.

The basic idea was to store digitally on a high-speed magnetic drum the destinations of mail and the concomitant routes. For example, a letter addressed to a specific geographical location, specified on the letter as an alpha-numeric code, e.g. L4N, 6B8 would automatically be routed by a series of relay switches to a specific bag for transportation to its destination. It is noteworthy that the Levy scheme, adopted as well a few years subsequently by the United Kingdom, is still in use today and is appreciably more flexible than the numeric system used by the United States Post Office. Operators transcribed the code into a bar code which could be optically scanned and the digital data thereby provided was identified on the magnetic drum storage and the corresponding route data obtained. The experimental prototype could sort more than 36,000 letters per hour. Several novel techniques were created, notably printed-wired circuit boards and on completion in 1956, about a year after I had left the department, it was one of the most elegant technological achievements of the period and not surprisingly received international attention. Indeed, in the words of J.J. Brown in a book published in 1967 (and I am grateful to John Vardalas[20] for this and other relevant information) "The United States sent a group of Congressmen to check on the Canadian system before Congress voted $5 million to fund a research laboratory in Washington, D.C. for a similar study."

Ironically, shortly thereafter, in spite of being the pioneer in automatic mail sorting the request by my department for a $1 million grant to build a full-scale system was denied. The government, in rejecting the request, referred to the project as the "million dollar monster." If the system already planned in detail in 1955 had been brought to fruition, the Canadian Post Office would have been several years ahead of other countries. I understand that the first computerized mail-sorting system in the United States went into operation in 1960 and Great Britain in 1966.

Within a few years of my departure, the department under the leadership of Kenyon Taylor and the unique creative talents of Fred Longstaffe, Gordon Lang, Tom Cranston and Les Wood, to name a few, achieved some notable successes. For example, the computerized seat reservation system based on the original ideas of Lyman Richardson, for the Trans-Canadian Airlines was one of the first in the field and concomitantly the design and building of the FP6000 medium size computer with time-sharing capabilities was a phenomenal success. A brief historical survey of the work of the department to which reference should be made has been published in the technical literature.

It was appropriate and indeed symbolic that the last visitors we entertained before leaving Canada were the Hartrees. Douglas had been

---

[20] John Vardalas, "From DATAR to the FP-6000: Technological Change in a Canadian Industrial Context," Institute of Electrical and Electronic Engineers Annals of the History of Computing," Vol. 16. No. 2, 1994

essentially responsible for our being there in the first place! Patricia and I were thrilled when Douglas, shortly to take up the prestigious Higgins Visiting Professorship at Princeton University, and Elaine spent a few days with us in June 1955. It was a delightful reunion and gave us plenty of opportunity to be briefed on recent developments in the academic world in Britain to which we were soon to become participants. It is sad to reflect, however, that this was the last prolonged get together between the Hartrees and the Porters.

In one respect, my mission to Canada was not as successful as I might have expected. I failed to convince the Canadian government with the exception of Omond Solandt, of course, that Canadian electronic technology was second to none in the world. Indeed, the dismal lack of foresight on the part of the federal and provincial governments of the day, as witness the fact that they had so little confidence in the superb creative teams of brilliant young Canadian engineers and scientists, one of which was the Ferranti Packard Research Department. The pattern was repeated again and again when Canadian developments were rejected in favor of equivalent or in some cases inferior products from the United States. Even today I find the extent to which opportunities for world-class technology innovations were squandered by incompetent bureaucrats quite incomprehensible.

But this should not detract from the fact that my relatively brief sojourn in the industrial environment was both stimulating and rewarding. To have had the privilege of being associated with the likes of Kenyon Taylor and our young colleagues was reward indeed.

I cannot refrain in concluding this chapter from paying a special tribute to Kenyon Taylor, my close friend and colleague. His incredible creative genius inspired all of us. Every time I see "flip-disk" display boards, which are ubiquitous in sports stadiums, airports, railway stations and major highways all over the world, I visualize Kenyon the inventor, pipe in mouth, soldering iron in hand at a laboratory bench. Although his invention reaped many millions of dollars for the company and the electronics industry, Kenyon's financial rewards were minimal. But he always reasoned that having been given the opportunities to create were adequate compensation. He was one of a kind and a man to whom I shall be everlastingly grateful. Sadly, Patricia and I were at his bedside in the Princess Margaret Hospital, Toronto, the day before he passed away.

At the farewell dinner held at the Old Mill Restaurant, a favorite haunt, I was presented with a pair of binoculars, suitable inscribed, and a very unique paper weight, which is one of the most treasured possessions of my family. It is a model of the transistor circuit board used in the Post Office mail-sorting system, complemented by a second circuit board inscribed on both sides using printed circuit techniques, are the initials of every member of that very wonderful group of young men and women with whom I had the privilege of being associated. On a platform of Union Station, Toronto, on a very hot summer afternoon in July 1955, many of them were present to wish Patricia, John and myself a fond farewell. I recall that Patricia shed a tear as the train pulled out of the station and headed for New York and the Cunard Liner that transported us to England.

As a fitting ending to this chapter, it is heartwarming to mention that during the last week of December 2002 I have received birthday greeting cards from four of my Ferranti colleagues, and a telephone call from Vincent Taylor, younger son of Kenyon. The note on George and Audrey Collins' card appeals especially — it reads: "Happy 92nd birthday from your crack team of razor-sharp co-workers, one of whom was George Collins. Sincerely and with many good memories."

Chapter 9

IMPERIAL COLLEGE OF SCIENCE AND TECHNOLOGY

IT was a perfect September day when we docked at Southampton and proceeded by train to Waterloo Station to start a new chapter in our lives. A wonderland of a different kind beckoned us. After all, London of 1955 was very different from the London of 1945, reeling after six years of war, which we had deserted. We had mixed feelings: on one hand excitement, on the other a sense of misgiving regarding the many uncertainties we faced. For me, a hiatus of six years in my erstwhile academic career; for Patricia and John setting up a new home, finding a suitable school in an entirely different environment to which we had become accustomed. Fortunately, our families and friends were readily accessible, especially Carol, my sister-in-law.

With her characteristic foresight and perspicacity, Carol had obtained temporary accommodation for us, bearing in mind the key parameters — comfort, location, transportation, schools, shops, etc. The top floor, intimidating today but by no means then, indeed just the reverse, of a typical Georgian town residence in Argyll Road off Kensington High Street, a stones-throw from the underground station. In marked contrast to Old Colony Road, on the outskirts of Toronto, it was in the heart of the Royal Borough of Kensington, a half mile distance from Kensington Palace, the future residence of the Prince and Princess, (Princess Diana) of Wales.. My family appears to have an affinity for royal residences, e.g. Kensington and Hampton Court. Not only were we conveniently located for the college, a 20 minute walk, but there was a small private school within a few hundred yards, Holland Park across the road was a walker's delight, and some of London's most illustrious shops, notably

Harrod's, within easy reach, a few minutes by bus. We were located less than a mile distance from the Albert Hall and the great National Museums of Science, Natural History, Archeology and Geology — a veritable wonderland of culture.

Before my arrival in London I had had few opportunities to obtain background information on the College. Although I was aware that it was the pre-eminent educational institution in Britain devoted exclusively to teaching and research in science and technology, I was woefully ignorant of its history. Established as a constituent college of the University of London in 1907, Imperial College[21] was in fact made up of three colleges — the Royal College of Science, the Royal School of Mines and the City and Guilds College. Each had a distinguished history. The latter, my college, was essentially a school of engineering with historic roots in the 19th century when the Guilds of the City of London of medieval origin, recognizing the importance of applied science and engineering, established educational facilities for their craftsmen. As an aside, it is somewhat disconcerting to reflect on the fact that, at the end of the 19th century Britain was many years behind Germany, France and the USA in technological education. The concept that engineering was craft rather than science took many years to eradicate. Ironically, it was Britain's role as progenitor of the industrial revolution of the 18th century, through the inventions and creativity of such men as Stephenson, Watt, Arwkright and Bernal, and not least Faraday that gave birth to the laissez-faire attitude during the 19th century which resulted in negligence of technological education.

But I was encouraged when informed that the lessons of WWII, which had demonstrated the critical role of science and engineering in both war and peace, had taken root and a renaissance of scientific and engineering education in Britain was in process. Indeed the creation of several new chairs in engineering, of which mine was one, was a direct consequence of the recognition that Britain was in the process of catching up with the foreign competition. Consequently, there was an air of excitement and expectation, reminiscent of my experience at MIT almost two decades previously when I took up the chair of Light Electrical Engineering.

The appointment, several months prior to mine, of Arnold Tustin as Professor of Heavy Electrical Engineering and chairman of the department, gave me considerable comfort and confidence. Formerly a

---

[21]Within the past decade i.e. late 90's, a medical faculty has been added. The College is now The Imperial College of Science, Technology and Medicine.

member of the research staff of the Metropolitan-Vickers Company Research Division and member of the Servo Panel, Arnold and I had common interests in the field of automatic controls. It was not coincidental moreover that we were both recruited from industry. There was to be an added incentive to bring the university into close contact with industry.

Two of my new colleagues deserve special mention — they both held readerships in the department. Dennis Gabor, a future Nobel Laureate in physics, circa 1971, a pre-WWII refugee from Hungary, had the adjoining office to my own. As a pioneer in electron-optics, his crowning achievement was the invention of holography (i.e. 3-dimensional imaging). The second was Colin Cherry, Britain's foremost exponent of information theory who had interests closely paralleling my own in advocating inter-disciplinary research. As well there was the ubiquitous and quite delightful, Mr. David Hopkin, a senior lecturer who had been on the staff of the College for well nigh 30 years — he was, as far as I was concerned, the dispenser of wisdom in all matters relating to administration and his advice proved to be invaluable.

Top priority in the list of jobs facing me during my first two weeks at the College, was my teaching schedule. The undergraduate classes were due to start early in October so there was not much time for preparation. At the time there were only two full professors in the department and Arnold Tustin, the senior, felt that one of us should give the first year course of lectures, the purpose of which was to introduce students to the basic concepts of electrical science. As the junior professor, I was the obvious choice. The title of the course was "Introduction to Electricity and Magnetism." For a graduate in honors physics, this should have been a relatively straight- forward assignment. However, it turned out to be quite a laborious and time-consuming task. I soon discovered that I had to delve much more deeply into the subject than I had imagined. However, it proved to be a rewarding exercise. The class of 60 young men and four young women, specially selected for their achievements in high school in mathematics and science, were eager and hard-workers. Contrasted with the undergraduates of today, they were well-dressed (blazers and slacks) and well disciplined. They were a joy to teach.

Reflecting on my teaching experiences during that first term, I soon discovered, for example, that the dead-lines I had been confronted within industry, were appreciably less stressful than the new ones. There was always an element of maneuverability — time schedules were more flexible and one's associates were never quite so intimidating as a class of eager and for the most part very perceptive undergraduates. Only the dedicated teacher appreciates the discipline required in meeting his or her class at a specific time on a specific day and being fully prepared.

Early in February 1956 we left our temporary accommodation in South Kensington and moved to a permanent home. It was a spacious semi-detached house in Melbury Gardens, Wimbledon, within a mile of the famous tennis courts. The move had important consequences for John and Patricia. Once again they had to adapt to an entirely different environment. One significant factor was John's schooling and fortunately Wimbledon was well-endowed with excellent schools. Furthermore, convenient bus and train services to London meant that we were by no means isolated.

To help John adapt to yet another change in his young life, we aquired a dog — a Welsh Corgi which we named Topper, an affectionate and lovable dog. Having Patricia's family close by — her mother at Twickenham, a short distance away, and her sister, Carol, who worked for British Airways in London, helped considerably in enabling us to adjust to yet another move. My brother Ronald and his wife, Mary, and cousins Elizabeth and Richard were a great support and John and Elizabeth became very close friends. We had missed our families more than we realized, and it helped to give John much needed security to have grandparents, aunts, uncles and cousins close by.

One of the most intimidating experiences facing parents and children of the day was the so-called 11+ examination. The examination covered the three R's — reading, writing and arithmetic. It was under the jurisdiction of a local educational authority and mandatory for all school children. A pass, regarded as a symbol of scholastic achievement and much coveted, guaranteed admission to a grammar school while a failure resulted in a student attending a technical school. One of Patricia's and my biggest thrills occurred when the official letter proclaiming John's success arrived. He had passed the 11+ at age 10 and had obtained a place in the most prestigious high school of the region — the King's College School in a grade one higher than the average, demonstrating that he had not only passed, but had passed with distinction.

During a period of dramatic change such as my family was experiencing, I reflect especially on John's stamina and courage. Subject to persistent attacks of allergic asthma, which had plagued him since the age of two years, he found the London environment even less friendly than Toronto. Molds in the fabric of Georgian residences were prevalent and caused allergic reactions. But compounding these distressful incidents was the problem of schooling. In retrospect, and I am literally writing this on my 92nd birthday, I have difficulty in comprehending how Patricia and John coped. The extent to which Patricia succeeded is manifest in John's subsequent academic and professional achievements. It is only with hindsight that these truths emerge and I understand now that my constant search for new challenges must have placed burdens on the family. On the other hand, however, perhaps these were responsible for the closely knit family that we have become. I've always argued that the "law of requisite variety" has been central to my academic career, but it's also been central to John's education. By the age of nine years he had already attended four schools with four more in prospect before he attended university.

A memorable occasion in the history of the University was the installation of Her Majesty, the Queen Mother as Chancellor on November 23-24, 1955. All professors and their ladies received formal invitations to attend the ceremony in the recently completed Festival Hall on the banks of the River Thames, and a Reception in her honor at the Senate House. Regrettably, I was suffering from a severe attack of influenza and missed the ceremonies. But Patricia attended and described it as being the most splendid ceremonial she had ever attended. The academic gowns of representatives from universities from all over the world were striking, and Patricia still recalls the delegates from the Commonwealth. Her Majesty rose to the occasion with her characteristic grace and dignity.

The university was indeed fortunate in having the Queen Mother, one of the most popular figures not only in Britain and the Commonwealth, but equally so in the United States, as Chancellor. During my tenure, Patricia and I were privileged to attend several receptions which she hosted. She always greeted us with obvious pleasure — a very great lady.

It was essentially through such ceremonials and receptions, some exclusively for the faculty wives, that Patricia met and became close friends with three ladies in particular — Marjorie Linstead, wife of the Rector, Marjorie Gabor, wife of Dennis, and Ingelisa Argyris, wife of John Argyris, professor of aeronautical structures. The extent to which these friendships benefited me professionally is difficult to assess. It was appreciable. After all, some of the most rewarding seeds of my imagination have been sowed during such social occasions as dinner parties, and Patricia has always been adept at organizing these. I have much to be thankful for in this respect.

My inaugural lecture proved to be a much more formal affair than I had anticipated. Elaborate invitations, public notices on boards around the College, and on the day of the lecture a notice appeared in the "Events of the Day" announcements in the *Times* of London. It is not surprising that when I entered the large Chemistry Lecture Theatre seating 400, accompanied by Professor Patrick Blackett I was nervous. Blackett, who was to introduce me came to the rescue once again. It was certainly the most distinguished audience I had ever faced — Lord Falmouth, Chairman of the Governing Council, the Rector, the Mayor of Westminister, my cousin Sir Vincent Tewson,[22] to name a few, and all my colleagues. Patricia sat with the Rector and Mrs. Linstead. My lecture entitled "The Control of Processes" which was illustrated by lantern slides anticipated the role of digital computers in the control of processes and in particular stressed the increasing importance of transistor circuit technology. I was well satisfied with its reception. Indeed my only regret was that my parents, for health reasons, were unable to attend. However, they were certainly present in spirit and I felt instinctively that their sacrifices had not been in vain. Hosted by the Rector, the dinner following the lecture was a fitting conclusion to a memorable occasion. The lecture was subsequently published in *Imperial College Inaugural Lectures 1955-56* and I am the proud possessor of a copy.

In addition to my teaching and research commitments in the College, as holder of a chair in the University of London, I was an ex-officio member of several inter-collegiate committees, most notable of which was charged with recommending computer facilities for the university as a whole. It was quite a responsibility because at the time, the dawn of the computer era, commercially available computers were rare and very expensive. Being one of the most influential universities in the country, our conclusions and recommendations would have broad implications. As chairman of the committee, we were fortunate to have Professor Hermann Bondi (later Sir Hermann) of University College, an internationally acclaimed cosmologist, co-author with Fred Hoyle and Tom Gold of the Steady-State Theory of the Universe. It was a fascinating experience especially because it gave me opportunities to meet like-minded scholars and scientists from other colleges.

Another committee which I enjoyed thoroughly was the College Admissions Committee. During the spring of each year we were required to sieve through about 200 applications from qualified high school students for admission to our department. Arnold Tustin and I took turns

[22]Sir Vincent was General Secretary to the Trades Union Council of Great Britain

chairing the committee. Our job was to identify 60 promising candidates. As well as their academic performances in the Higher School Certificate examination, the criteria for selection were based on such factors as the school headmaster's (or headmistress) letter of recommendation, leadership and social attributes, such as school prefect, participation in school societies, such as debating, and sports and recreational activities. Children of alumni of the department were given a slight preference. We were particularly anxious to attract women students because we anticipated increasing demand from industry for graduates with expertise in such emerging fields as computer software, and we felt that women graduates would make major contributions. It is difficult to assess our success rate in the admissions process, as judged for example, by subsequent career successes, but I know of several alumni whom we had selected who have had extraordinarily successful careers. Consequently, Admissions was one of my most rewarding activities at the College.

I believe that it was largely due to Patricia's friendship with Marjorie Linstead that I was invited to participate in two positively enchanting enterprises. They related to industrial research. Because it was only affordable by large companies, industrial research to assist small companies in a specific industry was carried out cooperatively. The so-called Research Association's (RA) were financed jointly by the participating companies and government. To ensure that the research programs were well balanced and consistent with established practice, two independent "visitors" were appointed, one academic and the other industrial. Their job was to visit their assigned R.A. bi-annually for a day or two and to report to the Council that administered the Associations. Much to my surprise, and indeed delight, I was invited, for some obscure reason to become academic visitor to two R.A.'s. The Hosiery and Allied Trades Research Association (HATRA) and the Lace R.A. A modest honorarium was provided. My industrial counterpart, David Traill, was a director of Imperial Chemical Industries Ltd., the largest chemical conglomerate in Britain, and incidentally possessor of one of the largest private wine cellars in the country. He turned out to be a delightful colleague.

The laboratories of both R.A.'s were located in Nottingham, a three-hour train journey from London. A remarkable coincidence was that the Director of HATRA was Dr. James Illingworth. He had been a member of my undergraduate class at Manchester and in fact placed second in the final examinations. Subsequently he obtained his PhD. for research in X-Ray Crystallography under Sir Lawrence Bragg at the same convocation as myself.

The days dedicated to the "visitors" inspections were quite special and David Traill and I were treated almost like royalty. Although neither of us was an authority in any aspect of the research, we nevertheless obtained an overall appreciation of what was going on. I was struck, for example, by the sheer complexity and speed of the knitting machines and by the studies relating to the tensile strength of fabrics. Incidentally, because of her life-long devotion to needlework and interest in fabrics, Patricia provided me with a host of relevant questions to ask during the visits.

Not unrelated to my work in operations research during WWII were the statistical problems related to the manufacture of hosiery. Correlations, for example, between such parameters as length of leg, size of foot and mid-thigh diameter were taken to ensure that the stockings would accommodate the whole female population. We were certainly treated to a fascinating display of experiments, the most spectacular of which I suspect were developed especially for our visit.

The Lace Research Association Laboratories were equally interesting with emphasis on the performance of modern versions of the "Jacquard Loom."[23] Our visits in many respects constituted a history lesson insofar as we learned that lace-making was a "cottage industry" even in medieval times and by the beginning of the 16th century, lace-pattern books were available. Lace-making had evolved into an art-form with marked societal implications. But the emergence of the power-loom during the late 19th century had completely changed the industry. To see modern looms weaving such intricate patterns was a revelation. However, the prestige of hand-made lace remains.

It is noteworthy that my Aunt Laura was addicted to the craft and fashioned an elegant tablecloth as our wedding present. As well, during the London Blitz Patricia shared an air-raid shelter with a doctor's housekeeper who, in spite of the bombing, continued to crochet a tablecloth which became another wedding present. Both beautiful artifacts are prized possessions.

During our visits to the research associations, David and I were always entertained lavishly at lunch and dinner. From every point of view I recall my brief encounters with research activities related to lady's apparel with great pleasure and satisfaction.

---

[23] Of interest is the fact that the loom invented by Jacquard early in the 19th century used punch cards which were the forerunners of the Hollerith punched cards utilized in early computer systems.

Bearing in mind my experience at Ferranti Electric it's not surprising that in formulating my research program at Imperial College I considered non-military applications of DATAR technology. In simplistic terms, my team had demonstrated the viability of interconnecting three special purpose digital computers in true time. It was essentially a sophisticated (for the time) digital information transmission, storage and retrieval system. In modern terminology, it was a miniature "internet." Furthermore, I had introduced some of the basic components and techniques in my Inaugural Lecture, and it was central to my thinking at the time.

Probably influenced by the fact that cancer was hereditary in my family medical history, I reflected on the possibility of creating a world-wide cancer information network. I reasoned, for example, if information relating to environmental factors such as air and water quality, soil constituents, tobacco consumption and diet could be correlated with the incidence of specific cancers for specific geographical locations, stored digitally and made available world-wide, it would be an important contribution to cancer research. After identifying the major cancer research institutes around the world, my idea was to interconnect them by digital transmission links and install special purpose computers with adequate storage capacity at each center. Originally, I envisaged a network of no more than 10 centers. The information would be continually updated and each center would therefore have available information relating to specific environmental causes of cancer world-wide. The idea was obviously ambitious, but in light of DATAR's success, it was feasible. Regrettably the tentative inquiries I made to governmental funding agencies for support were unsuccessful. Because the idea was so nebulous its publication was very problematical. However, I discussed the concept with Dennis Gabor who, while agreeing it was worth pursuing, at the same time raised the hypothetical issue of the varying qualities of information available from cancer research centers throughout the world. For example, would data originating from a developing country be compatible with that originating from an advanced industrial country? If not, then some method of weighting the information would be required. Gabor suggested that it might be worthwhile to investigate the viability of a computer system predicated on four-valued rather than binary logic. After a preliminary search of the literature, I discovered that many-valued logics had been studied by several logicians, one of whom was none other than Alan Rose of the University of Nottingham, whose parents had both taught at Ulverston Grammar School.

At the time it looked as though many-valued logics might prove useful in modeling information processing systems in which parameters are specified in terms of probabilities. Where, for example, the description of a process involved, logically speaking, not merely "white-black", but more correctly "shades of gray." I became so intrigued by the possibilities that I visited Alan Rose in Nottingham and suggested that his research may have practical applications — as a very pure mathematician, he was impressed, and subsequently undertook the study of relevant problems such as, for example, railroad signaling and switching systems.

But the potential of many-valued logics not only provided me with some fascinating problems, especially in the development of "truth tables," and their circuit equivalents, as well I attracted two outstanding graduate students as collaborators. Peter Vaswani, who pursued the concept in depth (as far as I know he was the only electrical engineering graduate to do so) obtained his Ph.D. and published the material. Jack Cowan was the other.

There is no greater thrill in academic life than to discover a brilliant student, to nurture him and to steer him into an outstanding career. I have been fortunate in this respect and I recall several students (Frank Stoneman was such a student and I will identify others subsequently) who have achieved distinction after graduating. But the student I shall single out for special mention is Jack Cowan in spite of the fact that he only spent a year with me at Imperial College.

Because of my association with Ferranti, I occasionally visited the company's laboratories in northern England and in Edinburgh, Scotland. It was during a visit to Edinburgh that I first met Cowan. Fortunately, that day, his boss was on vacation and his colleagues were attending demonstrations elsewhere. Accordingly, our meeting was serendipitous in so far as Cowan, the most junior, was the only person available to describe to me certain experimental procedures I was interested in. Indeed, Sir John Toothill, the general manager and my guide, even suggested that I should await the availability of a more senior engineer. Apparently Cowan was a recent graduate of the University of Glasgow and had only been hired a few weeks previously. But after a few minutes conversation I was convinced that he was "something special." As a matter of fact, I delayed my departure for London until the following day so that I could spend a couple of hours with him. The upshot was that I persuaded Sir John to grant Cowan a leave of absence on full pay in order that he could spend a year at Imperial College. Remarkably, he was unable to register for the master's degree because his academic qualifications were inadequate. But there was a loophole and he was registered for the Diploma of Imperial College.

Let me briefly summarize Cowan's subsequent phenomenal career. At the end of his year with me, 1957-58, having worked on many-valued logics and related problems, he was awarded a prestigious graduate fellowship to MIT. Incidently, of the eight applicants, he was the only candidate without a doctorate. At MIT he was soon identified as an extraordinarily bright student with a flare for mathematical modeling, and he was recruited by the McCullough-Pitts group. At the time this team of neuro-physiologists was one of the most renowned in the United States. (About a decade subsequently during a visit to Toronto, Bill McCullough gave me a glowing account of Cowan's contributions.) I lost touch with Cowan for a few years until one day I received a brief letter from him which stated: " You'll be interested to know that I've just been appointed Professor of Mathematical Biology at the University of Chicago in succession to Nicholas Rashevski." At the age of 29, Cowan had been appointed to one of the most prestigious chairs in one of the U.S.A.'s most renowned universities. It's interesting to note as well, that at the time, he did not hold a doctorate degree, but shortly thereafter, Imperial College awarded him a doctorate for his distinguished work in neuro-physiology. During the intervening years Cowan has been appointed to joint professorships in mathematics and neurology at Chicago. I know of no other such achievement. I look back on that day in 1957 when I met Jack Cowan with special pride.

It is a special pleasure to recall the blossoming of an idea first germinated at the Military College and mentioned in Chapter Seven — the mathematical laboratory. Most of the credit for the laboratory is due to John Barker, a lecturer in the Department of Electrical Engineering. Even at Imperial College with high admission standards, many engineering students exhibited a positive dislike of mathematics. In light of society's increasing reliance on the design of complex technical systems, this was a serious shortcoming. Essentially due to Barker's energy and drive, the deficiency was largely remedied by providing students with the means of simulating, both mechanically and electronically, basic mathematical procedures (the differential analyzer is a superb example). By identifying a mathematical methodology with a mechanical model, as I personally experienced as a graduate student, the mathematics are much more tractable and understandable. I believe the

Imperial College laboratory was a pioneer in this approach to teaching mathematics. The paper co-authored by Barker and myself, "The Role of A Mathematical Machines Laboratory in Education," published in the Bulletin of The Institute of Physics in 1959 gives an excellent summary of the experiments we developed.

There were several basic problems raised in my Inaugural Lecture which I was anxious to pursue further. One of these was pattern recognition — a fundamental property of complex control systems, and indeed basic to the learning process. The patterns innate in logical truth-tables were of special interest. In view of the advances in the technology of printed electronic circuitry, which were remarkable even at that time and which today are truly miraculous, I reasoned that it might be possible to print logic patterns on silicon wafers, which would perform arithmetical processes directly. For example, the binary addition pattern is very simple, but the real challenge was to develop patterns for binary multiplication involving for example, twenty digits and more. For optimum speed of operation it was necessary to incorporate "instantaneous carry." I collaborated with Jim Calderwood, a lecturer in the department and we wrestled with the problem unsuccessfully for many weeks. We reasoned that if pattern configurations emerged for six binary digital multiplication, we should be able to extrapolate them to n-digits. But we failed. However, several interesting developments emerged as the result of Calderwood and my collaboration and three papers were published in "Journal of Electronics and the Control". The most comprehensive was "Pattern Recognition in the Synthesis of Complex Switching Systems" published in 1958 in which we evoked the concept of "many-valued logics." We concluded that for complex switching systems our approach was more elegant and powerful than the classic Boolean Algebra approach. But time has proved that the ultra-high switching speeds achieved using silicon chip technology are more than adequate for practical purposes. However, we had probed untrodden territory and it was fun.

It was a surprise, early in 1957, albeit a pleasant one, to be invited to act as "external examiner" to the Mechanical Sciences Tripos Part II Examinations in the University of Cambridge. The Tripos, in sheer comprehensiveness and difficulty, without doubt is the pinnacle of engineering undergraduate education in Britain. There was no established curriculum and I was requested to set six questions in the field of control engineering (one question in each of six examination papers) bearing in mind that each of the three-hour examination paper was headed: "Candidates are expected to attempt only a few questions." In fact I learned that a candidate could graduate with high honors based on the answers to two or at most three very difficult questions in each of the examination papers. It was a daunting task and when, a few weeks later, I was requested to provide the University with my formal answers to my questions, I was surprised to discover that they were appreciably more difficult than I had intended. Quite challenging in fact. But that's what was wanted.

The final examiner's meeting was held during the early summer and it was a sheer delight to visit Cambridge at that time of year — the "backs" of the ancient colleges were spectacular. The traditional University "punts" were navigating the River Cam. To cap the experience the suite of rooms I was allocated for two days, in Trinity College, the largest in the University, were those of the senior Tutor — a four-poster bed no less. I attended dinner in the Great Hall at the high table seated next to the Master of Trinity — Nobel Laureate Lord Adrian. The lengthy grace in Latin, before dinner, recited by a scholar of the College still lives in my memory — I recall that my brother, Ronald, a scholar at Queens College, could recite the 100 word grace in Latin as recently as three years ago (1999).

Following dinner the high table adjourned to the Senior Common Room for port, cigars and conversation. What an experience! As well the visit was memorable in my being shown the University Achives where the Tripos Examination papers and the answers, for the past several centuries, are stored. Many years ago, opposite one question, was the response: "No answer to this question has yet been found" — apparently the examiner died before submitting his formal answer.

Shortly after my return from Cambridge I received the sad, but not unexpected, news of my father's death on July 4, 1957. Patricia and I attended his funeral held in the small chapel of Ulverston Cemetery. His grave, adjacent to mother's, is located within a few hundred feet of my paternal and maternal grandparents and many aunts and uncles. As well, Dr. Cousins, my beloved headmaster rests within a few yards. The view from the cemetery overlooks Morecambe Bay, the Plumpton Viaduct and Conishead Priory and is of unsurpassing beauty. It has been a joy to revisit on many occasions most recently in 2000. Another cause for sorrow was the untimely and unexpected death of Douglas Hartree early in 1958 at the age of 61 years. Douglas had been diagnosed with diabetes a few years earlier and this was the basic cause of the fatal heart attack which he suffered en route to his physician for a physical examination.

John Michel, a former differential analyzer colleague and his wife, drove Patricia and myself from Wimbledon to Cambridge for the funeral. It was held in Christ's College Chapel, and it was gratifying to identify many former friends and colleagues in the huge congregation. The chapel was filled to overflowing — among those present were Sir Harold and Lady Jeffreys (Bertha), Maurice Wilkes, Professor Lennard-Jones, and Patrick Blackett. Patricia and I paid our respects to Elaine Hartree and her family. Elaine had been a good friend since my student days. It was a very sad occasion. Subsequently, Sir Charle Darwin, who wrote the official Hartree obituary, for the *Proceedings of the Royal Society* requested me to fill in a few details of the Manchester and WWII years when Douglas and I had worked together.

One of the most rewarding and delightful associations of our brief sojourn in London was undoubtedly our friendship with the Raven family. It came about essentially because Ronald and Kathleen had been pupils at the Ulverston Grammar School and although Ronald was in his final year when I started the school and I only knew him as an outstanding athlete, his sister was in my class. As a matter of fact, Kathleen and I entered the school in Form 1A, in September, 1922. The Ravens were a well-known Lake District family who were resident in Coniston, within a mile or two of Water Yeat where my mother lived for many years. The Ravens had close connections with John Ruskin, the renowned Victorian author and literary critic who had been Professor of Poetry at Oxford. A maternal ancestor of the family was Miles Mason of Mason Ironstone Pottery and Mason Jar fame. Ronald's love of porcelain and pottery inspired the finest private collection in Britain.

I do not recall how Patricia and I met the Ravens in London, almost 30 years after our school-days, but it was fortuitous — he had a profound influence on my future career and on John's as well. During the intervening years, Ronald had become an internationally-famous cancer surgeon and oncologist. He was Senior Consulting Surgeon at the Royal Marsden Cancer Hospital, and Kathleen was the Chief Nursing Officer at the Ministry of Health and Home Security (in effect the head of the nursing profession in Britain).

Because Ronald Raven played such a central role in my early transition from "dyed in the wool" engineering scientist to an academic with much wider interests and sensibilities, it is fitting that I should recall some of the qualities of a man whom I admired so much.

To enter 29 Harley Street, Britain's most prestigious medical residential street, and Patricia and I did so on many occasions, was to enter a living museum. We were enthralled by the sheer beauty of the house. It was obvious that Ronald was a collector of rare and beautiful antiques. Indeed, he always emphasized the therapeutic value of collecting, especially for physicians when there is so often the need to escape the "realities of time for they can be heartbreakingly sad." Our son John obviously agrees, as witness the ardor with which he pursues the art, science and technology of antique automobiles, especially Bentley's.

Dominating his living room was a grand piano which he had played daily. In fact, as a young medical student, he taught piano and always stressed the importance of finger dexterity, induced at the piano, so necessary in surgery.

Patricia and I are the proud possessors of Episodes in My Life by Ronald W. Raven, F.R.C.S. (Faculty Royal College of Surgeons) with a Foreword by Dame Kathleen Raven. It was privately printed in 1998.

After we had made only a few visits to Harley Street, Ronald sensed my burgeoning interest in issues quite remote from electrical engineering per se, and suggested that I might be interested in participating in the work of two bodies which he chaired. One was the Board of the Marie Curie Memorial Foundation, the patron of which was Her Majesty Queen Elizabeth, the Queen-Mother. The Foundation was concerned with the education and rehabilitation of cancer patients as well as the welfare of their families. At the time there were six Marie Curie Homes in Britain. I served on the Board for two years. Because my father was suffering from terminal cancer during this period, I felt a strong personal attachment to the work. I recall during the last several months of my father's illness, when he was suffering intense pain, Ronald Raven contacted a neuro-surgeon in Lancaster who operated on my father and his pain dim-inished dramatically. The second council was that of Epsom College. The College is essentially a large private school dedicated to the pre-university education of physicians. I served on the Council for almost two years. It was an education in itself because my colleagues although for the most part notable physicians, included as well two Cabinet Ministers. It was fortunate at the time there was increasing interest in modernizing the science laboratories of the College and especially in consideration of the future role of computers. I was in my element.

In retrospect there is no doubt that the Ravens sowed a seed which ultimately germinated and blossomed at the University of Saskatchewan and in no small measure was responsible for John's decision to study medicine and to become the accomplished neurologist which he undoubtedly is.

We were fortunate at Imperial College, as indeed at all the institutions with which we've been associated, that the wives of many of my colleagues were gracious hostesses and we were entertained frequently. Three were close friends of Patricia's, but sadly, two are deceased. She is still in touch with Ingelese Argyris, whose husband is a distinguished professor of aerodynamics in Germany. Consequently, we were never lacking in companionship when attending College and University social functions. And there were many. Several were presided over by Queen Elizabeth, the Queen Mother — a gracious hostess who greeted us most cordially on these occasions. One in particular, a banquet held in the magnificent Guild-Hall in the City, for about 200 guests was spectacular — white tie and tails, naval and military full dress uniforms, the ladies wore elegant gowns with long white gloves, and a Toast Master in traditional dress.

During term time, one of the traditional activities of the College was the lunch-hour public lecture. The lecturers were eminent academics and public figures. I was fortunate to be invited to chair one of these during the fall of 1957. The guest lecturer was R.V. Jones, Professor of Natural Philosophy in the University of Aberdeen. We had met at a few meetings during the war when I was a member of the Army Operations Research Group. R.V., as he was universally known, was one of the most charismatic academics I have ever known. As an advisor to Winston Churchill, he had been a key figure in top secret enterprises. [24]

After an entertaining lunch spent mostly reminiscing about the war years, R.V. and I proceeded to the large Chemistry Lecture Theatre, to be greeted by a positively hilarious over-flowing audience of students and faculty. The title of the lecture, "The importance of Practical Joking to Physics," obviously had great appeal. And R.V. did not disappoint. Starting by producing an army revolver from his briefcase and laying it on the lecture bench, he proceeded to enthrall all present with a discourse on how practical joking had played a central role in war-time intelligence throughout history, especially during WWII. As well, he described the practical joking propensities of some of the world's greatest physicists. The lecture ended with thunderous applause. Sadly, R.V. is no longer living, and my last contact with him was in Toronto when we were guests on the widely broadcast Betty Kennedy radio show.

---

[24]"Most Secret War. British Scientific Intelligence 1939-45" R.V. Jones, Hamish Hamilton, London 1978. "Supreme Command" (pp.95-97) Elliott A. Cohen, The Free Press 2002

Another consequence of holding a chair at City and Guilds College was the close association of the College and the Guilds of London, which resulted in Patricia and me being invited to formal dinners held in the "hallowed halls" of several of the Guilds. Perhaps the most enjoyable, not least because the historic gold-plate and table ornaments which were on view, was at the Gold and Silversmith's Hall. The wine and food were excellent in the tradition of one of the oldest Guilds in the world.

The College dinners in Hall were also memorable insofar as faculty and students got together informally and the Lindstead's saw to it that we all had a good time. The other parties still fresh in my memory, were those given by the Gabors in their spacious apartment on the ground floor of a large residence on Queen's Gate adjacent to the College campus. Marjorie, Patricia's closest friend in London, was perhaps the most charming hostess I've ever encountered. She was certainly the ideal consort of a prospective Nobel Laureate and, like Patricia she loved parties. Always present was the ubiquitous Zsa-Zsa, a French poodle with no doubt impeccable credentials. Never having had children of their own, the Gabors were particularly attached to John, who had the kind of inquiring mind which delighted Dennis — two of a kind so to speak. After we left London, it is gratifying to recall that Marjorie remained a good friend of my mother-in-law and sister Carol until their respective deaths. Having Patricia's family in such close proximity was a great advantage. Carol, in particular, was very close to John and Patricia, and they enjoyed visiting many of the historic sites of London, the Tower, the Wren churches (many of which had been bombed) and the spacious and beautiful London parks. Of course, Patricia, the inveterate shopper, thank goodness, was in her element exploring the London shops — the likes of Harrods, Fortnum and Masons and Selfridges, all of which were familiar from her youth.

Despite continuing scholastic success, John continued to be predisposed to asthma attacks. Patricia bore the brunt of caring for him during this critical year of his life. However, during one of his relatively rare periods of remission, Patricia and I, together with Fred and Gladys Williams, were able to spend a few days in Paris as the guests of the Ferranti Company represented by Eric and Eva Grundy.

Neither Fred, who effectively launched the Ferranti Company into digital computers, nor I, at a much lower level, were regarded as paid consultants. But we were entertained, often lavishly, by the Grundys on behalf of the company. One such occasion was the visit to Paris during the spring of 1957. The excuse was the World Congress of Electrical

Power Engineers Meeting, but the main object was for us to enjoy the sights of Paris, especially the night life. Never having visited Paris before (and only a couple of times since) Patricia and I and our friends the Williams were introduced to such delights as the Folie Bergere, the Moulin Rouge, dinner at Maxim's, the Crazy Horse, and visits to the Eiffel Tower, Notre Dame and Montmartre. Four days and nights we shall never forget.

My visit to Montreal, Canada, during the summer resulted from an invitation by Omond Solandt, then Vice-Chairman of Canadian National Railroads, to act as a consultant on methods of freight car identification, and location, to optimize the utilization of railroad rolling stock. I spent a month on this project which comprised the initial step in the computerization of the railroad operations. (It is of interest that a year or two subsequently, Jim Williams, who had been a member of my team at Ferranti, became head of computer operations at the company.)

At the conclusion of my study Omond intimated that he was unwilling to let me "escape" from Canada and that I had an important role to play in Canadian affairs in the future. As events transpired, he proved to be correct and he continued to play a central role in my life. The invitation to present the prizes at the Wimbledon High School for Girls, probably resulted from my continuing efforts to attract young women into the electrical engineering profession. The date set for the ceremony was during the fall of 1957. That evening I was accompanied on the platform of the school hall by Patricia, the Headmistress and members of the teaching staff, and sitting on the front row in the midst of the prize-winners was John and his grandmother. There must have been at least 500 school girls present.

Because in those days high school teachers generally wore academic gowns, caps and hoods on such occasions, I decided to wear my doctorate regalia (bright red gown, gold silk hood and velvet cap). After my short address emphasizing the important part women would play in the future in such engineering enterprises as computer software development and ergonomics, I presented the prizes. As each prizewinner stood in front of me and literally curtsied, I responded by raising my cap ("capping" is the official term). I only hope that I was able to convince the girls that some of them had an exciting future in the world of engineering.

The fall of 1957, however, turned out to be a stressful period for John and Patricia. Adapting to a new school, especially a large prestigious school such as Kings College School Wimbledon, was in itself a traumatic experience. New boys are always subject to a degree of "hazing" by more senior classmen, and John, especially was considered to be a "foreigner" — the " Canadian kid." Coupled with his asthma attacks, which caused several absences from school — indeed an oxygen tent was required during one attack — Patricia and he were, to put it mildly, going through a difficult period. But relief was in sight from an unexpected source.

A letter from Dr. C. J. MacKenzie, the eminent Canadian engineer, arrived on my birthday, December 8, 1957. It had a profound effect on our lives. Early in his career C.J. MacKenzie had been Dean of Engineering at the University of Saskatchewan in Saskatoon. Pending the retirement of the current dean (Dean Fraser) he had been asked to recommend a successor. He wrote to ask "would I be interested in the appointment?"

Of all the decisions which have confronted us, this turned out to be the most difficult. Central to our reflections on the merits of a potential move from London to Saskatoon was John's health. Both Patricia and I were confident that we could settle in Western Canada. After all we had already proved to be a very adaptable family and from a professional point of view, the dean's job was an obvious challenge.

Life in London had many attractions, not least family ties and friends. Imperial College was a wonderful institution, probably the finest of its kind in the British Commonwealth, and we were settled in Wimbledon with excellent educational opportunities for John. But London and its environs obviously had a deleterious influence on his health. The many blood tests he endured to identify the allergens which gave rise to his asthmatic condition were convincing evidence that we were not living in a benign environment.

Before replying to the MacKenzie letter, Patricia and I made every possible effort to assess the risks of a potential move. Two sources of information provided us with most of the answers.

Sir Graham Sutton, my former colleague at Military College of Science, in the interim had been appointed Director — General of the Meteorological Office, and he was extremely helpful. I telephoned him and within a few days he had supplied us with detailed information relating to climate (much drier albeit colder in winter than London's) and other environmental factors. Through his good offices we were provided with the opinions of specialists in respiratory diseases, especially allergic asthma, regarding John's potential sensitivity to prevailing allergens in Western Canada. Their conclusions were very positive — Saskatoon would be a much more desirable place for John to grow up than London!

Insofar as information relating to living conditions, including costs, was concerned we benefitted greatly from the advice of the Saskatchewan Trade Commissioner in London. The Commissioner, Mr. Graham Spry and his wife provided a plethora of data and their good friendship as well. They were a delightful couple. We became convinced that a return to Canada would be beneficial.

While neither my family nor Patricia's were enthusiastic about our proposed departure from Britain once again, they nevertheless understood the circumstances and were very supportive. My mother, still adjusting to the death of my father less than a year previously, and my mother-in-law in poor health, must have felt sad, but they never admitted it. We were lucky to have parents who accepted their offsprings' decisions with such forbearance. As well, Carol, close as she was to her sister and nephew, was equally gracious. Although Patrick Blackett expressed a measure of displeasure, even suggesting that we should consider sending John to school in Switzerland (unthinkable!), he finally approved and my other colleagues were of like mind. It was gratifying that both the Rector and Arnold Tustin felt we were making the right decision, and so did the Gabors.

Incidently, shortly after my positive response to C.J. MacKenzie's letter, the president of the university, Dr. J.M. Thomson, wrote a delightful letter confirming my appointment and outlining the terms. During the all too brief period before his retirement I found him to be a delightful colleague and friend.

Not surprisingly, Patricia with her ususal acumen for managing our affairs, quickly got down to planning our second transatlantic move — even to the extent of getting in touch with a builder in Saskatoon, purchasing a lot and arranging for a four-bedroom home to be built. Being fully occupied completing research projects, preparing papers for publication and finishing my teaching commitments precluded me from active participation in the preparations, but that has been "par for the course" in the many moves we have undertaken! Fortunately, however, during our final few months in London, Patricia, John and Carol found opportunities to attend a few shows. Never having been a true theatre lover in contrast to Patricia whose dedication to all the arts was inbred during her school days at Twickenham County School where theatre played a prominent role in her education, I did not take advantage of the many attractions provided by the world renowned London theatre. Nor for that matter of many of the classical concerts that were available. But I recall a special occasion. Patricia, John and I attended the Drury Lane Theatre to see one of the first performances, after the New York premier, of *My Fair Lady* with Julie Andrews and Stanley Holloway. It was an unforgettable experience.

A farewell dinner at the College in June 1958 hosted by Arnold Tustin was a sad occasion. But everybody appreciated the reason for our comparatively early departure from London. I was presented with a beautiful leather bound and gold embossed booklet — "The Charter of the Imperial College of Science and Technology — on the occasion of the Golden Jubilee 1907-1957," signed by all members of the staff. The inscription reads: "Presented to Professor Arthur Porter by his friends at the Imperial College as a token of their esteem and regard and with their warmest good wishes for his future."

Our final appearance at the College was in June 2000. We were invited by the Pro-Rector to attend the Dennis Gabor 100th anniversary celebrations. They were attended by at least 100 invited guests, mostly former staff and graduate students. A National Holiday — Dennis Gabor Day — was declared in Hungary and a satellite radio link between the Royal Society of Hungary in Budapest and Imperial College had been organized. Many old friends, including Jack Cowan, who had made a special trip from Chicago, greeted us. The formal lunch, sitting with Jack Cowan, was a fitting conclusion to the celebrations — they closed a chapter in our lives which had left so many treasured memories, some sad but most happy.

In closing this chapter it is also fitting for historical purposes, to mention the fact that Patricia and I have just seen on television the Memorial Service, held on February 4, 2003, in Houston, Texas, to honor the Columbia seven who lost their lives in the shuttle disaster on February 1.

Huntsman with Lakeland pack of fox hounds.

*My mother and dad on their
wedding day at
Station House, Ulverston,
August 1908.*

*Aged three years, wearing a
velvet tunic sewn by my mother, 1913.*

Ulverston Victoria Grammar School prefects, 1929, 1930.
Dr. H.W. Cousins, headmaster, and myself as head prefect.

School Cricket XI, June 1930. Ronald and I, back row,
second and third from left.

The Differential Analyzer, 1934. I am operating the machine and Douglas Hartree, my professor, stands proudly by. This photograph was first published in the Meccano Magazine, June 1934.

The family and friends seeing me off at Liverpool, on board R.M.S. Laconia, September 1937.

My brother, Robert, 1937.

My brother, Ronald, 1937.

*Arthur Armitage
on board the Laconia.*

*Runkle House, M.I.T., November 1937.
Oscar Puls, Fred Merrill and I.*

*High Sierras, California,
Summer 1938. Yosemite
National Park.*

Mother and dad
at Birkrigg, 1939.

Best man at John and Elsa Dixon's wedding.
August 1940, during the Battle of Britain.

Our wedding day, July 26, 1941. From left to right: Dad, Mother, Robert,
groom and bride, Carol, Elsa Dixon, Mabel and Vernon Dixon.

My father-in-law Lt. Col. V. G. Dixon, centre front row, on the occasion of a visit by General Sir Frederick Pile, Commander in Chief, Anti-Aircraft Command, to his regiment.

Time cover photo of V. Bush, April 1944.

*Professor Douglas Hartree in his office at the
Cavendish Laboratory, Cambridge.*

*Professor Hartree and Dr. Vannevar Bush—prior to Dr. Bush's
receiving an honorary doctorate at Cambridge University, 1950.*

During World War II most people who flew across the Atlantic were designated "Short Snorters." The certificate of membership in the "Short Snorter Club" was a one dollar bill on which the signatures of other members were written. Life membership in the club cost $1.00 paid to the Short Snorter who performed the induction.

Arther Porter, Short Snorter, introduced by Cdr. Keith Walter, R.N., during a Boeing Flying Boat flight (Poole, Lisbon, Bathurst, Belem, Trinidad, Bermuda, Baltimore) February 6-9, 1945. Arthur Porter returned to the U.K. (Montreal, Goose Bay, Keflavik, Prestwick) in a Liberator, April 13-14, 1945.

Patricia and John
at Shrivenham, January 1948.

Military College of Science, visit of
Rt. Hon. Clement Attlee, Prime Minister,
1948. The Commandant Major General
Shapland, Dean Lander, and four Deans.
From left to right: Porter, Baughan,
Sutton, and Thompson with
Senior Staff Officers.

Kenyon Taylor and I, 1953.

The Ferranti Electric Research Department, Scarborough, Ontario, 1954.

Friend and mentor Omond Solandt, Chancellor of the University of Toronto. Formerly Chairman of the Canadian Research Board.

Dinner at the Dorchester Hotel, London, 1957. Patricia, Dr. and Mrs. W.S. Elliott (Bill and Berry), and I.

University of London Invitation

*University of Saskatchewan, meeting of all four Deans of Engineering
since inception of College of Engineering.
From left to right: C.J. MacKenzie (1922-1939), R.A. Spencer (1942-1953),
I.M. Frazer (1953-1958), A. Porter (1958-1961).*

*John on our "homemade"
ice rink at Saskatoon, 1960.*

Belfountain, our home in the Caledon Hills, 1962-1988.

Marshall McLuhan, director of the Center for Culture and Technology,
University of Toronto, with students.

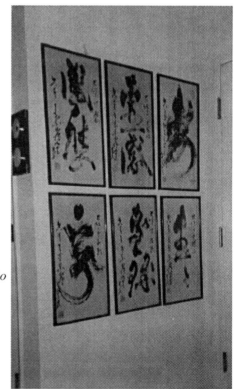

Calligraphies written by Bishop Kojo
Sakamoto, Kyoto, Japan
for me as a consequence of the
Canada Council Seminar, 1967.

Montreal World Exhibition, 1967.

University of Western Ontario, Academic Commissioner, 1969-1971, on the campus of the university.

*John's graduation ceremony, Queen's University,
Kingston, Ontario, June 1971.*

Proud parents with John after the ceremony.

Mother and her three boys at Water Yeat, 1978.

Her Majesty Queen Elizabeth II and the Rt. Hon. Lord Nelson, President of the Institution of Electrical Engineers on the occasion of the Centenary Celebrations, May 1971. Shortly after this photograph was taken, Patricia and I were presented to her majesty.

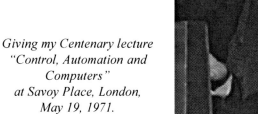

Giving my Centenary lecture "Control, Automation and Computers" at Savoy Place, London, May 19, 1971.

*Royal Commission on Electric Power Planning, myself as Chairman,
with Solanac Plourde-Gagnon and William W. Stevenson, at a hearing
of the Commission in Toronto, 1979.*

*My family at Wyndemere
Country Club, Naples, Florida.
Kathryn and I, John, Patricia,
and Ian and Gregory, 1986.*

*Order of Canada Investiture,
Rideau Hall, Ottawa, April 1984.*

A Caribbean cruise, 1994.

Reunion with Dartmouth "guys" at Pinehurst, North Carolina.
I'm between Bob Schwartz (l.) and Adrian Weiss, September 2001.

My grandchildren at Jennifer's wedding, October 2000.
From left to right: Ian, Jennifer, Trevor, Gregory.

My 92nd birthday with John and Kathryn.

Chapter 10

SASKATCHEWAN — RHAPSODY IN ACADEME

HAVING said our farewells to family and friends, oft times tearful, we headed for unknown territory 5000 miles away before the days of jet air travel. It was a daunting prospect, especially for Patricia and John. But as always we were optimists and survivors. We were determined to retain our most treasured possessions — the grandfather clock, antique furniture, paintings, ornaments and books — most of which had already survived two trans-Atlantic crossings. And as an after thought, especially because of John's attachment to it, the Berkeley, a small plastic-bodied 3-cylinder 2-cycle automobile which we had purchased during the fall of 1957. Apart from the car, most of the other items are still in our home here in Bermuda Village or in John and Kathryn's, a couple of miles away, constant reminders of our English roots and powerful endorsements of the survival quality of the furnishings crafted two centuries earlier.

The voyage to Montreal was uneventful, largely because we are all good sailors, and we continued from there by train to Toronto. Incidently, no longer immigrants, but Canadian citizens, we breezed through Customs and Immigration. It was a thrill to return to a city which had provided so much adventure and excitement, and especially to be welcomed by our friends the Corkums. We'd met Wynnis and Perry at a holiday resort in the Haliburton Lake Country during the fall of 1949. We stayed in their lovely home in West Toronto, Patricia and John for about four days, myself for a single day. I was anxious to get settled in Saskatoon.

I boarded the Canadian Pacific(CPR) Trans-Continental train in

Toronto. A bedroom had been reserved and superb meals were served in the adjacent dining car. In retrospect the two-days plus journey was a delight. A wonderland unfolded of quite different proportions to any I had encountered previously.

In spite of having explored, in 1938, a goodly trek of territory in North America, I was nevertheless enchanted during the train journey out west, to see first-hand the extraordinary size of my adopted country.

The first day we skirted the shores of the Great Lakes — the Canadian Shield. The outcroppings of granite, especially those north of Lake Superior, which have been deeply eroded by glacial action, are truly spectacular. This was "Group of Seven" terrain — my family and I now possess several large volumes of the works of these talented Canadian painters. Crossing the Ontario-Manitoba border on the second day brought about a marked change of scenery. This is the land of a thousand lakes beloved by fishermen who travel hundreds of miles to get there, often by private plane from the United States. The City of Winnipeg was a surprise — a veritable metropolis of half a million people emerged after many miles of desolate country. And then the prairies — Canada's most fertile land and one of the great wheat producing regions. It has been called the "Bread Basket of the World."

The prairies of Manitoba and Saskatchewen, in the early fall, presented an incredible vista — thousands of square miles of farmland. An ocean of golden wheat which rippled in the wind like waves stretching to the far horizons and in places, four abreast, huge combine harvesters were in operation. The wheat is transported to massive grain elevators that dot the landscape. So characteristic of the prairie scene — a scene with which we were to become very familiar during the three years of our lives in the Province of Saskatchewan. A scene incidently which is ever present in our living room in one of Robert Hurley's memorable paintings — a parting gift from the students of the College.

Saskatoon, a city of some 120,000 inhabitants can be likened to an oasis in a limitless desert of golden wheat. Only the train journey could really reveal such delights, and fortunately it was to be repeated on several occasions before we eventually left the city. But the railroad station dominated by grain elevators is of course characteristically prairie. Indeed almost plebeian — not an attractive foretaste of our future home. I reflected on arrival on the contrast between London's spectacular railway terminals and Saskatoon's railway depot. What would Patricia and John think? I anticipated, correctly, that their thoughts would parallel mine — What have we got ourselves into?

My disquiet was transitory. The warm welcome by President Thomson who drove me across the huge bridge spanning the South Saskatchewan River to what I still consider to be the most attractive university campus in Canada was all that was needed to reassure me. Even the sparse temporary accommodation assigned to us in the University Union complex, did not dampen my enthusiasm, especially after meeting Professor and Mrs. Abramson and their young son who were fellow residents. They were a delightful family — members of the faculty of the Department of Sociology and highly talented flutists.

Soon after our arrival we were fortunate to meet Dr. Irwin Hilliard and his wife, Agnes through the kind recommendation of our mutual friend Omond Solandt. Irwin and Omond had been classmates at medical school and the Hilliards had come to Saskatoon a few years previously. Irwin was chief of medicine at the medical school and through them we met many of the medical faculty. Agnes was active in the hospital auxiliary and introduced Patricia to this rewarding volunteer work which she continued in Toronto.

My first week in the dean's office was an education. First and foremost I had the support of a superb assistant dean, Bill Staples, without whose friendship and advice I would have floundered for many months. Bill knew all the angles and the "angels" as well! However, I didn't accept all his advice as witness, for example, the cases of two former students who having failed second year rather badly were denied readmission by the assistant dean after a two-year hiatus. They insisted on seeing me to plead their respective cases. On one hand, within a few days of my arrival, I obviously had to be loyal to Bill who was much more cognizant of the students' records than me, on the other, the students' futures were at stake. I gave them a sympathetic hearing and, in agreeing to their reinstatement, I stressed that if they failed once again, they would not only let down themselves but me as well. Three years subsequently at my last convocation in 1961, I was proud to note that both students had graduated, one with "distinction," and the other with the rarely awarded, "great distinction."

Another more entertaining encounter with a student also occurred during my early days in the dean's chair. Because my secretary was absent, I was not alerted to the fact that I had a visitor. Suddenly, without warning, my office door opened and a student, dressed in plaid shirt, jeans and cowboy boots, entered. He stood, looked at me, and said "Hi!" Being distracted trying to make some sense out of the College budget and somewhat perplexed by this apparent "breech" of etiquette, I hesitated before responding, "Hi." I shall always be grateful to that particular student. He had provided me with an instant education into the ways of the West. It was a "new ball game.".

The week-end after our arrival turned out to be the traditional Home Coming celebration, signaling the return of students to the campus after their almost five-month vacation. For many students these months had been spent working on family farms and most of the others, working on summer jobs in order to pay their university fees and living expenses. (I've always regarded the idea of summer jobs for North American students as a wonderful adjunct to their education — unfortunately they were non-existent in Britain when I was a student.)

Key events were the annual football game ("Varsity" versus another school in the "Western Conference"), college reunions and parties, and from our point of view, especially John's, the colorful parade of floats through the main thoroughfares of Saskatoon. Financed by local businesses and banks, and designed by students, these were quite elaborate affairs. One, in particular, caught our eye and thrilled us. It had been designed by the College of Engineering — against a background of pure white blossoms were the huge letters in black, reading: FAREWELL DEAN FRASER — WELCOME DEAN PORTER.

My first official meeting with fellow deans, notably the deans of Arts and Science (Francis Leddy) Law (Frederic Cronkite), Medicine (Wendell McCleod) was at a Disciplinary Committee meeting less than two weeks after my arrival. Three engineering students had been detained by the campus police after forcing an entry into the nursing students' dormitory with "felonious intent." In fact a "panty-raid!"

I regarded myself as their "defense attorney" and indeed, the Dean of Law congratulated me on my performance. My argument was to the effect that such activities were highly desirable for students' (both female and male) morale. But the "punch-line" of my defense was I had discovered that the co-conspirators who encouraged the "raid" were in fact the student nurses themselves. Verdict – "not guilty." I believe the general consensus thereafter among engineering students was "the new dean is OK."

While I was familiarizing myself with the College of Engineering in particular — six departments (civil, electrical, mechanical, agricultural machinery, geology and mining) — and the university administration in general, Patricia was fully occupied with furnishing our new home, 521 Bate Crescent, ready about a month after our arrival, finding a school for John and adapting to an entirely new environment.

Brunskill School turned out to be ideal and John did well because he had been well grounded in English schools. A classmate, another boy from England, John Crabb, son of the Principal of Emmanuel College, became a close friend and this friendship persisted for many years. As a consequence of the friendship, John was accepted as a member of the choir of St. John's Cathedral under the stewardship of Dean Wood. The choir-master, Kenneth Ansell, was a very special and talented musician, and a great favorite of our son. Indeed, John began to adapt to Saskatoon, even more quickly than his parents and even more importantly, the persistent asthma attacks he had suffered in England did not recur. He took on a neighborhood newspaper route which was an arduous undertaking in the bitter cold winters. The cold never seemed to worry John, and I recall that he would often return home on a late winter afternoon with his scarf frozen to his chin, but with rosy cheeks looking very different from the pale faced boy he had been.

Our neighbors were Professor Peter Forsyth and his family. I had met Peter in Ottawa during visits there in the early 50's. Peter and Lucille and their children, Leslie and Peter, became close friends and we enjoyed a warm relationship which compensated somewhat for the loss of our English relatives.

It was a real thrill, for Patricia and I to attend a school concert one evening, in which John played the guitar and sang "The Streets of Laredo," after only a few months instruction.

As I mentioned earlier the college budget for the 1959 university year required my urgent attention. With Bill Staples help and input from heads of departments, I prepared a budget which turned out to be about 40 percent greater than that for the current year. I emphasized, in particular, the urgent need to update departmental laboratories, acquire new faculty and an engineering library.

I was conscious of the fact that the influence of the great depression during which the Province had suffered markedly, was still paramount. In the past, departmental heads had been praised for limiting their budgets to absolute minimums. It was time to inaugurate a new era!

A few days after I had presented my budget to the finance committee and stressed that I was no longer seeking praise for frugality, I was accosted by Colb McEwan, the Vice-President. He announced — "Arthur, the honeymoon's over!" I replied — "Colb, it hasn't even started!"

After having achieved my immediate objectives for the primary needs of the College, I turned to the graduate and research component.

This was one of the major topics at the first faculty meeting which I chaired. Prior to the meeting I had briefed heads of departments and suggested that we should proceed by establishing standing committees on graduate studies, research programs and the possibility of setting up an engineering physics undergraduate program in order to encourage the academically inclined student. The whole faculty accepted the new ideas with enthusiasm and the new committees were approved and established during the meeting. It was a good start! Even though after the meeting I was mildly rebuked by the dean of graduate studies, John Spinks, (John and Mary subsequently became close friends) for being a "trifle dictatorial."

I then turned my attention to post-graduate education. In 1958 only five graduate students were enrolled for master's degrees in the College as a whole. This was obviously most unsatisfactory, especially in a period when technological advances were in evidence world-wide and when the need for trained specialists was escalating. A top priority, therefore, was to obtain funds for research. It was here that my contacts in Ottawa, notably the National Research Council (NRC) and Defense Research Board paid dividends. Accordingly I submitted a grant application for about $50,000 (a large sum in those days) to the NRC. A few days later I heard from Ottawa that the Council had not only approved my application, but had in fact increased it by $20,000. I was informed that this was very unusual. Every department in the College benefitted and a major drive began to encourage the top undergraduate students to consider undertaking post-graduate programs.

It was fortuitous that I had already procured a student for my personal research — an immigrant from London. In my last lecture to final year students at Imperial College, in anticipation of my move to University of Saskatchewan, I asked — "Would anyone be interested in joining me?" to my great surprise, one did. John Cook, another of my rewarding discoveries.

John Cook was a dedicated student with interdisciplinary interests and like myself he was willing to take risks. After obtaining his master's of engineering at Saskatchewan, he proceeded to take a Ph.D in psychology at an American university. I was agreeably surprised to discern how quickly John fell in love with western Canada and its people, both literally and figuratively. One Saturday morning during the fall of '58 there was a knock at our front door and Patricia answered it. A typical prairie farmer (he probably farmed at least 500 acres) quite forcefully demanded to "see the dean." Brushing aside Patricia's remark that I was extremely busy and could not be disturbed, he prevailed and I came upstairs from my study in the basement. "What did I know about John Cook?" was his opening gambit. "What for and why?" was my response! "He wants to marry my daughter (a student nurse) next month." I assured him that John had an unblemished character, came of a highly respected English family and had brilliant career prospects. He accepted my strong endorsement with gratitude and the happy couple were married in early 1959. Twenty-seven years later during our last visit to Saskatoon in 1986, Patricia and I were entertained for breakfast by the Cook family. At that time John was a full professor of psychology, a tower of strength in the university, and a father of six children, two of whom were married. We've rarely met a more devoted family.

As a matter of fact the project I had in mind for John Cook was an extension of the logical pattern research which Jim Calderwood and I carried out in London. Design, build and test a "logic computer" predicated on binary logic. It was probably through his work with this device that John eventually chose psychology for his career.

The onset of winter in the prairie is truly remarkable. One day it might be plus 70 degrees F and the next 0 degrees F, usually early in November, but rarely with snow — that comes in December. To those who've never experienced minus 40 degrees F wind chill, it's difficult to describe. Essential commodities are fur caps and fur lined boots, "long-johns" for men and "snuggies"for the ladies. For the automobiles, block heaters and wheel chains. During icy pavement conditions I found a ski-pole a valuable adjunct. During our first winter there were few episodes more memorable than "the dean's epic drive to work one brilliantly sunny but very cold morning in January."

I set off to walk via a short-cut inaccessible to motor vehicles which reduced the distance from home to office to about a mile. After about a quarter of a mile facing a 20 mph wind and with a wind chill of minus 25 degrees F, I quit!

Patricia had taken John to school in our newly acquired Ford car so the Berkeley was the only alternative. Fortunately it started, but I quickly discovered that, with no heater, visibility through windscreen and side windows was zero. No other option was available but to drive the car with the "top down." It was a horrendous three-mile drive. My arrival at the College coincided with the period for change of classes and I was cheered vociferously by the students as I drove into the shelter of the Agricultural Engineering Laboratory. The story is told on campus to this day (at least it was in 1986 when we last visited) of the dean who drove to work in a small convertible with the top down in minus 25 degree F wind chill weather!

Incidently, the Berkeley featured prominently in our first Saskatoon Christmas outdoor decorations. The idea was to "keep up with the Jones." It was probably John's idea to drive, and lift, the Berkeley on to the front lawn through a foot of snow. We acquired a life-size wood Santa as the "driver" with accompanying bags of brightly colored gifts and a huge sign "WELCOME SANTA." The whole display was illuminated by flood lights and together with our well-decorated home and the fabulous snow background, we had a very unique display which few, if any, of our neighbors could match! But nevertheless it was a pleasant surprise to see our display featured on the front page of the Saskatoon Star Phoenix which John proudly showed us a few days before Christmas.

Nor did the winter frolic subside until the end of March. Early in December 1958 we had flooded our backyard with the garden hose and set up a primitive ice hockey rink. The ice surface was renewable in a few minutes in those frigid conditions. Although by no means good skaters (I had some experience in Britain and during the winters of '37 and '38 in New England) John and I enjoyed our "hockey games" on our private rink.

There is an unexpected and little appreciated academic advantage associated with cocktail parties in university towns. We had a surfeit of them in Saskatoon, especially during the winter months. As a matter of fact I met both Bill Feindel and Marshall McLuhan at cocktail parties. Both have had a profound impact on my career and our family fortunes.

I met Bill Feindel at a party hosted by the President. It was a standing joke among senior faculty members that the President's parties were in fact faculty meetings during which members of the teaching staff were segregated in the east end of the Presidential house, while their spouses were diverted to the west end. After about a couple of hours the groups were reunited at a sumptuous supper.

Dr. William H. Feindel, who trained under the internationally-acclaimed Dr. Wilder Penfield at the Montreal Neurological Institute (MNI), was Professor of Neurosurgery at the time and presently holds the same chair at the MNI. But before detailing our relationship, let me comment briefly on the background.

In many respects the university was ripe for interdisciplinary activity. The reason was essentially that being comparatively geographically isolated, a spirit of improvisation and self-sufficiency pervaded the campus. This was not only a characteristic of the university community but of prairie communities in general. Isolation breeds creativity and creativity is, or should be, a major aim of all educational establishments, especially the university. Of all academic faculty interfaces, one of the most fertile is that of medicine and engineering, and Bill and I complemented each other perfectly. Having held a Rhodes Scholarship at Oxford for three years he was well attuned to academe in Britain. Our meeting was essentially the catalyst that sparked several joint research programs between the medical and engineering faculties, and which subsequently gave birth to "biomedical engineering" as a formal discipline in the university. It was encouraging as well that Dr. Irwin Hilliard gave us strong support. A few years hence Irwin was to play a key role in John's medical education and to become our family physician. The best we've ever had. There is little doubt in my mind that the University of Saskatchewan was the first university in Canada to formally establish the discipline and probably one of the first in the world.

At the aforementioned party, Bill and I reviewed several aspects of neurosurgery in which electronic engineering might contribute. The problem of monitoring blood flow in major arteries of the brain, during surgical procedures was one such. In order to compensate for variations due to cardiac pulse a comparatively simple electronic analog computing device was required. I knew instinctively that one of the best people in Canada to tackle such problems was Norman Moody, at the time an electronics engineer with the Defense Research Telecommunications Establishment in Ottawa. I mentioned this to Bill who immediately responded "Can you get him?" I said — "I'll try."

Because Moody was the senior electronic circuit designer, working on the first Canadian satellite — "Alouette," — I knew that it would be a difficult proposition to persuade him to leave Ottawa, where Joan and he were so well-established and to embark on an entirely different career at the University of Saskatchewan. But it was worth a try.

It was fortuitous incidently that at the time the chairmanship of the Electrical Engineering Department would become vacant because of the retirement of Professor Lovell. Although Moody had had no academic experience and indeed was not even a university graduate, I was convinced that he was eminently suited for what I had in mind. It was a tough selling job, but eventually after I had made two trips to Ottawa, he agreed to apply for the Professorship of Electrical Engineering and the Chairmanship of the department.

As required by university statute, the post was duly advertised in appropriate scientific and engineering journals and in national newspapers. The response was excellent. A dozen applicants many of whom had Ph.Ds. Under my chairmanship the Appointments Committee selected a short list of five candidates and I insisted that in spite of his lack of academic qualifications, Norman Moody should be included. His only professional qualification was an associate membership in the Institution of Electrical Engineers, but I stressed that this was a prestigious qualification.

Appointments to departmental chairmanships were made by committees chaired by the President and included the dean of the relevant college (myself), the Dean of Graduate Studies, two chairmen of departments and three members of the Governing Council of the university. The meeting started at 8 p.m. because two of the governors resided in Regina.

After a brief introduction, the President turned to me and said, "After reviewing the five applicants Mr. Dean, have you a specific recommendation?" I replied, "Yes, but I would prefer to hear the comments of the other committee members first." Not surprisingly, not a single member recommended Moody and another candidate was favored. Now it was my turn! When I recommended Moody, there was shock and disbelief on every face. I had a major selling job on my hands! One of the governors immediately pointed out that Moody's application was incomplete in so far as his C.V. did not show any education at university level and indeed that his formal education had been completed at the age of 17. I responded that in fact the C.V. was correct, but because of the outbreak of WWII in 1939, Norman Moody after high school graduation was posted to a radar research station where electronic technicians were urgently required. Subsequently he had a meteoric career in government laboratories in Britain and Canada and had published several important papers on the design of unique electronic circuits.

Fortunately the Dean of Graduate Studies (John Spinks, soon to become President of the university) backed me, although at times the discussion was acrimonious. To solve the undoubted problem of Moody's lack of academic qualifications, the President made a truly magnanimous gesture — Moody would be awarded the B.E. (Sask) degree, honoris causa on his taking up the appointment as Professor of Electrical Engineering. My intuition had not let me down, and indeed, Norman Moody has had a brilliant career in biomedical electronics culminating in his election as a Fellow of the Royal Society of Canada, his leadership of the University of Toronto Institute of Biomedical Electronics, and his retirement from the university as Professor Emeritus.

The story of what ensued as a consequence of the collaboration between the Colleges of Engineering and Medicine is much too lengthy to be included in these memoirs. I hope it will not be overlooked when the history of biomedical engineering is eventually published. But it may not be out of place to mention a few of the early studies:

- Measurement of blood transit times between carotid artery and various points in the brain. This has appreciably improved the diagnosis and surgical treatment of certain diseases of the brain.

- Cardiac diagnosis using improved vector electrocardiography

- Application of automatic control technology in improving the safety of heart-lung machines in "open-heart" surgery.

- Improvement of the tensile strength of delicate sutures used in eye surgery.

To familiarize myself with some of these problems I personally observed several surgical operations performed by Eric Nanson, Professor of Surgery. Standing on a "Porter's stool," looking over the surgeon's shoulder, I had an intimate view of the procedures which included open heart and abdominal operations.

But most memorable was the brain surgery. I attended several neuro-surgical procedures and saw first hand how important it was to obtain accurate monitoring of blood flow in the brain. On one special occasion Bill invited both my son John and myself to attend. It was a new procedure for Parkinsonianism. From that day John's future career was decided — he was enthralled, and his interest in medicine never faltered subsequently.

There were several important developments in addition to biomedical engineering, especially in research and graduate studies. These were made possible largely because of the generous financial support of the National Research Council and DRB. All departments benefitted and several bright young faculty were recruited. One name stands out — Peter Nikiforuk. He was recommended to me by Professor John West, Professor of Electrical Engineering, Queen's University, Belfast, with whom I had many contacts in the past through our common interest in automatic control systems, After much "arm-twisting" I persuaded John Mantle, head of mechanical, that Peter would be an admirable choice to teach thermodynamics. This was quite intuitive on my part because Nikiforuk had never studied thermodynamics in his life, but it worked. He was a resounding success in the College, spearheaded control system research, subsequently was elected a Fellow of the Royal Society of Canada and became Dean of the College. I'm proud to have launched him on his brilliant career in Canada.

As the premier educational institution in the province, members of faculty were frequently consulted on provincial affairs. During the first year of my deanship I was appointed to membership of the Saskatchewan Research Council and the Board of the Saskatchewan Power Corporation (with headquarters in Regina). These were worthwhile, albeit time-consuming, activities which gave me insights into the operation of high-level government agencies. Indeed, the chairman of the Power Corporation was a senior provincial cabinet minister and two other cabinet members were my colleagues. It was as a direct consequence of these "extra-curricular" activities that I assumed a friendly relationship with the Hon. Tommy Douglas, Premier of the province and subsequently a member of the federal parliament. He was the colorful leader of the New Democratic Party in Canada for many years. My final meeting with Tommy, as he always preferred to be called, was during the fall of 1961 when I met with him in the Members' Dining Room of the House of Commons in Ottawa.

Probably my most significant contribution to the Power Corporation was my strong advocacy of the role of a high speed computer, not only in power system operations, but also in governmental activities as a whole. As a direct result, a Ferranti-Packard FP 6000 computer was subsequently installed and held the record for length of high performance operations for medium range computers for 17 years. This not only benefitted the Power Corporation but the Ferranti Company as well.

By the time I gave my annual report to the university senate I was beginning to feel very much at home. Most of my original plans were well in hand and most importantly I felt that I had the confidence of both faculty and students. Not surprisingly therefore, I presented a vigorous assessment of the needs of my College and was by no means reticent in my choice of words. For example, I began by emphasizing the fact that my predecessors had been congratulated for keeping College budgets to minimum levels. In contrast I announced that I would not seek such plaudits, but would be seeking additional funds to remedy the obvious deficiencies in laboratories and research which had resulted. Not least because I was aware that several provincial legislators were members of

Senate, I emphasized the importance of provincial enterprise and concluded as follows: -

"In conclusion I hope I have succeeded in indicating in a general way, our forward thinking and planning and particularly how we hope the activities of the College as a whole, especially in the field of research, will be aimed at some of the more pressing technological problems with which the province will be faced in the future. And that, in so doing, we will play our part in the establishment of new industries in the province and in particular in insuring by modern methods of research that we are utilizing the resources of the provinces in man and materials to the full for the benefit of all."

I think the new dean made a good impression!

My first year at U. of S. ended with the convocation ceremony when, as dean, I presented over 100 candidates (many of Ukranian extraction with almost unpronounceable names) for the degree of Bachelor of Engineering. Because Convocation Hall was too small to accommodate several thousand graduates and parents, the ceremony was performed in the University's gymnasium. The temperature was well over 90 degrees F and I wore my Ph.D gown, hood and cap, and perspiration rolled down my back!

There was a subsequent ceremony which has the flavor of a secret society — the Iron Ring Ceremony. In many respects similar to the doctor's Hippocratic Oath, the ritual had been written by Rudyard Kipling. It had religious overtones.

Because I had never graduated in engineering it had transpired that I was ineligible for membership in the Association of Professional Engineers of Saskatchewan. This was obviously an unsatisfactory state of affairs and in the eyes of the pundits of the Association, quite unacceptable. But I was treated as a special case, ergo, I agreed to join the Engineering Graduating Class of '59 at the ceremony, and together, with the new engineering graduates, I held an endless chain of "cold iron" and swore in the presence of my peers to uphold the traditions of the engineering profession. Because of the secrecy of the ceremony, even Patricia was excluded. The traditional iron ring was then placed on the small finger of my right hand where it stayed for many years until rust took its toll. There is a great deal to be said for this ceremony which is uniquely Canadian.

The significance of the "iron ring" in the ceremony is to emphasize to all practicing engineers their responsibility for the safety of all structures which they build. Years ago there had been a serious accident in Quebec caused by the collapse of an iron bridge resulting in many fatalities. The early rings were made from iron used in the construction of that bridge.

Our 1959 summer vacation was memorable for many reasons. In various ways each one of us had had a stressful year and we were ready for a few weeks relaxation, preferably far removed from our prairie abode. With memories of my camping days at Bardsea Beach still fresh, I persuaded Patricia and John to plan a camping holiday in Montana, Wyoming and British Columbia. The investment in tents, sleeping cots, sleeping bags, stoves, cooking utensils and ancillary items was not inappreciable, but it was less than corresponding motel and restaurant costs, and certainly more fun. We purchased our supplies through Sears and to our dismay, we got a tent that I am sure had been in storage for years. Every time we erected it, some of the seams split. Patricia, fortunately, always travels with a sewing kit, so she was kept busy repairing the splits in the tent, and stitching through thick canvas was not an easy job. Our Ford sedan was roomy with adequate trunk space for the camping equipment, baggage and basic food needs for several days. As usual, I relied exclusively on Patricia's expertise in acquiring and packing the requisite materials.

Our overall plan was to drive south from Saskatoon, cross the border into the state of Montana, proceed west to the Watertown-Glacier International Peace Park, cross into Alberta, proceed west through the Rocky Mountains to Vancouver and take the car ferry to Vancouver Island. An ambitious trip involving driving more than 2,000 miles mostly through mountainous terrain. One of our objectives was to spend a few days with Gladys and Carl Patch, our former neighbors and first Canadian friends, now resident in Vancouver.

Our first night spent at a public camp site in Montana, was not particularly successful. The camp site was bleak and noisy with unattractive, indeed, primitive toilet and cooking arrangements. Loud speakers reminded campers of the danger of bears in the vicinity which did nothing to help create a peaceful pastoral environment. Thankfully, our initial disappointment was short lived and after such an inauspicious beginning we enjoyed every minute of our unique vacation. Let me summarize the highlights.

Flat Head Lake, Montana lingers in my memory as a camping wonderland. So much so that we decided to revisit it on our return journey. Comparatively small and peaceful, located in a wooded area bordering the lake, with excellent facilities, it was largely responsible for

Patricia deciding that a camping holiday had much to commend it. And John, after his enjoyable months at our Georgian Bay cottage was pre-conditioned for adventure in an entirely different environment. Swimming, fishing, exploring the woodlands and assisting his mother in the preparation of delicious feasts cooked on the camp fire were his main pursuits.

Our reunion with the Patch family in Vancouver lived up to expectations. Wonderful hosts, they accommodated us and gave us a comprehensive tour of this the most scenic of all Canadian cities. Snow-capped mountains in the background and the sparkling waters of Vancouver Bay in the foreground. After taking the car ferry to Nanaimo, Vancouver Island, we paid a fleeting visit to Victoria. Tea at the Empress Hotel was mandatory. Then we drove up a comparatively isolated road to the camping grounds at Qualicam Falls. This is Douglas Fir country. The trees can reach a height of 200 feet and a diameter of six feet. Our tent nestled between the trunks of these giants and we experienced the bliss of true solitude and a completely pollution-free environment. Every convenience of home was to hand. Much to the credit of the maintenance staff, the camp fire was refurbished daily with an adequate supply of firewood and the fragrance of those camp fires in such a pristine location still lives in my memory. Never before or since have we experienced the likes of those glorious days spent in Qualicam. Fortunately, in spite of being located in the rain forest we encountered "nary a drop of rain" during the week or so we spent on Vancouver Island.

The only notable feature of our return trip was an evening at Flat Head. The lake is a fisherman's paradise with steelhead trout the main attraction. However, on our earlier visit, John and I had been unsuccessful in our angling expeditions. Bearing in mind the fact that my father and younger brother were masters of the art, I was determined on our return visit to remedy our previous failures. Perhaps different lures would do the trick! But they didn't and after a couple of hours of futile casting flies and lures we gave up in disgust at sundown. We were extremely frustrated and figured the lake's reputation had been grossly exaggerated. But it hadn't! An hour after sunset a gypsy band, at least 30 men, women and children occupied the camp site adjacent to ours and within a few minutes of their arrival three young men with rods and tackle began fishing precisely where we had fished. Miraculously they proceeded to haul in one and even two pound steelheads with virtually every cast. They were friendly folk and were not reticent about their angling successes — after all they and their forebears survived largely because of these self-same hunting and fishing skills. John and I concluded that angling was not our forte. However, the family angling tradition is being upheld by our grandson, Gregory, who not only has a passion for fishing and hunting but ties his own flies, some of quite spectacular beauty.

Back in Saskatoon as the hot dry summer waned, we were treated to yet another novel experience. Huge tumbleweeds barreling down our street. During my monthly pilgrimages to Regina to attend meetings it was a common sight at this time of year to see them racing along the highways. Somewhat scary at times when "collisions" were inevitable. It's incredible how such comparatively trivial incidents stick in the memory. There were many more at U. of S. In fact so many that my only recourse is to identify some highlights before time runs out!

There have been few more delightful and indeed thought-provoking dimensions of our lives than our common interest in the arts, Patricia as an active practitioner and myself as a disciple. And it was our all too brief sojourn at U. of S. that provided a quantum impetus to these interests, especially through our association with Edith Ivan and Robert Hurley.

Edith Ivan and her husband Leslie had escaped in very dramatic fashion from Budapest, Hungary in November 1956 when the Red Army invaded. She had already established a reputation as a painter and her work had been exhibited in the Art Gallery of Budapest, while he was a neurosurgeon on the staff of the University Hospital. We met this delightful couple through our friendship with Bill and Faith Feindel.

In her late 30's, Edith was at the peak of her artistic powers and we were fortunate to count her as a friend within months of her arrival in Saskatoon. She was talented in portraiture, landscape and modern painting. Her pencil drawings of John, aged 11, which hang in our dining area are exquisite and complement her oil painting of our son which is displayed in his home. In total, our family possesses seven of her works.

I recall her as a vivacious lady, albeit diminutive in stature, who will always hold a special place in our memories, not least because she did so much to stimulate my interest in art.

Three of her paintings deserve special mention. The depiction of the group of grieving Hungarian women during the early days of the Soviet occupation is a powerful work. For me, a masterpiece. Hanging above the mantle piece in John's family room it occupies an honored place in our family collection. The other two "Clowns at Play," and "Indian Girl" hang in our dining area and my den respectively, are more personal and mean a great deal to us.

Early in 1960 Edith was diagnosed with a terminal cancer with a life expectancy of no more than 12 months. Aware of this, I arranged through my contacts at University of Toronto, for a Hart House Exhibition[25] of her work. This was providential in so far as it provided her with an incentive to complete and select paintings for the exhibition. The latter proved to be a great success and the review in the Toronto Globe and Mail was most gratifying. Edith was thrilled. All her paintings sold and we purchased the "Clowns at Play." In her gratitude, Edith gave me the "Indian Girl." Sadly she died a few months later, but not before she was reunited with her parents and two children who had been forced by the Soviet authorities to remain in Budapest.

The "Prairie Painter" is the sobriquet widely ascribed to Robert Hurley. Patricia and I met him through the Spinks — John Spinks had been his former boss when he worked in the Chemistry Department of the university. A Londoner by birth (in fact a real Cockney and proud of it), he left school at age 14 and never attended art classes. He emigrated to Canada at an early age. His first job as a laboratory assistant he told me did not require much skill and he spent most of his time "washing the bottles." But during the depression of the '30's, Hurley lost his job. This was fortuitous because he discovered a hidden talent — drawing and painting. In fact during those early days as well as doing "odd jobs" he fabricated and sold Christmas cards.

By the time we arrived in Saskatoon, Hurley had established himself in a modest way, as an artist specializing in prairie scenes. His small studio, located in the suburbs of Saskatoon, was unpretentious in the extreme. Patricia, John and I became frequent visitors. I recall how proudly he demonstrated some novel techniques which were particularly applicable in portraying the prairie landscape.

Robert Hurley loved to reminisce about England and London, and we struck up a real friendship. Regretfully we lost touch with him after we left Saskatoon in '61. But his memory lives on in the paintings that hang in both John's and our homes. Some of them are unique — gifts to us of some of his earliest paintings. Apart from our purchases, I was presented with a Hurley, with brass plaque, by the students of the College on my resignation. We are not only proud possessors of several of Robert Hurley's very distinctive works, but so is H.M. Queen

---

[25]Hart House Exhibitions are rare events. They are recognized as the most prestigious of their kind in Canada. A few years subsequently, I was to have a close association with Hart House.

Elizabeth II. She was presented with five of his paintings on the occasion of her official visit to Saskatoon in the late '60's. Suffice it to say, and this is by way of Sotheby's, Robert Hurley's paintings have appreciated greatly in value. It was a rewarding relationship in every possible respect.

Pride in their university was manifest especially during the Golden Jubilee Celebrations in September '59. The city as well as the university rejoiced. At the beginning of the century the debate, acrimonious at times, was being waged between Regina and Saskatoon as to which city would become capital of the Province and which host of the university. Regina was chosen for the former and Saskatoon for the latter.

A whole week was devoted to the celebrations which included a parade, convocation, banquets at which The Hon. T.C. Douglas, Premier of the Province and the Rt. Hon. John G. Diefenbaker, Prime Minister of Canada were the speakers, a formal ball, a classical concert, a football game and on Tuesday, September 29, a Jubilee Symposium. I was involved in one way or another in several of the events, notably the Symposium — "Memory, Learning and Language — The Physical Basis of Mind," held in Convocation Hall. Chaired by Dr. J.W. Spinks, President-Elect, this was a truly interdisciplinary affair — neurosurgery, psychiatry, the humanities, chemistry and engineering. My own paper "Mechanical Representation of Thought Processes" emphasized the limitation of so-called thinking machines. But for me the "tours de force" of the Symposium were the papers by Bill Feindel — "The Brain Considered as a Thinking Machine," and the renowned pioneer in brain surgery Wilder Penfield — "The Nature of Speech."

There was an overflow audience of faculty, students, politicians and public in Convocation Hall that day. They appreciated with a roar of applause when, on a lantern slide, Bill Feindel showed the "brain-waves" of a professor of neurosurgery (himself), a dean of engineering (myself) and a baboon without identifying them specifically. He then challenged the audience, "Can you identify the brain- waves of the baboon?" Incidently, the Symposium papers, edited by Bill, were published subsequently as a monograph and "the brain-waves" are presented therein. As a participant, my copy is beautifully bound with my name embossed in gold. On the cover page Bill Feindel has inscribed a hand-written note: "To: Arthur Porter, whose brain-waves contributed so much to the Symposium. The Editor." I still refer to the monograph on questions relating to the brain and I'm still in touch with Bill Feindel.

The Jubilee Celebrations gave me many opportunities to meet

several public figures including Health Minister Allan Blakeney. This proved fortuitous because during a critical phase in negotiations between government and university regarding universal health coverage for the citizens of the Province, I inadvertently provided a catalyst. At the time, Eric Nanson, the surgeon, was chairman of the university negotiating team committee and I personally arranged the meeting between Blakeney and Nanson which apparently resolved most of the outstanding problems. It transpired that the subsequent Provincial Health Plan introduced in the Province was the first in North America.

The plan approved by the government of Saskatchewan, headed by my friend Premier Tommy Douglas, was quickly adopted by the other provinces. When we took up residence in the Province of Ontario in 1961, for example, Patricia, John and I were beneficiaries under the Ontario Health Insurance Plan (OHIP). The sophisticated procedures associated with my cancer and subsequent radio-therapy, and Patricia's extensive plastic surgery for pre-cancerous skin lesions were covered completely and we were treated by physicians and surgeons with international reputations.

It is more than 40 years since OHIP was inaugurated and, contrary to a great deal of misinformation in the press and media, it has been a resounding success. Having been a consumer, until comparatively recently, I can assert without reservation that the plan continues to provide all residents with excellent health care, including choice of primary care physicians and free prescription drugs for seniors at minimal cost. I am proud to have played a very minor role in its formation.

On the homefront, Patricia created what was in effect a precedent in the university. Characteristically, she enrolled in an undergraduate course in "textiles" and passed with honors. This was an unusual achievement for the wife of a dean and impressed the faculty greatly. As well, John was equally successful in being admitted as a freshman to Nutana Collegiate of which the late Prime Minister John Diefenbaker was an alumnus. He was joined by his good friend John Crabb.

At about the same time I received a letter from Sir John Baker, head of the Engineering Department, University of Cambridge. Would I be interested in the Chair of Electrical Engineering, shortly to become vacant on the retirement of Professor Eric Moullin? I felt extremely flattered because Moullin was a renowned figure in British electrical engineering circles having served as President of the Institution and having many well-known inventions named for him. I responded positively and understood that I was short-listed. A few weeks later John wrote to say that the board of electors had decided on another candidate. In retrospect it was fortunate. Aware of my limited and it was very limited, knowledge of the discipline, especially power engineering, it would have been quite impossible to have replaced Moullin. As well, at the time I did not foresee the many prospects that would open up in Canada. My failure to obtain this highly prestigious chair was fortunate also for the whole family, especially John, whose health might have been at risk, as it had been in London, and whose future career in medicine might have been jeopardized.

Concurrently with the Baker correspondence, I received an invitation from the English Universities Press to become General Editor of their Electrical Engineering Series. Actually, I had been approached initially when I was at Imperial College, but I assumed this series had been abandoned. Fortunately, contacts with my former colleagues had been maintained because they were the prospective authors. I had no hesitation in accepting the invitation.

The series was intended primarily for electrical engineers and physicists who were employed in research and development. It was particularly gratifying when Professor John West, Queens University, Belfast, agreed to author the first volume. Like myself, John had been intimately involved with control systems since his student days and he had established an international reputation. His book, Analytical Techniques for Non-Linear Control Systems was a notable success and it provided a salutary launch of the series. Other volumes which followed were by friends and IC Colleagues, and I certainly enjoyed my one and only experience of being a General Editor.

The cordial relations that existed between the Colleges of Medicine and Engineering were essentially responsible for Ronald Raven's visit to Saskatoon during the summer of 1960. He stayed with us for several days, delivered two lectures and performed a surgical procedure at the University Hospital. It was very gratifying for Patricia and myself to renew our friendship with Ronald, and it is noteworthy that even John benefitted a few years later when at the invitation of Ronald Raven, he spent two months at the Royal Marsden Cancer Hospital in London as part of his medical training.

An unexpected but very welcome invitation reached me about the same time as Ronald's visit. During the intervening 12 years since he was my star student at Military College of Science, Frank Stoneman (then a major in the Army) had joined the Ultra Electronic Engineering

Company in Britain and had become chief engineer and a director. To celebrate the 25th anniversary of the company, four Jubilee Lectures were being arranged and I was invited to give the first on September 14, 1960. I accepted, and chose the title "The Evolution of Instrumentation."

The company provided first-class air travel, and accommodation at the Savoy Hotel for several days. The lecture was given in the ornate Recital Room of Royal Festival Hall with Frank Stoneman in the chair. It was most gratifying to identify several old friends in the audience — the Hon. T. H. Douglas, Ronald Raven, Sir Vincent Tewson (mother's cousin), the President of the I.E.E., and several former colleagues from Imperial College and the Ministry of Defense.

In my lecture, I surveyed the development in general terms of analog and digital computers, automatic control systems and introduced the idea of complementary biological and physical systems. As an example I described the monitoring and control of the behavior of a cat's brain. To explain my escalating interest in interdisciplinary research I stressed how much it had been stimulated by the creative environment of the Saskatoon campus. I ended the lecture thus: —

And we would do well to recall the words of Kelvin. "I sometimes say that when you can measure what you are speaking of and express it in numbers, you know that on which you are discoursing. But if you cannot measure it and express it in numbers, your knowledge is of a very meager and unsatisfactory kind." My former much beloved Ulverston Grammar School teacher George Calderbank would have approved.

I treasure several photographs of my Ultra Lecture in progress and of the audience. At the conclusion, Frank Stoneman graciously presented me with an honorarium and a beautiful pigskin wallet with gold inlays and my initials from the Queen's jeweler, Asprey's.

During my final year at U. Of S., Dr. John Hrones, formerly a friend in the Graduate School of MIT, and subsequently Vice-President, Academic, of The Case Institute of Technology in Cleveland, Ohio, had been in touch with me concerning some problems in control theory. (I recall incidently that we had entertained John and his family for tea in our home in Wimbledon just before we returned to Canada.) We had a particularly rewarding meeting in Washington, D.C., where we were joined by the president of Case, and we exchanged ideas on engineering education. John even suggested tentatively that I might be interested in joining him at Case. Indeed, within a few weeks of our meeting came an invitation for me to meet with the Board of Trustees.

The flight from Saskatoon en route to Cleveland that morning was appreciably delayed and I was obliged to take a later flight. As it happened, this flight was held up for several minutes in Toronto awaiting my arrival and I was the last passenger to board. One seat was vacant, at the extreme rear of the aircraft. Imagine my surprise when proceeding down the aisle of the DC-3 aircraft I spotted Omond Solandt sitting in the adjacent seat. Another example of the "being in the right place at the right time" phenomenon which has characterized my career. Unaware of any obvious associations between Saskatoon and Cleveland, he asked "What on earth are you going to do in Cleveland?" When I told him I was to meet and dine with the Board of Trustees of The Case Institute with a view to a potential appointment, he immediately responded — "Can you hold your decision for a couple of weeks?" I responded positively.

Because of his many close associations with the University of Toronto (he was to become Chancellor four years later) I was reasonably sure that he intended to look into possibilities there.

In the meantime the situation at Case proceeded smoothly even to the extent of my being shown residences in Shaker Heights and the location of the high school.

Decision day was July 3, 1960 when coincidently I received offers from both Case and Toronto. The former was a professorship in engineering and associate chairmanship of the Engineering Division of Case and the latter was a professorship in industrial engineering and chairmanship of the newly created department at Toronto. The starting date for both jobs would be September 1, 1961. This was another of the critical decisions with which Patricia and myself have been faced. Both offers were attractive and we reflected long and hard on the pro's and con's of each. Bearing in mind academic status and future prospects there was little to choose between them. But one consideration took precedence — John's education. Our virtually nomadic lives had not been conducive to any degree of continuity in his education and Patricia pointed out that "past was prologue to the future," and we might well be on the move again in three years time. Once again our son's education would be disrupted. She insisted quite justifiably that John's next school must be his last before university. Furthermore, familiarity with the Canadian educational system on one hand and life in Toronto on the other was a powerful magnet. The final decision, moved by Patricia, seconded by John and supported by myself, was that I should accept Toronto.

It was on the occasion of the Association of Professional Engineers of Ontario (APEO) annual banquet in Toronto which I attended as a guest of Omond Solandt a few days later, that I was finally convinced that our decision was correct. The main reason was that I met several U. of T. department heads, sat at the head table with them and got along famously. Ross Lord, head of Mechanical Engineering, with whom I was to become closely associated, was especially instrumental in my feeling very much at home again in Toronto.

I certainly did not relish the thought of informing my colleagues at U. of S., nor for that matter, my friend John Hrones, of my intentions. Fortunately, they were accepted with reasonable equanimity, except Bill Staples, the Assistant Dean. He was one of the first to know — I told him late one afternoon. The following morning, bright and early, with a doleful expression, he came to see me. "Mr. Dean (a form of address he had not used since the day I started at U. Of S.) I've had a sleepless night — are you really serious? If you'll forgive me saying so, I think you should see a psychiatrist!" And he was very serious! True westerners were never enamored of Easteners.

After informing John Spinks, the new President, I told him I had a potential replacement. Donald Booth was a computer pioneer and professor at Birkbeck College, University of London, with an international reputation. He took the dean's job two years later.

It may not be out of place to close this chapter with two quotations from "Thorough — A History of the College of Engineering, 1912-1982." They tell it all.

"As the 1950's drew to a close, Arthur Porter blasted off from England and, like a heat-seeking intercontinental ballistic missile, he hit The College of Engineering in Saskatoon in the fall of 1958."

"The most notable change during the year in the staff of the College was the loss of Dean Porter to the University of Toronto. Dr. Arthur Porter's contribution to the College during his three years as Dean have been notable. Under his guidance were initiated the Engineering Science Courses that have caught the imagination of many undergraduates of marked ability, and greatly interested the staff. Along with this and a logical outcome of it, he stimulated advanced training and research. This all meant more staff, space and equipment, matters that he forcefully pleaded for. We are all grateful to Dean Porter for initiating an important era in the history of the College."

The second quotation was taken from the 1961-62 academic year report of Dean Mawdsley, my immediate successor.

The Farewell Dinner for Patricia and myself was in many respects a sad occasion. We had become attached to the College and the College had become attached to us. I was presented with an elegant Sheffield Plate tray suitably inscribed by the faculty, and the afore-mentioned Hurley picture by the students.

Chapter 11

TORONTO AND ENVIRONS — RESIDENCES AND UNIVERSITY

WITH the possible exception of the war years, there have been few periods in my career more diversified than the years we spent in the Province of Ontario, for the most part Toronto and vicinity. We've certainly been a resilient family.

Because of this diversity it is impractical to proceed chronologically. Instead I plan to devote this chapter first to family matters and then to episodes that relate specifically to the University of Toronto during the period 1961 until I officially retired in 1976. Concomitantly, during the same period I worked on several Ontario and Canadian government projects of special interest and these are introduced in the next chapter. Chapter 13 is devoted to a unique assignment I undertook during the two-year period 1969-1971.

Even before we left Saskatoon during July of 1961, I had been approached by the Royal Commission on Government Organization, headquartered in Ottawa, to act as a consultant. On grounds which I shall outline in the next chapter, and having been granted a leave of absence by the university, I agreed, with Patricia's full support, to serve. Consequently, I did not take up my university job until January 1, 1962. This decision, although we didn't fully appreciate it at the time, placed a heavy burden on Patricia. My absence for several months, except for occasional weekends, resulted in Patricia once again having to handle the move from Saskatoon and much more.

By happy chance the Toronto housing situation in 1961 was much better than a decade earlier and Patricia quickly identified and rented an apartment in Rosedale, a delightful enclave of the city overlooking a wooded ravine and directly opposite the official residence of the President of the University. It was ideal from all points of view — transportation, schools, shopping, downtown accessibility, etc.

In the meanwhile, John passed the Upper Canada College Entrance Examination and was admitted as a boarder to Wedd's House. The housemaster was Tim Coulton, a wonderful master who was largely responsible for John's readily adapting to boarding school life. Incidently, Mrs. Coulton was the niece of George Athersmith, my favorite teacher at the Lightburn Council School, Ulverston, who had first introduced me to algebra when I was 10 years old. Another reason for John's comparatively rapid assimilation into school life was his compatibility with Harry Ditson, his roommate, an American student who eventually became an actor. Having completed school arrangements for John, including the purchase of books and requisite items for his room, Patricia furnished the Crescent Road apartment. She started with our old familiar pieces, including the grandfather clock which had traveled 13,000 miles including three Atlantic crossings, and then purchased all the furniture and equipment for a three-bedroom apartment, most expeditiously and economically — Patricia has always had a fantastic flare for a bargain! Even on "moving" day I was 200 miles away. It is noteworthy that a similar pattern applied during each of our moves to the plethora of homes in Toronto and environs which we occupied for varying periods during our second sojourn in Toronto — a total of seven. As John grew older he became adept at moving house and was a great help to Patricia.

Back in the city which had been our home a decade earlier, Patricia and John quickly renewed old friendships and savored the many attractions of one of the most attractive cities of its size in North America. During my comparatively rare visits, I too enjoyed exploring a city whose growth, physically and culturally since we'd left in 1955, had been truly spectacular. As well I had fleeting opportunities to meet my future colleagues at the University.

From time to time, especially during WWII, Patricia and I have been exposed to life-threatening situations, but few were more alarming than the fire that originated in a second floor apartment of the Crescent Road building. Fortunately, it occurred one Saturday morning during the fall of 1961 when I was at home. Suddenly, the smell of burning permeated our fifth and top floor apartment. Opening the door to the corridor we were horrified when dense acrid smoke enveloped us. It was so dense that we literally could not see anything — no lights, no walls, no floor. Hurriedly closing the door, not before a plume of smoke had entered, we packed wet towels at the base of the door, closed windows and stepped out onto the narrow balcony overlooking the ravine. By then the Toronto Fire Department, with many pieces of equipment, was in full operation. The fire was under control within an hour, but the smoke lingered for days. It was several weeks before our apartment was completely free from the after-effects. An elderly couple died in the fire which had been caused by a cigarette.

It was during a Friday evening flight from Ottawa where I had been attending a final briefing session of the Royal Commission, that another fortunate happening occurred. In those pre-jet age days the flight to Toronto took well over an hour and I'd read the Toronto Star in its entirety, except the real estate section. A casual glance revealed a "box ad" headed "Beautiful Caledon Hills Property" — 50 acres of "prime farm land" were for sale in the vicinity of Belfountain. I was intrigued and so was Patricia. In spite of the lateness of the hour, 10 p.m., I telephoned the agent and made an appointment for early Saturday morning.

In 1950, soon after our arrival in Canada, we had received an invitation to a wedding. Cyril Henderson, with whom I had shared accommodation in Cambridge, Mass. in 1945, was marrying a Toronto girl. The reception was held at the Caledon Mountain Trout Club in the beautiful hills of Caledon, part of the Niagara Escarpment. We both remembered the area and how it had reminded us of the English countryside.

By 11 a.m. we'd purchased the property after a superficial inspection. The price was right and we'd concluded that it would be an ideal spot for picnics during the summer months. We little realized at the time that Belfountain would become the most beloved of all the 35 homes we've occupied during our well-nigh 62-years of marriage. Beautiful country, fantastic neighbors and friends. During Patricia and John's brief visit to London in August, I spent a day or two reconnoitering the property. It obviously had great potential, but it would take Patricia's artistic talents to realize. An English squire surveying his estates could not have been more proud than I was that day.

After a year's residence in the apartment and having decided that Toronto would almost certainly be our permanent home, we purchased a house on Standish Avenue — a quiet, secluded enclave of Rosedale. It was an older house with several attractive features — fireplace, stained glass windows and a small garden. Not surprisingly, after furnishing the place, Patricia modernized the kitchen. John and I were always impressed by the manner in which she handled such projects — the Irish carpenter, after a well-deserved rebuke for sloppy work, would have agreed!

Our social membership in the Royal Canadian Yacht Club, which gave opportunities for swimming and occasional feasting during weekends and with occasional visits to Belfountain, complemented most admirably those early years back in Toronto.

It was coincidental as well that our next door neighbors, an elderly couple who dwelt in a small cottage, were John Peel and his wife Mary. Emigrants like me from the Lake District, they may have had ancestral relations with the famous huntsman. When we left Standish they gave us a delightful several centuries old tankard now in John's possession.

With her increasing participation in a variety of activities such as the Wellesley Hospital Auxiliary, Presidency of the Applied Science and Engineering Wives Association, and by no means least the symphony and theatre, Patricia soon realized that we needed more space to reciprocate growing social commitments. John and I fully concurred. After almost three years at Standish we decided on yet another move. Patricia, always the bargain hunter, discovered an ideal house on Rosedale Heights Drive. After literally no more than 10 minutes in the house, we submitted an offer and purchase was completed within 24 hours. Situated contiguous to Rosedale, the house was, at the time, located in one of the city's most desirable residential areas — the ubiquitous ravines dominating. The only reason we acquired it for such a modest price was the fact that although the Georgian exterior was very attractive, the interior required major renovation. But Patricia regarded it as an irresistible challenge. Even the fact that there were three floors and hence an abundance of stairs, and the major bathroom was on the second floor, did not deter her. With the help of the most wonderful housekeeper we've ever had, Jean Gillies, she succeeded in restoring the house into a very elegant residence. We will never forget Jean — a devout Scottish spinster — for her many kindnesses and extreme generosity. She had a particularly soft spot for John and several years later when he was interning at Toronto's Western Hospital and had an apartment which he shared with four other interns, Jean took care of their household needs. She used to refer affectionately to her boys as "my young doctors."

Not only had we acquired a beautiful home, but wonderful neighbors as well, all lawyers, especially the Sullivans — Mike, Joan and their five delightful children were special friends. Indeed, Mike became our family lawyer and financial advisor for many years until his untimely passing. We still keep in touch with Joan and family.

With large living and dining rooms on the ground floor, our Rosedale Heights home was perfect for entertaining. A Porter characteristic, still extant, we loved parties. One in particular was to honor a house guest, to give him his full title, the Rt. Hon. Lord Bowden of Chesterfield, (Vivian, a friend of many years dating back to the Ferranti days). Among our guests were the presidents of the Universities of Toronto and Western Ontario. As usual on these occasions, Jean Gillies was ever-present, and I can't resist recalling her subsequent comment to Patricia. In her pure Scottish burr — "I canna understand why such eminent gentlemen tell such naughty stories!" Another memorable party held for the most part in the backyard was on the occasion of our 25th wedding anniversary — July 26, 1966. About 20 guests attended and the toast was proposed in his inimitable style by Marshall McLuhan.

The Belfountain Saga

Though we'd purchased the Belfountain property in the spring of 1961 and enjoyed many picnics there, we didn't build a country home until the fall of 1966. Many weekends thereafter were spent planning and developing our future permanent home. It was a labor of love because our 50-acre estate had many natural attributes — 40 acres of bush which incorporated hard maple trees, clumps of silver birch, many pine and several pink crab apple trees. Nestled beneath the trees were spacious beds of glorious trilliums (the provincial flower of Ontario) and violets. Almost unbelievably, a small stream with marsh marigolds and water-cress, a poet's as well as a gourmet's delight. In fact, the only disquieting feature was the dead elm trees (killed by the Dutch Elm disease) which dotted the landscape. I dealt with them eventually.

By the summer of 1970, when we built an extension to the cottage, almost doubling its area, we had installed two up-to-date bathrooms, a large brick fireplace, a fair-sized library and a modern kitchen.

Because most of our homes in Britain and Canada have been readily accessible to the sea or lakes, we were determined that Belfountain would not be an exception. Accordingly, we contracted a small local company, consisting of two brothers and their elderly mother, to dig two half-acre sized ponds, one in front and the other in a dip behind the cottage.

Before starting, the brothers insisted that their mother should "witch" (i.e. water-divine) the appropriate area. Patricia and I drove the dozen or so miles to pick up the lady — she was in her 80s. Vivid in my memory is the sight of her "witching" our property. The process consisted of walking to and fro gesticulating "the wand," a wire coat hanger suitably bent, until she stopped and with an imperious gesture announced, "Here." She repeated the process for the second pond.

Happily there were several natural springs on our property and after the deep holes (about eight feet) were dug, it was fascinating to see them gradually fill with pure Caledon Mountain water. (This spring water was, and may be still, used for the original Canada Dry Ginger Ale.)

The ponds were perfect for swimming and trout — eventually smallmouth bass — and we fabricated small docks. I spent many moments on one of the docks fascinated by the male bass swimming tirelessly around and around the small fry protecting them from predators, especially the adult bass, and perhaps the bullfrogs whose male chorus resonated day and night, notably during the spring.

Another hazard which appeared a few years before we left Belfountain were the "snapping turtles." They killed the young ducks and geese which frequented the ponds. On more than one occasion I had the unpleasant and by no means simple task of disposing of them. One was over two-feet in diameter and weighed almost 20 pounds.

An essential requirement before winter set in was a driveway. Situated as we were some 400 feet from the 5th Line of Caledon, and necessitating a small culvert, this was a major undertaking. But our local contractor completed the job expeditiously and our once-a-week handyman, Cecil, albeit in his 70's, assisted in tarmacking the surface. Incidently, Cecil, by profession, was a "post-hole digger" and this talent proved of inestimable value when we erected fences and assembled our main and subsidiary gates.

Having made the cottage livable, which required, the installation of a complex water-softening and conditioning system, Patricia concentrated on beautifying the landscape. As an extension of the Niagara Escarpment — a distinctive feature of the previous Ice Age with primitive fossils of sea-life scattered around to prove it — we were privileged to have a historic, albeit rocky, site.

Our arable and wetlands property was advertised as category-3 farm land, translatable as marginal for grazing and some crops. But in fact, because of the abundance of small rocks, it was very difficult to cultivate. We decided therefore, to reserve about one-quarter acre for a kitchen garden, about five acres for rough lawn which at peak season required bi-weekly mowing, and various fringe areas as herbaceous borders. The remaining acreage was planted with yearling pine trees, about 20,000 of them, under a government reforestation program at a cost of one cent per planted tree. We eventually had a veritable forest of Christmas trees about 12-feet tall.

Our son John was instrumental in creating a park like setting for our new home. He and his friends moved and planted many young saplings from the back woods, around the house and ponds. These thrived and when we eventually left, they had grown into large handsome silver birch and ash trees transforming the rather barren farm fields.

The conversion of that 50-acres from essentially wilderness to a beautiful country estate was our dream and together we worked long and hard to bring it about. Eventually our efforts resulted in a bountiful vegetable and fruit bush plot, a plantation of ornamental trees, an extensive lawn, and flower beds and borders which were Patricia's pride and joy. Never forgetful of family traditions, she planted a "host of golden daffodils" beside our back pond "beneath the trees" (to paraphrase Wordsworth) and they certainly "fluttered and danced" in the ever-present breeze. In fact the only distraction from that idyllic scene in the summer months were the mosquitoes. We named the narrow pathway between pond and wetland bush — "mosquito alley." It was their favorite breeding and feeding ground and we rarely lingered there.

The remote portion of the property, mostly wetland, provided a real haven for the wildlife and wonderful trails for walking and in winter — snowshoeing. The fall colors were spectacular. Indeed, our only concern was the threat of flooding caused by a beaver dam. In spite of heroic efforts on our part to discourage these incredibly energetic animals, we waged a losing battle. At the time we left Belfountain, the damage to the deciduous trees, notably the poplars and some maples, was immaterial, but our neighbor Marg Bell was not so fortunate — within the span of a year or two, she lost most of the trees on her property.

With the help of a huge amount of fertilizer and a roto-tiller, we succeeded in producing all our vegetable and fruit requirements. The delectable gooseberry, red and black currant, plum and rhubarb pies which Patricia baked were a gourmet's delight. Indeed, they still are although the fruit is by no means as tasty as the fruit we grew at Belfountain. Our new potatoes, asparagus, tomatoes and salad ingredients were equally scrumptious. A very necessary project which Patricia and I shared in the garden was the control of weeds, especially dandelions. The bane of my life!

There was wildlife galore. Some attractive and much appreciated such as the deer, fox, jack rabbit and garter snake, others attractive but much less appreciated such as the skunk, ground-hog, raccoon, squirrel and beaver. One afternoon, above the back pond, I was cutting the grass using our trusty Massey-Harris riding mower when a fox, with resplendent tail, emerged from the bush a mere 30-feet away. Eyeing me rather disdainfully, she headed for her den quite unperturbed. I subsequently located her den — a huge hole with small bones and other detritus spattered around in a glade within a copse of pine trees. Although my ancestors were not enamoured of the fox, I must confess on that occasion I was on the fox's side and relieved to know that our property was off-limits for the local Hunt because of the preponderance of ground-hog holes!

One of our neighbors was Major and Mrs. Charles Kindersley. Charles was the Master of the Caledon and Eglinton Hunt and was responsible for the rearing and care of the hounds. He always reminded us of our family link with the Master of Hounds of the Eskdale and Ennerdale Hunt in the English Lake District.

The wild bird population in our comparatively secluded property was the most prolific we'd ever encountered. We cooperated by installing large feeders and an elaborate purple martin mansion — 15-feet high, it had 12 "apartments." Unfortunately, we didn't attract a single purple martin because, as we learned subsequently, the elevation of our property (about 1000 feet above sea level) was above the bird's altitude limit. This was a disappointment because we understood purple martins are major consumers of mosquitoes. On the other hand, the common swallow, soon took over the mansion and together with the barn variety, nesting as they did on the walls of our garage, did a reasonably good job in this respect.

Our favorite birds, especially in winter, were the chick-a-dees, cardinals, rose-breasted grossbeaks, snow buntings, and on rare occasions red-headed and pilated woodpeckers. Even rarer were the occasional glimpses of a golden eagle, and a pair of red-tailed hawks on the property. The beautiful blue jays and the quarrelsome grackles were the least welcome because they were such greedy and wanton feeders. To minimize the loss of bird seed to the ubiquitous grey squirrel we designed various contrivances and strategies, but to no avail.

I should mention also our perennial tenants — mother goose (Canadian) and her mate who returned every spring and reared an average of eight goslings — they were as regular as clockwork. We were also visited by a wide variety of ducks who also nested near the ponds, their arrival the first harbinger of spring.

Many of our new found friends in Belfountain were, like ourselves, imports from Toronto, and we had many interests in common. Several were enthusiastic gardeners and in particular Patricia, Vivian Sturdee and Norma Dattels were co-founders of the Credit Forks Garden Club. Vivian was the first president and Patricia the second of a club, still extant, with upwards of 30 members. It has had an impressive record during the past 40 years. It was essentially through the club activities that we acquired many new friends — the Dattels, the Smiths, the Willoughbys, the Kindersleys — to name a few. Some of the most memorable parties of our lives, especially New Year's Eve, were held in our respective homes. Even the not infrequent snow and ice storms did not deter our friends — indeed, on one occasion the Willoughbys arrived complete with snow plow.

Our property was in fact ideal cross-country skiing terrain and together with snowshoeing in the bush, we were dwelling in a winter wonderland. We even succeeded eventually in clearing much of our hinterland of the unattractive vista of dead elm trees which had dotted the skyline.

As a wedding present, Patricia and I were given a very attractive leather-bound Visitor's Book. All of our guests signed it and as well we put on record most of the significant events that have occurred since we were married. I've referred to it frequently in preparing these memoirs. In the 60 completed pages more than 40 are devoted to Belfountain. Let me summarize a few of the entries.

Not surprisingly, albeit happily, our most frequent guests were family — John, our daughter-in-law Kathryn and our three grandchildren in particular. Jennifer, Ian and Gregory liked nothing better than having grandad drive them around the property, beside the ponds and through the woods. They could all get into the large trailer pulled by my reliable tractor — which I usually used to haul fire wood.

Other family staying with us from time-to-time were my brother Ronald and his wife on several occasions, Patricia's brother John and his wife, Elsa, my youngest brother Robert and wife, Georgie, my nephew Andrew and Patricia's cousin Jeremy Marks (who stayed with us for two weeks while he purchased a herd of Holstein cattle which were shipped to his farm in England). Close family friends included Victoria Attwood and her daughter Daphne and husband, her grandson Michael, Kathleen Raven and her brother Jack, Ted and Johnnie Lee, and Olive and Jack

White. As well we welcomed the McLuhans, Lord Bowden, Herta and Oscar Puls and our American friends, Bob and Jean Schwartz whom I first met during my travels in 1938. John also enjoyed bringing his friends home and putting them to work on the tree planting operation.

Events of note which occurred during our residence at Belfountain included the following:

- I was inducted as a Fellow of the Royal Society of Canada at the University of Manitoba in Winnipeg at the end of May 1970.

- Patricia and I attended the Convocation at Queen's University when John knelt before the Chancellor who conferred the degree with the words "Rise Doctor of Medicine." It was announced at the same ceremony that he had been awarded the Lillian Zhbar Prize for the best clinical case report of his year.

- During a visit to England, accompanied by Patricia, I presented the prizes and addressed the school on Speech Day at my old school — the Ulverston Grammar School. We were greeted by Margo Cousins, daughter of my headmaster. The occasion brought back many happy memories.

- John married Susan Smith in June of 1972 and our first grandchild, Jennifer, was born on October 26, 1974. Three years later John and Susan were divorced.

- John married Kathryn McClone at the Anglican Church in Delafield, Wisconsin.

- Our first grandson, Ian John Arthur, was born in Milwaukee on April 14, 1979, and his brother Gregory Patrick Harris, was also born in Milwaukee on February 25, 1982.

- The entry in our Visitor's Book for July 6, 1987 reads: "On this day very sadly we sold our beloved Belfountain home to Ann and Robert Burr."

During our residence at Belfountain I have to report with great sadness the deaths of several family members. Patricia's sister Carol died suddenly June 1967 at the young age of 45, followed by the death of her mother in July 1969. My sister-in-law Mary, my brother Ronald's wife, died earlier in 1963 of breast cancer and my brother Robert in May 1984. My mother was with us until her 98th year when she too passed away.

Their deaths left a large gap in our lives.

It is fitting that I should conclude the Belfountain story with the entry which our son John wrote in the Visitor's Book in August 1987. It reads:

> *BELFOUNTAIN EPILOGUE*
> *Belfountain that wondrous matrix of brick, wood and mortar-fields, woods, plants and ponds. We came here for a score of years and with our vision and our toil, we wrought this place. As we watched it grow, the saplings to trees, the fields to ponds and lawns, and this house to our home, we grew too – as we had not done before. We three became seven, and we grew not just in number but in insight, training and intellect — and in our chosen field of education, industry, government and the healing arts went out and touched the future of two great nations that make up this continent. Thus was nurtured here this clan of Porters who leave here with thanks and who as usual have left their mark behind.*
> *J.A.H. P. August, 1987*

Hanging on the wall of the sun room of our home at Bermuda Village is a watercolor depicting the cottage and surroundings, part of the lawn and one herbaceous border. It was painted by Patricia in January 2003 from a photograph. It is a constant reminder of the Belfountain home which gave us so much pleasure.

University of Toronto

Although my work with the Royal Commission on Government Organization (July-December 1961) precluded much contact with my future department at U. Of T. I spent several Saturday mornings familiarizing myself with the campus. It is scattered over a large area mostly adjacent to Queen's Park, the site of the Ontario Provincial Legislature. Fortunately, the Department of Industrial Engineering is located centrally on a street car route, only two-hundred yards from the Queen's Park Subway Station and a mere hundred yards from Simcoe Hall Administrative Center.

A few words about the origin of the department is appropriate. About 15 years prior to my appointment, during the 1950's, because of increasing interest of many engineering students in management, a unique course called Engineering and Business had been introduced in the Department of Mechanical Engineering. Its object was to prepare a few undergraduates for careers in business administration. But it had transpired that the course had not been successful because it was lacking in depth in both business and engineering. An obvious alternative was to establish a Department of Industrial Engineering. When Omond Solandt appeared on the scene on the lookout for a job for me he persuaded the university to offer me the chairmanship of the newly created department.

It will not pass unnoticed that once again during my career I had accepted a job for which my qualifications and experience were minimal. But once again the challenge had been irresistible and Patricia was all for it.

The embryonic department in January 1962 when I joined it consisted essentially of three people. Associate Professors Clough and Anderson were the academic staff and Lois Hefford the administrative assistant. Regretfully the former are both deceased, but Patricia and I retain a warm relationship with Lois and Barry Smith. As a matter of fact. Lois until her marriage in 1965 was the "lynch-pin" of the department. She handled all the paperwork and counseled the students as well. Not only was Lois a star performer, but a very attractive young woman, indeed, Patricia likened her to Jackie Kennedy, but better looking!

At the time of my appointment no other degree program in industrial engineering existed in Canada or Britain and as far as I am aware, in few of the U.S. universities and certainly not at MIT. Its relationship, in the early days, to Time and Motion Studies resulted in the subject being taught in technical colleges. Indeed there was at the time considerable debate as to whether or not industrial engineering was worthy for recognition at the university level. This was one of the first issues with which I was confronted. Clearly it was necessary initially to formulate my ideas on industrial engineering as a university discipline.

There's no better way to learn about a subject than to teach it or more simplistically, prepare a lecture on it. At both Imperial College and the Military College of Science I'd been faced with a not dissimilar situation. I'd found it extremely helpful to structure my ideas by giving an Inaugural Lecture. Accordingly, I approached the Dean of the Faculty of Applied Science (Roland McLaughlin, a truly delightful person who became a close friend) with the idea. He was not overly impressed on the grounds that it would create a precedent — never before, nor I understand since, had a newly appointed departmental chairman delivered a formal Inaugural Lecture. Notwithstanding the lukewarm response, I persisted with the idea and pointed out that my new department was the first of its kind in Canada and that I had already given two Inaugurals — why not a third? He agreed. The Dean also agreed to have the lecture published in pamphlet form in order to publicize the creation of the new department. The agreed date was February 15, 1962. My final report for the Royal Commission was also due about that same date, and a very hectic few weeks ensued. Fortunately, Lois Hefford helped enormously with the diagrams and slide preparation.

Because of its novelty, my Inaugural, which I entitled "Industrial Engineering in Retrospect and Prospect," attracted quite a lot of attention and even Claude Bissell, the President, attended. I was told subsequently by Roland McLaughlin that when Lois and her friend, the Dean's secretary, entered the lecture theatre the President whispered, "Who are those two very attractive young women?" To which the Dean replied, "Porter's and my secretaries." And the President responded, "Trust you G-D engineers!"

In emphasizing the interdisciplinary nature of industrial engineering I pointed out that its basic components were — engineering, psychology, computer science, accountancy and business administration. Indeed, operational research summed it up admirably. However, instead of attempting to define the discipline formally I preferred to exemplify it in the words of philosopher and mathematician Alfred North Whitehead who had written:

> *"A factory with its machinery, its community of operatives, its social service to the general population, its dependence on organizing and designing genius, its potentiality of wealth to the holders of its stock is an organism exhibiting a variety of vivid values. What we want to train is the habit of apprehending such an organism in its completeness."*

I suggested that "factory" should be interpreted in the broadest sense to include the university, the hospital, the bank, the insurance office, etc. I intimated that Whitehead had in effect propounded the justification for a department of industrial engineering, and had answered the question "What is industrial engineering?" in a very elegant way.

After publication by the university the lecture was subsequently published in its entirety in the Journal of the Institute of Industrial Engineering. As a direct consequence of the latter I was invited to give lectures, notably at the University of Florida (Gainsville) and to the Engineering Department of the R.J. Reynolds Tobacco Company in Winston-Salem, North Carolina. Patricia accompanied me on both occasions little realizing that in the future we would dwell in Florida for 17 years and we would eventually live in North Carolina. Indeed, Bermuda Village is within a few miles of where the lecture took place and where as guests of the chief engineer and his wife, we spent a few happy days.

Since the early days of radio, a traditional feature of Christmas Day celebrations in Britain and the Commonwealth has been the Queen's Christmas message to her subjects. The message is broadcast from Buckingham Palace around the world. Her Majesty's speech is followed immediately by short contributions from several Commonwealth countries. In 1962 I, a comparatively new Canadian, was especially gratified to deliver Canada's portion of the broadcast. As a topic I chose the then emerging field of computers. My talk was recorded at the studios of the Canadian Broadcasting Corporation in Toronto on October 30, 1962 and broadcast on Christmas Day 1962. The text was as follows:

> *It is twenty-eight years since we built a computer for solving problems in higher mathematics at the University of Manchester. It was the first in Europe. It cost two hundred dollars. Today there are six thousand computers working in North America and the average cost of each machine is a quarter of a million dollars. And the story is only just beginning to unfold because the technological and sociological challenges of our times increase in complexity daily. And, although we have computers which can carry out arithmetical operations a million times faster than man, they still cannot do some things we would like them to do.*
>
> *Take scientific weather forecasting, for instance, we require faster computers with a hundred times the speed of existing machines to deal with the mass of data being collected by the weather satellites. I believe we will have such machines within five years.*
>
> *In another field some of us at the University of*

Toronto are trying to simulate, using computers, some aspects of human behavior. Our computers can already learn to recognize simple patterns and sounds. But we have a long way to go before we can design a machine with the thinking capacity of a mouse! However, this research is already leading to some important new ideas about the process of adaptation, and this is tremendously important in biology and medicine.

I am confident that computers will play an increasingly important part in all branches of education. For instance, in my department all senior students can program these machines. And lately, we have been wondering how to use computers as teaching machines. Of course they will never replace teachers, at least I hope not, but they will help to solve pressing educational problems.

In the business world, I predict that, within a few years, computer centres will be established as public utilities, similar to the telephone systems. Companies will be able to transmit problems over teleprinter lines and will obtain answers perhaps within minutes.

It is quite certain that computers will have an enormous impact on man's future. To the scientist they constitute an immense challenge. But they are also lots of fun.

To the illustrious names of Calderwood and Cousins at Ulverston, Bragg and Hartree at Manchester, Bush at MIT, and Blackett at London must be added McLuhan at Toronto. To these men, I owe a tremendous debt of gratitude.

Few people during my career have had a greater impact on my sensibilities than Marshall McLuhan, Companion of the Order of Canada, Professor of English Literature in the University of Toronto. Described by "Life" magazine as the "Oracle of the Electronic Age," McLuhan's influence has been profound.

I met Marshall at a small cocktail party hosted by a mutual friend in Toronto. As was his usual wont, he bombarded me with ideas on science, philosophy and media, using a mystifying language. Returning home from the party, I said to Patricia — "I met a delightful but completely incomprehensible character at the party" (or words to that effect). This impression persisted for about three subsequent meetings. But during our fourth meeting it suddenly struck me that Marshall and I were on the same "wave-length." He actually understood the basic concepts of information theory as enunciated, for example, by my friend Claude Shannon, and that was highly unusual for a professor of English — an authority on modern authors such as James Joyce and T.S. Elliot. From thence our friendship blossomed. I attended several of his renowned Monday evening seminars and we met frequently for lunch. A devout Christian, who had converted to Roman Catholicism, he rarely missed attending noon-day mass.

Among a host of attributes, what endeared Patricia and me most to Marshall was his fantastic sense of humor. He was the perennial punster.

It has only been during the last few days (April 2003) in revisiting the "Gutenberg Galaxy" published in 1962, a masterpiece in my opinion, have I at last discovered the basis of our mutual empathy. Not only did he understand information theory, but his literacy and understanding embodied the works of such geniuses as physicists Werner Heisenberg, biologist Pierre Teilhard d' Chardin, economist Adam Smith, and historian Jacques Barzun. He also was influenced by neuro-anatomist J.Z. Young's book *Doubt and Certainty in Science*.

The following quotations from the Galaxy exemplify the breadth of McLuhan's interest:

- For the renaissance it was the infinitesimal calculus that enabled arithmetic to take over mechanics, physics and geometry.

- The new electronic inter-dependence recreates the world in an image of a global village — The Newton Laws of Mechanics, latent in Gutenberg typography, were translated by Adam Smith to govern the laws of production and consumption.

- The modern physicist is at home with Oriental field theory.

- Money is metaphor in the sense that it stores skill and labor and also translates one skill into another.

- Terror is the normal state of any oral society for in it everything affects everything all the time.

Like all celebrities the number of anecdotes relating to Marshall are countless. Many are apocryphal, but the following to my certain knowledge are true.

It is virtually a truism that McLuhan changed the culture of advertising — contrast the ads of the 1950's to those of the 1970's. Madison Avenue adored him — he was an icon. I cannot refrain from recounting an episode relating thereto.

After the publication of *Understanding Media* in 1963, the Madison Avenue moguls arranged a party in Manhattan to honor the author. On the day of the party the organizer had arranged to meet Marshall at the LaGuardia Airport. However, he failed to arrive on the designated flight from Toronto, nor on a subsequent flight. Accordingly the organizer telephoned Toronto and McLuhan answered the phone. The exchange went as follows: "Marshall what the hell's going on — you're supposed to be in New York for the dinner in your honor." To which Marshall responded, "Sorry but I'm grading exam papers!" We treasure a copy of *Understanding Media*, 1963 in wich he wrote, "in friendship and esteem, dreams need drivers."

A second incident related to a nationally televised show on McLuhan broadcast in March 1967 by NBC-TV. The producers of the show arrived at the university campus in an enormous transport loaded with equipment. At Simcoe Hall they asked the receptionist to direct them to the "Center for Culture and Technology." "Never heard of it," was the response! "Where can we find Professor Marshall McLuhan?" The girl checked the faculty list and responded, "St. Michael's College" and gave directions. (In order to keep McLuhan in Canada at a time when many U.S. universities were tempting him, the President convened a small committee, of which I was a member, who devised a mechanism to ensure that Marshall stayed in Toronto. We created the "Center for Culture and Technology.") It worked.

Arriving at St. Michael's, the girl at the college switchboard then directed the TV people to 96 Joseph Street, an old red brick house. Having driven the transport from New York City this in itself must have been a surprise. But more surprises followed. Locating their objective on the ground floor, it was identified as "Center for Culture and Technology" printed on a narrow strip of aluminum. But the door was locked with a large padlock and chain. It was lunch-time and Marshall appeared within a few minutes. The incongruity of the situation still causes me to chuckle!

The third episode was another delight. The occasion was a dinner hosted by the Principal and his wife of Erindale College (a college of U. of T.) Carl and Peggy Williams. The guests included the President and other heads of university colleges. The dinner was to honor McLuhan's appointment as a Companion of the Order of Canada. The dinner, preceded by a cocktail hour, was timed for 7 p.m. but the McLuhans had not put in an appearance. Par for the course, I reflected. Indeed, the honored guests did not arrive until 8 p.m. when we were at the dessert stage. Marshall's initial remarks were unforgettable — "Carl, where's your television. I must see "Hogan's Heroes"!" He enjoyed the most unlikely programs!

But in spite of, or perhaps because of, such eccentric attributes, Marshall's influence was quite extraordinary. For the first time in my life I appreciated the equivalence of thought processes such as metaphors in poetry and models in science. This was a major step in bridging science and the humanities including religion. And of profound importance when subsequently, as outlined in the next chapter, I became involved in activities which ranged from environmental concerns to the creation of theme pavilions for a World Fair. I had become a McLuhan disciple and I'm grateful for it.

An important manifestation of our collaboration was in publicizing the increasing role of technology in societal evolution. I recall in particular two lecture series which we organized. The first was sponsored by the Royal Ontario Museum on "The Arts as Communication" and the second sponsored by the university's Extension Department was entitled "Technology — A Restructuring of Human Sensibilities."

In addition to Marshall and myself the lecturers included Tommy Lewellyn Thomas, the artist Harley Parker, and the author and broadcaster Peter Newman. Patricia and her friend Jean Cowperthwaite attended several of the lectures.

McLuhan's appointment to the Schweitzer Chair at Fordham University for the 1967-68 year required a major reassessment of the Center. In fact, Marshall was the Center and there was good reason to close down the activity during his absence. But much to my surprise and gratification, he insisted that the work of the Center should proceed with me as acting director. By this time my own department was running smoothly, undergraduate and graduate programs had been established and I felt that with the able assistance of Ben Bernholtz, I could undertake both chairmanship and acting-directorship of the Center. Indeed, I benefited greatly from the challenge. Another plus was the fact that Margaret Stewart, the Center's secretary, was a tower of strength and she handled most of the administrative chores. However, I ignored Marshall's instruction that "Mrs. Stewart would, as always, handle the budget." I did, and as a consequence, new accommodation was acquired and an adjunct professorship approved.

My main contribution to the Center was the organization and conduct of the traditional Monday evening seminars. When Marshall was in charge these had been little short of sensational and I was rather apprehensive about following in his footsteps. Be that as it may, I chose as a topic "Technology and Society" and hoped for the best! Because of McLuhan's absence, only a few humanities and arts graduate students registered for the seminar, but the registration of scientists and engineers was remarkable — the total seminar class averaged 20 students. As guest speakers I invited Buckminister Fuller, Llewellyn-Thomas, Bill McCullough, the eminent physiologist from MIT, and well-known painter Harley Parker.

At the conclusion of the first seminar I was approached by one of the participants. Bill McElchron, subsequently one of Canada's most distinguished sculptors. At the time he was a lecturer in art at the Ontario College of Art. He was holding a ball of wax, and to my astonishment, I identified it as an effigy of my head! Bill turned out to be one of my brightest students. He told me that when attending classes his concentration was always enhanced when he created, virtually unconsciously, images of the teacher. To cut a long story short, both Patricia and I agreed to sit for Bill and he created the two beautiful bronzes which grace our living room. As well, a few years later we purchased a complete set of six bronze relief's titled "Protest." These exemplify the infamous protest demonstrations by the students of Kent State College when several students were killed by the police, and I believe we own the only full set. The student disturbances, typical of the 60's were in full swing during my directorship of the Center and a fascinating dimension was added to the seminars. For instance, several students were leading activists on the campus and they certainly enlivened the proceedings. I recall that the leadership of "Energy Probe," probably the most effective public interest group of the period, may have been spawned during my seminar. Ironically, a decade subsequently, "Energy Probe" became the most eloquent anti-nuclear advocates during the public hearings I held as Royal Commissioner.

During March 1968, Marshall was admitted to the Presbyterian Hospital in New York City for urgent brain surgery. A non-malignant tumor the size of an orange, had been detected at the base of his brain. By no means an ideal patient, he nevertheless survived a surgical procedure which lasted for 20 hours. On recovering consciousness he was asked by the surgeon — "How are you feeling, Professor

McLuhan?" Replied Marshall, "It depends how you categorize feeling!" As a matter of fact my dinner companion at a reception in my honor prior to my delivering the "John Kershman Memorial Lecture" was the neurosurgeon who carried out the procedure, and he told me the story.

I visited Marshall in the spring of that year and stayed for a couple of days. He was in great form. On the second day we were invited to meet several directors of I.B.M. at their corporate headquarters on Madison Avenue. At lunch Marshall astonished the half-dozen directors by predicting fabulous growth for computers. In particular he announced that within 20 years most homes in the United States would possess a computer. At that time there were probably fewer than 1,000 computers in the whole country. One of the directors whispered to me — "Surely he's not serious!" But of course it turned out that his prediction was pretty accurate.

One of the activities at the Center which I had not anticipated was the comparatively large number of invitations I received to deliver after-dinner speeches and lectures. To give some idea of the diversity of my talks let me summarize a few of them. At a Divinity Seminar at Trinity College I gave a talk on"Linguistics and Tool-Making;" at a labor-management workshop, I spoke on "Labor Implications of Automation;" at an American Institute of Industrial Engineering, meeting in Buffalo, NY, I spoke on "The Nature of Information Science;" at the Royal Ontario Museum Lecture Series in 1967 I spoke on "Restructuring of Human Sensibilities;"and spoke on "Space, Science and Religion" at a meeting of the Rotarian Club in Orangeville, Ontario (one of the audience was the famous metropolitan singer Jon Vickers, a Belfountain neighbor and friend of Patricia and myself.) Complementing these was the Metropolitan Educational Television Association special program on "Automation and Social Change" in which I participated with such eminent authors and officials as Sir Geoffery Vickers, V.C., author of *The Undirected Society*, Dr. John Dunlop, Chairman, Department of Economics, Harvard University, and Ewan Clague, Commissioner of Labor Statistics, U.S. government. This special TV program entitled "Are People Necessary?" was an extremely provoking and exhilarating experience. An invitation to address the"Third World Congress for the Theory of Machines and Mechanics,"hosted in Yugoslavia in September 1971 at Dubrovnik, had regretfully to be declined at the last moment because of illness.

An even more prestigious occasion arose during the spring of 1963 when I received a letter from the President of the University inviting me to deliver the Convocation Address in early May. Having been interested in the process of adaptation for so many years, I decided that it was a suitable topic for the address. Furthermore, Rachel Carson's book *Silent Spring*, had been published comparatively recently, so I felt on secure grounds. Patricia and John sat on the front row of Convocation Hall that afternoon, and as I rose to give the address, capping the Chancellor, I was very conscious of John's eyes being riveted on me. Beginning with "Those to whom the harmonious doors of science," a quotation from my favorite poet Wordsworth, I half-read and half-extemporized a 15 minute talk. The audience of rather more than 4,000 graduates together with their families seemed to approve. It was encouraging to hear from Patricia that when the academic procession passed them by, the President winked at John — a good sign.

The address, which retains a degree of relevance even today, and which was not published at the time, is given below:

Adaptation in a Rapidly Changing Environment

When the President invited me to give this Convocation Address, I was much exercised over the choice of a subject which would justify me addressing so distinguished and vital an audience. My strictly limited horizons precluded most suitable topics, and I have had, perforce, to fall back on some aspect of "engineering philosophy."

When Wordsworth, and I would be a traitor to my native English Lake District if I referred to another poet, wrote,
"Those to whom the harmonious doors
Of science have unbarred celestial stores,
To whom a burning energy has given
That other eye which darts thro' earth and heaven."
he clearly anticipated a dramatic evolution of science and technology. It is doubtful, however, if he would have the same ecstatic reaction today. Certainly, he would not condone the rampant commercialization of applied science and its associated threat to the balance of nature. But more of this anon.

The theme of my address is "Adaptation in a rapidly changing environment." The engineering implications of this subject have interested me for several years. It is a truism that the intellectual, cultural, social and physical environment, which man and nature have created, is changing more rapidly than at any time in history. Perhaps the major reason is that education, on an ever-expanding scale, is regarded as essential to the evolution of nations. And the proliferation of the arts, letters, sciences and applied sciences, which we are witnessing, and enduring, is a direct consequence of the raising of educational levels. Society must continuously adapt itself to these changes.

Throughout the history of life on earth, there is evidence of a continual increase in the perceptual acuity and accuracy, with which the higher animals can evaluate their environment. A corresponding progressive development of the structure of their central nervous systems, especially the brain, has enabled them to reach a practical understanding of it. This is the process of adaptation. It is fundamental to life, and, like breathing, although motivation is essential, it is effectively an unconscious process. Consider as an example, the appreciation of art. Probably fewer than one percent of Canada's population would admit to a liking for surrealistic and abstract forms of art, and yet comic strips, especially Pogo, and modern advertisements in the press, and on television, frequently display a high degree of abstraction. Compare the advertisements of 50 years ago, and there is no doubt what a powerful impact modern art is having on our everyday lives, nor any doubt that we are adapting to the changing visual environment. Similarly, in literature, in architecture, in industry, in our homes, the adaptive process proceeds inexorably.

To some environmental changes we adapt very rapidly, for instance to changes in temperature. To others, for instance the change from an agrarian to an industrial society, we adapt very slowly, albeit often with violence, as exemplified by the Industrial Revolution in England and the Civil War in the United States, and the revolutions in Russia and China. Indeed, the present racial situation, looming so ominously in South Africa and, to a lesser degree, in the United States, are not unrelated to the agrarian-industrial-automation transformation. These problems are not likely to be resolved quickly.

Superficially, it appears paradoxical that, although adaptation to the environment is essential to life, there is nevertheless, in nature, inherent resistance to change. Such resistance is a manifestation of tradition, and, to a high degree, tradition determines our present and future behaviour. But, on the whole, it is a stablizing influence, and hence beneficial. However, over-emphasis on tradition, corresponds to a state of over-stability, and it is not conducive to speedy adaptation.

I am reminded of the operations research study carried out during World War II, when movies of British Army 25-pounder gun crews in action were studied in order to improve the gun drill. In all cases it was found throughout the action, that one man stood at ease, some 50 yards from the guns. Apparently, the gun drill had been developed before World War I, in the days of the horse artillery, and the extra man was there "to hold the horses."

It is perhaps not immediately obvious why some engineers should be interested in the process of adaptation. It is a field normally regarded as the preserve of geneticists, archaeologists and sociologists. But, during the past few years, engineers have become intensely interested in the mechanism of self-adaptation. This interest stems essentially from the spectacular developments in large-scale electronic computers. For instance, we have reached a stage in applying computers to the control of complex physical and mechanical processes in which it is desirable for the process to be capable of adapting its behaviour to elementary changes in the environment. Let me give a simple example. The behaviour and efficient performance of a large scale oil refining process depends very much on the outdoor temperature. Thus, if there is a 20 degree change in temperature over a 24-hour period, it is necessary for various automatic regulating loops in the process to take this into account, otherwise grade 1 gas may become grade 2. In like manner, out bodies adapt to a change in temperature when we walk out of our heated homes, and step into an environment in which the temperature may be 90 degrees lower. The adaptive processes, which go into action in our bodies to cope with such sudden changes, are far, far more complex and efficient than the most sophisticated computer-controlled process operating today.

Our investigations suggest that there appears to be five basic requirements for self-adaptive behaviour. First, an ability to memorize imformation; second, an ability to recognize patterns of behaviour in both space and time; third, an ability to establish cause-effect relationships — this is essentially the feedback process; fourth, an ability to carry out experiments or, as we say, to probe the environment; and fifth, an ability to time events. We have built self-adaptive systems which embody these characteristics. And we believe that the mechanism of self-adaptation in all processes, whether physical or biological or sociological is predicated on similar concepts.

Suppose we translate these simple requirements into the language of social history and sociology. It is not difficult to deduce that the adaptation of a society depends essentially on history and tradition, on the carrying out of economic, technological and sociological experiments, on the assessment of the results of these experiments and on the general patterns of behaviour which emerge from the correlation of new knowledge.

Our very simplified model of the adaptive process does not take into account, however, the fact that society itself is having an increasingly important influence on its environment. And as a result the environment will probably tend to become more and more hostile, especially if man persists in misusing the tools and materials which science and technology are providing.

A few weeks ago, the fourth volume of the Royal Commission Report on Government Organization was published. About half of it is devoted to the government's role in scientific research and development. The opening sentence of this section of the Report reads — "The conduct of scientific research and development is today universally recognized as having a profound effect on the development of nations and the well-being of their peoples." And it may not be out of place to comment that, measured in terms of press and TV reaction to the Report, the profundity of the effect corresponds roughly to about 10 percent of that evoked when Canada won a gold medal for swimming at the Pan-American Games.

Although science and technology have certainly improved the standard of living of nations, there can be little doubt that large-scale commercialization of science is responsible for our increasingly hostile environment, and to increasing concern. For example, we cannot predict the long-term, and probably deleterious, effects on society of such technological breakthroughs as modern cars and their effluents; new detergents; the mass production of television sets and cigarettes; the ubiquitous telephone; the production of nuclear energy; and the multiplicity of new drugs, to mention just a few. There is obviously an alarming tendency for the reckless and dangerous exploitation of scientific discoveries. In a recent book, Miss Rachel Carson has drawn our attention to the deleterious effects which are already evident as a result of the indiscriminate use of insecticides and the like. Indeed, in the fields of insecticides and antibiotics, our existing models of the self-adaptive process suggest that the present models of utilization are "playing directly into the hands of the enemy." Resistant strains are proliferating rapidly, and the development of more and more toxic agents may not provide a solution, not least because a potentially serious health problem is already evident. What can be done about it?

I suggest that scientists and applied scientists must resist the commercialization of potentially dangerous chemical agents and technological processes until the results of extensive research on the long-term effects have been assessed, and until the adaptive process is better understood. The degree of beneficence to society, or science, surely rests with the scientists.

Perhaps it is man's unrivaled ability to adapt to hostile environments, and his unrivaled ability to create more hostile environments which are the root cause of many of the difficult economic and sociological problems which confront us today. Our dynamic environment can be likened to motion in ever-decreasing circles — one important manifestation of it is the man-made phenomenon of the "rat race."

Clearly the only hope of resolving the dilemma is through education. The complexity of our environment has been due in large measure to the fruits of specialization. And the universities, the cradles of basic research, have fostered, and indeed, encouraged the specialist. But effective probes of the environment, essential for adaptation, must, I believe, be inter-disciplinary probes, and the responsibility for their creation and execution rests with the universities. In one sense we created the problem and it is up to use to try and solve it. But time is short.

The arts, letters and humanities, on the one hand, and science and applied science on the other, are often regarded as having a mutually exclusive relationship one with the other. This attitude, this dangerous doctrine, must be exorcized as quickly as possible. I recall the story of a famous scientist noted for his absent-mindedness, who, on one occasion immediately prior to delivering an important lecture to an engineering society, was asked by the President of the Society to refute the idea that mistrust existed between scientists and engineers. In the lecture which followed, the scientist fulfilled his promise by saying "We hear a great deal at present about the unsatisfactory relationship, bordering on hostility, which exists between science and engineering: Mr. Chairman, it is untrue, absolutely untrue; indeed, it can't be true — they have nothing whatever to do with each other."

In concluding, Mr. Chancellor, may I reiterate the

*conviction of many of us, that the effective adaptation of
society will be increasingly dependent upon the efforts of
the universities in stimulating the cross-fertilization of
scholarship and science. The seeds, when sown, may
give rise to more profound concepts with which to probe
the environment, and to increased wisdom for the
exacting task of interpreting the resulting patterns and
charting society's future course. But the first step will
necessitate a critical appraisal of our own house.*
"Tempora mutantur et nos mutamur cum illis"
All things change, and with them we too change.

As President of the Canadian Operational Research Society, 1963-
64, I was required to present a Presidential Address, to be delivered at
the Annual General Meeting. Coincidentally, it was the year when the
American Operations Research Society held their Annual Meeting in
Montreal, and the decision was taken to combine our conventions.
Regretfully, neither Patricia nor John were able to attend. The meeting
remains a delightful and unique memory, not least because I met the
Beatles — John Lennon, Paul McCarthy, George Harrison and Ringo
Starr — during the morning prior to my addressr — in the elevator of the
Queen Elizabeth Hotel. Alerted by their obvious "Liverpudlean" dialect,
not dissimilar to my own, I struck up a conversation with these delightful
young men. Their hair was long and their laughter infectious. They told
me that they were on their way to New York City to appear on the
internationally acclaimed "Ed Sullivan Show!" The rest is history.

I took advantage of my encounter with the Beatles when I introduced
them into my Presidential Address. I suggested that many operations
research problems lent themselves to identifying imaginative catalysts, in
the sense of devising new techniques in McLuhanistic terms, this can be
described as "finding suitable anti-environments!" As an example I
raised the question of how most effectively the crime problem in the
Liverpool docks might be solved. I suggested that the Bealtes had helped
by encouraging the young "thugs"to exchange their "knuckle-dusters"
for guitars. If the Beatles could do it why not they? I pointed out that
social workers had been addressing the problem for years unsuccessfully.
In other words the Beatles were the anti-environment. The following
morning the Montreal Gazette on account of the P.R. value of the
Beatles, headlined a story "Professor praises Beatles."

As a matter of fact, operations research, largely because of my early involvement during WWII, was a key component of the Department of Industrial Engineering Research program. It will be recalled that I emphasized its importance during my inaugural lecture. Many situations, commerce, industry, health care and defense, lend themselves to the technology. To name a few — hospital administration, transportation systems, communications and merchandise retailing. Ben Bernholtz and Jim Templeton, new members of the faculty, were pioneers in these fields and we quickly had a highly-productive research group. An application of special interest was the Toronto Transit Commission's streetcar and subway system. One by-product of this resulted in a summer job for John. It was probably one of the most demanding jobs of his career because it involved two shifts. The first was for the period 5 a.m. — 9 a.m. and the second for the period from 4 p.m. to 7 p.m. His summer job on the street cars was to enumerate the number of passengers entering and leaving a street car at each stop. The job was as stressful for Patricia as for John because of the working hours. But they both accepted the situation cheerfully and John's earnings gave him a degree of independence not hitherto achievable.

Although not strictly describable as such, John's summer job was in fact operations research, and it provided valuable statistics relating to the frequency of streetcar stops during the rush hours. There was another dimension as well — human factors. To what degree was it desirable to combine driver and conductor jobs? These were by no means trivial questions and it's gratifying that John's data provided the basis upon which such decisions were made.

I was fortunate in identifying and subsequently hiring, one of the leaders in Canada in human factors engineering — often referred to as the man-machine interface. Pat Foley, a psychologist by training, became a tower of strength in my department. He pioneered research in several fields, notably nuclear power controls, automobile design and, in partnership with "Tommy" Edward Llewellyn-Thomas, was responsible for liaison between industrial engineering and the Faculty of Medicine. Shortly after my retirement, Foley assumed the chairmanship and indeed, was the first psychologist in the history of the university to be appointed chairman of an engineering department.

My membership of the Board of Governors of Seneca College of Applied Arts and Technology, 1969-75 was an exhilarating experience. It could not have been otherwise with such outstanding colleagues as Dr. Fred Minckler, the chairman, Bill Newnham, the President, and Grace Cronin (nee Carter) a fellow member who was destined to become chairman within a few years. I served during a period of dramatic growth of the college not only with respect to the number of students, faculty and accommodation, but most importantly in stature. Indeed, it is no exaggeration to assert that Seneca was and probably still is the pre-eminent community college in the Province of Ontario.

Of the many imaginative programs and events in which I participated, I can identify three of special interest.

For many years the education of nurses in the Province had been based in the hospitals, and I suggested that it would be more appropriate for the education of nurses to be transferred to the community colleges. Following up on this idea, the Board established a task force on Nursing Education chaired by Grace Cronin. Their recommendations eventually gave rise to the transfer. Noteworthy is the fact that in the College of Nursing final examinations, Seneca students were ranked in the top echelon.

It also played a strong role in the Board decision regarding the Aviation and Flight Technology Program. The advisory committee on which I served was established in cooperation with Air Canada whose chief training officer was a prominent member. It was decided to base the program at the Buttonville Airport. We acquired seven airplanes for training purposes. Within three years the College had first and second officers in several air lines. It is gratifying to note that more recently the Seneca program was allied with that of the University of Toronto and is now a degree granting course.

Another program of special interest related to "Underwater Skills" at the King Campus. My personal involvement albeit minimal resulted from my knowing Dr. Joe MacInnis, Canada's leading underwater specialist. As a matter of fact, at that time Joe was a member of the Canadian Environmental Advisory Council which I chaired. Graduates of the program were sought after by the major oil companies and several of them worked on the oil exploration diving platforms in the North Sea, the Beaufort Sea and the ocean in the vicinity of Newfoundland.

Some of my happiest memories of Toronto relate to Seneca College and I keep in touch with developments through my contacts with Bill Newnham and Grace Cronin. The warm friendship of these two wonderful people also resulted in my receiving a singular honor. At the Fall Convocation of 1977, I was appointed the first Honorary Fellow of the College. After giving the Convocation Address I was presented with a beautiful embossed brass plaque which presently hangs in my den. The inscription reads "In recognition of his many contributions to the

College, the University Community, the Province of Ontario and Canada."

Patricia's activities during our many years at the University very much complemented mine. In addition to her herculean work at Belfountain, she undertook such activities as the presidency of the Faculty Wives Association and the vice presidency of the Wellesley Hospital Auxiliary (if we had stayed an additional year in Toronto, she would have been appointed president with a seat on the Board of the Hospital). She even enrolled and graduated in a diploma course in Real Estate at George Brown Community College in Toronto. In the meanwhile, John had graduated at Upper Canada College, obtained admission to the Medical School at Queen's University and was happily embarked on his career in medicine.

In an earlier section I mentioned my acting directorship of the Center for Culture and Technology and my involvement with several of the leading lights in the student protest movement. But more was to come when I was appointed to the Board of Stewards of Hart House. The House is essentially the social center of the University where students, faculty and governors can debate, dine and socialize. I was privileged to be a steward during most of my tenure at the University. The Board under the chairmanship of the Warden, consisted of about 12 members, three faculty and nine students. Surprisingly, in debating some issues, the students were more conservative than the faculty. In particular I recall the acrimonious debate on the question of whether women should be admitted to membership of the House. Fortunately, with the strong endorsement of the faculty members, the motion to admit them was carried by a single vote. Subsequently a dinner hosted by the Rt. Hon. Vincent Massey (a former Governor-General of Canada) was held to celebrate the occasion. Incidently the Massey family had financed the House many years previously in memory of Hart Massey, who was killed during WW1.

A notable Hart House event which I organized during the fall of 1968, was a "teach-in" on "Basic Requirements for Leadership," It's too long a story to recount how I became involved in a political issue, but suffice it to say that I was persuaded to do so by the noted Canadian political columnist Dalton Camp. The teach-in was timed to coincide with the Progressive Conservative Leadership Convention and obviously had important political implications. Being politically independent I was considered to be an ideal chairman for such an affair. I invited some of the leading Canadian politicians of the day, together with a few well-known academics such as Marshall McLuhan, to give presentations. The teach-in was well attended by students and faculty and was given prominent media coverage. It lasted for an entire weekend. I suspect that this event singled me out as a prospective advisor to government and Chapter 12 of these memoirs proves the correctness of my suspicions!

Towards the end of the 60's, as a result of my work at the Center for Culture and Technology, I decided that an elementary book on cybernetics would be worthwhile. The subject had evolved spectacularly since Norbert Wiener had introduced me to it two decades previously and I felt even as early as 1968 that the subject should be introduced to high school students in their senior year. Accordingly, I arranged with the Principal of Forest Hill Collegiate Institute to give a course of 10 lectures at the school. It was attended by about a dozen students as an "extra-curricular" activity. Of the students who attended six subsequently registered for the bachelor's degree in industrial engineering. Two of these students deserve special mention — Harvey Schipper and William Cass. They achieved high honors in the undergraduate engineering program and subsequently with my encouragement pursued outstanding careers in medicine. And it was undoubtedly their early exposure to cybernetics which stimulated their interest in both engineering and medicine. With a little stretch of the imagination, it is probable that our son John's career was stimulated in this way as well. In 1969 my book Cybernetics Simplified, was published with a foreword by Marshall McLuhan. It was based entirely on my Forest Hill lectures. McLuhan's foreword concluded with the paragraph:

> *"Professor Porter's book will be of the utmost service in promoting an understanding for the need for the wedding of science and technology and of politics and the art."*

The most memorable event of my last two years at the University of Toronto was the faculty of Applied Science and Engineering Centennial. Of the many events celebrating the Centennial year the most memorable for me was the Centennial Lecture Series, "The Next Hundred Years." I was privileged to be one of the eight lecturers. The lectures were presented at approximately monthly intervals throughout the year.

The inaugural lecture was presented by my good friend and former colleague at Imperial College, Dennis Gabor. It was an especially notable occasion when he delivered the lecture in January 1973 because only a month previously he had been presented with the Nobel Prize for physics. It was a special treat for Patricia and me to entertain Dennis and Marjorie Gabor as our house guests for several days, not surprisingly since Marjorie had been Patricia's best friend during our three years at Imperial College. They sat together on the front row of a crowded Convocation Hall as shown in a photograph of the occasion published in the Centennial Lecture volume.

In the lecture series that followed I recall especially the lecture by my friend Llewellyn-Thomas who presented a brilliant discourse on the evolution of biomedical engineering. As both professional engineer and physician he was in a particularly strong position to present the case and of course my own department's interest in human factors engineering was related. It had not occurred to me before that the two most dangerous places in our homes are the kitchen and the bathroom. This fact is rarely mentioned in treatises on preventative medicine.

The second lecture that appealed greatly was by Herbert Simon on "Engineering Design." It was he who stressed that we should be concerned with the future only when it is relevant to the present. His lecture complemented perfectly the previous lecture on biomedical engineering. Herbert Simon was a man after my own heart, a true inter-disciplinarian who within a decade would be awarded the Nobel Prize for economics,. At the time he was both Professors of Computer Science and of Psychology at Carnegie Mellon University.

My own lecture, the last in the series, given in December 1973 was entitled "The Education of an Engineer." This title was chosen by the Committee on Academic Events for the Centennial. It is noteworthy that the inaugural and final lectures in the series were delivered by physicists. For my part I felt very privileged to have been given the responsibility of providing guidelines for the education of engineers for the next century. But I enjoyed the challenge.

Chapter 12

COUNCILS AND COMMISSIONS

THE consequences of my chairing the University of Toronto's "Teach-In" referred to in the previous chapter were extraordinary. I found myself involved in a plethora of activities which for the most part were only remotely related to industrial engineering. But there were benefits as well, especially working with personalities the likes of whom I had only encountered on television and radio. I am devoting this chapter and Chapters 13 and 14 to these essentially extra curricular activities.

I justified my involvement on the grounds that since the university was largely dependent on government funding, it was virtually obligatory to help wherever possible. Furthermore, I reasoned that my dedication to interdisciplinary endeavors would be enhanced by such work. This chapter and Chapters 13 and 14 will be devoted to six of the nine independent, albeit government related, projects in which I played an important part. The first was my appointment as a project officer attached to the Canadian Royal Commission on Government Organization (usually referred to as the Glassco Commission). Starting in July 1961 I would be committed virtually full time for at least six months. In view of the importance of the Commission I was granted a leave of absence from the University of Toronto. I was assigned to the Scientific Research Division with special responsibility for the organization of defense research. Other members of the group were Rennie Whitehead, whose career had closely followed my own, and Dick Dillon, Dean of the Faculty of Engineering at the University of Western Ontario.

At the preliminary briefing I discovered that the scope of the inquiry would involve a considerable amount of traveling. My office would be located in Ottawa and I commuted from Toronto on a weekly basis —

Saturday at home and returning on Sunday evening. As I pointed out in the previous chapter, this imposed a considerable load on Patricia in the process of the family settling in Toronto.

I was, of course, by no means unfamiliar with the government defense organization because of my previous work in Toronto as described in Chapter 8. Of primary significance was my friendship with Omond Solandt and this gave me a good grounding. But a great deal had occurred since I had last visited Ottawa in 1955.

The main establishments I visited are listed below:

- The Canadian Armament Research and Development Establishment, CARDE, was the first. I chose it because it provided the family an opportunity to partake of a 10-day holiday in one of the most attractive regions of Quebec before John started his new school. It was a day's drive from Toronto. The Establishment is located in the vicinity of Lac Beauport and we were fortunate to obtain accommodation in La Gete, an attractive cottage adjacent to the hotel. While I visited the Establishment, Patricia and John enjoyed swimming in the lake, fishing and especially sunbathing. As recently as the fall of 2001, during a St. Lawrence cruise, Patricia and I revisited the hotel. CARDE is largely concerned with research related to ballistics, armored fighting vehicles, proximity fuze developments, etc. I was warmly received by my French Canadian hosts and my mission was completed according to plan. The "Belle Provence," as it is usually referred to, provided us with wonderful food and entertainment, and by no means least, an introduction to "Le Bal" a ball game played by the locals. Regarding the latter, I've rarely seen such enthusiasm and excitement on the part of the elderly male participants as when they played the game every evening.

- Atomic Energy of Canada Ltd. at Chalk River, Ontario, was second on my list of visits. It is the center of the country's nuclear power industry and was responsible for the development of the CANDU, heavy water-moderated nuclear reactor with which I was to become very familiar in the future. My hosts were Lorne Gray, General Manager and Chief Scientist Ben Lewis. Of international stature the work undertaken at the laboratories was truly breathtaking. I shall have more to say about it in Chapter 14.

- The Defense Research Telecommunications Establishment at Shirley Bay is within a few miles of Chalk River and was next on my list of visits. The laboratories were responsible for the development of novel radio communication systems notably utilizing so- called troposcopic scattering technology. I recall that Peter Forsyth, a former colleague at the University of Saskatchewan was a pioneer in this field. Of special interest was work on the communication satellites. Indeed, the Canadian "Alouette" series of satellites were already some of the most reliable in the world. In no small measure this was the result of Norman Moody's wizardry with transistor circuitry. Although I was unaware of it at the time, this visit, which lasted about a week, was of special importance because within a few years I became personally involved with a specific satellite communication system in collaboration with the Ontario Educational Communications Authority.

• My visit to the Research Station at Suffield, Alberta was memorable for several reasons. Situated in the "Badlands" of the Province, I encountered for the first time of my life, a region in which dinosaur fossils had been located. It was fascinating to observe at first hand archeologists at work. It was rather incongruous that a few miles away the research station is devoted almost exclusively to the study of the impact of high explosives. In fact, I was fortunate to be present for a test, the object of which, was to simulate the effects of a nuclear bomb explosion. Several tons of TNT explosive material were arranged as a small pyramid, and a variety of artifacts, small buildings, electrical equipment and of sundry vehicles were arranged within a circle of about 800 yards radius. The control and observation station was located about two miles from the site of the explosion and I was one of the observers. It was an unforgettable experience to see, hear and be exposed to the blast of the explosion. By no means in the same order of magnitude of an atomic explosion, indeed three orders of magnitude less, it was nevertheless a tremendous spectacle. I had never before or indeed since seen anything like it.

• My fifth and last official visit and one of the most important, was to the Pentagon in Washington, D.C. This building, at the time the largest office building in the world, covers 29 acres. It is a very impressive sight. Arrangements had been made for me to meet the Deputy Secretary of Defense, the Hon. Harold Brown. In particular we discussed joint programs of defense research in which Canada and the U.S.A. collaborated. For example, the Distant Early Warning System (the DEW Line) consisting of massive radar, computer and communication facilities was one of the most important defense installations on the North American continent. It was by far the most significant example of U.S.-Canadian collaboration, and was one of the topics we discussed. It was a pleasure as well to revisit a city for which I've had so much affection.

- The final briefing of the advisory committee and members of the Royal Commission, were held in Ottawa during December 1961. They were enjoyable affairs during which I was able to renew friendships and lay the groundwork for future collaboration with a diverse group of government scientists.

Women and Technology

One of my main objectives serving on student admission committees at the Universities of London and Saskatchewan had been to ensure that women were well represented in the freshman class. I had been aware for several years of the persistent and unfair practices manifested in occupational segregation and discrimination based on sex, race and age that existed. I was concerned that there was no reason why women should not participate on equal terms in such fields as management science, computer software and the health sciences, indeed, at the very cutting edge of technology and its applications. Probably because I had given several public lectures on the urgency of this problem, I was approached by the Chairwoman of the Royal Commission on the Status of Women in Canada inviting me to undertake a study on "The Impact of Technology on Women's Employment." I accepted, fully aware that it would be a major commitment during the summer months of 1968.

To facilitate the study, I incorporated a consulting company, Arthur Porter Associates with myself as president, Patricia as vice-president, and my friend Phil Lapp, with whom I was to have close relations in the future, as a director. In fact Patricia handled all the paperwork and hired university students seeking summer jobs to help with the statistics. The contract placed by the Royal Commission covered consulting fees, part-time help, travel costs, etc.

During the 60's the so-called "cyber-revolution" was in its infancy and hence women's employment essentially was restricted to school teaching, nursing, clerical work and domestic work. Few women worked, for example, at senior levels in the medical and legal professions and fewer still in top-level management of business. My plan was to develop statistics demonstrable in the form of bar graphs relating to age, formal education and job training. In particular, I attempted to extrapolate future trends, especially in light of the emerging role of computers. But I stressed that contemplation of the future course of women's employment calls to mind an appropriate metaphor, (simile is perhaps more correct) the tragedy of the "Titanic." The disaster would have been averted if earlier warning of the fatal iceberg, dead ahead, had been given and the ship's rudder had been rotated hard to port. Large ships sailing at full speed, however, (like large complex societies) respond only slowly to changes in rudder, however drastic, and it is vitally important that the ships' captains are fully aware of the time taken to change course. Likewise governments, after deciding on major policy changes and the appropriate rudders, must take into account how long it will take for the changes to be effective. Naturally the "rudders" will be "bi-sexual."

I stressed that technology is by no means a novel commodity. Indeed, it has always been humankind's major support; society and technology are complementary — mirror images one with the other. Humans create technology and unquestionably technology has profoundly influenced the human psyche, through the arts and sciences, social and natural that have sprung from it. In my final report to the Royal Commission I suggested that no one exemplified technological change better than Leonardo da Vinci. He has been described as the last "universal man" — painter, sculptor, physician, scientist, engineer and above all humanist. His painting of the "Mona Lisa" is renowned for both its sensitivity and for its technical innovations. As well he anticipated a host of scientific theories and engineering developments that included the circulation of the blood, flying machines, the construction of canals and the submarine. It's not surprising that I singled out Leonardo as the "icon" of the age. Let me hasten to add that the relevance of his highly creative life to the impact of technology on women's occupations I left to the Royal Commissioners! But it certainly sounded convincing in my report.

I summed up my report with the words: "In the opinions of virtually all scholars and scientists of the day, the next decade or two will be crucial — if corrective steps, manifest in drastic changes in the directions society is inexorably moving, are not taken, civilization will be at risk as never before. Hopefully, if the talents of outstanding women, presently not being utilized to their full potential can be mobilized, the risk would be minimized."

It was largely as a result of the "women-technology" study that several years subsequently, as a member of the Board of Governors of

Seneca College, together with my good friend Grace Cronin, the chairman, we sponsored the introduction of senior level courses in nursing into the College curriculum.

Montreal World Exhibition Expo '67

Expo '67 has been acclaimed internationally as the most imaginative and breath-taking World Fair of the 20th century. And I was privileged to play an important role in its creation. The site itself was a miracle of civil engineering. During a period of 10 months, rock and earth amounting to 15 million tons were brought to the site. The two most powerful dredgers in the world brought up 6,825,000 tons from the bed of the St. Lawrence River. The rest was trucked virtually day and night. The site of the exhibition was literally built up from this material and ready by the end of June 1964. In less than three years Expo '67 was completed and incorporated a major metropolitan subway system and the Expo Express Monorail. The panorama of architectural marvels, some of which are still extant, will live forever in my memory.

The theme of Expo '67 was "Man and His World." A group of distinguished Canadian scientists and scholars, of which I was fortunate to be one, brought the concept into relationship with plans for the exhibition at a conference in the spring of 1963. It was a great thrill, a few months subsequently, to be invited to become chairman of the "Advisory Committee for Science and Medicine." The committee was responsible for advising on the nature of the exhibits to be housed in a chain of Theme Pavilions.

My committee consisted of 20 members — scholars and scientists from virtually every province in Canada, many of whom were household names. Let me mention a few. Tuzo Wilson, the Vice-Chairman, was the renowned geo-physicist who postulated and measured inter-continental drift; Gerald Halpenny, the other Vice-Chairman, was Physician-in-Chief at Montreal General Hospital; Frank Scott was Canada's most revered poet; Helen Hogg was Canada's premier astronomer; and other members included heads of university departments and chief executive officers of industry. As well, my good friend Omond Solandt was a member. During the period 1964-67 the committee met on a monthly basis and we established cordial relations with the exhibition administration. In particular Bob Shaw, the Deputy Commissioner General, was a tower of strength.

There was so much at Expo '67 that deserves mention as well as the six Theme Pavilions for which my committee was responsible. For example the Rose Garden, covering five-acres of ground, was heralded as one of the most beautiful rose gardens in the world. On display were a hundred varieties of outstanding roses of many types, a grand total of 10,000 plants — mostly donated by other countries.

The Theme Pavilions included: Man and Life; Man, His Planet and Space; Man and the Oceans; Man and the Polar Regions; Man and His Health; and Man in the Community. Other advisory committees were responsible for such themes as Man the Producer, Man the Creator and Man the Provider.

For me two themes were of special interest. "Man in Control" and "Man in the Community." With regard to the former, I stressed the importance of portraying the burgeoning implications of the high-speed digital computer. Even 36 years ago there were indications that it would play a central role in our lives. Accordingly, demonstrations of specialized applications were developed. I have vivid recollections of two of these — a computer used as a design and teaching aid, and a talking computer. Early days but pretty accurate progenitors of what was to come.

But it was the second theme, "Man in the Community," perhaps not surprisingly because of its subjectivity, that gave rise to the most controversy during committee meetings. It was essentially a tug-of-war between scholars and scientists. After several lengthy debates we had reached no firm conclusion concerning the story-line, let alone specific exhibits only 12 months before the official opening! Then a consensus was reached. Consult McLuhan! Having declined an invitation to join the committee two years earlier (Marshall hated committees) I knew it would be a "hard sell." [26] However, we were close friends and it was worth a try.

Together with a couple of designers, I arranged to meet Marshall at the Board of Trade Club in downtown Toronto. The previous evening in Chicago, he had been guest speaker at a dinner celebrating the 25th anniversary of the Continental Can Company. It was a white-tie affair for everybody but Marshall. Because it was summer, he wore his seersucker suit. Knowing he would be late for lunch because of his flight from Chicago, I left instructions with the club steward requesting him to ask Marshall to join us on arrival. However, he didn't appear for lunch at 2 o'clock so we returned to the meeting room to find him asleep on a sofa.

---

[26]This anecdote is reported more parochially in <u>Who Was Marshall McLuhan</u>; Barrington Nevitt and Maurice McLuhan, Comprehensive Publications.

But he recovered rapidly and what followed was a three-hour outpouring of McLuhan creativity. At the end of the meeting the designers had a complete framework for "Man in the Community," and Marshall invited the three of us for a drink at his home. Before we left I asked, "What about your suitcase?" Marshall pulled out a plastic bag containing his shaving kit and toothbrush from his jacket pocket. That's all he had taken to Chicago. He had obviously not taken seriously the request that he should wear a white tie. Incidently, the Community Theme Pavilion was an outstanding success.

Expo '67 was opened formally in April by the Rt. Hon. Lester Pearson, Prime Minister of Canada. There were about a thousand invited guests and Patricia and I were allocated seats next to the Chairman of the Advisory Committee on Architecture, John C. Parkin and his wife. At the time John Parkin was probably the most eminent architect in Canada. After the opening ceremonies, we joined Dr. and Mrs. Wilder Penfield, whom we had met previously in Saskatoon and Dr. and Mrs. C.J. MacKenzie, who had been responsible for our return to Canada from London in 1958. The six of us toured the Theme Pavilions expedited by the Expo Express.

Of the virtually 100 national and cultural pavilions, which I recall, those of Britain, France, The United States and the Soviet Union were the most spectacular. I remember especially the Soviet Space Exhibit, which included the Sputnik capsule, and an exhibit which literally allowed visitors to experience the sensation of space travel while comfortably seated in arm chairs. The United States exhibits were equally sensational. Housed in a huge transparent "geodesic bubble" which contained a multi-level system of exhibit platforms interconnected by escalators, they reflected different aspects of the country's folk art, cinema, fine arts and technology, as well as a space exhibit which could be reached by a 125-foot escalator. The space exhibit incorporated a lunar landscape together with lunar vehicles. The "bubble" was of special interest to me because it was designed by the renowned American architect Buckminster Fuller. As I will indicate subsequently, "Bucky" Fuller and I became good friends and served on several panel and discussion groups together.

On the occasion of the National Day of Italy, I attended a luncheon in the Italian Pavilion in honor of the President of the Italian Republic. There were 64 guests and I still have the formal invitation requesting the pleasure of my company.

The final dinner hosted by His Excellency Pierre Dupuy,

Ambassador and Commissioner General of the Exhibition was held the evening after Expo '67 closed in late September. All I can remember about it is my one minute speech in French (always my "Achille's heel" at the Grammar School). It must have been a distressing minute for the Ambassador.

The Canadian Environmental Advisory Council

About a year after serving as Deputy Commissioner General of Expo '67, Bob Shaw became Deputy Minister for the Environment. Bearing in mind the success of the advisory committees associated with the World Exhibition, he decided to set up a group of physical and social scientists to advise the government on environmental problems. This became the Canadian Environmental Advisory Council. With the approval of Prime Minister Pierre Trudeau, I was appointed chairman.

This was another challenging commitment because of my unfamiliarity with the subject on one hand, and the fact that the majority of the 16 member council were authorities on environmental issues on the other. Indeed, Pierre Dansereau of the University of Montreal, and Patrick MacTaggart-Cowan of the University of British Columbia were giants in the field. However, in retrospect my three-year chairmanship proved a rewarding experience — new friends and education and several interesting topics for graduate research programs. It was a delight as well to act essentially as scientific advisor to the Honorable Jeanne Sauve, the Minister responsible for the Department for the Environment. In large measure the work of the Council was predicated on the urgent need to protect the world's and specifically the Canadian eco-system and hence life support systems. For example, processes such as deforestation interfere with the carbon, nitrogen and hydrological cycles, and we discovered that Canadian forests were being denuded at an alarming rate. Furthermore, the impact of acid rain on agriculture and on the fish populations, especially in the fresh water lakes of Ontario and Quebec, was a serious topic for discussion. The fact that the prevailing southwesterly winds carried polluting agents from United States factories and power plants had important political implications.

As well, at the time the environmental impact of oil spills was another topic which transcended international boundaries. But of all the diverse environmental matters we discussed none was debated more thoroughly than the potential impact of natural gas pipelines on the migration patterns of the caribou herds of Northern Canada. MacTaggart-

Cowan was an authority on the caribou and their habitat and I recall how vehemently he presented the case. Apparently, the herds would not pass beneath pipelines and this had a profound effect on their migration.

It is gratifying to recall that shortly after my term had expired, the Minister was elevated to appointment as the first woman Governor-General of Canada.

I am also proud to say that many years later my granddaughter, Jennifer, chose environmental studies as her university major, and after graduating from the University of Guelph went on to obtain a master's degree in the environmental sciences. Jennifer is working in Northern Ontario together with her husband, Trevor Griffin on environmental affairs for the Government of Ontario. Jennifer is specializing in Indian Affairs and working for the interests of the First Nation's people in the far north, and Trevor is superintendent of several Provincial parks, including one of the only two Polar Bear parks in North America and probably the world.

Chapter 13

A SATELLITE, A SCIENCE CENTER AND A SEMINAR

The Ontario Educational Communications Authority

My long association with the Authority began in the fall of 1963 when I chaired an Ontario Commission on Automation and Employment. The director of the Authority, Ran Ide was a member of the Commission and we became close friends. Noteworthy was a special TV program on which we collaborated entitled "Automation and Social Change." The specific topic debated by a panel of eight who included Omond Solandt; David Archer, President, Ontario Federation of Labor; Dr. John Dunlop, Chairman, Department of Economics, Harvard University; and Sir Geoffrey Vickers, V.C., was "Are people necessary?" Each panelist gave a 10- minute presentation. My contribution related to automation per se and I outlined the burgeoning implications of the man-machine interface. I little realized at the time how much the Commission and subsequent TV program had influenced the Ontario government. In fact, through Ran Ide's organization, it triggered a fascinating investigation, in which I played a central role on the possible utilization of satellite communications in Northern Ontario.

The investigation was in fact an exercise in operational research and consequently fitted perfectly into the research program of my department at U. of T. The major objective was to design experiments which were intended to assess the communications and educational implications of a so-called "Communications Technology Satellite" in northern Ontario. While southern Ontario was blessed with a plethora of radio and television facilities, the existing communications facilities for the northern region inhabited largely by native people, were extremely limited.

The satellite (CTS) was designed and built at the Communications Research Center, Ottawa to which I made reference previously. It was sponsored jointly by the Canadian Department of Communications and the United States National Aeronautics and Space Administration (NASA).

The main purposes of the experiments were to ensure the involvement of the native peoples and in particular:

(a) to determine the viability of satellite communications in northern Ontario and to assess the relative merits of various forms of communications e.g. interactive television, broadcast television, radio, telephone and combinations of these;

(b) to demonstrate and assess the impact of specific educational and social uses of these systems.

In a paper which was published in the "Proceedings of the Royal Society of London" Volume 345, pp. 459-475, I summarized the technical characteristics of the proposed satellite communications network in northern Ontario and discussed briefly the social and political background of the native peoples of the region. I also outlined the planning of the experiments and how they would facilitate the education, social well-being and maintenance of the culture and languages of the native peoples. Needless to add, in a project of such magnitude I received not only the help of O.E.C.A. technical staff, but most importantly that of Dr. P.A. Lapp, the project consultant with whom I was to have so much collaboration in the future. Phil Lapp still remains a friend and colleague.

As I have noted previously, I was co-author with Douglas Hartree and others of several papers published by the Royal Society, but I had never before authored and presented a paper at a conference held at the Society's headquarters in London. The conference on "The Introduction of a Satellite into Education Systems" was held in October 1975. It was a rare privilege to speak in those hallowed halls with a history dating back three centuries. It was particularly gratifying as well to be welcomed by a former colleague at Imperial College, Professor Colin Cherry who opened the discussion on my paper.

The Ontario Centennial Centre for Science and Technology

To those who have survived the reading of these memoirs so far, the importance of interdisciplinary activity in my life will be obvious. In virtually every field of endeavor I have contrived to cross disciplinary boundaries. This was especially manifest in my work as a scientific advisor to the Board of Directors of the Ontario Centre for Science and Technology.

Of the many major projects associated with Canada's Centennial and sponsored by the government of Ontario, the Centre was the most ambitious, the most lavish, and the most creative. My involvement in this enterprise was almost certainly due to the fact that Expo '67 had been such a success and I had participated in it.

For many years the Royal Ontario Museum, located in downtown Toronto and devoted essentially to natural history, had dominated the museum scene in the Province. Under the directorship of Bill Swinton, to whom I owe so much, the ROM, as it was affectionately called, had become internationally famous, especially for its exhibits of dinosaurs, fossils and a fantastic collection of artifacts relating to the ancient Chinese dynasties. But no complementary museum of science, technology and industry had been established in Canada. Furthermore, science and technology were expanding at such a bewildering speed and most people were finding it increasingly difficult to cope with the new knowledge and the new environments which were being created. No expense would be spared by the government of Ontario to establish a world-class institution in the Toronto area.

In the words of the Hon. James Auld, the cabinet minister responsible for the project:

> *"The Centennial Centre of Science and Technology will be a unique public institution — combining many characteristics and functions of museum, school, university and exhibition. It will be devoted to helping people of all ages understand the scientific revolution and the impact of technological advances on their lives."*

The original consultants hired by the Board were essentially traditionalists, not surprising in view of the fact that virtually all the great science museums in the world were predicated on historical scientific and technological artifacts. Exhibits of 19th century technology — fruits of the industrial revolution — being dominant. There was no doubt that a highly impressive collection of exhibits would have been developed for the Centre on these traditional lines. But one very influential member of the Board, Dr. William (Bill) Swinton had other ideas. He suggested that the basic purpose of the Centre should be to complement the Ontario education system by augmenting the science courses given in the schools. It would therefore, become a valuable and popular aid to both student and teacher. Bill stressed that what was required was a relaxed and pleasant atmosphere in which young people could absorb important concepts in science by participating in demonstrations and "do-it-yourself" exhibits. The emphasis would be on "Please Touch" rather than "Do Not Touch." He convinced the Board that this should be the basic concept for the Centre. Consequently, the government appointed a Scientific Advisory Committee consisting of Bill Swinton, Tommy Llewellyn-Thomas, and myself.

Because our paths had crossed on numerous occasions we were not only colleagues but close friends. From the beginning we realized that as a first priority the Centre must nourish continuing enthusiasm for learning among the growing public, including students at all levels in the Ontario educational system. The dynamic nature of science and technology called for building new bridges of communication in order that the public would be kept in touch with and accept modern concepts. And the Centre would be such a bridge. I cannot emphasize too emphatically the sheer elegance of the buildings of the Centre and their location. Designed by the outstanding Canadian architect Raymond Moriyama, the buildings were tailored into the rugged ravines of the Don River some 12 miles east of Toronto. Three large interconnected buildings covering more than 20 acres were situated in parkland consisting of 180 acres.

Simplifying our task of defining in a general way the nature of the exhibits in such broad fields as pure science, the health sciences and technology was the appointment of an acting director of the Centre who had previously been deputy head of the British Museum in London. It was not coincidental that prior to Bill Swinton immigrating to Canada, the two had been colleagues at the British Museum.

With a superb team of technicians and equally superb woodworking and metal working shops, the exhibits were fabricated within a period of three years. During the spring of 1970 the Centre was formally opened by the Hon. John P. Robarts, Prime Minister of Ontario. Patricia and I were guests of the Prime Minister who presented each of the three members of the Scientific Advisory Committee with lifetime passes for individuals and families. The pass is an engraved sterling silver rectangular plate suitably engraved. I believe only four of these (the

Chairman of the Board was the fourth) were presented.

Another memorable day was August 19, 1970 when Astronaut Captain James Lovell commander of the famous Apollo XIII mission, came to the Centre to open our space exhibit. Only four months previously on April 17 together with two other astronauts he had splashed down in the Pacific Ocean after surviving a dangerous re-entry of the capsule. At an official lunch after the opening ceremony James Lovell presented each of the eight members at the lunch with a photograph of "the first sighting of Apollo XIII" which showed the space capsule suspended by three parachutes appearing through the clouds. A caption under the photograph describes the event. Incidentally, the photograph now hangs in my study.

A Canada Council Seminar

One of the most imaginative creations of the Canada Council was the summer seminars held in Stanley House, situated on the shores of the Gaspé Peninsula in the Provence of Quebec. Originally the house had been the hunting lodge of the Governor General of Canada. Excellent free accommodation and gourmet food and wine were provided for participants. The seminars were awarded by the Council to applicants presenting novel interdisciplinary topics. Gordon Parr, Dean of Applied Science, University of Windsor and a friend and colleague in various subsequent activities, was a successful applicant in 1967 and convened a seminar on "Science, Technology and Society." The invited participants were:

Mr. David Bartlett,
Secretary General, Canadian Commission for UNESCO

Professor B.C. Binning,
Professor of Fine Arts, University of British Columbia

Dr. J. C. MacDonald,
Professor of Sociology, Trent University

Dr. Cyrias Ouilett
Professor of Chemistry, Laval University

Dr. Arthur Porter,
Professor of Industrial Engineering, University of Toronto

Dr. D. B. Scott,
Professor of Computing Science, University of Alberta

Professor D.W. Smythe
Professor of Social Sciences, University of
Saskatchewan

Mr. David Spurgeon,
Science Editor, the Globe and Mail

Dr. J. Gordon Parr,
(Convenor)
Dean of Applied Science, University of Windsor.

During the period July 10-14 we held discussion groups, presented papers and dined together. It was a fascinating experience. But for me it was especially memorable because of the presentation by Bert Binning. He was a well-known Canadian painter and architect with many exhibitions to his credit. There is a permanent collection of his drawings and paintings in the Vancouver Art Gallery which Patricia and I visited during our Alaska cruise in 1997.

At the time Bert had recently returned from spending several months of his sabbatical leave resident in a Buddhist monastery in Kyoto, Japan. During his stay he had spent many hours with Bishop Kojo Sakamoto, an internationally renowned calligraphist, observing his technique. In fact, the topic which he presented to the seminar at Stanley House related specifically to Japanese calligraphy. We learned, for example, that the Bishop might spend up to four hours kneeling on a pad, large brush in hand and ink pot full of black ink at his side. In a state of contemplation, he remained in an upright posture until suddenly the brush was thrust into the pot and within a few seconds, a unique calligraphy was written on a sheet of rice paper. It must have been an amazing sight to see the Bishop who was then aged 93 years execute the calligraphy. Bert Binning, through an interpreter, informed the Bishop about his prospective talk to be given at the Stanley House seminar whereupon the Bishop presented him with nine copies of a calligraphy — "Word Used in the Praying for World Peace" and together with a like number of catalogs portraying the works of the Bishop which were displayed in art gallery exhibitions in Los Angeles, San Francisco, Seattle and Vancouver. It was a beautiful gift.

At the end of his talk Bert presented each of the seminar participants with the calligraphy and the catalog. On my return to Toronto I wrote a letter to Bishop Kojo Sakamoto and informed him that I was so impressed with the calligraphy that I had had it framed. I learned subsequently that I was the only one of the nine participants who had written. The quite unexpected consequences of my letter were as follows: A few weeks later I was delighted to receive a reply from the Bishop. Accompanying it was a set of five calligraphies, which we had framed and now hangs in our hall. The letter was written calligraphically on a 40-inch long, eight-inch wide strip of rice paper together with a translation into modern Japanese. I had the letter translated into English by a member of the staff of the Department of East Asian Studies at the university. Incidentally, I was informed that there was nobody on the staff who could translate the original calligraphic writing and that there were probably very few people in the world who could do so.

Because of its unique character and the great pleasure Patricia and I have derived from the Bishop's work I am including the translation of the letter below.

September 3, 1967

Professor Arthur Porter,
University of Toronto

Dear Prof. Porter,
Your letter has been received with much appreciation.

I am very grateful to you for the honor of your presence at my lecture given under the auspices of Prof. Bert Binning. I also esteem it a great honor that you not only placed some of my calligraphic writings on display at the place where seminar was held, but also you and some of the other spectators received inspiration, courage and vigour from my writings. If there is any merit in my calligraphy, however, it should be attributed to the founder, Kobo Daishi, whose teachings I am simply following.

I was so deeply impressed by your letter that I made another calligraphy copying some of the words of Kobo and am presenting it to you as a token of my gratitude. I request the honor of your inspection.

Yours sincerely,
Kojo Sakamoto

P.S. Please give my best regards to Professor Binning when you see him. I am also presenting you a collected letters of Prof. Tessai for your inspection.

The collected letters of the Master Tessai, (who I understand was the Japanese equivalent to Piccaso) were received in a beautifully linen-bound volume with ivory clasps — a wonderful treasure. It is exceptionally noteworthy that the calligraphies were written by Bishop Kojo Sakamoto when he was 94 years old.

Needless to say I wrote two more letters to the Bishop expressing my gratitude for his kindness and my appreciation of the wonderful calligraphies which he had written especially for me. Once again the reply was written calligraphically with a modern Japanese translation and once again I had the letter translated. The second letter is presented below:

October 10, 1967

Prof. Arthur Porter
University of Toronto

Dear Sir:
I have received three letters of yours with much appreciation.

I was deeply moved by your true feeling expressed in the act that you put my writing in a frame in order to inspect it all the time. I appreciate your sympathy with my adoration of the Great Master Kobo, whom I look up to as the founder of Shingon-Sanpo Sect.

I would like to express my heartfelt gratitude toward your hearty response to the calligraphy of Emperor Goyozei and your treatment of my writing. Though it is inexpert one, as a prayer for peace, both of which were displayed in Toronto.

According to your letter you are invited by the University of British Columbia to give lectures on October 22. I imagine that you will have a joyful time meeting Prof. Binning.
With much thanks.

Sincerely yours,
Kojo Sakamo

In light of the rather unique nature of the above correspondence, and the impressive calligraphies, the Bishop dedicated to me personally, Patricia and I feel that they should be preserved. Accordingly, it is our intention to bequeath them to an appropriate museum or art gallery.

Chapter 14

AN ADVENTURE IN ACADEME

THERE have been few, if any, experiences and opportunities in my life to match those I encountered during 1969-1971, the period when I was the Academic Commissioner at the University of Western Ontario (U.W.O.), London, Ontario. Writing these memoirs rather more than three decades subsequently, I can reflect on the freedom I had to roam uninhibited the highways and byways of a modern university campus, and to ponder on its academic structure, its vitality and its relationship to the community that provided its sustenance. They were heady days at Western.

For several years dating from 1962 I had had increasingly close relations with Carl Williams, who was the recently appointed President of the University. In particular, Carl and I were close friends and colleagues of Marshall McLuhan, especially during my term as Acting Director of the Center for Culture and Technology, and we had many informal discussions on academic affairs in general. It was a period of uncertainty — innovation in university governance and burgeoning developments in information technology. When Carl was appointed President of U.W.O, he decided that the time was ripe for an overall assessment of the University's academic structure and programs. The Senate concurred.

The concept of an Academic Commissioner emerged. It was obviously innovative and a manifestation of the University's willingness to undertake "academic experiments." The formal terms of reference of the Academic Commissioner as established by the Senate of the University were:

"To serve full time and to make a serious thorough and significant study of the structure and interrelationship of the academic programs of the University; to consult regularly with the Vice-President (Academic) and to report to the Senate within two years of his appointment."

Subsequently, Dr. Roger Rossiter, the Vice-President, elaborated on the formal terms of reference as follows:

"It is hoped that he will act as a catalyst to promote free and full discussion on all aspects of our University teaching. This will include (a) formal structures with the hope that more flexibility may be achieved together with more sophisticated counseling services, (b) course content, with the hope that the material presented will be more relevant to today's society, and(c) new teaching methods, including television aides, audio-visual aides, computer aides, etc. "

My appointment as Academic Commissioner meant obtaining a two-year leave of absence from the U. of T., and this was granted without reservation. I still marvel at the scope of the inquiry because I was given *carte blanche* and essentially diplomatic immunity by all estates of the University.

For its part, the University did everything in its power to make my two years on campus a pleasurable experience. A wonderful office in Middlesex College was provided as well as a hard-working secretary.

I had no illusions when I arrived on the campus early in July 1969 about the magnitude of the task confronting me. I was conscious of the fact that not all members of the faculty were happy about their work being subjected to assessment by an "outsider." I am certain, for example, that it was not particularly comforting for scholars in the humanities and social sciences to have their programs and lectures scrutinized by an industrial engineer. But let me hasten to add in retrospect that it is gratifying to recall the high level of collaboration I received and as well how close my relationships with key faculty and administration members became.

Almost immediately I was challenged concerning the object of the exercise. In particular a member of the School of Business

Administration insisted that I should spell out in detail the purpose of "my study." Because the question was so central and revealing of how I interpreted the terms of reference I can do no better than to quote a few lines from my final report: [27]

> There are, of course, a host of related questions which are relevant in any discussion of the purpose of the study. Some of them are:
>
> (a) How can the spirit and reality of a true university community be achieved in spite of burgeoning growth?
>
> (b) How can the University expedite, first, its major roles of scholarship and research in the liberal arts and sciences tradition, and thereby help to resolve some of the pressing problems of contemporary society, and secondly, the education and training of specialists and professionals to fit them for an increasingly uncertain future, albeit a future in which the roles of such specialists and professionals will probably be less specialized than today?
>
> (c) Bearing in mind the above questions, how can the resources of the University (human, cultural and physical) be optimized? A related question concerns the problem of facilitating communication within the University.
>
> Ideally, therefore, the major purpose of the study was to seek viable answers to the above questions and to hope that some of them could be implemented. Obviously the problem was complex. Not least because the majority of institutions of higher education were characterized by conservatism, in spite of the fact that they had given birth to discoveries of major proportions. However, it was in their approach to teaching, rather than to research, that the universities were more characterized by conservatism. But there may be some justification for this because the effects of innovation in educational systems cannot be assessed quickly, indeed, they may take several years.

---

[27] Arthur Porter. "Towards a Community University," University of Western Ontario; 1971

The normal procedure at the time in investigations such as mine was to hold "public hearings" during which evidence would be obtained from all estates of the University. But this did not appeal and I preferred a much more informal approach and decided a priori on a "participational commission." For example, I attended normally scheduled lectures and laboratories without giving the lecturer advance warning and I gave numerous lectures and conducted many seminars in a range of disciplines ranging from economic geography to dentistry and physical health education in order to clarify my mission. But the most rewarding were the lectures in which I participated as a student.

Especially memorable was the day I attended senior classes in a local high school and obtained a first-hand impression of a student's interests and aspirations. It was quite an experience to be seated in a classroom together with about 30 teenage students 40 years my junior. The extent to which this high school visitation assisted my investigation is problematical, but it lives in my memory.

Complementing the high school experience was the full day I spent with two freshmen, male and female, on campus in order to assess the trauma and such it was, of registration. The three of us stood in long queues to register for individual classes and athletic programs, to obtain such ancillary items as library cards and locker allocations, and to obtain lunch in the campus cafeteria. There was a measure of incredulity on the part of many faculty members and University staff to observe a senior academic surviving the first day on campus as a freshman. But it was well worthwhile. Not only was I able to assess the level of frustration involved in registration processes, but as well I got to know two young people during a major transition in their lives. A physically and mentally tiring day ended with a delicious dinner prepared by Patricia in our apartment. A few days later we invited eight more students, randomly selected, for coffee and donuts. During the course of my investigation I kept in touch with them and from time to time received valuable commentaries on various aspects of their lives on campus.

Certain it was during my early days on campus that the major consequences of the student protest movement of the late 60's lingered. I welcomed them. Students were questioning many aspects of higher education. Not surprisingly, therefore, as a precursor to my study of academic structure and curricula, I decided to direct my attention to some of the students' concerns, especially to such questions as the relevance of the curricula, academic freedom and University governance.

The issue of relevance bedeviled most debates on course content.

During the registration process for example, I identified a central concern in the minds of the students — is the material of this course relevant? I pointed out that the demand by students for relevance to their needs and desires and to techniques and methodology which may be relevant today may be irrelevant tomorrow. In other words, there would be a danger of investment in the present regardless of the future. Education for a changing environment must be the university's basic mission.

I concluded that in the minds of many students relevance in education is interpreted as "study and involvement with contemporary problems," without, apparently, much understanding of the relevance of the underlying basic concepts. Undergraduate curricula which do not recognize contemporary problems are obviously undesirable, but so also are curricula which do not adequately emphasize basic discipline and structure. This was certainly a knotty question which tormented me for many weeks. But I always insisted that the conventional and classical education systems of the past, predicated as they had been on comparatively highly structured and disciplined teaching and learning processes had had great successes.

"Academic freedom" was another topic which gave rise to passionate debate. Many faculty members were incensed by the prospect of their freedom to teach and carry out research being threatened by the bureaucracy. "Freedom" was a frequent rallying cry for some students who did not appreciate the educational value of the liberal arts and pressed for more freedom to choose.

While there was undoubtedly some justification for faculty concern about potential threats, on the other hand I concluded that academic freedom should not be interpreted as "academic license." For example, I was aware that some professors neglected their teaching because it interfered unduly with their research. No doubt this was understandable because all too frequently a professor's promotion depended on his research output and not on his teaching excellence.

But the above should not imply that I endorsed a policy which reduced the power and weakened the right of any member or group of members of the University from criticizing either government or University. Not surprisingly I endorsed the general consensus that academic freedom must not be readily compromised.

One of the major aftermaths of the period of student unrest was the urgent desires on the part of the more politically oriented student to become involved in university governance. The more vociferous students even went so far as to advocate a seat on the Board of Governors!

However, I made it abundantly clear that I was opposed to students being involved in the formulation of educational policy and academic curricula. I argued that students had neither the knowledge nor the experience to participate in such activities. I fully subscribed to the views of Kingman Brewster, former President of Yale:

> *"I am convinced that representation (of students) is not the clue to university improvement, indeed if carried too far it could lead to disaster -- Most students would rather have the policies of the university directed by the faculty and administration than by their classmates."*

On the other hand I subscribed to the idea of regular consultation on a formal basis at departmental levels between faculty and students interested in educational policy.

Controversial topics such as those outlined above and several others, which I identified during the first few months of my study, lent themselves to informal discussion in workshop formats. Accordingly I conducted a series of "weekend workshops." Everybody was invited, and although the average attendance was only about 12 people, who included faculty members, students, administrators and a representative group of "interested outsiders" (which included a Provincial Government Cabinet Minister, a senior trade unionist, a TV news analyst, a Director of Education, several secondary school principals, a housewife, several secondary school students and a senior academic administrator). The topics under discussion included: "Why the University?" "The Improvement of Teaching and Learning;" "The Development of Interdisciplinary Programs;" and "Management Problems in Universities."

Complementing the workshops, departmental commentaries and attendance at many committee meetings, I obtained information from every "nook and cranny" on campus and beyond, ranging from cocktail parties to political conferences. With respect to the latter I should point out that through my involvement in a broad range of government activities I had acquired the confidence of several key members of the cabinet, notably John White, Provincial Treasurer, and the Premier, Bill Davies, who on occasion referred to me as his academic "guru."

The database I accumulated was awesome. The material filled several filing cabinets. Perhaps at this stage of the investigation I might have made more use of a computer and electronic printer, but I was always conscious that the majority of the evidence was essentially subjective and its interpretation did not lend itself to normal analytical procedures. On the other hand, information relating, for example, to student admissions, student profiles and performance, library holdings and acquisitions, etc., and I assembled a great deal, does lend itself to statistical and probability analysis and even in some cases to risk assessment. But I considered such issues as being beyond the scope of my investigation.

In preparing my final report I identified five primary objectives and structured it accordingly. They were:

- Achievement of more flexible admissions criteria with more emphasis on extra-curricular activities and experience of the work-place.

- Enhancement of students' educational horizons by introduction of Junior and Senior Divisions. (My idea was to delay a student's career decision-point from the beginning of freshman year to the end of sophomore year.)

- Improvement of teaching with increasing emphasis on the use of information technology. (e.g. TV and computer).

- Encouragement of interdisciplinary studies and mission-oriented research — how might departments and faculties be restructured to encourage inter-faculty cooperation?

- Facilitation of continuing and community education.

In total I probably spent four months exclusively on the writing and then a few hours reflecting on a suitable title.

Perhaps "Towards A Community University" was not the most appropriate title because in the minds of some it obviously had community college connotations. However, I justified it on the grounds that the enhancement of communications between university and community, interpreted in the broadest possible sense as consistent with each one of my objectives. These had been approved, and indeed endorsed, by some of the most respected members of the University who included Roger Rossiter, the Vice President Academic, Ian Brooks, President of the Student Council, and Horace Krever, Professor of Law, and subsequently a justice of the Supreme Court of Ontario.

I'll never forget the Friday afternoon in July 1971 when I presented the report to the Senate. Gratifyingly, there was standing room only in the 200-seat chamber. In addition to members of Senate, several guests, notably Patricia and Hon. John White, attended. According to Patricia, and she should know having attended numerous similar events, I did a good job. It was certainly encouraging subsequently to read a note passed by John White to Patricia when he left the meeting early. It's still in my files:

> *Mrs. Porter:*
>
> *Please tell Arthur how much I enjoyed being here. It was a memorable experience. I will congratulate him and thank him more adequately some time shortly after your trip is over. Have a good time!*
>
> *John White*

The reference by John White to "our trip" referred to the fact that at the end of my presentation, jokingly, I mentioned that Patricia and I would be leaving almost immediately after the meeting to fly to England where I was due to present the prizes at my old school — consequently I would escape any brickbats for at least two weeks.

The Saturday edition of the "London Free Press" was especially praiseworthy of my report and its major recommendations. It was heartening to read some of the editorials just prior to our departure for England.

On revisiting the paper several years after it was written I am struck by its continuing relevance. This is obviously debatable, nevertheless to ensure that my "dust" ridden report remains a pleasant memory in my mind and that of my family, I am including in this memoir a copy of my letter of transmittal to the President of the University. Sadly, Carl Williams died about a decade ago.

Belfountain, Ontario

Dr. D.C. Williams
President and Vice-Chancellor
The University of Western Ontario
London, Ontario

Dear Dr. Williams:

Report of the Academic Commissioner

On February 14, 1969, you wrote, on behalf of the Senate of the University to confirm my appointment as Academic Commissioner. Prior to this I had intimated that if offered the appointment, I would accept with alacrity. I have had no cause to regret my decision. Instead, the past two years have been highly intellectually stimulating and enjoyable, and it is with some measure of regret that I herewith submit my report.

My terms of reference have been very broad — in your own words I have been given carte blanche. I can assure you that the University has played its parts splendidly in ensuring that my study could be undertaken with maximum openness and with minimum constraint; the extent to which I have fulfilled my part remains to be seen. You will be aware, for instance, of many shortcomings in the report, and for these I beg the indulgence and goodwill of Senate — they have in no way resulted from a lack of cooperation on the part of the many members of the University with whom I have had discussions, but perhaps rather from the sheer magnitude of my task. I am only too conscious, for example, that there have had to be many omissions, many overly superficial treatments of important topics and many failures to balance, wisely, conflicting opinions.

In consequence, some of my conclusions will not be viewed with enthusiasm by one or other constituencies of the University, but by this fact alone I will have stimulated some academic controversy, and, in part, this was the object of the exercise!

As you know, my commission has not been conducted along the traditional lines of governmental and educational commissions (i.e., the formal presentations of briefs, the holding of public hearings, etc.) but much more as a "participational commission," perhaps the first of its kind, in which the emphasis has been on my participation in the day-to-day activities and affairs of the University. As a result, I think I have avoided viewing the University in an artificial light. In

McLuhanistic terms, and I do not apologize, especially to you, Sir, for invoking McLuhan's insights, I have sought "antienvironments," in the sense of seeking means to illuminate the diversity of environments which make up the University.

It is unfortunate that those who criticize the University as a tradition-bound cloister, haven for scholars and scientists, have not had my opportunities to explore it without let or hindrance. They would find, taken by and large, especially in the administration and faculty, an extremely hard-working community of dedicated people. Trying to keep abreast of a single sector or one discipline today is tough and time-consuming. I sometimes reflect on how few laymen and politicians really appreciate this.

In this, my letter of transmittal, it may not be out of place to outline, albeit briefly, some of the guidelines upon which the study has been based. It is perhaps not surprising that an applied scientist, with a strong propensity to problem-solving in the study of regulatory systems, should begin by outlining his basic aims and aspirations. These have been several:

(a) I have tried to project the University into the mid-1970s, and the majority of my suggestions and recommendations relate to 1974-75, rather than to 1971-72.

(b) I have tried to develop arguments based essentially on academic values without being unduly prejudiced by economic factors. I believe, however, that my suggestions are realistic from an economic standpoint.

(c) I have tried to interpret the ideas and hopes of as broad a spectrum as possible of members of the University. But achievement of a consensus on several key issues has been virtually impossible and I have been obliged to rely on value judgments rather than on more objective assessments.

(d) All evolutionary processes embody historical patterns, as well as the "probes" necessary to keep them updated. Accordingly, I have tried to maintain a realistic

balance between conservation (in the sense of retaining relevant structures but keeping them continually under critical review) on one hand, and innovation (in the sense of experimentation) on the other hand.

(e) Healthy evolutionary systems embody a degree of diversity and, in recognizing that some measure of "diversity of approach" will continue to be essential for the well-being of the universities of Ontario, I have tried to ensure in my reflections the continued individuality of Western. But I sense, intuitively, a disturbing level of activity aimed essentially at a defensive posture on the part of most universities, including Western. And, of course, the defensive posture is unlikely to stimulate healthy academic growth, only a leadership posture can do that.

From the onset of the study it was obvious that a detailed review of curricula would be impracticable — at present in the undergraduate programs alone more than 1,500 courses are offered. Instead I have attempted to consider curricula in a general sense with special emphasis on interactions between courses from the standpoint of conceptual structures and orderings. I have been particularly conscious of the importance of evolving flexible and diverse learning environments.

Coincidentally, during the course of my study, I have noted a variety of academic innovations on the campus. In some degree these have already anticipated some of my suggestions and recommendations, and they have certainly strongly influenced my thinking. Such developments lend credence to my belief that the mere existence of an "Academic Commissioner" on campus may have a salutary influence — "The medium is the message!"

My report is perhaps more discursive in character than is normal in reports of this kind; a single investigator in such a study must continually "wage a battle with himself." As a result, it will be noted that some redundancy between chapters is evident — in part this has been intentional because few readers will be interested in the report as a whole, most will be concerned with particular chapters. Another idiosyncrasy is that only major recommendations have been presented as such; in addition, numerous suggestions which may, or may not, be of interest to specific departments and Faculties are included.

It is perhaps presumptuous of me even to mention the implementation of these suggestions and recommendations, embodied in my report, of which Senate approves. If, for example, my recommendation to the effect that a major standing committee of Senate, the Educational Policy Committee, is in fact approved by the Senate, this would clearly be the appropriate mechanism. May I re-emphasize, however, that it would be unrealistic to anticipate implementation of some recommendations (e.g., the Associateship) before1973-74, although, on the other hand, I believe it would be desirable for a Dean of General Studies to be appointed in 1972.

It is obviously impossible to record all of the contributions and assistance I have received from many members of the University. Suffice it to say that my study has been a truly communal operation, only made possible through the unstinting support of administrators, faculty and students.

With the publication of this report I hope that discussions which originated in the several workshops I conducted in 1969-70 will be stimulated and that the level of controversy so obvious on those occasions will not be diminished.

Yours sincerely,
Arthur Porter
Academic Commissioner
Professor of Industrial Engineering,
University of Toronto

While on the whole I was not dissatisfied with the initial response of the University to my report, it soon became apparent that as the implications of many of my recommendations sunk in so did the degree of resistance to change. The prospect of "the boat being rocked" to the extent I suggested was not on the agenda of many senior faculty members

Let me reflect on just a few of the proposals which were unacceptable to the faculty committees established to review the report. To encourage cross-disciplinary dialogue, I recommended the appointment of a University professor to act in effect as a catalyst. In other words, an academic who would literally extend the work of the Academic Commissioner by facilitating interaction between faculties and departments, and by identifying key academic issues of the day and potential issues of the future. Admittedly it would have been a daunting task, but could have been very rewarding. Imagination would have been the key requirement. At the time it seemed to me so obvious that the university was probably the unique agency in society whereby novel linkages between disciplines could be forged and might prosper. For example the burgeoning fields of medical engineering and information technology, both spawned in academe, have had profound implications for society and civilization. But clearly at the time Western had doubts about the viability of such an appointment.

My recommendations relating to changes in the structure of academic programs and in particular to the formation of Junior (freshman and sophomore) and Senior (junior and senior years) Divisions and the award of an associate diploma at the end of the second year obviously did not appeal. Still I felt that my objectives were basically sound. Let me outline them.

After a two year exposure to campus life, a student would have three options open. First, assuming she or he had reached a sufficiently high academic standing, proceed to an honors program in the arts, social sciences, or natural sciences faculties or to professional programs in medicine, engineering, business administration, etc. Second, for less qualified students, proceed with studies leading to an ordinary degree in the liberal arts and sciences. Third, delay academic aspirations e.g.students who felt that more exposure to the outside world would enhance their future prospects in one of the professions. A student having obtained the Associateship might obtain a job and consider returning to university after a hiatus of perhaps two or more years.

As far as I know there has never been a serious debate relating to the virtue or otherwise, of the associateship concept. In retrospect it should have been obvious to me at the time that Western was not the institution where such a reform should have been initiated. But not for the first time, I was carried away with enthusiasm and lacked the necessary judgment. My recommendation that the existing Faculty of Engineering Science should be re-structured as a Faculty of Environmental Engineering was one of the most controversial. For several years I had become increasingly interested in environmental issues and I felt that the elements for building up a faculty or even a division of environmental science/engineering were extant at the university. Cooperative programs with the Faculties of Social Science, Medicine and Business Administration seemed to me to be worthy of consideration. These would have been pioneering programs, perhaps even the first in any university. The case I presented to Senate for creation of such a faculty was powerful and persuasive. It concluded:

> *"All environmental studies epitomize general systems theory; the environment is not particularly conscious of departmental boundaries! The programs I envisage will call for a tremendous effort and goodwill on the part of the Faculty and students, and of other Faculties, but the making of some exciting developments exist and the time is right."*

Unfortunately, my recommendation was rejected. The University preferred to leave the Faculty of Engineering Science virtually unchanged, and together with at least 30 other schools of engineering in Canada to continue on traditional lines.

I will not dwell on other disappointments — suffice it to say the University was unwilling to pursue the most radical of my proposals. Not surprising in light of the innate conservatism of the school. But what was surprising was the fact that U.W.O. had embarked on the experiment in the first place. However, bearing in mind that the new president had proposed the idea, it would have been difficult for the Senate to reject it. Carl Williams, no doubt influenced by his friend Marshall McLuhan, was anxious to reform some of the more reactionary aspects of the University, especially in light of the recent student/faculty unrest. His motto was clearly that if changes were necessary, the sooner the better! This sentiment was somewhat at odds with the thoughts of one dean who remarked that my ideas were 20 years ahead of their time — as it transpired 50 years would have been nearer the mark!

Fortunately, there was one president of another Canadian university, Prince Edward Island, who agreed on the whole with my conclusions and recommendations. It was particularly gratifying to read in "University Affairs," February 1972, a lengthy review of my report by Dr. R. J.

Baker entitled "Oh, Mr. Porter, What Shall I Do?"

A few excerpts from the review are worth quoting. First, Baker clarifies the heading which was in fact the title of a London stage vaudeville song:

> *"In the old song, the 'silly young girl' asked another Mr. Porter to help her back to London. As far as I remember, she didn't get an answer. The University of Western Ontario, as befits a dowager soon to be a 100, has received a much more substantial reply, one that will help her stay in London and avoid her predecessor's fate."*

Following on, he commented:

> *'I suspect that Dr. Porter is right when he says 'that the mere existence of an academic commissioner on campus may have a salutary influence — the medium is the message.' — But the 'participational method' of the commissioner and now the report itself must have made everyone at Western consider these matters and re-think whatever is being done at present."*

I was particularly happy to read one comment that I felt hit the "nail on the head." It was:

> *"The obvious enthusiasm for cybernetics and McLuhan that runs throughout the report augments a wide-ranging interest in and sympathy with nearly every aspect of the university."*

It's interesting to note that the only genuine doubt Dr. Baker had related to my recommendation that a Faculty of Information and Communication be created incorporating such disciplines as journalism, secretarial science, linguistics, library and information science and computer science. Clearly the developments of the past three decades in these disciplines have borne out the rationale of my reasoning, essentially because of the central role in each discipline of the computer and information technology. In common with Buckminster Fuller, I anticipated the increasingly important role of women in management and the information professions.

But I must not knit-pick because the Baker assessment of my study at Western was to my way of thinking the most objective of all. But of course I was prejudiced. His final paragraph appealed most of all:

> *"Other universities live in somewhat different contexts, and are different contexts in themselves, but everyone in a university could profit from this book and all the universities I know could profit from following a similar procedure — if they can find someone as multi-talented as Arthur Porter."*

As far as I know, three decades subsequently, no other university has had the temerity to appoint an Academic Commissioner!

It was coincidental that within a few weeks of completion of the investigation, my son John completed an arduous six years studying medicine. As a newly graduated M.D. I sought his input on some of the medical school conclusions I had formulated. They were very perceptive. Here's a sample:

• Medical sciences rounds, to correlate basic science teaching and ideas with clinical problems are most worthwhile from a student interest point of view and as a teaching exercise in first year. Demonstration of respiration, hemodynamics, endocrine function in patients and their abnormalities stimulate the student's interest and will help him try to use his basic science knowledge in evaluating clinical problems later on.

• The amount of laboratory time spent in gross anatomy in the first medical year is totally unreasonable in this day and age and is twice that given at other universities. But 16 hours spent in first year on the history of medicine is excellent.

• The fact that history-taking is not covered in second year is deplorable. It is ridiculous to give training to students in bed-side manner and talking with patients in third year when only nine months from then they will be functioning as 'clinical clerks.' These skills are an integral part of clinical medicine and take time to acquire. Second year is the time to do it.

• A physician's every encounter with a patient can be either psychologically beneficial or detrimental. In order to make it as beneficial as possible, one must practice one's skill at 'talking with patients at every opportunity and as soon as possible.' It is far, far better to treat a confident and happy patient than a depressed one and indeed this very skill may do a patient more good than all the drug therapy on earth.

The last few lines of the above is an extract from Dr. W.F. Connell's lecture to meds' 71- Queen's University, November 18, 1968.

As far as the Connell doctrine is concerned, it is gratifying to his very proud parents to know that John's philosophy of clinical medicine has never deviated from Dr. Connell's teaching. Several patients of our acquaintance all confirm that his patience and courtesy in his office are exemplary.

Two events during my sojourn at Western are worthy of special mention. First I was delighted during the spring of 1970 to be informed by the Royal Society of Canada that I had been elected a Fellow in the Academy of Science. A new division of Applied Science and Engineering had been established in 1969 and I was fortunate to be elected the following year.

The initiation ceremony for the election of new Fellows in 1970 was held at the University of Manitoba, Winnipeg. After the citation had been read, I was formally admitted as a Fellow of the Society and presented with my diploma, an elegant document inscribed in Latin. Subsequently I was proposed and elected a member of the Council of the Academy. Several of my oldest friends in Canada were Fellows and at annual meetings, usually held in July, I was able to keep in touch with them, especially the Forsyths, the Feindels and Brenda Milner.

The Centenary of the Society celebrated in the Senate Chamber of the Houses of Parliament, Ottawa, were very special. Patricia accompanied me and it was a thrill to get together again with Sir Andrew and Lady Huxley after the ceremony. It will be recalled that Andrew and I had worked together on the anti-aircraft gun sites during the London Blitz in 1940-41. He was President of the Royal Society and one of the very few honorary Fellows to have been appointed to the Canadian Royal Society.

Secondly the UWO. Convocation of 1970 was unforgettable. I had the honor of giving the address. About 1200 people attended. Because a Rabbi offered the final prayers and being a Friday he was required to be present in the synagogue before sundown, I was instructed to limit by address to 15 minutes. Accordingly, although I did not read the address, I had prepared a set of six "prompt" cards — two minutes a card. Attired in my resplendent PhD. gown, all went well during my address until in the middle of recounting an anecdote I discovered to my horror that card number five was missing. For a fraction of a second I was speechless, but recovered rapidly and turned completely around to face the Chancellor. I raised my cap and said, "Mr. Chancellor, at this point in my address I regret that a prompt card is missing and hence there will be a discontinuity." The reaction of the assembly was spontaneous — there was a roar of laughter! At the presidential reception after the convocation a few of my friends suggested that I had deliberately staged the affair to liven up the proceedings. Quite untrue of course.

In July 1971 I looked back on two fantastic years. In many respects unmatched during my academic life. We departed from London, Ontario without fanfare, but with a measure of sadness. Only Suzie, our much beloved cat, was delighted!

As a fitting conclusion to this chapter I record an event which in retrospect profoundly affected the lives of our family. Almost immediately after his graduation, John began his internship at the Toronto Western Hospital and had the good fortune to serve under Irwin Hilliard, the Physician-in-Chief. Irwin had returned to his alma mater as Professor of Medicine. John's progress as a clinician not only impressed Irwin, who regarded him as the most promising intern of his class, but resulted essentially in his being accepted as a resident in neurology at the School of Medicine, University of Colorado. The neuroscience program at Denver was regarded as one of the most prestigious in the U.S.A. The letter of acceptance arrived on August 17, 1971 shortly after we'd left London. We little realized that it would be a landmark.

Chapter 15

A CENTENARY CELEBRATION

WITH the possible exception of the Investiture Ceremony on the occasion of my appointment as an Officer of the Order of Canada, as described in Chapter 18, the Institution of Electrical Engineers, Centenary Celebrations in London during May 1971 were the most impressive and undoubtedly the most glamorous that Patricia and I had ever attended.

My invitation to participate in a Centenary Technical Congress, the theme of which was "Electrical Science and Engineering in the Greater Service of Man," was a wonderful surprise.

Because of the international character of the Institution the eight Centenary lecturers came from different parts of the world — three from Britain, two from the United States and one each from India, the Netherlands and Canada. I, a Fellow of the Institution, was the Canadian.

Patricia and I traveled to London during the weekend prior to the celebrations. We stayed at the Waldorf Hotel as guests of the Institution. But apart from sleeping and breakfast, we were only in residence there transiently. Most of our time was taken up with official events. I'll try to summarize them.

On Sunday, May 16 I attended a briefing session at the headquarters of the Institution at Savoy Place. The impressive Georgian building had been suitably decorated for the Centenary. One of the first to welcome me was John Coales who had been responsible for my participation in the first place. It is interesting how frequently the Servo Panel of WWII of which John was a founder member, influenced my life, even three decades subsequently. I did not have any appreciation of John's role in planning the celebrations until a year or two later. With his characteristic modesty he had not given me any intimation that he had been responsible for the sheer grandeur of the occasion. Unknown to many of his friends, he was a shooting companion at his estate in Scotland, of H.R.H. the Duke of Edinburgh. It was obviously through their relationship, as I will relate subsequently, that the I.E.E. Centenary became a Royal Occasion. Indeed, every aspect of the celebrations was planned with dignity and in the highest of British traditions. It was a rare privilege for Patricia and myself to attend.

A fanfare of trumpets echoing through Westminister Abbey launched the celebrations on the morning of Monday, May 17, 1971. It was 100 years to the day from the original meeting of a group of men who were to form what was then the Society of Telegraph Engineers.

As we entered the Abbey west door that morning, Patricia and I reflected on the fact that we were entering the most hallowed shrine in Britain and the Commonwealth. All English monarchs since William the Conqueror in 1066 had been crowned in the Abbey and many of them entombed there. As well the tombs of some of the country's most famous citizens including Chaucer, Newton and Darwin are located there. Poets' Corner, memorializing Shakespeare, Wordsworth and other famous men and women of letters, nestles there. To be seated with the other Centenary lecturers and their wives in the Choir Stalls was a thrill. Many historic events had been enacted within a few yards of us, the likes of Sir Winston Churchill had worshiped there.

The hundredth anniversary Thanksgiving Service was opened by the Lord Mayor of Westminister and following prayers, special hymns and an anthem, the sermon was preached by the Chaplain to the I.E.E. Council. The service concluded with the presentation, by the Secretary of the I.E.E., to the Sacrist of the Abbey of the book containing the minutes of the first meeting. It will be preserved for all time in the Abbey.

In the afternoon, the celebrations continued in the Royal Festival Hall across the River Thames. This was the occasion when the Institution received commemorative gifts from more than 30 learned Societies of the UK, Europe, the USA, Israel and South Africa. All the dignitaries were resplendent in academic dress and the atmosphere was reminiscent of a state wedding — the ladies providing a gay scattering of color and the gifts were displayed for all to see.

The so-called "coruscant" opening address was delivered by Lord Hailsham, the Lord Chancellor who spoke of professional electrical engineers as the "creative artist of modern society." In conclusion he stressed that "it is high time that the professional classes of the world unite — whatever we stand to win or lose the world cannot afford to do without our brains." This made all present feel very self-satisfied. In concluding the session, Lord Nelson, the President, read a telegram of congratulations from H.M The Queen in response to the loyal greeting which Her Majesty had received previously.

The Centenary Technological Congress got under way on Tuesday, May 18. I've had opportunity to review the eight lecturers recently and I have been struck by their sheer brilliance (and even in the case of my own lecture I regard it as one of the three most important I have delivered in my life). Three decades ago each one outlined an almost uncanny prediction of technological developments in its respective field. It would be remiss if I did not include in this memoir, and I do injustice to all of them, a brief synopsis:

- The opening lecture was given by Professor Sir Brian Flowers, chairman of the UK Science Research Council and subsequently Chancellor of the University of Manchester and Rector of Imperial College. He spoke on "The Scientific Basis of Electrical Engineering in 2000 A.D." Among other things Brian Flowers speculated on the widespread introduction of push-button telephones, world-wide satellite communication systems and appreciably higher radio frequencies by the year 2000. He stressed the need for the universities to produce engineers who will combine the life sciences, physical sciences and mechanical sciences. He concluded with the remark that "we will need primroses as much as power stations."

- "Energy, Progress and Man" was the theme of Walker L. Cisler, chief executive officer of the Detroit Edison Co. of the United States. He was a strong advocate of nuclear power and indeed, a pioneer in its introduction in the U.S.A. He stressed the peaceful use of nuclear power and of international co-operation and pointed out that energy was the key to the productivity that must be achieved if "the human potential within the less developed and more heavily populated countries was not to be lost. The present imbalances of much of the political, economic and social unrest in the world relate to people, natural resources, energy and systems of production. We must go forward together or else we will all ultimately go down together. Nature has never dealt gently with the failure of a species."

- The third lecture on May 18 was by Dr. A. E. Pannenborg, director of research at the Phillips Research Laboratories, Eindhoven, Holland, probably the largest electronics research organization in Europe. His subject was "Solid-State Physics and Its Impact on the

Electrical Engineer." After briefly reviewing the impact of solid-state research on electronic engineering, he assessed its potential in electric power engineering. The objectives were to achieve high reliability, low energy dissipation and low price. He pointed out that the design of large-scale integrated circuits was increasingly dependent on the use of computers. In other words, "computer-aided design." I was particularly struck by Dr. Pannenborg's final remark. "Perhaps even more important, the consequences of the vastly increased reliability and useful life through the use of solid-state technology which make electronics viable in many branches of technology hitherto closed to it, have hardly been faced yet." How extremely perceptive he was!

- The fourth and final lecture of the first day of the Congress was delivered by Dr. John Pierce, executive director of the Bell Telephone Laboratories. His subject was "How Communications Change Man's World." He dwelt at some length on changes and the future, saying that revolutionary changes are infrequent, but that wise support of science may favor them. He went on to describe some of the new discovery and inventions created at the Bell Labs whose potentialities have been sensed but not tapped, he forecasted for example, the widespread installation of cable television systems for cities. Stressing that engineers have great resources in computer and communications, he emphasized that the challenge is that of identifying problems and grasping opportunities. Freeing people for tasks which are less routine and more rewarding must continue to be a tremendous challenge and opportunity for electrical engineers.

- The second day of the Congress opened with a lecture by Dr. P. K. Kelkar, director of the Indian Institute of Technology (the equivalent in India to MIT). His subject was "Disparate World: Challenge to Education." He reviewed the current experiences of India in transforming its technology through research and education and he stressed the role of the educationist in preserving the quality of life during material progress. In India he asserted that the latest industry to be established is the "knowledge industry," and that with electronics and other aids, education is making the nation a less labor intensive society. Dr. Kelkar pointed out that there is no direct relationship between the quantity of knowledge and the understanding to which it leads, and there should be teamwork between promoters of technological change and agents of social change. "Electrical engineering education is potentially capable of developing an ethos which will embrace scientific, technological and social considerations."

• As I reflect today on Dr. Kelkar's lecture I am struck by the fact that the Institution which he headed is today acclaimed as a "combination of MIT and Princeton." Its prestige in computer software technology, for example, is unsurpassed anywhere in the world.

• Alan Hodgkin, professor of physiology at Cambridge University, President of the Royal Society and Nobel Laureate, gave the sixth lecture. "The Physical Basis of Nervous Conduction." His lecture was a striking example of interdisciplinary research — it bridged physics, mathematics, physiology and electrical engineering. After introducing the historical background and in particular the early knowledge of the biological effects of electricity known several centuries ago, he described the mode of signaling in nervous systems. I was surprised to hear that the mechanism of conduction was poorly understood in systems which did not contain metals. For example, the electrical resistance of small nerve fibers may be in the order of a trillion ohms per meter. Hodgkin then described his work with Andrew Huxley when they investigated the conductivity of nerve fibers in the giant squid He pointed out that if similar devices could be made they might lead to great reduction in the power consumption of computers. This proved to be a very perceptive observation. The Hodgkin lecture revived memories of the very happy and productive relationship I had had with Andrew Huxley during WWII.

• My own lecture "Control, Automation and Computers," the seventh, was delivered immediately after lunch at the Savoy Hotel on May 19. I was by no means alone in advocating the importance of interdisciplinary research. It will not come as a surprise that it was a central theme in my lecture with special reference to control theory. It was appropriate that I should open the lecture by introducing the simple servo-mechanism for two reasons. First because it was a paradigm for all goal seeking systems and secondly because the work of the servo-panel during WWII had been greatly facilitated by the Institution, not least by providing us with an ideal location for meetings. Indeed, I mentioned that it was not coincidental that the panel had held all its meetings in the self-same lecture theater in which I was speaking. In a dynamic discipline such as control technology it is important to identify the "conceptual" structures upon which the discipline is based. They include pattern recognition, decision-making, stability and adaptive behavior. The interaction between man and machine epitomizes the technological environment. I was at pains to stress that the principles of control theory lent themselves to educational systems and that this would be even more so with the burgeoning introduction of computers into the classroom.

- The eighth and last Centenary lecture was delivered by The Right Honourable Lord Nelson, president of the I.E.E. It was a brilliant summing up of the Congress in which he showed how each of our individual contributions had demonstrated the centrality of electrical engineering in modern society, and especially how the Institution had, during the past century, played such a pivotal role in the evolution of the profession. As a professional engineer who was in fact a fellow of each of our sister institutions, Lord Nelson epitomized the chief executive who "knew what he was talking about!" I was extremely impressed with a man who had achieved the stature of the top industrialist in Britain. Not a financier, not an accountant, not a lawyer, but an engineer.

Two illustrious social events were held during the evenings of May 18 and 19.

The Centenary banquet, the most formal and splendid we've ever attended, was held in the Guildhall of London. In bygone days it had been the meeting place of the master craftsmen — the goldsmiths, the silversmiths, etc. — of the city. It is one of the city's most colorful landmarks. The hall where countless monarchs of England and their courts dined with the Lords' Mayor and Aldermen of the city.

About 600 members and guests were seated at five long tables, including the head table. It was a quite unforgettable affair with men and women wearing orders and decorations and, of course, white ties for men and evening gowns, long white gloves for women. I recall that Patricia always loved "dressing up," especially for an occasion such as this and few of the ladies present, if any, could match the creation she had designed. Background music was provided by the band of "Her Majesty's Royal Electrical and Mechanical Engineers."

After we had dined and wined the Toast Master entered the hall and proposed the first of about five toasts. "OYEZ, OYEZ, OYEZ. Your

Excellencies; Your Graces; My Lord Archbishop; My Lords, Ladies and Gentlemen, pray silence for the Prime Minister of Great Britain and Northern Ireland, the Rt. Hon. Edward Heath."

Coincidently, Patricia and I were seated with my friends from Manchester days, Sir Bernard and Lady (Joyce) Lovell, and the occasion was marked as well by our meetings with old friends from Imperial College and the Royal Military College of Science. Patricia and I revelled in the ancient and historic environment and considered that we had been very fortunate to have been able to attend.

The Centenary Conversazione was held at the Royal Festival Hall on the evening of Wednesday, May 19. It was well and truly a royal occasion. After dining in a private dining room of the Festival Hall, the Centenary lecturers and their wives, together with the Institution's senior officers and the members of the organizing committee, were ushered into a small reception room for after-dinner refreshment. At about 10:30 p.m. it was announced that Her Majesty the Queen and entourage would be joining us shortly. Whereupon we literally lined the walls of the room expecting the distinguished visitor to walk around and greet us en masse. But it was not to be. Immediately after arriving, the Queen proceeded to the refreshment's table in the middle of the room and each lecturer and his wife was presented by Lord Nelson to Her Majesty, the Duke of Edinburgh and Lord and Lady Mountbatten. When it came Patricia and my turn to be presented, we performed the traditional bow of the head and curtsy and were treated to a few minutes of royalty. The Queen, wearing a beautiful gown and tiara with the Order of the Garter and several other orders and decorations, was vivacious and extremely beautiful. She inquired about my lecture and then proceeded to tell us about the vicissitudes she had endured during a recent journey from Vancouver to London and especially the effects of the nine hours jet lag. Afterwards we met briefly with the Duke of Edinburgh and then had a long conversation with Lord Mountbatten with whom I had had several meetings at the Military College. I recall that at the beginning of the conversation Mountbatten was rather remote, partly I suspect because he knew that I was one of the scientists who had deserted Britain, but he thawed appreciably when I turned the conversation to television. During the previous months he and Prince Phillip were featured in a long television series of which he was inordinately proud. He waxed eloquent when I praised the series. That glorious evening concluded when Patricia and myself were joined by Dr. and Mrs. Pierce and we walked together along the Thames Embankment, across the river to our hotel on a warm, moonlight summer evening. An unusual occasion for those used to the more traditional English weather. I recall that John Pierce told us that he had had an almost acrimonious discussion with the Duke relating to the role of computers in the translation of language. The Duke was very excited about the possibility but John took the opposite point of view. As it has turned out, it was the Duke, not the very eminent scientist, who was the more perceptive in his prediction.

Those were five days to remember, days of inspiration and Patricia and I still reflect on them with nostalgia and delight. The Centenary celebrations left the Porter family with two wonderful souvenirs. Fifty presentation copies of the lectures were printed of which mine is No. 19, and a sterling silver bowl inscribed "Institution of Electrical Engineers Centenary Congress May 1971."

Chapter 16

A ROYAL COMMISSION

A TELEPHONE call to my office early in March 1975 triggered off a sequence of events which had a profound impact on my life. It was from the office of the Hon. Allan Grossman, Provincial Secretary of Resource Development. Calls from this office were not uncommon because being located in Queens' Park a mere 200 yards from the Ontario Legislature, I was frequently called in for consultation. Would it be possible for me to meet the Minister in his office at 11. a.m?

I remember the occasion very well. A beautiful spring morning and a helicopter carrying a huge vertical structure was approaching over Lake Ontario. Having heard from various sources that the government was considering setting up a committee to review the planning of Ontario Hydro I assumed, correctly, that the Minister wanted to talk about it. Ontario Hydro was legendary — a crown corporation which was, and probably still is, the largest electrical utility in Canada. Its name was based on the fact that when established early in the 20th century, virtually all the power was derived from Ontario's massive hydro-electrical resources of which Niagara Falls was a major component.

After outlining the government concerns relating to the projected growth of the utility and the urgent need for an independent review of the future demand for electrical power, he mentioned that it was the government's intention to set up a Royal Commission with extremely broad terms of reference to consider the matter. As the meeting progressed I became increasingly convinced that I would be invited to participate in an investigation which would obviously be of several years duration. The closing of the Minister's remarks was dramatic. He stated almost casually, "we want you to chair the Royal Commission." In view of the fact that this Royal Commission would be the largest of its kind ever undertaken in Canada and the fact that there were many senior scientists and engineers who were certainly as well if not more qualified than me, I was, to put it mildly, astonished, but delighted. Mr. Grossman then stated that an official announcement would be made in the Ontario Legislature within a few days.

On descending the steps of the Legislature, my "head in the clouds," I literally saw the final stage of the "topping of the CN Tower," the tallest free standing structure in the world — about 1200 feet. It was an incredible sight to see that Sikorsky helicopter, the most powerful in existence, hovering above the tower with the 100 foot antennae structure in place. As far as I was concerned at the time this was a symbolic event because during the following six years many radio and television transmissions of the proceedings of the Royal Commission would originate there.

On March 12, 1975 the Government of the Province of Ontario issued an "Order-in- Council which stated:

> *"Upon the recognition of the Honorable the Provincial Secretary for Resources Development, the committee of the Council advise that pursuant to the provisions of The Public Inquiries Act, 1971,*

> *Dr. Arthur Porter*

> *be appointed to inquire into the long range planning of Ontario's electrical power needs, to have all the powers under The Public Inquiries Act of summoning any person and requiring him to give evidence under oath and to present such documents and things as the Commissioner deems requisite for the full investigation of the matter and to make recommendations thereon for the information and consideration of the Provincial Secretary for Resources Development.*

> *Certified*
> *J.K. Young*
> *Clerk, Executive Council.*

During the afternoon of the following day March 13, Patricia and I sat in seats A-19 and A-20 of the Speaker's Gallery in the Ontario Legislature to hear the official announcement. This was the first time in our lives we had attended a session of Parliament and it was fascinating to see the traditional ceremony enacted. After the prayers were read by the Speaker, the business of Parliament was opened with the reading of the afore-mentioned Order-in-Council and it was intimated at the end that Patricia and I were seated in the Speaker's Gallery. After the announcement, the leader of the opposition, Hon. Robert R. Nixon, rose to express the satisfaction of his party with the recommendation. But I was particularly happy when Stephen Lewis, the head of the New Democratic Party rose to say how delighted he was with the appointment — this was very encouraging because the New Democratic Party had not been especially supportive of government policy regarding Ontario Hydro.

It was not until July 17 that a more comprehensive Order-in-Council was published in which the terms of reference of the Royal Commission were spelled out in full and the names of the four commissioners who would serve under my chairmanship were announced. My colleagues were Robert E. Costello, an engineer and Vice-President of a large paper company; Solange Plourde-Gagnon, a journalist; George A. McCague, a farm executive; Dr. W. W. Stevenson, economist. The commission was officially designated The Royal Commission on Electric Power Planning (RCEPP). As terms of reference I was empowered to consider:

- A long-range planning program in relation to Provincial planning;

- Domestic, commercial and industrial utilization of electrical energy;

- Environmental, energy and socio-economic factors, including such matters as electrical load growth, systems reliability, safety, management of heat discharge from generation stations, export policy, land use;

- General principles on siting generating stations and transmission corridors, efficient use of electrical energy and conservation through wise management of primary energy resources;

- Power generation technology, interconnecting and power pooling with neighboring utilities, security of fuel supplies and operation considerations;

- The broader issues relating to electric power planning;

- And report on a priority basis on the need for a North Channel nuclear generating station, a second 500 kV line from Bruce, a 500 kV supply to Kitchener, London and the Ottawa- Cornwall region.

Of the many issues I was confronted with immediately subsequent to my appointment, the most important was the recruitment of senior staff. In this respect I was extremely fortunate. Before the end of March I had appointed Ron Smith as Executive Director (essentially chief of staff); Robert G. Rosehart as Scientific Counselor, and Robert Scott, Q.C., as Legal Counsel. These three men proved to be "towers of strength" during the formative period of the RCEPP and during the first year of our investigation. It is with profound regret however, that I must record that Robin Scott only served about 18 months — he was killed in the aircraft tragedy of September 6, 1976 while he was working for the commission. I shall describe the disaster later in this chapter.

Ron Smith who served full-time during the life of the commission was in every respect my "right arm." It was he who acquired accommodation for a staff which finally totaled about 50 people. He interviewed and hired secretarial personnel and as well handled the very important question of public relations consultants through whom many press, radio and television interviews ensued. Incidently, I quite enjoyed my sudden "rise to fame" as a result of many interviews on talk shows and the like! The commission was identified from those early days as the Porter Commission. So the die was well and truly cast and I was facing the most formidable task of my life. Put simply it was to investigate the operation of a corporation with assets of about $7 billion, annual revenue of about $1 billion and 23,000 employees which served two and a half million customers in the province.

There is no doubt that Ontario Hydro was eager to capitalize on my appointment as soon as possible. Within a couple of days of its announcement I was being entertained at the executive offices of the corporation by Chairman Bob Taylor and his senior advisors for tea. The main topic of conversation was the priority items. The Hydro executives stressed repeatedly that it was essential for a decision to be in the hands of the government within a month. For my part I expressed great interests but did not commit myself. Quite frankly I was appalled at the prospect of making a snap judgment on projects valued at several billion dollars. Unknown to myself at the time was the fact that preliminary planning was already in progress before authorization had been given.

I should stress that at the time these events were taking place I was still actively teaching at the University. Indeed with the end of term approaching it was a particularly busy time. Final examinations to be set, graduate students' theses scrutinized and as a department head, many meetings to attend. Furthermore, the government was still negotiating the terms of my severance, timed for July 1, 1975, with the University. But this fact did not deter the Hydro "priority projects" enthusiasts and they even persuaded the Deputy Secretary (my erstwhile friend Dick Dillon, the former Dean of Engineering at the UWO) to intervene on their behalf.

We met for lunch at one of Toronto's premier restaurants — The Scala on Bay Street. Dick stated the case very succinctly and pointed out that the government was as anxious as Hydro for a decision by the Royal Commissioner to be promulgated as soon as possible. I should point out, and perhaps should have previously, that the designation "Royal" implied that my commission was independent in every since of the word and not to be influenced by political implications — indeed "de jure" the title implied that I was responsible only to H.M. the Queen!

In spite of Dick's eloquent pleading, I persisted in my refusal to concur on the grounds that I would need many months to arrange public hearings and to consult with authorities before a realistic decision was possible. At one stage during the lunch I was convinced that my long friendship with Dick Dillon was ending. In fact, for several months subsequently our relations were strained. In retrospect it is obvious that my position was correct. To this day one of the priority projects (a nuclear power station) is still in abeyance and the need for additional bulk power transmission lines was not announced by my commission until 1979. The task confronting me in March of 1975 was well summed up in a speech delivered at the beginning of April by Chairman Taylor. It was an extremely thoughtful address in which he outlined Hydro's long term aspirations and his confidence in the process which was being implemented. It may not be out of place to mention a few highlights:

> *"Based on his past record, Dr. Porter may take some innovative approaches in his review, going beyond the formal hearing of briefs and arguments by technical experts and interested groups and individuals. His task, and it is a daunting one, is not to bring in a verdict but to achieve a consensus, a general agreement on new guidelines for Ontario to follow in planning its electrical power system."*

> *"The establishment of the Porter Commission is an important first step in examining alternatives, exploring*

*their consequences and in making choices. I personally
believe that it represents a watershed in Hydro's long
history of service to Ontario."*

*"Dr. Porter will hear from environmentalists,
conservationists, zero growth philosophers, anti-nuclear
groups who are concerned, and sometimes dismayed at
the direction of life in these complex times."*

The summer of 1975 was a period of intense activity when we developed plans and procedures. Indeed, early in the fall of 1975 we initiated a series of preliminary hearings to identify the basic issues. As well we established procedures for widespread public participation which included educational programs on television and in the schools. The first of the preliminary hearings was held in London, Ontario and we had a good reception — there were about 150 people in attendance. Immediately prior to this hearing the stage was set by Norman Webster, a highly respected columnist of the Toronto Globe and Mail. I must confess to feeling a glow of satisfaction when I read the following excerpts:

*"The curtain rises tomorrow on one of the more
important public sessions in Ontario's history. It will
deal with vital issues. It will influence the future of
everyone in the Province. There will be controversy and
debate, presided over by a gentleman of wisdom and
humor."*

*"The commission under the chairmanship of Arthur
Porter begins its public hearings in London today, and
don't let its unsexy name fool you. It's mission is nothing
less than to chart the future of Ontario."*

Norman Webster's column in a newspaper which was nationally distributed did a great deal to stimulate interest in our work and it certainly encouraged me personally.

Although during my long career in academe I had delivered countless lectures and many public speeches to service clubs and the like, I had never before chaired a public hearing convened under the authority of "the Public Inquiries Act." I must confess to a feeling of apprehension when I faced several television cameras as well as the crowded hall in London, Ontario.

I was aware at the time, for example, that most public inquiries, such as mine, involved court-room-like procedures, and were essentially "adversarial." But probably true to form I created a precedent. I pointed out that the hearings of my commission would have a marked futures orientation, and that for the most part, a courtroom-like environment would not be conducive to the creation of innovative learning environments and I announced that since our hearings would involve speculations concerning the future, we would adopt a more inquisitorial-like approach. It would be informal. Issues would be identified and clarified during informal preliminary public meetings of which the London hearing was the first. Thus, I made it abundantly clear that we would in fact be staging public seminars across the province.

It transpired that the preliminary meetings were invaluable in the identification of many issues worrying the public. Arising out of them we published a series of nine Issue Papers which were widely distributed. One issue clearly dominated the minds of the public — the safety and cost of nuclear power. Because of its centrality throughout my investigations and the fact that my personal involvement in nuclear power was not limited exclusively to the work of the Commission, I have devoted the next chapter of this memoir to the topic.

Of the many information hearings we staged during the ensuing months none was more dramatic and in outcome more tragic than the meeting we held in the Town Hall of the small town of Orangeville on July 21, 1976. Incidently, Orangeville is a mere 12 miles from Belfountain. It was a warm summer's day I recall, and the air conditioning of the Town Hall had not been designed to handle a meeting of almost 100 people. Prominent among the attendees who submitted briefs was a young Ojibway, Harry Achneepineskun who represented Grand Council Treaty No. 9. As a matter of fact, Harry was a brilliant university student — the first in the history of his band — to attend university. He was studying political science at Trent University. His brief stressed the urgent necessity of preserving the native lands in northern Ontario, the life, people, animals, birds, fish — their way of life. It was extremely eloquent. He ended by, in effect, challenging my Commission to visit the native communities and to "see for ourselves." Without hesitation I accepted the challenge in spite of the fact that the primitive nature of the territory precluded travel by conventional means. But I was confident that Ron Smith with his talents for improvisation would solve the problem. And he did.

A visit to Northern Ontario was planned for the week August 29 to September 4. The visit would encompass six native communities scattered throughout a vast area of Northern Ontario and transportation would be first by Air Canada and secondly by specially chartered float planes. Our party consisted of myself (the four members of my Commission were unavailable), Ron Smith, Bob Rosehart, Robin Scott, Mark Couse, Delores Montgomery, all of the staff of the Commission, four members of Grand Council Treaty No. 9, three members of Ontario Hydro and a representative of the press.

During the evening of Sunday, Aug. 29, the Toronto-based members of the party, a total of 10 which included two women, flew to the city of Timmins by Air Canada. We were joined by the remaining four members at the Holiday Inn where we dined. Departure was scheduled for 9 a.m. Monday, Aug. 30 when the party would proceed by road to the village of Mattagami and later that day by two float planes to Attawapiskat. However, one of the party, myself, did not make it. Here is what happened.

After dining together at the Inn, the party retired for the night at about 10 p.m. At 5 a.m. or thereabouts, I awakened with a severe case of laryngitis. I was literally speechless. If ever there was an episode of "*divine intervention*" in my life, it was on that occasion. Never before nor to my certain knowledge since, have I suffered such a throat illness. I immediately roused Ron Smith, in the adjacent room, and by signs and gesticulations I conveyed to him the nature of my predicament. Unless the condition improved within a few hours, it was unlikely that I would be able to continue, and he would have to lead the party in my place.

After "seeing the party off," at the front door of the hotel, arrangements were made for me to fly back to Toronto on the Air Canada flight leaving at noon. Patricia had a shock when I appeared at our Belfountain home at about 6 p.m. I had been unable to communicate with her, indeed continued to be virtually incommunicado for two days. I was fully recovered by Friday, Sept. 3 and in fact, actively participated in a Symposium held in the Toronto City Hall in which the cities of Toronto and Milan, Italy, participated. It was organized by the University of Toronto. Incidently, I had originally been invited but declined to participate because of the Northern Ontario trip.

In the meantime, the Commission's hearings in five native communities of Northern Ontario proceeded on schedule. At each village the party was welcomed by the Chief, Counselors and Elders of the

Ojibway and Cree bands. They turned out to be highly successful. The final hearing on Friday, Sept. 3 was in Winisk on the shores of Hudson's Bay, about 200 miles west of James Bay. It was here that the party split up. Ann Dyer, Ron Smith, Bob Rosehart and Mark Couse had arranged to spend two days fishing in the region and used the small float plane. The majority flew from Winisk to Moosonee on James Bay and spent the night there.

On the Saturday morning the party of 10 departed in the larger float plane en route to Timmins, but tragedy struck in the Abitibi Canyon. In attempting to locate his position in foggy conditions (at the time charter planes operating in the vast area of Northern Ontario were not equipped with navigation equipment, nor, because of the distances, with radio communications) the pilot descended to too low an altitude and the floats of the plane struck an electrical power line. The crash, which was not discovered for several hours and then most improbably by two loan hikers who spotted a wisp of smoke. All nine passengers and the pilot, Douglas Clifford of the Austin Airways Limited, lost their lives.

It was especially tragic for one member of the Hyrdro delegation, John Wesley James because he was the engineer responsible for the design of the high voltage transmission line several years earlier.

At midnight on that tragic day at Belfountain our telephone rang. Patricia and I had retired an hour previously and were asleep. It was the most shocking telephone call I've ever received in my life. The caller announced that he was an officer of the Ontario Provincial Police. Was he speaking to Dr. Arthur Porter? Was my heart in sound condition because he had shocking news. I braced myself for the inevitable. Then he proceeded to read the names of those who were associated in one way or another with my Commission. I confirmed that they were. The names Smith, Rosehart, Couse and Dyer, all of whom had participated in the mission, were not included and I knew that they would not be returning to Toronto until the following day, Sunday, Sept. 5. They were completely unaware of the tragedy until the following evening when I telephoned Ron Smith. I still tremble to recall the shock of hearing the names read and after each one, the question can you confirm that he or she was on the aircraft? The police also informed me that they were responsible for informing the next of kin, whereupon I insisted that Patricia and I would inform Mrs. Robin Scott and family and the relatives of Delores Montgomery.

After a sleepless night and in a state of shock, Patricia and I drove into Toronto on that Sunday morning. It was the Labor Day holiday weekend. The Scott family, the widow and two children saw Patricia and me walking up their driveway and they knew immediately that Robin had been lost. For Patricia and me, and the Scott family, a harrowing moment, but the bravery of Dorothy Scott and her children was considerable. We afterwards visited the home of Delores and the grief of her live-in fiancé was so great that he virtually collapsed. The following morning I flew back to Timmins for a memorial service to honor the three members of the Grand Council Treaty who had been killed. They were:

Harry Achneepineskum
Douglas C. Sheppard
Xavier Sutherland

The service was conducted in the Ojibway language by Grand Chief Andrew Rickard. At the end of the service I was handed a plain envelope. It contained a non-headed sheet of paper with a few hand-written lines of poetry. It read:

"Like a flock of geese
in the fog they passed
then returned home
this morning
in a flock of small birds
I saw them
they left me a feather
the feather is heavy with our grief
may it lighten as their work is realized"

These lines, some of the most beautiful and moving I have ever read were by an anonymous member of the native community.

During the afternoon of Wednesday, Sept. 15, 1976 a memorial service for those who lost their lives "in service to the Province of Ontario while participating with the Royal Commission on Electric Power Planning" was held in the Cathedral Church of St. James in downtown Toronto. The church was crowded with several hundred people standing at the back of the sanctuary. Attending were the Premier of the Province, the Hon. William Davis, several members of his cabinet, the Mayor of the City of Toronto and several other mayors, the Grand Chief and many counselors as well as all members of my Commission. I read the first lesson — Revelation 2:1 — "I saw a new heaven and new earth — -- he that overcometh shall inherit all things; and I will be his God and he shall be my son." The second lesson was read in the Ojibway language by the Grand Chief (I have a copy of this reading). The service was conducted by the Bishop of Toronto; the Pastor of St. Michael's Cathedral and the head of the Presbyterian Church of Toronto.

A few months after the memorial services my Commission published a special memorial report "The Meetings in the North" which was dedicated to:

Harry Achneepineskum	*Grand Counsel Treaty No. 9*
Douglas Clifford	*Austin Airways Limited*
John Richard Houston	*Tilley, Carson and Findlay (Counsel for Ontario Hydro)*
Bryan Rolland Isbister	*Ontario Hydro*
John Wesley James	*Ontario Hydro*
Joe McClelland	*London Free Press*
Delores Montgomery	*Public Interest Coalition For Energy Planning*
Robert Allen (Robin) Scott	*Ministry of the Attorney –General (Counsel to the Royal Commission on Electric Power Planning)*
Douglas C. Sheppard	*Grand Counsel Treaty No. 9*
Xavier Sutherland	*Grand Counsel Treaty No. 9*

During the spring of 1977, together with the Minister of Energy, the Hon. Rene Brunell, we unveiled a large bronze plaque at the site of the tragedy in the Abitibi Canyon — a large group of Ojibway and Cree people were in attendance.

Shortly after the tragedy the government appointed Fred Hume, a prominent Ontario lawyer, to take the place of Robin Scott as counsel for the Commission. During the remaining years of our investigation, Fred steered me through some, to put it mildly, treacherous situations.

To recapitulate the status of the Commission after a full year of operation, we had undertaken a total of 17 Province-wide information meetings which were attended by more than 6,000 people. We had identified the key issues which were of concern to Hydro customers, and we had published nine comprehensive issue papers. As well, we had succeeded in setting an informal, almost casual style of operation which greatly facilitated public participation. Indeed, more than 300 individuals and interest groups contributed coherent verbal submissions at the meetings. We had, as described above, conducted a special tour of five remote communities in Northern Ontario. Most importantly we had demonstrated that of all the issues identified the most outstanding related to nuclear power (See Chapter 17), the financing of electric power, the demand for electricity, the generation of electricity using conventional and alternate technologies, the transmission of electricity and land use.

To give an indication of the scope of the inquiry, let me reflect on some of the above. With respect to finance, for example, the assets of Ontario Hydro by 1983 would total more than $15 billion. Questions we examined were — "can the corporation obtain sufficient capital in Canadian money markets? — what pricing mechanisms can be used to encourage conservation?" These were not trivial problems. In so far as future demand for electricity was concerned, we noted that the power needs of Ontario had been growing at almost seven percent each year and that had necessitated a doubling of generating and transmission facilities every 10 years. The critical questions facing the Commission were: "Would the demand for electricity continue to increase at this rate? What were the implications of population growth and burgeoning urban transportation on electrical demand? To what extent would energy conservation reduce power demands? Because of the primacy of agricultural production, especially in the southern regions of the province, the issue of land use was central. The farmers of Ontario had banded together to ensure that there was minimum encroachment on their property by, for example, electrical power transmission lines. To familiarize myself with this situation, I inspected, from a helicopter, the extent to which power lines were in fact intruding on prime farm land. It was obvious as well that land was needed for new industrial plants, housing, recreation and wildlife preserves. A complex issue which we were obliged to address.

To complement the information meetings the Commission initiated several other departures in public participation and public communication to encourage maximum opportunity for the people of the province to join in the debate. These activities included:

- Co-operation with TV Ontario on the production of a two-hour special program on energy aimed at the Ontario school system.

- Displays at the Canadian National Exhibition, the International Plowman's Match and Farm Machinery Show, and numerous festivals around the province.

- A three-day symposium aimed primarily at obtaining information from the academic and industrial communities, and most importantly from international authorities from Britain and the USA.

- Workshops were arranged during the spring of 1977 to reflect on future life-styles. Notably the need for future electrification of the home.

- A Schools Program to communicate information about the work of the Commission.

The above activities in effect laid the foundation for the final hearings of the Commission which took place between May and October 1977. Although slightly more structured than the previous information hearings, they were nevertheless predicated on the avoidance of courtroom- like procedures so that individuals and groups were not in any way inhibited or intimidated. Furthermore, as an indication that the government of Ontario was in full accord with the concept of "intervener funding" we awarded grants totally $357,317 to public interest groups and individuals.

There is no doubt that these financial incentives enhanced appreciably the intellectual level of the debates.

During the 50 final hearings, we introduced several innovative concepts. None more so however than the three day symposium during which experts in particular subjects made presentations and the public were allowed to cross-examine them following each presentation. For me this hearing was especially rewarding in so far as we invited three prominent scientists to present papers. They were Lord Ashby, with whom I had had numerous contacts — he was a Commonwealth Fund Fellow (1929-31) and had been chairman of the British Royal Commission on Environmental Pollution; Alvin Toffler, author of the New York Times bestseller *Future Shock*; and Kenneth Hare, university professor of geography and chairman of the Hare Committee on Electric Power Line Routing. This was a formidable group of scientists and they made a lasting impression.

Another landmark in the Commission's activities occurred in December 1977 when, in order to expedite our decisions relating to nuclear power stations, the government issued an amending Order in Council requesting the Commission to complete examination of the issue and to prepare an interim report on its opinion and conclusions. This resulted in an intense effort being devoted to the nuclear power question and a corresponding diminution of work on the major part of our mandate. Accordingly a period of eight months was devoted to nuclear power and resulted in the major report which is introduced in Chapter 17.

Underpinning the holistic planning of Hydro's future needs for generation and transmission was the critical question of the demand for electric power. Not surprisingly this was a topic which gave rise to many hours of in-depth discussion.

On one hand Hydro's projections through the year 2000 was based on a growth in demand of about 5.5 percent per year while on the other the Commission concluded that four percent would be more realistic. I will not dwell on the outrage and disbelief on the part of Hydro and the electric power industry as expressed in press and media, when my conclusions were announced. But subsequent events proved that I was much nearer the mark than the corporation.

The year 1979 was one of frantic activity. We had literally many thousands of pages of evidence to analyze, many consultants' reports to digest and several important deadlines to meet. However, with a staff who was willing to put in many hours of overtime, without pay, and many patient spouses, we succeeded in producing a final report consisting of nine volumes. With the exception of a single chapter on "economics and finance," I wrote the whole of Volume I "Concepts, Conclusions and Recommendations." My secretary Margaret James performed miracles and so did Ron Smith and Ann Dyer and the other gallant souls on the Commission staff. During the writing period, I was grateful for the solitude of Belfountain and for Patricia's management and editing skills. And the sterling work of Phil Lapp, who acted as editor-in-chief of the report, is gratefully acknowledged.

I will not dwell on the content of Volume I of the report which I regarded, and still regard, as my most important literary effort. During the period of three to four months writing I completely immersed myself in the data we had assembled during the four years of the life of the

Commission. The fact that literally billions of dollars were at stake was certainly a highly motivating factor. Obviously the demand for electrical energy could be reduced through conservation, and the peak power requirements on the electric grid could be mitigated by appropriate pricing policies and through the use of solar energy to help heat homes in winter and swimming pools in summer. These were concepts we advocated. We even went further as exemplified by the following quotation from the Preface to the report:

> *"Our philosophy for survival, albeit survival with comparatively high living standards, is based essentially on the need to live within environmental constraints (i.e. the Spaceship Earth concept), to ensure adequate food supplies for all people and to optimize our utilization of energy. Societal values are in a continuous state of evolution, and technological developments are clearly a primary cause. Central among these are contemporary developments in energy and communications."*

While agreeing in general with such percepts, Ontario Hydro and the electrical industry were always conscious of the dire consequence of power short-falls and advocated a more conservative margin of safety in their planning. I reasoned that we had achieved a realistic compromise, but not unexpectedly there were strong voices, some politically motivated, on the one hand that we had not gone far enough to minimize demand and on the other that we had gone too far.

The report itself, quite apart from its literary and technical merits, or otherwise, stands out as a superb production. It incorporated elegant design, production management and photo composition carried out by members of the staff of the Commission and a team of brilliant commercial designers. I shall always be grateful to them.

A press conference was held on March 26, 1980 at 2 p.m. on the occasion of the formal submission of the report to Her Honor the Lieutenant-Governor of the Province of Ontario. I circulated a 17-page statement to members of the press and there was a room full of attendees. Needless to add, I did not read the statement in full and gave only a 10-minute summary, but the first and last paragraphs are worth recalling:

> *"During a period of intense concern with the security and price, of future energy supplies, especially oil*

supplies, it is not surprising that my Commission has been faced with an incredibly complex task. Indeed, our mandate, which was amended on two occasions, covered an extraordinary range of issues, so much so that we felt compelled to devote the first chapter of Volume 1 of the report to its interpretation. When we were established in July 1975, the western world was grappling, and still is, with the aftermath of the OPEC oil embargo and the many-fold increase in the world price of crude oil. The writing was on the wall. But worse was to come — the economic and political implications of recurrent energy crises have been compounded since we began our hearings, and have been manifest in such events as the Three-Mile Island accident and the Iran Revolution. These have impacted to a greater or lesser extent on Ontario's (and Canada's) energy expectations to the end of the century and perhaps beyond. And by no means least on the planning of the Province's electric power system. As well, and closely related, we have witnessed economic slow-down in most industrial nations, including Canada, and, an increasing recognition on the part of the public that the world's non-renewable resources, especially of oil, are strictly limited and that they are being depleted at an unacceptable rate. "

In conclusion:

"In concluding this statement I want to stress that in completing its task, the Commission is very optimistic concerning Ontario's energy future. We hope our Report reflects this optimism and that it will help to 'shape the future.' We believe most profoundly that the Province's key resource is its people. "

I was particularly happy with the conclusion of Volume 1 in which I introduced a brief "postscript." I felt that it was fitting to close my press conference statement with the last two sentences:

"We have been exposed to the ideas of many imaginative people, people who are concerned, people whose

attitudes reflect the values of a new society that has become aware of the world around it, of the environment in which it lives and of the value of natural resources. If we have succeeded in fashioning even a fraction of their creative inputs into a framework that will facilitate the future planning of the Province's electrical power system we shall be well content. "

The following morning there was extensive press and media coverage of the event and on the whole it was fair and gratifying. The next question — how would the government react? A Progressive Conservative government with close ties to the financial and industrial sector of the Province. It would not have been surprising if they had rejected many of my recommendations (cf. my report as Academic Commissioner, see Chapter 15). But after a hiatus of some 15 months the verdict was announced — quite favorable to my Commission as witness the following extracts from a speech delivered by the Hon. Robert Welch, Deputy Premier and Minister of Energy, in the Ontario Legislature on June 2, 1981 (incidently it would have been my father's 101st birthday):

"I am pleased to advise the House that, following this review, the Government accepts 77 of the 88 recommendations. "

"Therefore, the Government is requesting Ontario Hydro to proceed with the next stages of the planning and approvals process in such a way as to conform to the spirit and intent of the Royal Commission's recommendations.

"I would like to take this opportunity once again to thank Dr. Porter and the other members of the Royal Commission for the important contribution they have made to energy policy-making and electric power planning in Ontario.

"In particular the Government notes the Commission's success in facilitating a reasoned, open and fair public debate on nuclear and other complex technological and

social issues.

"Unquestionably, the Commission had a major impact on electric power planning even before it submitted its final report. The fact that the Government itself is in agreement with most of the Commission's recommendations emphases the valuable contribution it has made.

"Thank you Mr. Speaker."

But the final word with respect to this incredible saga — the Ontario Royal Commission on Electric Power Planning — must be given to the editor of a Listowel newspaper who wrote after our appearance in the town:

"We've said it before and we'll say it again. Whatever decisions are finally reached by the Royal Commission on Electric Power Planning the Commission deserves only the highest praise for the way it has conducted its hearings."

"To watch this Commission in action under the chairmanship of Dr. Arthur Porter is an inspiration. Those in attendance are treated with courtesy and respect. As a result, the Commission sessions are long ones. They are also dignified and exceedingly informative."

I feel rather embarrassed by including this final quotation, but as I reread it today, it leaves a glow in my heart.

Chapter 17

THE QUESTION OF NUCLEAR POWER

MY INTEREST in nuclear power stemmed from my early work on automatic control systems and servomechanisms during the 1930's and WWII. The subject is of prime importance in the operation of nuclear power stations. For example, the control of a nuclear reactor requires a high level of precision and dependability. It exemplifies servo-technology at the very cutting edge. The safety of a nuclear power installation depends essentially on the efficacy of automatic control and regulation systems. It was one of the most important topics I discussed in my graduate classes at the University of Toronto during the 1960's. I expanded on my ideas in a paper I presented in June of 1972 to the Annual Conference of the Canadian Nuclear Association in which I stressed as well the significance of socio-economic factors in system design philosophy. Accordingly, it is not surprising that the issue which intrigued me most of all during my almost six years involvement with the Royal Commission was the question of nuclear power. It is important to note that at the time the majority of people identified nuclear power quite closely with nuclear weapons technology. Suffice it to add that nuclear weapons exemplify uncontrolled nuclear fission reactions while nuclear power exemplifies controlled reactions. This chapter is devoted exclusively to the conversion of the energy innate in the nucleus of uranium atoms into electrical power.

Not only did my theoretical background in control and safety problems hold me in good stead for the forthcoming hearings of the Commission, but as well my chairmanship of the Canadian Environmental Advisory Council provided insights into the potential impacts of radioactive waste on the environment.

The many hours of public debate we conducted during 1976-77 were characterized by an overwhelming desire on the part of the public to discuss issues related to nuclear power. It was clear that these were complex and far-reaching in terms of their probable impact on the future shape and well-being of society. Emotions ran high. Much of the public concern, I concluded, resulted from the undoubted veil of secrecy which had historically surrounded information related to all matters involving nuclear power. This resulted inevitably in the debates being conducted in an atmosphere of acrimony and distrust.

But as the debates evolved, the level of objectivity increased. In no small measure this was due to the intervenor funding program which my Commission organized. Consequently, in spite of much comment to the contrary on the part of the nuclear industry as a whole, I was impressed by some of the arguments put forward by several of the "notorious" anti-nuclear advocates. For example, two well-informed nuclear critics, Gordon Edwards and Ralph Torrie demonstrated, quite dramatically, that the number of loss of regulation "incidents" occurring at a specific nuclear power plant was six within a period of four years. This compared very unfavorably with the design target of one incident in 100 years. It was as a result of such revelations that, although my personal assessments of the safety of the automatic controls of nuclear power stations was more than adequate, on the other hand there were certainly problems associated with the manual control aspects. My interest in human factors in engineering design, of course, dated back many years to WWII and more recently had resulted in the establishment of a powerful human factors group in my department at U. of T. Not surprisingly I turned to Pat Foley to undertake an investigation of human performance in nuclear power central control stations. In fact, it was a direct consequence of these human factors studies, at the Pickering Nuclear Power Plant by a former colleague in the Department of Industrial Engineering that precipitated the most disturbing event of my life as a Royal Commissioner. A "whistle-blower" no less!

A telephone call one Saturday afternoon triggered off the incident. It was from my former colleague, Professor John Senders. His opening gambit to put it mildly was dramatic. "Because there was a possibility that my telephone might be tapped, would I call him at his home using the public telephone in the village of Belfountain?" I well remember that call because it was raining heavily and the floor of the telephone booth was covered to a depth of about an inch in water. His message was to the effect that one of his former students working at the Pickering plant had, on a strictly confidential basis, informed him of several incidents affecting reactor safety which had occurred. Senders had assured him that he would pass this information on to me. Incidently, it still escapes me as to how my home telephone phone line could possibly have been tapped! But it unquestionably emphasized the importance of the allegation. As well it came at a critical period in my inquiry.

About a month previously the Government of Ontario had decided to appoint a select committee to review the Province's nuclear commitment. Suspecting a move on the part of some members to minimize the importance of my findings, I requested the Government, under a specific section of the Order in Council, to issue an additional Order in Council which would empower me to prepare, on a priority basis, above all other priorities, an interim report on those aspects of nuclear power which had been under consideration by my Commission. This request had in fact been granted, and I was already in the early stages of preparing an interim report. What the impact of the "whistle blower's" allegations would have had on public opinion is not difficult to imagine. The fact that the person had a master's degree in human factors engineering suggested that his information must be taken very seriously.

My first move was to consult Fred Hume, the commission counsel in whom I had the greatest confidence. But there was a problem. Fred was on vacation in Venice, Florida. I will not bore the reader with the frustrations I suffered in that telephone booth. My feet were soaked and it took almost half an hour to locate my colleague. Fred confirmed that legally our only recourse was to hold a public hearing as soon as possible. However, after returning home on that dreadful Saturday afternoon I had second thoughts. There was no doubt in my mind that a public hearing would seriously erode public confidence in nuclear power and the consequences would have been unimaginable.

Perhaps there was an alternative approach. I sought the advice of a close friend and colleague at the University. Jim Ham was Dean of Graduate Studies and had personal experience of a Royal Commission having chaired a commission on "Mine Safety" a few years previously.

After briefing Jim privately in his office I suggested that Senders should join us. We had a lengthy and at times acrimonious discussion. In my jacket pocket I held a subpoena, duly signed by myself and countersigned by a judge requiring Senders to appear at a future hearing of my commission. Fortunately, it was not served. I pointed out during the meeting that I was under an obligation as a Royal Commissioner to ensure that all information relating to the safety of nuclear power stations should be made available to the public, in spite of the fact that the divulgence of this information might threaten the entire nuclear power program in which more than $20 billion had been invested by the government. Furthermore, the comparatively recent Three-Mile Island (TMI) debacle did not help the situation. I was confronted by a situation charged with "political dynamite." And Senders remained adamant in his refusal to divulge the name of the whistle-blower and was determined to protect him at all costs.

The compromise I proposed proved to be acceptable. I suggested that Senders' former graduate student should appear before the Canadian Atomic Energy Control Board (AECB) and present his allegations and that consequently my commission would not be required to hold a public hearing until the findings of the Board had been published. In fact, the subsequent inquiry by the AECB turned out to be acceptable to both Ontario Hydro and the whistle-blower, and several misunderstandings were cleared up. But I had a few "sleepless nights" wrestling with what appeared at the time to be a very intransigent situation. It is still comforting to reflect that the only subpoena document I had ever initiated was never activated.

My mandate necessitated consultation with nuclear agencies in other countries. For instance, I was particularly interested in measures being introduced to ensure maximum safety, to determine the extent to which the public participated in decisions relating to nuclear power and to learn as much as possible about the management of radioactive waste. Accordingly, with Bob Rosehart and Ron Smith, I visited the United States Nuclear Regulatory Commission in Washington, D.C., the Commonwealth Edison Company in Chicago and the headquarters of the Pacific Gas and Electricity Company in California. It is noteworthy that all the nuclear power plants in the US are light water reactors (LWRs) in contrast to the heavy water moderated reactors (CANDU) of Ontario Hydro. Furthermore, while CANDU reactors, albeit of varying sizes, are essentially of standardized design, this does not apply to the LWRs. Indeed, there is no standardized LWR design in the United States essentially because different vendors, architect-engineers and utilities have produced custom-built plants for each site. As well, the pace of development from prototype to about 100 commercial reactors had been very rapid. All these factors had given rise to new safety issues being identified with the concomitant changes in regulatory requirements. As a result, in the United States we discovered that there was a wide range of nuclear power plant performance, ranging from excellent to poor. While the former had capacity factors ranging up to 80 percent for years on end, others had been plagued with continual hardware problems which had led to low capacity utilization. It was noteworthy as well that although the safety record of nuclear plants up to that time had been very good, the accident at TMI had raised concerns about the ability of all utilities to maintain this record. Consequently, we concluded that the CANDU reactor had safety and reliability features which appeared to be superior on average to the LWRs. What was refreshing during our visit to the United States agencies was the friendly and extremely open manner in which we were greeted and accepted.

Clearly, the issues of safety and economic viability, as in Ontario, dominated the nuclear debate. Surprisingly, however, the problem of radioactive waste management was raised infrequently. In common with my experiences during the debates in Ontario, I learned that, in the U.S., organizations such as the Sierra Club, the Friends of the Earth and the Union of Concerned Scientists were well-funded, articulate and knowledgeable. Most of them had given evidence during my hearings in Ontario.

Our visits to nuclear installations in France and Great Britain were equally successful. We felt these were essential because at the time the technologies under development differed appreciably from those being adopted in North America. The French program was the most ambitious and indeed, probably the most advanced in the world at the time. We were privileged to visit a nuclear power station and a fuel reprocessing plant. The Super-Phenix reactor utilizes uranium fuel enriched with plutonium-239, and is correspondingly more efficient in uranium utilization. We visited the one and only uranium separation plant and were struck by the steps taken to ensure environmental cleanliness. For example, during the visit we wore special clothing and boots. Especially noteworthy was the number of times the alarm bell sounded, but we were assured this was normal. The end product — pure plutonium-239 — is one of only three known fissionable isotopes and because of its toxicity, was handled by remote control in specially designed chambers. French government hospitality was extraordinary. Rosehart and I were accommodated in a suite in a French chateau. The view was spectacular. So were the food and wine served at dinner.

The United Kingdom experimental nuclear facility I visited is located in the north of Scotland, adjacent to Scapa Flow, one of the most famous naval bases in the world. Having at an early stage of my career had close association with the Admiralty, the visit was fascinating. I flew at low altitude over the Scottish highlands and had an aerial view of

Loch Ness and Ben Nevis (highest mountain in the U.K.) and many smaller lochs. The terrain was familiar, reminiscent of my native heath. The lakes and granite crags and verdant valleys were, albeit on a rather larger scale, a carbon copy of the Lake District. It seemed rather incongruous at the time that Britain's premier nuclear power research facilities should be located adjacent to such beautiful country. I spent a full day being shown around the establishment. I must confess that most of the research in hand was beyond my comprehension, but it helped provide me with an overview of nuclear technology at the cutting-edge. To spend several hours enjoying the hospitality of a very friendly group of Scottish and English scientists and engineers was in itself very worthwhile. Being comparatively isolated geographically, they went out of their way to make my visit both scientifically and socially a huge success. As I gazed across the frigid North Sea waters to the Orkney and Shetand Islands, I reflected on the naval history that had been enacted there. The tragic loss of H.M.S. Royal Oak in the early months of WWII, and the dramatic hunt for the "Bismarck" which was launched from there. Incidently, my flight back to Canada involved a stop-over at Aberdeen and an "aerial visit" to a North Sea drilling platform. Our small plane allowed us to descend to within a few hundred feet of the oil drilling platform. My nephew, Richard Porter, had spent some time as a meteorologist on one such platform.

On returning from Europe, having assembled many relevant facts on the nuclear issue, I proceeded with writing the interim report. With the invaluable help of Bill Stevenson, especially on the economic impact of nuclear power, I completed the job in little more than three months. The title, "A Race Against Time" was chosen because at the time there was strong evidence from impeccable sources, that before the end of the century the supply of crude oil would fall behind the potential demand. In such circumstances nuclear power would have a significant role to play in the transition from an oil-rich to an oil-impoverished society. (Because of major advances in oil exploration and recovery technologies, unforeseen at the time, the dire predictions of the "experts" have proven to be far off the mark, and at the time of writing it appears that oil and natural gas supplies are secure for at least several decades.) There were other reasons as well. Assuming an accelerated nuclear power program, the security of Ontario Hydro's uranium requirements was problematical, and the development of a credible long-term nuclear waste management program was not in sight. Incidently, the title certainly epitomized my personal efforts to meet the deadline specified in the order-in-council. I missed by a few weeks.

The report was undoubtedly a sound piece of work — praised internationally. In the British House of Lords, for example, thanks to the support of Lord Ashby, it was described as a model of clarity and unambiguity. Dr. David Rose, professor of nuclear science and technology at MIT was equally praiseworthy. Incidently, it was as a direct consequence of Professor Rose's enthusiasm for the report that several years later I was invited to become a member of a U.S. Congressional Advisory Panel on "The Future of Conventional Nuclear Power."

The credit for the production of such a splendid volume and in my prejudiced opinion it has few if any equals in the field, with such superb illustrations, is due to Ken Slater and Ann Dyer of the Commission staff, to Shirley Birch of Alphatext Limited, to Joe Stevens, Brent Cowie of Artplus Limited for the graphics and to Alger Press Limited for the printing. The volume is proudly displayed on my shelves.

In the foreword, I stated the aims of this report thus:

> *"We have in the report provided, for the people and the Government, the commission's findings and conclusions to date about the future of nuclear power in the Province. Indeed, it is a sincere effort on our part to put you fully into the picture concerning the nuclear story. We have attempted to balance points of view on major issues that are on one hand ethical, socio-economic, environmental and political, and on the other hand scientific and technical."*

I shall refrain from attempting to summarize our conclusions. But perhaps a statement of the pro's and con's of nuclear power extant 25 years ago may be helpful in the light of present day opinions.

The Case for Nuclear Power

- The arguments for nuclear power rest on the assumptions that the demand for electrical energy will continue to experience growth in the foreseeable future. Energy conservation and alternative, renewable energy technologies (solar, biomass, wind, etc.) will have a marginal and uncertain impact on this demand by the year 2000. An assured and reliable supply of electricity provides substantial economic and social benefits which would be at risk if shortfalls are allowed to develop in the supply of electrical energy.

- Oil and natural gas, which are not resources indigenous to Ontario, have important uses (chemical feed-stocks, liquid transport fuels) for which they should be increasingly preserved as their price escalates and supplies become depleted. Therefore the answer is to substitute electricity whenever possible.

- Coal, with which Ontario is not well endowed, is the principal alternative to nuclear generated electricity, but has escalated rapidly in price and carries with it heavy environmental health costs.

- Uranium is indigenous to Ontario and is available in significant quantities elsewhere in Canada, thereby minimizing Ontario's dependence on uncertain and increasingly expensive imports and maximizing its potential for self-reliance.

- The CANDU technology developed independently by Canada over the last 25 years represents an unparalleled achievement in an extremely competitive high technology field. It is a proven technology which is available now.

- The CANDU reactor burns natural uranium which not only is available in Ontario, but obviates the problems associated with the acquisition of uranium enrichment services. This is a costly, complex and sensitive (from a proliferation point of view) technology available to few countries, albeit necessary for all current light water reactors. Furthermore, CANDU reactors consume uranium more efficiently than any other first generation reactors available and, therefore, help to conserve a non-renewable resource

- Many human undertakings involve some risk to individuals and society as a whole, and nuclear power is no exception. However, the safety of CANDU and indeed nuclear power stations of all types, has been well demonstrated. Indeed, the safety standards and record of the nuclear industry are unequaled and provide a model for other industries. Nuclear power, therefore, represents a risk to society which is vanishingly small, particularly when compared to the risk to which we are already, often voluntarily, subjected.

- Nuclear power is environmentally more benign when compared with currently available alternatives, especially coal. Radioactive emissions from nuclear power plants during routine operations are negligible when compared to natural background radiation to which we are also subjected or to the radiation dose which the average person receives from medical X-rays. Although the wastes created by nuclear-generated electricity are highly radioactive for very long periods of time, they are much smaller in volume and can be more easily contained and isolated from the environment than the bi-products of coal-fired generation.

- CANDU generated electricity has proven to be highly reliable and is independent of uncontrollable factors such as weather.

- Based on life-cycle costs, nuclear -generated electricity is less expensive than currently available alternatives such as coal. The nuclear industry anticipates that the cost advantage that nuclear energy now enjoys will tend to increase with time.

- A Canadian nuclear industry, based largely in Ontario, with the capacity to fabricate and supply 80 percent of the equipment and material required for CANDU plants, has been put in place over the past two decades. This industry employs 30,000 people, many of them highly skilled professionals and technicians. If an orderly domestic market of sufficient volume for CANDU plants is forthcoming, the future employment and investment offered by nuclear power is impressive.

- Although there is no economic incentive to recycle and reprocess spent fuel from current, highly efficient, once-through natural uranium CANDU reactors, CANDU can be adopted to other fuel cycles based on plutonium or thorium. This flexibility could greatly extend the life and viability of both the CANDU systems and finite uranium supplies thereby providing a Canadian alternative to the fast breeder reactor.

The Case Against Nuclear Power

- The critics of nuclear power are confident that an effective program of energy conservation and efficiency improvement is possible and could significantly reduce the growth rate for electricity without altering existing life styles and living standards, thereby making nuclear power unnecessary. They argue that an energy conservation program would be cheaper, faster and less environmentally destructive, while creating more jobs where they are needed than by increasing nuclear generating capacity. Such an approach would buy time to re-evaluate energy supply strategy leading in the long run to a sustainable, resilient energy system based on indigenous renewable energy technologies (solar, biomass, wind, etc) which can be more appropriately and efficiently matched to the end-use for which energy is needed.

- The safety of nuclear power stations, especially CANDU stations with their limited operational experience on a commercial scale, has not been proven beyond reasonable doubt. The health and environmental consequences of a major accident at a nuclear plant could be both long-lived and catastrophic. The probability of such events is higher than the low risk levels which the nuclear industry has publicized.

- Public health and the health of workers across the entire nuclear fuel cycle- mining, milling, refining, fuel fabrication, plant operation, spent fuel management and decommissioning may be at risk due to chronic exposure to low-level radiation, the aggregated effects of which may not be detectable for many years.

- The mining and milling of uranium ore produces very large volumes of long-lived low-level radioactive tailings which have leached into waterways in the vicinity of Elliot Lake, Ontario, thereby posing serious health and environmental problems which have yet to be adequately addressed.

- No method for the safe and permanent disposal of the toxic and long-lived high-level radioactive nuclear wastes has been demonstrated. These wastes must be isolated from the environment and people for periods of time longer than the records of the history of human civilization, and may, therefore, present a threat to future generations who will not have received any of the benefits of nuclear-generated electricity.

- The current cost figures for nuclear-generated electricity do not reflect true costs because of various forms of government subsidization or hidden or externalized costs which society as a whole will pay. Nuclear power is also extremely capital intensive, a situation which will result in fewer jobs per dollar invested than an alternative. Therefore, a heavy commitment to nuclear power will limit the availability of capital for social and other uses and for the development of alternative energy systems whose costs and benefits seem more sensible and sustainable.

- Nuclear power is a centralized, highly capital-intensive and complex technoloogy which few people understand. It is "hard" technology requiring very long lead-times, highly sophisticated controls, extensive planning and regulation and unending vigilance to ensure safety. It is therefore, a technology which demands and tends to increase further the centralization of society, thereby eroding further our potential for diversity, resilience, self-reliance and adaptivity.

- Nuclear power is based on an uncritical and unimaginative extrapolation of historical trends into the future. The length of the lead-times required to deploy nuclear stations provide little flexibility to cope with future social, economic and political uncertainties.

- If a major commitment is made to expand nuclear power in Ontario, the reprocessing of spent fuel to extract plutonium and the deployment of second-generation advanced fuel cycle technologies will become inevitable due to the finite nature of uranium resources. The massive human and financial resources which will have been committed over the next two or three decades will provide an added and perhaps irresistible momentum. These second-generation nuclear technologies will dramatically escalate the safety, environmental and proliferation risks associated with nuclear power.

- Nuclear power will lead to greater local and international tension and instability because (a) raw materials and basic technologies for nuclear weapons will be more widely available; (b) by providing further potential targets to terrorists, the inevitable response to which will negatively affect our civil liberties; and (c) by forcing competition for an increasingly strategic but finite raw material, i.e. uranium rather than oil.

- Nuclear power should be considered a technology of last resort and the option of phasing out of this technology before it becomes irreversibly established should be preserved. A temporary moratorium on further expansion of nuclear energy should be immediately adopted while an extensive education program is undertaken to better inform the public of the full range of implications which would accompany a large future commitment to nuclear power in Ontario.

- Measures to ensure the continued viability of the nuclear industry during a temporary moratorium should be developed. The moratorium should be accompanied by serious programs of energy conservation and renewable energy development.

Having delineated the issues as above, I went on in the report to make the following comment:

> *"As is generally the case in the course of human affairs, particularly when issues are of such importance that they are intensely and frequently emotionally debated, the truth may well lie between these two seemingly polar positions. When an issue is at once as complex and as crucial as is the case with nuclear power, then a responsible dialogue and extensive, wide-ranging public participation are fundamentally important if wise and just decisions are to be made. This is especially important at this point in our history when public trust and confidence in traditional institutions and government in Ontario and all western industrial democracies may be decreasing."*

It is noteworthy, but not unexpected, that we sided in general with the nuclear industry with respect to the risks and economic viability of nuclear power, but on the other hand, with the anti-nuclear interveners with regard to the questionable safety and reliability of long-term storage of radioactive waste. Both positions have stood the test of time insofar as during the past quarter century there has been no serious accident at a CANDU power station, but as far as I know, no suitable site for the ultimate disposal of spent nuclear fuel and other high-level radioactive wastes has been identified.

On purely economic grounds we concluded that there was no convincing evidence to suggest that a large nuclear reactor, in the capacity range of 1250 MW should be adopted. In recommending that no further development, even at the concept stage of this reactor, we probably saved the Ontario tax payer a considerable sum. But at the time I do not recall the commission with being credited with this. One internationally recognized publication, the "New Scientist," in the November, 1978 issue was very generous in an editorial which included the comments, "indeed in some respects the Porter report is in a class by itself, not least because it carries the arguments of the Flowers

Commission[28] two years farther forward, refining and developing them with clarity and insight."

A few months after the publication of the interim report, a nuclear accident occurred which electrified the world and which had a profound impact on the debate. No single incident relating to the commercial use of nuclear power had a more profound impact on the general public, and indeed on nuclear-power-oriented electricity utilities, than the TMI accident. On one hand the proponents of nuclear power contended that the accident demonstrated that, in spite of its serious nature, and essentially because of the reliable operation of critical control systems (i.e. shut-down systems) and effective "defense in depth," not a single fatality or injury occurred. Furthermore, it was asserted that the lessons to be learned would facilitate the safe operation of nuclear power stations in the future. On the other hand, those opposed to nuclear power contended that the accident demonstrated that nuclear power stations are basically unsafe, that the situation at TMI was potentially extremely dangerous, that the regulatory procedures and licensing processes were inadequate and that the public was ill-informed with respect to the threats of nuclear power.

The TMI accident, from the standpoint of my inquiry, could not have happened at a more appropriate time. It provided a classical example of how an operating nuclear power station could be put at risk by a combination of simple causes. A relief valve failing to close, an indicator failing to operate, two isolating valves which should have been open were in fact closed. It is interesting to speculate on the probable impacts of a TMI-like accident on an Ontario CANDU -based power station. This question was considered in some detail in Vol. I of my Commission's final Report pages 61-62.

My initial involvement with the media and press coverage of the TMI accident had been restricted to Canada until one afternoon early in April, 1979 when I was interviewed by "Good Morning America" at Belfountain. It was by far my most impressive TV appearance. The large transport, housing all the TV paraphernalia made it through our drive gates with only inches to spare, and had trouble negotiating the bends in our driveway. Then they proceeded to completely reorganize the furniture in our living room and assembled huge flood lights and cameras. Fortunately I was well briefed on the TMI incident and the interview went extremely well. To emphasize the rural nature of the

---

[28]Royal Commission on Environmental Pollution chaired by Sr. Brian Flowers 1973-76

landscape in which the interview took place, the final stages were telecast with the interviewer and myself sitting on a bench beside our front pond in the sunset. This event, together with the occasion when I was deposited from a helicopter on our grounds certainly intrigued our neighbors.

Arising as it did during the final few months of my commission when the final report was being planned, the TMI phenomenon virtually ended my involvement with issues related to nuclear power except for one — the management of radioactive waste. Although the topic was touched on in my interim report, when I did little more than state the problem, it remained a bone of contention. How could public confidence in light of the socio-economic implications of managing the waste be ensured?

We concluded that, because we were dealing with wastes that will be potentially hazardous for at least 500 to 1000 years, socially acceptable steps on a continuing basis must be taken to ensure that the long-term risks are minimal. Indeed, the social, health, psychological and political aspects of the problem may be more important, in arriving at an acceptable solution, than the geographical, ecological and engineering aspects of management. In my final recommendations I "stuck my neck out" much to the chagrin of the nuclear community by stating:

"The future expansion of the nuclear power program in Ontario and in particular the uranium mining and milling portion of the fuel cycle should be contingent on demonstrated progress in uranium tailings waste disposal problems, as judged by the provincial and federal regulatory agencies and the people of Ontario, especially those who would be most directly affected by uranium mining operations. It would be unacceptable to continue to generate these wastes in the absence of clear progress in the efforts to minimize their impact on future generations."

I certainly had no intimation of any kind that some six years subsequently I would be involved in a study of the problem of managing low-level radioactive waste. Because it was undertaken during my "retirement," I shall talk about it in the next chapter.

Insofar as the management of the high-level waste associated with spent nuclear fuel elements was concerned, because these wastes remain extremely radioactive and toxic for hundreds of years, very toxic and radioactive for thousands of years and moderately toxic and radioactive for tens of thousands of years, the issue was even more contentious. And be it noted that, as in the case of the mining wastes, these wastes had been accumulating for several decades as a consequence of the proliferation of nuclear weapons programs in the United States. Consequently, my recommendation was even more forceful and indeed, intimidating. It read:

> *"If progress in high-level nuclear waste disposal research and development, in both the technical sense and social sense, is not satisfactory by at least 1990, as judged by the technical and social advisory committees, the provincial and federal regulatory agencies, and the people of Ontario — especially in those communities that would be directly affected by a nuclear waste disposal facility — a moratorium should be declared on additional nuclear power stations."*

At the time I believe I put the question of nuclear power quite succinctly in the final three paragraphs of my interim report. They were:

> *"The fundamental decisions about nuclear power are all political. They have to do with quality of life, with quality of the environment and with the energy options we want to leave our future generations. These are hard decisions which ultimately must be made by government. But government requires the benefit of the public's view on these far-reaching public policy issues. New and imaginative forums must be found to involve the public, whose input must be sought at every step of the fuel cycle. Education and information will be essential.*
>
> *The government and the public can no longer sit back and be relatively uninterested in the generation decisions made by the utility. We must become knowledgeable about the proposed technologies, their environmental, societal and political implications and their capital and fuel requirements both in the short and long term. We must all enter the debate in a process designed to give political direction to the utility.*
>
> *The range and polarity of views about nuclear power indicate some deeply felt concerns that in all likelihood*

will lead to a prolonged and ongoing debate. But we believe that an informed public debate might make the achievement of a just and wise consensus possible. Perhaps our Commission is the beginning of a process of education and discussion which will allow society to form and to shape a mature and sophisticated understanding of nuclear power and thereby give an informed input to the decision-makers. We believe that armed with such public understanding we might move more quickly to rational and sustainable solutions to the energy planning problems."

There have been few problems during my career which have challenged me more than the question of nuclear power. It would re-emerge during my retirement.

Chapter 18

IN RETIREMENT

ACCORDING to Patricia I've never really retired. In fact, I officially retired as Professor of Industrial Engineering from the University of Toronto on July 1, 1976, and as President of Arthur Porter Associates on December 31, 1988. Subsequent to the submission of my final report as Chairman of the RCEPP in 1980, I've certainly led a much more tranquil, but by no means inactive, life than hitherto.

In this last chapter of my memoir I shall recall episodes in my life that have occurred since 1980. I categorize the years 1980-88 as those of semi-retirement when I retained APA Ltd. essentially as a conduit for consulting work. Indeed, during the Royal Commission period 1975-80, APA, under the diligent supervision of Patricia, handled the financial aspects of my appointment.

Although my consulting work and associated government activities occupied a fair portion of my time during the semi-retirement years, I was able to devote much more time to helping Patricia pursue her goal of beautifying Belfountain. The work associated with the burgeoning plantations, lawns, herbaceous border, the orchard and vegetable garden, even with the help of our trusty Cecil Foster seemed to be never ending. I recall, for example, the week when the three of us resurfaced our lengthy driveway in the summer heat. But I've already portrayed the Belfountain story in Chapter 12. It only remains to say that the transformation of many acres, including a fair amount of wetlands, to a virtual paradise continued until 1988 when we regretfully departed.

The decade 1980-1990 was one of diversity from both domestic and professional points of view. While Belfountain was our main residence, as the decade progressed we spent an increasing amount of time in Florida and as well spent a few weeks each summer in Oconomowoc,

Wisconsin, close to John and family. Our decision to spend winter months in Naples, Florida was one of the most propitious of our lives. Naples ranked with Belfountain as our most beloved place of residence. Actually we were introduced to Gulf Shore Blvd. in 1976 when we spent two weeks as the house guests of Gordon and Jean Cowperthwaite in their "Diplomat" condo. At that time we were greatly impressed with the city and its glorious beaches. Not surprisingly we purchased a home, also on the boulevard, in 1983.

During a brief period in early 1981 I rented a small office adjacent to P.A.Lapp Associates, and in the process of moving a small amount of furniture from Belfountain to Toronto a rather scary incident occurred. To facilitate and minimize the cost of the move, I had rented a commercial van. Patricia and I loaded the furniture one rather unpleasant Sunday morning in March with freezing rain in the weather forecast. We drove to the city by our usual route — the Mississuaga Road and then the four-lane highway 401. After driving a mile or two on the major highway, the freezing rain started and within a few minutes the road surface was covered with a sheet of ice. A gear change was advisable — down to second. But unfortunately the gear indicator of the van was "haywire." When I shifted to second the gearshift actually engaged reverse and Patricia and I were subjected to the craziest motor vehicle gyrations we had ever encountered. We skidded every which way across the east bound lanes of the highway and ended up pointing in the wrong direction on the grass verge. Miraculously, it being a Sunday morning, traffic was light on that normally very heavily traveled highway. The closest car was about a 100 yards behind us. Incidently, it was quite a feat to return to the hardtop and to "baby" the vehicle into the center of the city in atrocious conditions. When we reached our destination, Patricia and I breathed a collective sigh of relieve. We had had a very narrow escape.

Within a few months of this incident I accepted an associateship with Hickling-Johnson, a Toronto consulting company with offices on Yonge Street just north of a Metropolitan subway station. In fact, the journey by car and subway took only an hour and I was not restricted to the rush-hours.

My association with Hickling-Johnson provided office and secretarial assistance and I became involved in consulting mostly related to the electrical industry with educational implications. Although I did not find these studies particularly exciting, I was provided with a convenient base — a free-wheeling operation which suited me admirably, especially after the stressful situations I had encountered during the 1970's.

Let me digress and leap from Toronto to MIT and associations there which eventually gave rise to my being appointed a member of a U.S. Congressional Advisory Panel.

Since my good fortune in having Dr. Vannevar Bush as my advisor, and my friendship with Harold Hazen, Dean Emeritus of Graduate Sudies and Gordon Brown, who became Dean of Engineering and incidently, one of the most illustrious engineering educators in the U.S., I had always regarded MIT as my academic home in America. These early associations were supplemented during Project Lamp Light when I was fortunate to work with Jay Forrester and Jerry Wiesner, the prospective president of MIT. However, it was my involvement with nuclear power that brought me into contact with David Rose, professor of Nuclear Science and Engineering, which had unexpected consequences.

During the spring of 1983, the U.S. Congress, through the Office of Technology Assessment (OTA) established an advisory panel "The Future of Conventional Nuclear Power Advisory Panel." It was chaired by George Rathjens of MIT, and through the good offices of David Rose, a member, I was invited to become the only foreign member of the panel. It consisted of 18 members embracing a broad spectrum of nuclear interests and included representatives of major electric power utilities; universities (MIT, Stanford, Berkeley); electrical industry; financial institutions; and public interest groups. Three senior government officials from the U.S. Nuclear Regulatory Commission and the Department of Energy acted as observers. The study had been requested by the House Committee on Science and Technology and endorsed by the Senate Committee on Energy and Natural Resources. Its object was to assess the future of nuclear power in the U.S. and how the technology "might be changed to reduce problems now besetting the nuclear option."

The panel met during the summer and fall of 1983, at monthly intervals, in the OTA offices located at 600 Pennsylvania Ave, S.E. Washington D.C. For me it was a fascinating experience because I obtained an overview of the nuclear power industry in the U.S. and its future prospects. The outlook was not propitious largely because the credibility of the industry in the eyes of the public was so low, not least because of the TMI accident.

My personal contributions to the discussions related specifically to the potential of heavy-water reactors, notably the CANDU. Although my argument to the effect that the safety and reliability features of CANDU had been demonstrated over a period of 20 years was persuasive, it was obvious that the adoption of the system in the U.S. was highly improbable. It was considered that a switch from a light water to a heavy water system would have been too drastic to even contemplate! On the other hand, it was gratifying to hear the laudatory remarks of several of the panel members concerning the high management skills inherent in the operation of CANDU-based power plants in Ontario.

The final report of the advisory panel was published in February, 1984 under the title "Nuclear Power in an Age of Uncertainty."

In spite of the fact that several nuclear plants had been very successful in producing reliable and low cost electricity, we reported that in general too many plants presented financial risks as a result of uncertainties in electrical demand growth, very high capital costs, operating problems, increasing regulatory requirements and growing public opposition. We concluded that "the future of nuclear power poses a complex dilemma for policy-makers. It has advantages that may prove crucial to this nation's energy system in the coming decades, but at present it is an option that no electrical utility would seriously consider."

In retrospect, in light of the continuing successful operation of nuclear power facilities in France, Germany and Japan, the validity of this conclusion might be questionable. But undoubtedly at the time it was fully justifiable. One thing is clear — the nuclear debate in North America is likely to continue into the foreseeable future.

The year 1983 was memorable not only because of the advisory panel and our purchase of the Beacon House condo in Naples, but most importantly, my appointment to the Order of Canada.

There have been few more exciting moments for Patricia and myself than that at Belfountain when I received notification of the honor. It was early in October not long after our return from England where we had been visiting friends and family.

The Order, Canada's highest civilian award, was established in 1967 by H.M. Queen Elizabeth, the queen of Canada, to recognize outstanding achievement and service in various fields of human endeavor. Appointments were made bi-annually on January 1 and July 1 (Canada Day). They are made by the Governor General on the recommendation of an Advisory Council chaired by the Chief Justice of Canada.

The Investiture Ceremony took place in the Ballroom of Rideau Hall, the residence of the Governor General in Ottawa on April 11, 1984. Twenty-five Officers and 46 Members were invested by the Governor General. They included a former Cabinet Minister, the Hon. Mitchell

Sharp, the chief executives of two of Canada's largest corporations, and two friends, the Rev. John Kelly, a colleague of Marshall McLuhan's and Arnold Edinborough, publisher of a large Canadian newspaper with whom I had had several contacts. Former Prime Minister Pierre Trudeau was a guest and Patricia sat immediately behind him.

The program started with a fanfare and their Excellencies entered the Ballroom in procession. Then followed the Vice-Regal Salute and the Invocation. Members of the Order were then invested. I recall that, after a brief resume being read by the Clerk of the Order, the Governor General hung the ribbon and badge of the Order around my neck and shook my hand.

After all members had been invested, remarks by the Governor General, and the singing of *O Canada,* all recipients and their guests adjourned for a buffet dinner. During the event and the following day, Patricia and I enjoyed the company of Tish and Arnold Edinborough and Corrine McLuhan, widow of Marshall. Patricia has put together an album of photographs and documents as a record of a day to be remembered.

As an addendum to the OC appointment perhaps I should mention the medals that had been awarded previously — the Canadian Centenary Medal; the Canadian Confederation Medal; and the Queen's Silver Jubilee Medal. Subsequently, in 2002, the Golden Jubilee Medal. These medals and miniatures and the OC badge are in a display table in our home, together with WWII medals awarded to Patricia and myself and as well the miniatures of the medals awarded to Lt. Col. Vernon Dixon in World Wars I and II.

A consulting assignment of special interest, albeit far removed from nuclear power issues, arose during the spring of 1985. My friend and former colleague Phil Lapp, at the time a director of McDonald Dettwiler and Associates (MDA), a Vancouver-based company specializing in the development of digital image processing systems, recommended to the board that Arthur Porter Associates should be given a contract to "investigate and determine the degree to which the work undertaken by the company should be categorized as research and development. Such an assessment was required for Canadian income tax purposes."

During visits (MDA) in May and June, I had opportunities to meet the scientific and engineering staff and to inspect laboratories and computer facilities, etc. Over a six- week period I received an education in cutting-edge technology related to high performance radar and infra-red sensor techniques required for surveillance aircraft and satellites. I still recall how very impressed I was with the airborne real time data processing systems. These necessitated meticulous design and packaging in order to meet the stringent weight and volume constraints. I learned, for example, that information processing systems operating at speeds of 500 million logical operations per second were being designed. The advances which had been made in data processing since my first exposure to the technology some 30 years previously had been truly remarkable. I shall always be grateful to MDA for providing me with such an exciting experience. Within a span of about six weeks I completed the assignment and wrote a report on my findings. I understand that my report satisfied the Canadian income tax authorities.

But my visits to Vancouver were not only of value professionally and indeed financially, but they gave me opportunity to explore a little of the city's hinterland, especially Grouse Mountain.

One evening in early June, accompanied by the director of research, I ascended the mountain via the gondola elevator system. Patricia and John had undertaken this trip during our visit to Vancouver to see our friends, Carl and Gladys Patch in the summer of 1959. The view of the harbor and of the several islands which dotted the bay were spectacular, especially during evening hours as the sun was setting. Several of our fellow passengers were carrying skis — some of them had probably been sun-bathing a few hours previously on the beaches, a mere 10 miles distance. As a matter of fact, the upper slopes of Grouse Mountain provide an excellent year-round ski resort. The magnificent restaurant at the summit provided both gourmet food and wine and magnificent views. I was very fortunate to have been invited to undertake the MDA assignment.

There are few more attractive provinces to visit in Canada than British Columbia. It was a delightful surprise, therefore, within a few weeks of my completing the MDA job to be invited to address the Association of Mining Executives at their annual convention to be held at Harrison Lake, B.C. about 150 miles east of Vancouver, up the Fraser Valley. It was to be an adventure of a different kind because I had not the faintest idea why I should have been invited to give one of the four plenary session addresses. My personal interests seemed to be so remote from those of the executives who were concerned largely with the leasing and mortgaging of oil exploration properties But my foreboding turned out to be ill-founded because Patricia, who had been invited with all expenses paid, and I had a wonderful time. It was a three-day convention with special tours arranged for the wives during the working sessions. Two occurrences stick in my memory.

At dinner the evening prior to the plenary session, Patricia and I were joined by another of the guest speakers and his wife. Like us, they were immigrants from Britain. However, what was remarkable was the fact that we had both attended the Ulverston Grammar School although he had been a student there about 20 years after me. The probability of such a coincidence must have been extremely slight — two of the four guest speakers attended the same grammar school in a small town in the north of England about 6000 miles away! This getting together greatly facilitated our enjoyment of the convention. Not least because both our presentations were well received.

For the final evening a boat tour of Harrison Lake and adjoining lakes had been arranged. It culminated in a delicious dinner accompanied by excellent wines, served on board a large steamer to at least 200 people. But what was truly memorable were the rock formations which bordered the lake shore and reflected colors as the sun went down — browns, greens, yellows and vermillion. It was a watercolorist's paradise.

My retirement years at this stage were obviously being enlightened by new experiences such as the visits to British Columbia and I felt as though I was embarking on a new career. This was further enhanced on my return to Belfountain when I received an invitation to participate in a meeting to be held in Yellowknife, capital of the Canadian North West Territories. The meeting was being held to discuss the impact of oil pipelines from Prudoe Bay in the Arctic to Alberta. No doubt my chairmanship of the Environmental Advisory Council in the 1960's was the reason for my being invited. Because the pipelines had generated a great deal of controversy involving the industry on one hand and environmentalists on the other, there had been a powerful political lobby in operation. To obtain an impression of this latter dimension, I was invited to attend a debate in the Legislative Assembly of the North West Territories. It turned out to be one of the most passionate and illuminating events of its kind I'd ever attended. It was true democracy in action — multi-lingual, the languages of English, French and Inuit were used and an excellent simultaneous translation and communication system provided. I spent an enthralling couple of hours in the debating chamber, the most northerly in Canada.

Never having visited the Territories previously, I was enthusiastic about my visit from several standpoints — the nature of the environment, the town itself, the native population and their customs. The city of Yellowknife is located on the shores of the Great Slave Lake with mining camps in the vicinity. Notably it was linked with the Klondyke Gold

Rush of the late 19th century and provided a major base camp.

Several things impressed me about this northern city by no means least the water supply pipes which were located about eight feet below street level and which were heated electrically. Otherwise during the winter months they would freeze solid. Apart from attending several meetings, I was invited during my visit to give a public lecture in the Town Hall. Gratifyingly, it was well attended and my topic "Energy and the Environment" appeared to be appropriate for the occasion. I talked about the environmental "insults" resulting from energy exploration, transportation and transformation. It was a fairly sophisticated topic for an unsophisticated audience..

After my return from Yellowknife, Patricia and I headed for Naples in the expectation that the winter and spring of 1987 would be spent beach-walking, swimming in the Gulf and playing tennis at Wyndemere Country Club. However, for me this was to be delayed for several months. I became immersed in the ubiquitous issue of disposing of low-level radioactive wastes. It was to be the last of the series of government inquiries in which I'd been involved since leaving Saskatoon in 1961. In fact, it was the third inquiry relating to nuclear technology in which I'd participated. The Ministerial Task Force on Low-Level-Radioactive Wastes Disposal was established in December 1986. I was invited to become a member. At age 75 it would have been understandable if I had declined the invitation. But I was flattered and intrigued. It turned out to be a more time-consuming and in many respects more arduous project than I'd bargained for. But it had compensations.

The Task Force was comprised of six independent members and a senior government official who acted as coordinator. It was a diverse group and included professionals in the fields of environmental management, economics and real estate and three academically-based members. Our terms of reference related specifically to designing a process for siting a disposal facility within Ontario for the existing, on-going and historic waste located in the Port Hope District. The latter is adjacent to a major nuclear materials processing plant.

Radioactive waste had in fact been accumulating in the area since the early 1930's and the volume had escalated markedly during the early 1940's when Ontario was a major supplier of refined uranium for the nuclear weapons programs in the United States. In the meanwhile, the Port Hope area residents had become increasingly concerned about the hazards associated with the waste and this was essentially the reason for the establishment of the Task Force.

The most knowledgeable member was Michael Chamberlain, Chief of Nuclear Medicine, at the University Hospital and Professor and Chairman of the Division of Nuclear Medicine at the University of Western Ontario in London. The visit to Michael's laboratories proved to be one of the highlights of the Task Force activities, and I obtained an education in a fascinating field. Visits to the low-level radioactive waste facilities at the Bruce Nuclear Development, the Chalk River Laboratories, and a U.S. facility in South Carolina were also undertaken and also an extensive examination of the waste sites in Port Hope. As well, to gain an impression of the views of local residents, municipal councils, etc, who had been most affected by the siting of radioactive waste, the Task Force visited Swan Hills and Riley in Alberta. The social and political issues involved in siting the waste dominated discussions and were obviously more difficult to resolve than the technical issues. This was manifest in the many hours of meetings we held at the Constellation Hotel adjacent to Toronto airport. I recall that it was not uncommon for a meeting to begin at 7 a.m. and to conclude at 9 p.m. with brief intervals for meals. Not exactly the kind of activity I had envisioned for my retirement. But in spite of being the senior member in age by about 30 years, on the whole I enjoyed the challenge.

Perhaps our ultimate findings were predictable, but nevertheless are worth noting. Briefly, the most important were:

- The general public, having been excluded in large measure from decision-making, has become cynical and distrustful of governments, the nuclear industry and the regulatory agencies.

- Public acceptance and support for waste management initiatives will require reorientation of the decision-making process from top down.

- Low-level radioactive waste management and facility siting issues will not be readily resolved and there must be a willingness to question conventional wisdom.

- Appreciable social disruption in the siting of a low-level radioactive waste management facility is inevitable, and communities accepting such facilities must be compensated in a way that offsets all costs and leaves the community better off than it was previously. In effect, the service that the community is providing must be acknowledged and paid for.

The final report of the task force was written by Jim McTaggart-

Cowan and his support staff. I am extremely grateful to them for doing such an outstanding job. "Opting for cooperation" is a concise and readable statement of the problem. It identifies the technologies available at the time for transporting and containing low-level radioactive waste and most importantly it outlines a process for site selection with emphasis on public participation in decision-making. In reviewing the report in retrospect it is especially encouraging to recall the high level of support we received from so many government departments and agencies as well as from local authorities and the private sector.

As a final word it is a truism that the problem the Task Force confronted will not "go away." Society must recognize that the fruits of nuclear science and engineering have been highly desirable, notably in nuclear medicine and in the generation of electric power. But a price has to be paid. For example, a major component of the Port Hope radioactive waste under investigation arose from uranium refining processes undertaken to create the nuclear weapons, which in the minds of many people including myself, has saved the world from WWIII. Eternal vigilance in protecting the environment from the encroachment of radioactive waste is absolutely essential.

While I spent those months in wintry conditions up north, Patricia was in Naples. I managed to get away for the occasional weekend and our sister-in-law, Georgie, widow of my younger brother, came out from England to keep Patricia company. Like us, she fell in love with the beautiful beaches of the Gulf and the warm sunny weather of southwest Florida.

It was appropriate that the last of the many lectures I had given during a time span of 60 odd years was given in the Department of Computer Science at the University of Manchester in May 1998, and that the topic was virtually identical with the one I introduced at a Junior Colloquium 64 years previously. It was on the occasion when a memorial board honoring Douglas Hartree was unveiled. Patricia and I were greatly privileged to be present and we spent a few hours being enchanted by a wonderful group of creative computer scientists. During the afternoon of that day we were shown, at the Manchester Museum for Science and Technology, a major portion of the McDougall Differential Analyzer actually operating. Ted Edgar, the engineer who assembled the machine during 1935-36 had been brought out of retirement to reassemble it 60 year subsequently. During the evening Patricia and I were honored at a dinner hosted by the Department.

Although the impression may have been given that my retirement years have been "more of the same" let me hasten to reassure all who have survived this memoir that Patricia and I have had many years of real relaxation thanks in no small measure to our membership of Wyndemere Country Club and our residency at the Imperial Club on Gulf Shore Boulevard in Naples, and here at Bermuda Village. But before I summarize some of the highlights, let me pause and reflect on an episode that was one of the most, if not the most, traumatic experiences of our lives, albeit with a silver lining.

I will not go into the details of the first few weeks of Patricia's serious heart condition except to say that her first heart attack occurred when we were playing tennis together at Wyndemere one Sunday morning in April 1994. After several procedures, culminating in by-pass surgery at St. Luke's Hospital Milwaukee, which followed a dramatic air ambulance flight in a Lear Jet from Naples, she rested at John and Kathryn's home in Delafield. But her recovery was much slower than hoped for and, much to our chagrin, the surgeon and several other physicians attributed this to the fact that she was not "trying hard enough!" Both Patricia and I knew that this was nonsensical and the following proved how right we were.

About a month after the surgery, in spite of marked deterioration in Patricia's strength, we decided to move from Delafield to a villa we had rented for two months at the Holiday Inn Resort, Oconomowoc, with the expectation that the change would be beneficial. But it didn't help and after a few days Patricia was unable to walk more than a few steps.

The morning when her collapse occurred I was preparing her morning tea in the small kitchen. Suddenly there were distressing sounds from the bedroom and I discovered Patricia lying unconscious on the bed. I immediately called John and 911. The volunteer paramedics, members of the local fire department with oxygen facilities and an ambulance arrived within a few minutes only because a maintenance worker at the resort, himself a volunteer, on receiving the emergency call immediately stationed himself at the gates of the resort and directed the vehicle to our villa which was in a comparatively remote location. Otherwise, a delay of at least 10 minutes would have been inevitable. Patricia's pulse rate had fallen to 25 per minute when life-saving oxygen was administered. She had suffered a major pulmonary embolism. John and Kathryn, who arrived within minutes, drove to the Oconomowoc Hospital where coincidentally, John was chief of staff, and all was ready in the emergency room when Patricia arrived 10 minutes later. It was certainly the most stressful few minutes of our lives and the fact that

Patricia came through with flying colors was a miracle. Her failure to respond normally after the by-pass, which had revealed a 90 percent closure of her main coronary artery was due to the development and subsequent invasion of her lung by a massive blood clot which had remained undetected for a month.

For a decade prior to the surgery, Patricia and I had become tennis enthusiasts. The fact that we didn't take up the game seriously until we were in our mid 60's and 70's respectively meant that we were by no means experts. But we had many hours of activity on the Wyndemere tennis courts. Patricia played three or four times a week with a group of ladies in her age bracket and I did likewise with a group of men. We were fortunate to have wonderful tennis professionals in Rob, Kevin and Chris. They were superb teachers, so much so that I was nominated the "Most Improved Player" for two years and have trophies to prove it, while Patricia and I were finalists in the Over 80's Mixed Doubles Club Championship. Most rewarding of all were the friendships which blossomed on the tennis courts and which have endured ever since. Notably with Max and Mary Clark, Howard and Rosemarie Bossa, Cis Bronson and Ann Jacobson.

Wyndemere also provided us with wonderful exercise facilities in the fitness center, with countless dinner parties and social gatherings, and even with intellectual stimulation in the form of a men's reading group with nine members which is still extant. The latter was largely the result of Patricia's insistence that we males were insufficiently challenged except on the tennis court. For her part, Patricia was a very active member of the Naples Garden Club and won numerous awards at the annual flower show and as well worked hard for the Philharmonic League which raised funds for our fine symphony orchestra.

Complementing our club activities we spent many hours on the fantastic gulf shore beaches, walking and swimming in the gulf, a mere 200 feet distant from our building. Remembering those many years of exposure to the Florida sun and seawater I'm happy to say that our arthritic aches and pains were minimal. Even the ubiquitous sting-rays were not a threat when we learned how to treat them with respect, nor where the sharks which were around on rare occasions. The bird population at Naples was very different from the species we had in Belfountain. Unforgettable was the bald eagle's nest located on the top of a large pine tree enmeshed in a bower of brilliant foliage and situated

less than a quarter of a mile away. On my morning bike rides[29] I often
dwelt several minutes gazing in wonder as three or four young eagles
awaited the arrival of their parents flying in with fish clutched in their
claws. The pair of bald eagles used the same nest year after year and
during the summer months when they flew north the Naples fire
department strengthened the nest so that it would survive the force of
hurricane winds. How many times Patricia and I have paused during a
morning beach walk to admire the antics of the seabirds? The graceful
glide and sudden dive of the pelicans, the advances and rapid retreats of
the sanderlings into the flowing tide, the beautiful egrets and herons.
Even the cacophony of raucous cries of seagulls, reminiscent of camping
days at Bardsea, and of the day when my brother Ronald and I climbed
that treacherous Dow Crags gully.

Like ourselves, John, Kathryn and our grandsons enjoyed staying
with us in Naples. Ian and Gregory enjoyed playing on the beach,
building sand castles in the fine silver sand, collecting sea shells and
swimming in the Gulf. As they grew older, their interests changed and
Ian, like his mother, played tennis while Gregory loved to go fishing.
There are also antique car enthusiasts in the area to share John's love of
antique Bentleys. Needless to say we loved having them visit us,
although as educational demands become greater, their visits became
fewer.

Another dimension of retirement, the Coach Tours to exotic places
and the many cruises we've enjoyed deserve special mention. Our most
extensive land tour of Europe, which lasted 10 days, began in Leicester,
England. Dunkirk, of WWII beaches fame, was our first port-of-call and
we subsequently followed the route, marked by mile-stones, of the U.S.
infantry through the Low Countries and Luxembourg on their final thrust
into Germany. After Strasbourg, a focal point in the Battle of the Bulge,
we penetrated into Bavaria and Austria. Spectacular scenery. As music
lovers, Patricia and I were thrilled to visit Saltzberg, birth place of
Mozart, and to explore this historic city and its several museums. We
were not disappointed with Vienna in spite of the "Blue" Danube not
being quite so blue as we had anticipated because as the birthplace of
Beethoven and Johann Strauss Jr., it is a veritable shrine for all music
lovers. We stayed in the city several days and had an opportunity to visit

---

[29]Patricia, my editor-in chief, has just pointed out that in spite of the fact that I was
addicted to biking for many years, especially in the Lake District and Florida, this fact
has scarcely been mentioned in my narrative. Suffice it to say that I've spent many hours
on a bicycle saddle and loved every minute.

the Opera House and the birthplaces of famous musicians as well as a special visit to the baroque building that houses the Royal Society of Arts and Sciences of Austria. I had the privilege of standing at the lectern of the great lecture hall in which scientists such as Einstein, Heisenberg, Planck, Bohr, Rutherford and many others, the creators of modern physics, had stood and lectured.

The Austrian Alps were our next destination and we spent a couple of hours discovering Berchtesgarten and the environs where Hitler vacationed and entertained many historic figures, by no means least Neville Chamberlain. Hilter's Wolf's Lair is situated in one of the most beautiful locations in the Alps. After a brief visit to Northern Italy via the Brenner Pass, we proceeded to Innsbruck and obtained a "skier's-eye" view of the Olympic ski-jump. The highway passed within a 100 yards of the site.

A visit to the Normandie beach heads and the adjacent national cemeteries and memorials concluded the tour. We were particularly impressed by the museums and memorials which recalled most poignantly, for Patricia and myself, D-Day, June 6, 1944 — a day when we anxiously waited for news of the Allied invasion of Europe. The United States memorial in particular, surrounded as it is by a myriad of white crosses marking the graves of thousands of American service men is the most beautiful and moving we have ever seen.

Our other major Coach Tour during the fall of 1989 included visits to several of the National Parks of Western USA which I had visited during my epic adventure in 1938. The main purpose was to introduce Patricia to the wonderlands which had thrilled me so very much a half century earlier. (See Chapter 6)

After spending two days in Las Vegas, a city which had grown literally a 100 fold since my earlier visit, we boarded a coach for a 10-day tour of six National Parks and monuments. They included Zion Canyon, Bryce Canyon, Grand Canyon, Yellowstone National Park, Grand Tetons, and Mount Rushmore. Of special interest was my return to Zion and to the spot where Arthur Armitage and I had met the three Dartmouth men who with the exception of Jerry Ullman, who died in the late 1980s, have played a prominent part in my life since our reunion in 1986.

During the past two decades Patricia and I have taken a total of 17 cruises, most of them as "Captain's Circle" members with the Princess Cruise Line. Indeed, the last cruise of the Western Mediterranean Sea and the North Atlantic, beginning in Barcelona and finishing in New

York, was completed as recently as 10 days ago on September 21, '03. Coincidently, it was the 66th anniversary to the day of my first arrival in the city. I've selected four cruises for special mention.

In spite of the rigors of a 28-hour flight from Fort Myers, Florida, to Sydney, Australia, the ensuing cruise was one of our most memorable. After spending three days, including Christmas Day, in the delightful city of Sydney, with its magnificent opera house, monorail transportation system and beautiful harbor, we embarked on the Pacific Princess. After calls at Brisbane, the Great Barrier Reef and Papua, New Guinea, we reached the Isle of Bali in Indonesia. I recall especially the attractive young women, some carrying large flower bouquets on their heads, and the long climb we undertook to a Buddhist temple.

During the voyage from the island to Singapore we crossed the equator and participated in the traditional ceremony when first-timers, including ourselves, were initiated by Father Neptune.

Our 10 hours stay in Singapore, the most pristine city we have ever visited, was one of the highlights of the cruise. We visited Raffles Hotel and had glasses of beer at the "Long Bar." As well, I visited the famous cricket ground which fortunately had not suffered during the Japanese occupation. Of very special interest to Patricia and myself was a visit to the building where the Japanese surrendered in 1945.

The last two days of the cruise were spent sailing across the South China Sea headed for Bangkok. I reflected on the fact that it was in these waters that the mighty British battleship H.M.S. Prince of Wales and the battle cruiser Repulse were sunk by Japanese torpedo bombers three days after Pearl Harbor, and what a shock we suffered at that time.

Bangkok, capital city of Thailand, proved to be a very dynamic modern metropolis. The skyline was dominated by huge cranes in process of building commercial towers. In this regard, we little appreciated at the time that Patricia's nephew Tim, within a few years, would be building a factory in the suburbs of the city for the Mars Confectionery Company of America. Our return flight to San Francisco departed at an early hour and we were surprised to note that rush-hour traffic, bumper-to-bumper was in evidence as early as 3 a.m. — exemplification of the dynamism of the city and country.

Probably the most exciting and uniquely spectacular was the Princess cruise of September 1998 which started in Rome, Italy, and ended in Istanbul, Turkey. Neither Patricia nor I had ever visited Rome and providentially we had reserved two days prior to embarkation for a tour, albeit superficial, of the city. Our hotel was located within a quarter of a mile of the Vatican. A favorite lodging of Cardinals attending meetings of the College and notably for the conclave associated with the election of a new Pope. It was superb in every respect. Rarely, if ever, had we dined in a room with a frescoed ceiling of such splendor.. The building dated from the 15th century and was a palace at that time and later a monastery. We were fortunate as well to obtain a guide and driver to make the most of our brief visit. It paid off handsomely because we avoided the long lines, especially to view the Sistine Chapel and Michaelangelo's masterpiece. Our comprehensive tour of the Vatican and St. Peter's Basilica remains one of the most moving experiences of our lives. More was to follow.

During our visit to Naples, because we had visited the ruins of Pompeii on a previous occasion, we spent a few hours exploring the ruins of Herculaneum. The city was completely destroyed by the eruption which literally blew the top off Mount Vesuvius in August, 79 AD.

Two Greek islands were next in our itinerary. Santorini was of special interest because York Wilson's painting of the island has for many years dominated one of the walls of our living room. The ancient Greek ruins at Rhodes presented a physical challenge. Access to the ruins necessitated a climb of many deeply eroded steps with no handrails. But the ruins were worthy of the effort and so were the views.

Ephesus, in ancient times an important Greek port and presently Turkish, was our next port-of-call. In many respects the ruins of the ancient city were the most impressive we've every seen. The excavations, begun almost two centuries ago, have revealed several temples, one of which the temple to the goddess Diana was one of the seven wonders of the ancient world, public buildings, include the great library, a vast amphitheatre and the ancient mile-long marble surfaced avenue. We were fascinated to learn that Saint Paul had trodden this avenue during the first century AD when he established a Christian congregation and preached in the amphitheatre. This enhanced the majesty and mysticism of Ephesus.

I should stress, however, in parenthesis, that the ancient Greek ruins including, for example, the Parthenon and Acropolis of Athens, which we explored during two East Mediterranean cruises, are all so awe-inspiring that any attempt to grade them in terms of their beauty and historical value would be futile.

After Ephesus we sailed through the Dardanelles Straits, with Gallipoli on the port side. It was here that one of the great campaigns of

WWI was conducted and I reflected sadly, as a Moseley Prizeman on the loss of the great British physicist H.G.J. Moseley, in this campaign.

Next came the Sea of Marmot and we entered the Black Sea with calls at Odessa and Yalta. The former city had suffered extensive damage during the German occupation and my only recollection is of the magnificent opera house which had survived virtually unscathed. Our visit to Yalta had historical overtones. It was the site of the meeting in February 1945 of the Allied leaders when they discussed the future of Europe. The layout of the conference room remains exactly the same as it was almost 60 years ago. To those of us who had endured virtually six years of war, we recalled the sense of relief we experienced at the time of Yalta because the end was in sight.

This fantastic cruise terminated in Istanbul from whence we flew to the USA. The city is dominated by the fabulous Blue Mosque and beautiful palaces.

Both our cruises to Alaska were blessed with perfect weather and the many photographs in our albums are proof. The highlights were Glacier Bay on the first and Tracy Canyon on the second. The spectacular glaciers, from time to time depositing huge icebergs into the sea, were unforgettable sights and sounds. We were enchanted as well by the antics of the harp seals and the occasional whale. During our recent Alaska cruise in May '03 we attended a talk in Juneau by Libby Riddles, the first woman to win the Iditarod Dog Sled Race across Alaska. The year was 1985. After the talk we met and photographed this delightful lady, an attractive blonde in her early 40s and obtained an autographed copy of her book, a tale of incredible courage and stamina.

Several other cruises, notably the one from San Diego to Fort Lauderdale when we traversed the Panama Canal accompanied by a nuclear submarine, and from Copenhagen to Stockholm when we visited the fabulous Hermitage Museum in St. Petersburg deserve more than passing reference. However, Patricia insists that this final chapter should not degenerate into a travelogue.

Essentially, for reasons of age and health, Patricia and I decided early in 1998 that a move from the Imperial Club to a retirement center with health care provisions would be desirable. We had already inspected several facilities in the Naples area. However, within a month of selecting a suitable residence we received word from John and Kathryn that they had decided to move to Winston-Salem, North Carolina. During their 20-year sojourn in Delafield, Wisconsin John's practice had expanded appreciably and he had opted for a life devoted to clinical medicine rather than one devoted to administrating a large medical practice. He went into partnership with Ed Hill at the Salem Neurological Center and association with Forsyth Hospital.

Our subsequent move from the Imperial Club to Bermuda Village, a retirement resort situated about two miles distance from John and Kathryn's home in Bermuda Run, took place in May 1999, and from every possible point of view we have made a wise decision. After so many years of geographical separation, being so close to our family has brought many blessings. Who could wish for more than the love and care of a devoted family. But there has been much more, not least the fact that John and Kathryn have taken charge of our health needs with resounding success. The visits of our grandchildren, albeit comparatively rare, have brought much joy and happiness.

We have watched with pride the three of them grow and develop and become talented and delightful human beings. Jennifer and Trevor live in Cochrane, Ontario, too far away for frequent visits. After graduating from George Washington University, Ian lives in Georgetown and is active in the field of investment banking and is studying for his M.B.A. Gregory is in his third year at North Carolina State University and has just completed a semester at the American University in Dublin, Ireland.

After the mandatory five years waiting period subsequent to being admitted to the United States as legal residents (i.e. possessors of the "green card") and after successfully passing the citizen's examination, Patricia and I were sworn in as United States citizens on September 28, 2000. Coincidently, and most appropriately, our dear friends Mary and Max Clark who were staying overnight with us en route to their home in Naples, were able to attend the ceremony in Charlotte, North Carolina.

An equally joyful occasion and a fitting termination to my narrative occurred yesterday afternoon, December 2, 2003. I was literally editing this final chapter when the fax machine at the side of my desk was activated. A copy of a letter to Dr. John A. H. Porter emerged. It read: "The American Board of Psychiatry and Neurology is pleased to inform you that you have passed the 2003 examination for sub-specialty certification in pain medicine." This is a coveted accomplishment achieved by few. Patricia and I are very proud parents.

Bermuda Village has proved to be truly a haven for our retirement. Because of our wonderful friends, diverse communal activities and a staff dedicated to help in every possible way. We are grateful to all of them.

The writing of these memoirs has been fun. I've devoted an average of about three hours a day to them during the past two years. It has been an exercise which has been especially desirable in keeping my cerebral neurons dancing and interacting. There is something about writing with a pencil and yellow pad that stimulates the memory and I've been grateful for that.

EPILOGUE

DURING the afternoon of October 10, 1929 at the Annual Prize Giving of the Ulvertson Victoria Grammar School, I was awarded the Headmaster's Prize "for taking First Place in Senior Physics Advanced Course 2nd Year, during the session 1928-29." It was signed H. W. Cousins, Headmaster.

It was a beautiful volume of the poetry of William Wordsworth. Today, October 10, 2003, 74 years later I opened the volume at random and read the following lines from "Peter Bell-A Tale."

Taken from Part The Second

"I've played I've danced, with my narration;
I loitered long ere I began;
Ye waited then on my good pleasure;
Pour out indulgence still, in measure
As liberal as ye can!"

A fitting closure to the pleasure I've enjoyed in writing this narrative.

INDEX

CPSIA information can be obtained at www.ICGtesting.com
Printed in the USA
242527LV00004B/9/A